Discourses on Strauss

KIM A. SORENSEN

Discourses on Strauss

REVELATION AND REASON IN LEO STRAUSS
AND HIS CRITICAL STUDY OF MACHIAVELLI

UNIVERSITY OF NOTRE DAME PRESS   NOTRE DAME, INDIANA

Library of Congress Cataloging-in-Publication Data

Sorensen, Kim A., 1974–
Discourses on Strauss : revelation and reason in Leo Strauss and his critical study of
Machiavelli / Kim A. Sorensen.
p. cm.
Revision of the author's thesis (doctoral)—University of Adelaide.
Includes bibliographical references and index.
ISBN-13: 978-0-268-04117-5 (pbk. : alk. paper)
ISBN-10: 0-268-04117-2 (pbk. : alk. paper)
1. Strauss, Leo.   2. Religion and politics.   3. Political science—Philosophy.
4. Strauss, Leo. Thoughts on Machiavelli.   5. Machiavelli,
Nicoolò, 1469–1527. I. Title.
JC251.S8S67   2006
320.1—dc22

                                    2006003880

All the hopes that we entertain in the midst of the confusions and dangers of the present are founded positively or negatively, directly or indirectly on the experiences of the past. Of these experiences the broadest and deepest, as far as we Western men are concerned, are indicated by the names of the two cities Jerusalem and Athens. Western man became what he is and is what he is through the coming together of biblical faith and Greek thought. In order to understand ourselves and to illuminate our trackless way into the future, we must understand Jerusalem and Athens.

—Leo Strauss, "Jerusalem and Athens"

The clear grasp of a fundamental question requires understanding of the nature of the subject matter with which the question is concerned. Genuine knowledge of a fundamental question, thorough understanding of it, is better than blindness to it, or indifference to it, be that indifference or blindness accompanied by knowledge of the answers to a vast number of peripheral or ephemeral questions or not.

—Leo Strauss, "What Is Political Philosophy?"

For us, the god would be the measure of all things in the highest degree, and far more so than some "human being," as they [for example, Protagoras] assert. He who is to become dear to such a being must necessarily do all in his power to become like him.

—Plato *Laws* 716c–d

Contents

PART TWO
Strauss's Machiavelli on Religion: Neither Christian Nor Pagan

PART THREE
Strauss's Machiavelli on Philosophy: Political Virtue

Preface

To ask what is "modern" may seem anachronistic to those who would say we live in a "global," "postmodern," or "postcolonial" epoch. To examine the highest things, whether articulated in a religious or philosophical manner, may seem a regressive step into a "grand narrative." And turning to Leo Strauss, who reopened a path to the study of the highest things, may seem to raise the specter of a conservative revolt against modernity. Yet, as I argue in this book, confronting the core of modernity as found in the thought and teaching of Niccolò Machiavelli enables anew the meaningful consideration of the good life.

The importance of the revelation-reason question in the works of Leo Strauss is central to an understanding of his thought. This central question poses two fundamental alternatives—religion and philosophy—for understanding the good life. The elucidation of these alternatives and their shared opposition to modernity are key themes in Strauss's oeuvre, particularly in his critical study of Machiavelli's teaching, as this book will show.

Part One offers a close reading of Strauss's idea of history and his conception of the revelation-reason question. Chapter 1 shows why he thought it critically important to undertake the study of the history of political philosophy. Chapter 2, which examines how Strauss considered revelation and reason as fundamentally different worldviews, refutes arguments that his position on the authority and truth of religion was basically atheistic.

Parts Two and Three explore Strauss's critical study of Machiavelli's teaching. Exploring Strauss's thesis that Machiavelli is neither Christian nor pagan, Part Two examines Machiavelli's teaching on the nature and efficacy of religion. Chapter 3 focuses on his critique of Christianity, while chapter 4 focuses on Strauss's response to Machiavelli's critique of religion in general. Part Three—chapters 5 to 7—explicates Strauss's thesis that Machiavelli's teaching on morality and politics is a revolt against not only biblical religion but also classical political philosophy as found in Plato, Socrates, and Aristotle. Strauss's effort here is to demonstrate that Machiavelli based his notions of goodness, virtue, and governance in the "effectual truth" of all things, in the empirical realm, not in the abstract realm of eternal verities.

The close examination of Strauss's critical study of Machiavelli's teaching in Parts Two and Three shows that Strauss identified his own work as a commentary on classical political philosophy. Nonetheless, as a critical engagement with the precepts of biblical religion, it was a contribution to philosophical tradition. Strauss's open, if not precarious, stance with respect to these two traditions is fundamental to understanding his critique of modernity. Strauss maintains that "the crisis of our time" is the apogee of a modernity that has its point of origin in Machiavelli's rejection of biblical and classical morality as a guide to the efficacy of political virtue.

Acknowledgments

This study has its origins in a Ph.D. thesis I wrote in the Department of Politics at the University of Adelaide. I acknowledge the financial support of an Australian Postgraduate Award. The generosity of the Department in the form of a Visiting Research Fellowship from 2003 to 2005 made possible the revision of the thesis in its present form.

I would like to thank my principal Ph.D. supervisor, Associate Professor Paul Corcoran (Department of Politics), and my co-supervisor, Dr. Wayne Cristaudo (Centre for European Studies) for their unflagging patience. I am grateful to Dr. Vicki Spencer (Department of Politics), who was of great assistance as a temporary supervisor in July–December 2000.

The Political Theory Group in the Department provided a welcome opportunity for discussions about Machiavelli, Strauss, and political philosophy. Thanks in particular are due to David Olney for his helpful criticisms of the introduction and Part One in their original form.

I thank the following people for their support: Chris McElhinney, Tina Esca, Mel Pearson, Peter Newnham, Dominic Stefanson, and the interlibrary loan staff at the Barr Smith Library. I am indebted to the examiners of my thesis, Professors James V. Schall, S.J., and Harvey C. Mansfield. I am also grateful to Professor Walter Nicgorski and the anonymous readers at *The Review of Politics* for their comments on my "Revelation and Reason in Leo Strauss"; the article, published in the Summer 2003 issue, is an earlier version of chapter 2 of this study. I thank Michael P. Jackson for permission to quote from his "Leo Strauss's Teaching: A Study of *Thoughts on Machiavelli*" (Ph.D. diss., Georgetown University, 1985), and I thank Andrea Ciliotta-Rubery for permission to quote from her "Evil Teachings Without Remorse: An Examination of the Question of Evil Within Machiavelli's 'Exhortation to Penitence' and 'The Life of Castruccio Castracani Of Lucca'" (2 vols., Ph.D. diss., Georgetown University, 1994). Quotations from Dante Alighieri, *Inferno*, trans. Allan Gilbert (Durham, N.C.: Duke University Press, 1969), are reprinted with the permission of the publisher.

I thank the editors and the anonymous readers at the University of Notre Dame Press. Thanks to Jeff Gainey for expressing initial interest in the book, and to Barbara Hanrahan and Charles van Hof for guiding it through the stages of approval, review, and revision.

I dedicate this book to my parents, Peder and Lesley Sorensen, and to my twin brother and his wife, Julian and Belinda Sorensen.

Abbreviations of the Works of Leo Strauss

AAPL	*The Argument and the Action of Plato's Laws*
AE	"An Epilogue"
CCM	"Correspondence Concerning Modernity" (exchange of letters with Karl Löwith)
CCWM	"Correspondence Concerning *Wahrheit und Methode*" (exchange of letters with Hans-Georg Gadamer)
CM	*The City and Man*
COT	"The Crisis of Our Time"
CPP	"The Crisis of Political Philosophy"
ET	"Exoteric Teaching"
Exi	"Existentialism"
FMM	"Freud on Moses and Monotheism," in *JP*
GA	"A Giving of Accounts," in *JP*
GH	"Greek Historians"
GN	"German Nihilism"
HBS*GP*	"How to Begin to Study *The Guide of the Perplexed*"

HPP	*History of Political Philosophy*, 3rd ed.
HSMP	"How to Study Medieval Philosophy"
HSS	"How to Study Spinoza's *Theologico-Political Treatise*," in *JP*
IEHC	"Introductory Essay to Hermann Cohen, *Religion of Reason out of the Sources of Judaism*," in *JP*
IPP	*An Introduction to Political Philosophy*
JA	"Jerusalem and Athens," in *SPPP*
JP	*Jewish Philosophy and the Crisis of Modernity*
LAM	*Liberalism Ancient and Modern*
LCGP	"The Literary Character of *The Guide for the Perplexed*," in *PAW*
LE	"Letter to the Editor," in *JP*
LHK	"Letter to Helmut Kuhn"
LR*K*	"The Law of Reason in the *Kuzari*," in *PAW*
LSEW	*Leo Strauss: The Early Writings (1921–1932)*
LSPS	*Leo Strauss on Plato's Symposium*
MCL	"Machiavelli and Classical Literature"
MITP	"The Mutual Influence of Theology and Philosophy," Part III of POR
MP	"Marsilius of Padua," in *HPP*
NCS	Notes on Carl Schmitt, *The Concept of the Political*
NM	"Niccolò Machiavelli," in *HPP*
NRH	*Natural Right and History*
OCPH	"On Collingwood's Philosophy of History"
OCPP	"On Classical Political Philosophy," in *WIPP*
OFKW	"On a Forgotten Kind of Writing," in *WIPP*
OIG	"On the Interpretation of Genesis," in *JP*
OIR	"On the Intention of Rousseau"
ONI	"On a New Interpretation of Plato's Political Philosophy"
ONL	"On Natural Law," in *SPPP*
OPS	"The Origins of Political Science and the Problem of Socrates"
OT	*On Tyranny*, revised and expanded edition
PAW	*Persecution and the Art of Writing*

PGS	"Perspectives on the Good Society," in *JP*
P*HPW*	"Preface to *Hobbes Politische Wissenschaft*," in *JP*
PIH	"Preface to Issac Husik, *Philosophical Essays*," in *JP*
PL	*Philosophy and Law*
PM	"The Place of the Doctrine of Providence According to Maimonides"
PO	"Plato," in *HPP*
POG	"Preliminary Observations on the Gods in Thucydides' Work"
POR	"Progress or Return?" in *IPP*
PPH	"Political Philosophy and History," in *WIPP*
PRS	"Philosophy as Rigorous Science and Political Philosophy," in *SPPP*
PS	"The Problem of Socrates"
P*SCR*	"Preface to *Spinoza's Critique of Religion*," in *JP*
RCPR	*The Rebirth of Classical Political Rationalism*
Rel	"Relativism," in *RCPR*
R*HH*	Review of *The History of History*, vol. 1, by James T. Shotwell
RSW	"Replies to Schaar and Wolin" (no. 2)
SA	*Socrates and Aristophanes*
SCR	*Spinoza's Critique of Religion*
SPPP	*Studies in Platonic Political Philosophy*
SR	"Some Remarks on the Political Science of Maimonides and Farabi"
SSH	"Social Science and Humanism," in *RCPR*
SVC	"The Strauss-Voegelin Correspondence, 1934–1964" (exchange of letters with Eric Voegelin)
TM	*Thoughts on Machiavelli*
TPPH	*The Political Philosophy of Hobbes*
TWM	"The Three Waves of Modernity," in *IPP*
UP	"An Unspoken Prologue," in *JP*
WILE	"What Is Liberal Education?" in *LAM*
WIPP	"What Is Political Philosophy?" in *WIPP*

WIPP	*What Is Political Philosophy?*
WWRJ	"Why We Remain Jews," in *JP*
X*A*	"Xenophon's *Anabasis*"
XS	*Xenophon's Socrates*
XSD	*Xenophon's Socratic Discourses*

Introduction
Leo Strauss on the Permanent Problems
and the Predicaments of Modernity

Whether in his interest in medieval Jewish and Arabic philosophers, his early Zionist writings, his exegeses of ancient Greek philosophers, or his accounts of the moderns, the tension between revelation and reason as mutually exclusive but compelling responses to the predicaments of modernity is never far away in Leo Strauss's oeuvre. The same is true for his numerous journal articles, lectures, book reviews, and private letters, especially those to Eric Voegelin. The revelation-reason question puts forward the two fundamental alternatives of religion and philosophy for understanding the good life. The elucidation of each alternative, that they are immiscible, and the path they both offer out of the morass of modernity are important themes for Strauss.

Central to the revitalization of political philosophy for Strauss is the effort to excavate the obscured bases of the serious understanding of political things. His "primary" interest as a scholar, David Bolotin notes, was "the *history* of political philosophy"; "he was too modest," though, Allan Bloom points out, to describe himself as "a philosopher."[1] In "Why We Remain Jews" Strauss stated, "Everyone is a specialist, and my specialty is (to use a very broad and nonspecialist name) social science rather than divinity."[2] In "On the Interpretation of Genesis" he explained, "I want to begin with the remark that I am not a biblical scholar; I am a political scientist specializing in political theory." He continued, "Political theory is frequently said to be concerned with the values of the Western world. These values, as is well known, are partly of biblical and partly of Greek origin. The political theorist must, therefore, have an inkling of the agreement as well as the disagreement between the biblical and the Greek heritage."[3] In "Jerusalem and Athens" Strauss posed this core issue of political theory in a candid manner: "We are confronted with the incompatible claims of Jerusalem and Athens to our allegiance. We are open to both and willing to listen to each."[4]

Strauss himself was open and willing to listen to both Jerusalem and Athens. To explicate his openness, I focus on his critical study of Machiavelli's teaching, in the final chapter of *Thoughts on Machiavelli*. That focus is not for brevity alone, nor is it because *Thoughts on Machiavelli* is a pivotal work in his corpus.[5] The density of religious *and* philosophic themes in his critical study makes it a good example for an analysis of how Strauss dealt with the revelation-reason question.[6] In this book I focus on that question; but to locate Strauss in his intellectual or scholarly milieu, it is helpful to examine how he has been, and continues to be, read, criticized, and understood in academe.

Strauss and his Critics

Whether critics or students, Strauss's readers are compelled to come to terms with the gravity of his lifework.[7] Readers necessarily ask, Who was Leo Strauss and what did he teach?[8] Recent vociferous critics of the influence of his lifework, who reduce the range of their inquiries to the influence of his scholarly output on American conservatism, for instance, identifying him as the mastermind—"the Grand Inquisitor"—behind United States foreign policy and the war on Iraq,[9] fail to understand him on his own terms. Yet, despite heated and often ad hominem debates about his work, an abiding interest with political philosophy is at the core of his oeuvre.

Shadia Drury claims in her *Leo Strauss and the American Right* that Strauss and his followers have given American neoconservatism "its sense of crisis, its aversion to liberalism, its rejection of pluralism, its dread of nihilism, its insistence on nationalism, its populism, its religiosity, and more."[10] Drury's claim is convenient but simplistic; it misses the point of Strauss's critique of modernity.[11] In "Perspectives on the Good Society" Strauss claimed that the "ills" of America are its "tendency toward homogeneity or conformism, that is, toward the suppression by nonpolitical means of individuality and diversity."[12] "Liberal relativism," he said in *Natural Right and History*, though it preaches "tolerance," "is a seminary of intolerance." He continued: "Once we realize that the principles of our actions have no other support than our blind choice, we really do not believe in them any more. We cannot whole-heartedly act upon them any more.... The more we cultivate reason, the more we cultivate nihilism: the less are we able to be loyal members of society. The inescapable practical consequence of nihilism is fanatical obscurantism."[13] According to Drury's critique in her *The Political Ideas of Leo Strauss*, described by Peter Emberley and Barry Cooper as a "bizarre splenetic,"[14] Strauss felt contempt for morality; he believed the philosopher to be a near godlike being beyond good and evil and not subject to moral or legal norms. Thus for Drury, Strauss was a nihilist.[15] Of the charge Emberley and Cooper level at Drury, Laurence Lampert explains, "Such mindless dismissals excuse their authors from facing the fact that Drury's book contains many fine skeptical readings of Strauss's texts and acute insights into Strauss's real intentions." But, Lampert concedes, Drury's "own missionary tone" undermines her book.[16]

For Stephen Holmes, a "mindset" of "non-Marxist antiliberalism" links Strauss with theorists such as Alasdair MacIntyre, Christopher Lasch, and Roberto Unger. That mindset can be traced back, Holmes says, to Carl Schmitt, Martin Heidegger, and to the "nineteenth century enemies of the Enlightenment," Joseph de Maistre and Friedrich Nietzsche. "They all engage in *Kulturkritik*, for example, and their criticisms of modern culture follow a fairly standardized format whereby 'disparagement of liberalism forms part of a general lamentation over the moral and spiritual degeneration of modern society.'"[17] Holmes is quoting from Francis Coker, "Some Present-Day Critics of Liberalism," an essay published in the March 1953 issue of the *American Political Science Review*.[18] That Holmes uses the essay to describe Strauss is curious, for Coker did not mention Strauss; moreover, Coker concluded that criticism of liberalism is necessary. "Liberalism needs criticism. A liberal may have exaggerated notions of man's capacity and disposition to think and act justly and intelligently.... Liberals should also recognize that in their open-mindedness they may have exaggerated notions of the possibilities of freedom and variety."[19]

Of Holmes's claim that Strauss belongs to an antiliberal tradition of thought, Thomas Spragens remarks, "every group of bedfellows does not add up to a tradition."[20] It would be a mistake, Peter Berkowitz observes, to see Strauss as an out-and-out antiliberal: "Holmes' decision to analyze Strauss as an antiliberal is a strange one. For—as Holmes grudgingly acknowledges in the very last footnote of his chapter on Strauss—the fact is that Strauss defended liberal institutions."[21] In "Progress or Return?" Strauss wrote, "I share the hope in America and the faith in America, but I am compelled to add that that faith and that hope cannot be of the same character as that faith and that hope which a Jew has in regard to Judaism and which the Christian has in regard to Christianity."[22] Thus, Strauss was opposed to a modernity that began with Machiavelli, but was sympathetic to certain strands in modern thought—freedoms of speech, thought, and expression; Strauss regarded these liberal freedoms as necessary for a life of "attachment" to scholarship.[23]

To comment on Strauss's legacy is to risk being accused of partisanship; to interject into heated debates about Strauss is to risk being branded a Straussian or an anti-Straussian. In some academic circles, to be a Straussian is to have a conservative, illiberal, and antidemocratic worldview.[24] Against the charge of illiberalism, though, Gary Glenn argues that "a political program for today's circumstances" could be "based on Strauss' diagnosis" of the ills of liberalism. The program "would shore up liberalism" by "strengthening religiously based self-restraint on the passions" and by "promoting economic innovation and abundance," for example. The program, then, would "preserve the practice of liberal democracy against the destructive practical consequences of its own principles."[25]

In a less vehement tone, the critiques of Strauss offered by both Robert Devigne and Ted McAllister provide a contrast to the bleak critiques penned by Drury and Holmes.[26] Contemporary American conservatism, Devigne explains, does draw from Strauss's diagnosis of the ills of America. That conservatism was a response to, and a reaction against, what in the 1980s and 1990s academe would label postmodernism. In a postmodern society, "political theories have lost all faith, not only in God, but in the human power of transcendence as well."[27] In the 1960s and 1970s, growing alarmed at the ascendancy in the American academy, and in the wider social and political landscape, of the notion that politics is the will to action for its own sake, Straussians turned from their studies "to become political commentators and contributors to a new American conservative political theory." Straussians and neoconservatives call for "public policies and institutions that conduce to public standards of a political and moral good and bad."[28]

Shared concerns aside, one can question the specific influence of Straussians over conservatism. For André Liebich, "the relation" between them "is neither one of subservience nor of identity."[29] Steven Smith notes that, although "a number of Strauss' students (or students of his students) went into government service during the Reagan and Bush years," "to what extent" they "actively shaped" or "took advantage" of "the conservative agendas of their respective governments" is "unclear."[30] McAllister claims that Strauss and Voegelin, through their critique of modernity and call for a return to the classics, gave American conservatism its intellectual underpinnings. Although McAllister concedes that Strauss and Voegelin were not active in the resurgence of American conservatism in the late 1960s and early 1970s, he stresses that conservatives gave them "honorary memberships."[31] Yet, Steven McCarl says, rather than disclosing "the influence of Strauss and Voegelin on specific conservative thinkers," McAllister "considers them to be vital philosophical critics of modernity and therefore sources of clarifying insight for conservatives."[32]

The Critique of Modernity

Leaving in abeyance the continuing debates over Strauss's "conservative" influence, James Schall and others have focused critical appraisal on his core concern with the predicament inherent in modernity. According to Schall, Strauss's "very project is to attack the roots of precisely the ideological structure of modern thought over against faith and reason."[33] Harry Jaffa reflects, "No one can guarantee happiness. But one can deserve it. If success could be guaranteed . . . no one would deserve it. To guarantee success means to abolish human freedom. . . . The abolition of the possibility of failure may be said to be the heart of the Machiavellian project. Strauss rejected this project with all his heart, and all his soul, and all his mind."[34] In a memorial article on Strauss, published in December 1973, Herbert Storing wrote, "Strauss's constructive project was to recover sight of the ends of political life for a profession that had blinded itself to such considerations." To reach those ends, "he opened up the great alternative of classical political philosophy."[35] His critique of modernity, Susan Orr explains, is a critique of the "malaise" produced by the collapse of political philosophy and "Western Civilization" into uncertainty, relativism, and nihilism. "Leo Strauss made his contribution to the field of political science by uncovering the roots of modern political science and the intellectual barrenness of the remains of the modern project."[36] Paradoxically, Orr implies that Strauss is an ally of the postmodernists insofar as he foresaw their critique of modernity.[37]

It is beyond the scope of this book to determine whether, and if so, where, Strauss should be located within a tradition of crisis-thinking. Nevertheless, I would argue that his view of modernity—as marked by "decay," "decline," and "crisis"[38]—should be, as Dante Germino remarks, looked at "from the inside" of his self-understanding.[39] In the words of Strauss, "An adequate interpretation is such an interpretation as understands the thought of a philosopher exactly as he understood it himself."[40] If one takes heed of his dictum, an effort to amplify Strauss's self-understanding should guide discussion of his oeuvre. Encapsulating that understanding is what he called the "theological-political problem."[41] That "problem," as will be seen in chapter 2, is the challenge of the fundamental alternatives, revelation and reason.

Reflections on the core problems of modernity, especially the blindness to the above problem, pervade Strauss's corpus. The inadequacy of historicism and relativism, Hadley Arkes explains, "hovers over everything."[42] In *Spinoza's Critique of Religion*, first published in German in 1930, Strauss's effort in both parts of the work was to show as untenable the attempt by Spinoza (and others) at a historically minded critique of revealed religion; in Part I Strauss examined the historical study of the Bible and the predecessors to Spinoza— Uriel da Costa, Isaac de la Peyrère, and Thomas Hobbes; in Part II he examined Spinoza's critiques of orthodoxy, Maimonides, and Calvin.[43] In contrast to modern rationalism, medieval Jewish rationalism accepted that divine revelation is *the* defining mark of Jewish heritage, and set out to defend philosophy as sanctioned by the divine command to know—to apprehend the reality of—God.[44] As Strauss wrote in 1935, in the introduction to *Philosophy and Law*, "To awaken a prejudice in favor of this view of Maimonides [that he stands for "the true natural model" of "rationalism"] and, even more, to arouse suspicion against the powerful opposing prejudice [of the Enlightenment], is the aim of this present work."[45] In "What Is Political Philosophy?," a series of lectures he gave in December 1954 and January 1955 (published in 1959 as chapter 1 in the work of the same name), Strauss traced that prejudice to Machiavelli,[46] that is, to his rejection of both biblical religion and classical political philosophy as false and inefficacious guides to life.[47] Of this rejection as it relates to modernity as a whole, Strauss had stated in 1952, in *Persecution and the Art of Writing*, "The most fundamental issue—the issue raised by the conflicting claims of philosophy and revelation—is discussed in our time on a decidedly lower level than was almost customary in former ages."[48]

Although the revelation-reason question underlies Strauss's works on the ancients and the moderns, the "ancients versus the moderns" theme represents his entire corpus; the theme "is his way of organizing the history of political philosophy."[49] It is worthwhile to consider here the general features of modernity that Strauss outlined in mapping its terrain against the backdrop of western political thought. I say "general features" because in Parts Two and Three of this book I examine the "specific features" of Machiavelli's founding of modernity,[50] of how he anticipated and partly brought about the modern turn—or flight—to this-worldly concerns.[51] The core of modernity, Strauss proposed in "The Three Waves of Modernity," is Machiavelli's root-and-branch rejection of both biblical and classical morality as fundamentally untenable; Machiavelli and Hobbes initiated the first wave of modernity; Rousseau, the second; and Nietzsche, the third. "Machiavelli had completely severed the connection between politics and natural law or natural right." The restoration of that connection, Strauss noted, was Hobbes's contribution to modernity. "One can describe the change effected by Hobbes as follows: whereas prior to him natural law was understood in the light of a hierarchy of man's ends in which self-preservation occupied the lowest place, Hobbes understood natural law in terms of self-preservation alone."[52]

Rousseau, in seeking to link the origin of society with a state of nature, opposed, Strauss explains, "the degrading and enervating doctrines" articulated by both Machiavelli and Hobbes. Rousseau's own legacy is the idea of history as "a singular or unique process which is not teleological," Strauss points out. "The concept of history, i.e., of the historical process as a single process in which man becomes human without intending it, is a consequence of Rousseau's radicalization of the Hobbesean concept of the state of nature." For Rousseau, only that habituation induced by "civil society" and "the general will" overcomes the basic irrationality of human nature.[53] He is explicit in Book IV, Chapter 2, of the *Social Contract:* "The Citizen consents to all the laws, even to those passed in spite of him, and even to those that punish him when he dares to violate any one of them. The constant will of all the members of the State is the general will; it is through it that they are citizens and free."[54]

The modern study of history, as it emerged in the third wave of modernity, rejects philosophy and religion as inimical to the use of history for life.[55] Strauss explains, "Just as the second wave of modernity is related to Rousseau, the third wave is related to Nietzsche." This Nietzschean wave had "a new understanding of the sentiment of existence: that sentiment is the experience of terror and anguish rather than of harmony and peace, and it is the sentiment of historic existence as necessarily tragic."[56] Thus, Nietzsche "ushered in the second crisis of modernity—the crisis of our time."[57] The difference between the second and third waves of modernity is shown by "the discovery of history; the century between Rousseau and Nietzsche is the age of historical sense." In a "secularized" version of Christianity, Hegel perceived history as "rational," "progressive," and moving toward "a peak and end." But to Nietzsche, Strauss then noted, "The insight that all principles of thought and action are historical cannot be attenuated by the baseless hope that the historical sequence of these principles is progressive or that the historical process has an intrinsic meaning."[58]

History and Philosophy

Strauss's concern with modernity and history, and especially with the Nietzschean–Heideggerian wave of modernity, is evident in the introduction to *The City and Man*, published in 1964, twelve years after *Persecution and the Art of Writing*. "It is not self-forgetting and pain-loving antiquarianism nor self-forgetting and intoxicating romanticism which induces us to turn with passionate interest, with unqualified willingness to learn, toward the political thought of classical antiquity. We are impelled to do so by the crisis of our time, the crisis of the West."[59] According to David Lowenthal, "Strauss certainly does want to help guide the 'practice' of the modern world. But what motivates him is the wish not simply to do this, or even to save the West: it is to discover the true principles required for the guidance of human life generally—principles that must necessarily be related to an understanding of realities beyond human life."[60]

It is instructive to remember here that Strauss devoted the latter years of his life to exegeses of Aristophanes, Aristotle, Plato, Thucydides, and Xenophon. "The mature Strauss's lifework [on those thinkers] . . . seems," Gregory Smith notes, "to be built around the attempt to recover the [natural] experiences out of which philosophy initially grew."[61] In the main, commentators recognize that an abiding concern with this approach to history, namely, the necessity of painstakingly studying the classics, is an important leitmotif in Strauss's oeuvre.[62] His views emerged through lifelong reflection, and did not take the form of a complete, final, absolute philosophy of history. That philosophy maintains that the role of the historian is to elucidate the causes of historical phenomena and to discover patterns in, and laws of, history.[63] "The term 'philosophy of history,' " Karl Löwith explains, "was invented by Voltaire, who used it for the first time in its modern sense, as distinct from the theological interpretation of history. In Voltaire's *Essai sur les mœurs et l'esprit des nations* the leading principle was no longer the will of God and divine providence but the will of man and human reason."[64]

Strauss's own idea of history is akin to a "critical" philosophy of history, insofar as he critically questions the speculative approach to history. Perhaps that is the point Jaffa is making when he states, "To put Leo Strauss among those who thought that history was primarily a subject of thought, and not at all one of action, would be to put him among those who held a view of history like that of Marx."[65] By using the term, *idea of history*, I do not mean to place Strauss in the company of R. G. Collingwood. Strauss took issue with the underlying concept of modern thinking on history in Collingwood's 1946 book, *The Idea of History*. "The deficiencies of Collingwood's historiography can be traced to a fundamental dilemma.... [He] rejected the thought of the past as untrue in the decisive respect. Hence he could not take that thought seriously, for to take a thought seriously means to regard it as possible that the thought in question is true."[66]

Regardless of whether one speaks of Strauss's *idea of history* or of his *critical philosophy of history*, they are terms he did not use to describe his lifework. According to his well-known dictum, one must seek to understand thinkers as they understood themselves.[67] Yet, it is appropriate to use the term *idea of history*, for Strauss did have such an idea; he regarded the turn to history, to the attentive reading of the history of political philosophy, as critical in the effort to counter modernity. I will argue, then, that he had an idea of what history is and how and why one studies it.[68] At times, that argument may seem less of an argument than a statement of the obvious, of the surface of the matter. However, as Strauss said in *Thoughts on Machiavelli*, "There is no surer protection against the understanding of anything than taking for granted or otherwise despising the obvious and the surface. The problem inherent in the surface of things, and only in the surface of things, is the heart of things."[69] Strauss's point here is that readers who delve too far into the depths of a text without also explicating that which first comes to sight in a text—its surface, its form—may fail to grasp the scope, import, and substance of the author's meaning.[70]

Studying Strauss "Between the Lines"

Studying Strauss's own texts presents the reader with a "twofold problem." As Orr has explained, "His writing is usually in the form of a commentary on a given text, written to bring the ideas within that text to life. It is, therefore, difficult at times to distinguish between his elucidation of any given text and his own thought, to separate the philosopher being analyzed from the analyzing philosopher." Orr continues, "The second problem is the one for which Strauss and his school have been most excoriated: his teaching on esotericism, or reading between the lines."[71]

M. F. Burnyeat likewise maintains that there are "two ways" to read Strauss; but he recommends neither of them. The first is to read Strauss's "fourteen books and a multitude of learned papers"; the second is to "sign up for initiation with a Straussian teacher."[72] Burnyeat proceeds then to heap further scorn upon Strauss's rediscovery of the exoteric-esoteric distinction: "It was Maimonides who started it. It was from him that Strauss drew his idea of 'esoteric literature.' . . . Strauss's fantastical supposition is that, whether we are dealing with the allusiveness of Machiavelli and other Renaissance writers, . . . or with the dialogues of Plato and Xenophon, in each case Maimonides' instructions to his twelve-century readers will unlock a secret teaching."[73]

Like Burnyeat, Orr regards esotericism as an important theme for Strauss. Orr says the idea is part of "his appeal." However, unlike Burnyeat, Orr does not take Strauss to task for the idea: "Strauss consistently showed his contemporaries that in their failure to read texts carefully they had, in fact, misunderstood many philosophers. . . ." Orr goes on, "Fundamental to Strauss's teaching on reading between the lines is that only a few will be sufficiently intelligent and diligent enough to discover any hidden meaning in a text. As he states in *Thoughts on Machiavelli*, 'to speak the truth is sensible only when one speaks to wise men.' "[74] Elsewhere, Strauss says that in modern times, from Lessing and Kant onwards, "the question of exotericism seems to have been lost sight of almost completely."[75] The key word here is "almost"—Strauss, too, had great interest in the same "question"; for instance, he dealt with it in his critique of modern historical writing and in his own approach to hermeneutics and the art of writing.[76]

The attendant obstacles in studying Strauss represent a Gordian knot: should one unravel it or cut through it in one clean sweep? Kenneth Green advises, "In unraveling the mysteries of Leo Strauss, we may perhaps be quite well-advised to proceed first through the obvious perplexities."[77] Critics who accuse Strauss of harboring Machiavellian views on religion and morality,[78] and critics who dismiss him as a godfather of the American conservative revolt against modernity, cut through the Gordian knot; but they neglect the core of his project, namely, his contemplation of the revelation-reason question. Condemning Strauss as a closet Machiavellian, or as an "authoritarian antidemocratic,"[79] is to "use [the tactic of] guilt by dubious association."[80] That tactic has more in common with reductio ad absurdum than a reasoned attempt to do full justice to his oeuvre.

According to David Novak, a reader encounters a thinker as a disciple, student, or opponent. "The disciple believes that everything (or almost everything) this thinker says and writes is the truth," whereas "[t]he student . . . believes that some of what the thinker says and writes is true and some of it is not true. Even what the student does not believe is true in the words of the thinker is still respected as a challenging alternative that calls for a respectfully reasoned response." However, "there is the opponent who believes that nothing or almost nothing that the thinker says or writes is true. The response of the opponent is usually one of dismissal, often involving personal ridicule or contempt."[81] Indeed, Conal Condren remarks, "Leo Strauss, distressed at the decadence of the modern world, stood togaed for a generation in the image of a latter-day Cato and bemoaned the abandonment of classical political theory." Shadia Drury says that "proclivities" of "purposeful obfuscations, cold-blooded lies, and fearful mediocrity" characterize "Straussian scholarship."[82] Among Straussians, Novak continues, "there are disputes over what exactly is true in Strauss's teaching and can be accepted, and what is not true in it."[83]

Of the intra-Straussian "disputes," Orr explains, "The split between the West Coast and the East Coast Straussians is much more than a geographical division. It is a dispute over ideas, over the legacy of Leo Strauss." According to Orr, "His East Coast students, such as Allan Bloom and Thomas Pangle, have collapsed the distinction between ancient and modern philosophy, claiming that the real dispute is between philosophy and poetry, poetry being simply the code word for the spiritual realm or revelation."[84] Orr aligns herself with Jaffa, a West Coast Straussian. "For Jaffa, Strauss may have been a skeptic, but he was anything but a dogmatic skeptic. . . . [T]here are passages in Strauss's work that suggest that Jaffa's interpretation is correct." Shortly afterwards, and alluding to the limited usefulness of the East-West Straussian typology, Orr admits, "we cannot turn to Strauss's students—at least immediately—to obtain an accurate understanding of him."[85] To understand Strauss one must read his works "carefully," paying particular attention to "what he writes, the order in which he considers items, and what he fails to mention . . . . Only then can we hope to understand what Strauss himself can teach us."[86] Orr echoes what Bloom says of the effort to understand Machiavelli: "One must constantly stop, consult another text, try to penetrate another character, and walk around the room and think. One must use a pencil and paper, make lists, and count. It is an unending task."[87]

Re-reading Strauss

In its approach to understanding Strauss's contemplation of the revelation-reason question, this book is divided into three parts. Part One addresses the "obvious perplexities" in Strauss, that is, about his thoughts on history and his contemplation on religion and philosophy. I will propose that his idea of history has two main aspects: the speculative and the analytical; the former pertains to what the truth of history is; the latter pertains to practical concerns of how to study it. I will then examine how Strauss depicted the fundamental alternatives as mutually exclusive; paradoxically, he said that an adherent of one alternative must be open to the challenge of the other alternative.

Parts Two and Three of this book take up Strauss's critical study of Machiavelli's teaching—on religion and on morality and politics. To examine one or the other or both of these teachings is to travel over well-worn ground. Yet, no work hitherto written has examined Strauss's critical study to learn how Strauss himself grappled with the revelation-reason question. Part Two examines Strauss's critical study of Machiavelli's teaching on religion. I will treat Machiavelli's critique of Christianity (that it has made men weak and servile) and his reflections on biblical/Christian theology (for instance, on the doctrines of divine providence and creation *ex nihilo*) before probing the core of his general hostility to religion. Apart from his instrumental views on the limited usefulness of religion, Machiavelli's judgments on cosmology and the utility of religion demonstrate a fundamental opposition not to Christianity alone but to all religion; he replaces God with *Fortuna* as the divine being and, in turn, replaces Fortuna with mundane chance.

Part Three turns to philosophical matters. Strauss regards Machiavelli as having defined his notion of virtue against the classical conception of moral virtue. Whereas Aristotle defined virtue as the mean between the extremes of too much and too little, Machiavelli spoke of a mean between virtue and vice that varies with the exigencies of the times. A further examination of Machiavelli's notion of what virtue is and how it shapes human action will show that he directs the common good and governance not toward a higher—viz., transcendent and otherworldly—good but toward man's own will and desires.

Strauss's critical study of Machiavelli's teaching serves to elucidate Strauss's religious and philosophical "presuppositions"[88] and casts light on his understanding of modernity. Strauss's inclination to the "old-fashioned" view of Machiavelli, as "evil," "immoral," and "irreligious," is, George Mosse says, "based upon certain philosophical presuppositions."[89] Felix Gilbert observes, "According to Mr. Strauss Machiavelli indicates through *The Prince* that he is a new Moses, bringer of a new code, and through *The Discourses* that he wants to destroy the authority of the Bible and is imitating Jesus." Gilbert concludes, "The question left—and it is a question that makes Mr. Strauss's book significant—is to explain why Mr. Strauss arrived at this strange interpretation of the meaning of the writings of the great Florentine."[90] For Robert McShea, the answer to that question can be described thus: Strauss offers "not so much a study of Machiavelli" as he does "the exemplification of an ideology"; his presuppositions or "assumptions" point to an "ideological quintessence."[91] But, though Strauss is concerned with the crisis of modernity and with examining, indeed with recovering, the fundamental problems, he does not claim to present concrete solutions or ideological answers for the modern abandonment of revelation and reason; he seeks understanding of the fundamental problems, and commitment to an ideology would foreclose genuine awareness of the problems.

By closely examining Strauss's critical study of Machiavelli's teaching one learns how Strauss dealt with the revelation-reason question. This position agrees with Orr's succinctly stated view: "The key question for the serious student of Strauss to answer is whether or not he held the door open to revelation."[92] Although I agree overall with both Jaffa and Orr, particularly with their conclusions that Strauss the political philosopher was open, not closed, to the possibility of revelation, this book takes its own exegetical, interpretive, and thematic path to that conclusion. Strauss, as Shadia Drury notes, is "a man of ideas"[93]; and he offers, as Charles Larmore explains, a "root-and-branch criticism of modern thought."[94] However, the Strauss that emerges from the critical study is not a man of atheistic, nihilistic, or ideological ideas who poses a radical challenge to Western civilization; he is a philosopher who, in response to the crisis of modernity, seeks to help his contemporaries to return to the fundamental alternatives, to the very origins of Western civilization.[95]

PART ONE

Approaching Leo Strauss

What has taken place in the modern period has been a gradual corrosion and destruction of the heritage of Western civilization. The soul of the modern development, one may say, is a peculiar "realism," the notion that moral principles and the appeal to moral principles—preaching, sermonizing—is ineffective.

—Leo Strauss, "Progress or Return?"

CHAPTER ONE

Leo Strauss's Idea of History

It would be no exaggeration to say that Strauss felt impelled to guide his perplexed contemporaries away from unbelief in moral norms and towards
reconsidering the possibility of both revelation and reason—the two fundamental alternatives that disclose knowledge of the good life. To guide his contemporaries, he needed an idea of history.[1] This idea contains two aspects: the
speculative and the analytical. One can speak of a speculative aspect, for
reflection on the truth or very meaning of history pervades Strauss's critique
of the ontology of historicism. In that critique, he does not dwell upon actions
committed in fulfillment of the ends or problems of history; instead, he dwells
upon the truth of history. One can speak of an analytical aspect, for his
hermeneutic advice is concerned with the proper and necessary study of the
history of political philosophy.[2]

Historicism on the Meaning of History

Modern reflection upon history encompasses issues of historiography and
ontology. The former issue, Michael Murray explains, "is possible only for an
historical being such as man." The latter issue is about historicity—which "has
its existential condition of possibility in the temporalizing of temporality"—
and a fundamental concept of History—of "Being-as-History." Murray goes

on, "the academic conflation of history with historiography...we shall call *historicism*. Epistemologically expressed, historicism claims that all serious philosophical questions about history can be reduced to questions about the methods and disciplines of historiography."[3] Debates about historiography or methodology, Barry Cooper notes, invariably turn into debates about its ontology; and "Strauss compressed the two dimensions of the question. Historicism, he said, is 'the assertion that the fundamental distinction between philosophical and historical questions cannot in the last analysis be maintained.' "[4] Historicism, though, is more than an "assertion"; it is a doctrine of the close relation of reason, knowledge, and existence to time-bound history.[5]

When Strauss dealt with historicism, which he defined as the doctrine that *the* ground of thought is not nature but history,[6] his intent was not to provide a full account of its genesis and development, but to elucidate its tenets and lay bare their inadequacies. Nor was it his intent to examine at length the metaphysics of historicity. In a letter to Eric Voegelin dated 17 March 1949 he remarked, "Your surmise regarding my article 'Political Philosophy and History' is correct: the article is to be thought of as one of the introductory chapters of a publication on classic principles of politics." Strauss's article, a précis of historicism and modern political philosophy, was published in the January 1949 issue of the *Journal of the History of Ideas* and was reprinted in 1959 as chapter 2 in *What Is Political Philosophy?* In the letter Strauss continued, "But heaven only knows if I will manage with this publication: on the decisive questions, there are no preliminary studies, so that one would have to first lay the groundwork through a series of specialized investigations."[7]

Strauss would go on to lay such groundwork in *Natural Right and History*.[8] At the end of its introduction he stated, "Present-day social science rejects natural right on two different, although mostly combined, grounds; it rejects it in the name of History and in the name of the distinction between Facts and Values."[9] Although Strauss elsewhere spoke of Popper and his "washed-out, lifeless positivism,"[10] Strauss's "primary opponent" is "a historicism he believed to be *the spirit of our time*, and a historicism he identified as the forgetting of eternity."[11] In chapter 1 of *Natural Right and History*, shortly after having said that "[t]he genesis of historicism is inadequately understood," Strauss observed, "The historical school emerged in reaction to the French Revolution and to the natural right doctrines that had prepared that cataclysm."[12] Historicism has its roots in the historical school's perception of "the need of preserving or continuing the traditional order." The original inspiration of "the founders" of the "school" was the effort to protect the belief that knowledge of "universal principles" is possible. Thus, they claimed that the "actual here and now is more likely than not to fall short of the universal and unchangeable norm."[13] Strauss then states (again not naming names) that "the eminent conservatives who founded the historical school were, in fact, continuing and even sharpening the revolutionary effort of their adversaries."[14] In his chapter 6 essay on Edmund Burke, Strauss explains that Burke articulated his principles in response to the wake of the French Revolution; Strauss, however, did not mention "historicism" or its "derivatives."[15]

This shift or weakening of faith in knowledge, Strauss explains in chapter 1, modified the notion of the natural held by the French revolutionists. That notion had equated nature with individuality, but had situated the rights of the individual within "local and temporal variety" to avoid the dangers of "antisocial individualism and unnatural universality." The modification of the historical school was its argument "that the local and the temporal have a higher value than the universal." This argument would prove to be problematic. Strauss states, "By denying the significance, if not the existence, of universal norms, the historical school destroyed the only solid basis of all efforts to transcend the actual."[16]

In its effort to formulate "historical principles" that would be "objective" yet "relative to particular historical situations," the historical school turned to "historical studies." These studies, Strauss explains, "assumed" that every nation is characterized by its own "folk minds[et]," that historical changes proceed by "general laws," or "combined both assumptions." When those "assumptions were abandoned, the infancy of historicism came to its end." "Historicism now appeared as a particular form of positivism," as it eschewed "theology and metaphysics" for "positive science."[17] Positivism, past and present, is not entirely empirical, though. Of its metaphysics of historicity, Strauss notes in "Why We Remain Jews," "the object of science is everything that is—being. The belief admitted by all believers in science today—that science is by its nature essentially progressive, and eternally progressive—implies, without saying it, that being is mysterious."[18] Early historicism, he continues in chapter 1 of *Natural Right and History*, did not turn to "the methods of natural science" for empirical knowledge of reality. It turned to "history," to "knowledge of what is truly human, of man as man," not to natural science, in which historicism saw the dubious assertion of universality. Early historicism began by aping the methods of science but later disavowed the purpose and premises of science.[19]

Early historicism was itself, however, riddled with problems. There was a marked disjunction between its assumptions, aspiration, and results. Its aspiration to educe "norms from history" was a failure. Strauss points out, "no universal principle will ever sanction the acceptance of every historical standard or of every victorious cause: to conform with tradition or to jump on 'the wave of the future' is not obviously better." For "the unbiased historian," the course of history is shown by "the meaningless web spun by what men did, produced, and thought"; one sees in history "only standards... of a purely subjective character." Yet, to affirm thus a subjective basis to history renders impossible, Strauss retorts, "the distinction between good and bad choices. Historicism culminated in nihilism."[20]

Strauss means that early historicism led to nihilism but was not itself wholly nihilistic. He notes in chapter 1 that early historicism, though it declaimed universal standards, lingered over the idea that progress underpins the course of history.[21] Here Strauss implies that laws of progress are a latent tendency to view nature in a theistic or deistic manner.[22] In chapter 2, however, he explains that "the historical school ... had tried to establish standards that were particular and historical indeed, but still objective.... It is the recognition of timeless values that distinguishes Weber's position most significantly from historicism."[23] Tied to that recognition, according to Strauss, is Weber's apperception that revealed religion conveys truth about what it means to be.[24]

By claiming that history is the ground of all thought, early historicism had replaced belief in universal norms with belief in the experience of history.[25] Strauss states, "*The historicist thesis is self-contradictory or absurd.* We cannot see the historical character of 'all' thought—that is, of all thought with the exception of the historicist insight and its implications—without transcending history, without grasping something trans-historical."[26] The "radical historicist" is characterized by his adamant denial of "the trans-historical character of the historicist thesis" and by his recognition of "the absurdity of unqualified historicism as a theoretical thesis." The "radical historicist" Strauss has in mind is Nietzsche. Referring to his *Vom Nutzen und Nachteil der Historie für das Leben* (written in 1873, published in 1874), Strauss explains that Nietzsche's denial of the theoretical focus of early historicism signals the emergence of radical historicism.[27]

Nietzsche asked readers of his essay to think about the thesis: "The unhistorical and the historical are necessary in equal measure for the health of an individual, of a people and of a culture."[28] Insisting that history must serve life, he identified three ways to study and to use history. The *monumental* way sees in history monuments of great deeds, by men of action, that instruct men in the present who desire to be great but have no teachers to guide them. The *antiquarian* way protects the past as a source of identity for the masses, who lack the strength of mind and will to be inspired by the present. The *critical* way also seeks to serve life, but fulfills that aim by laying bare the truth of existence, namely, its violence and instability.[29] Nietzsche warned, however, against a surfeit of reflection on the meaning of history. Following on from his précis about the uses of history, he wrote, "modern man drags around with him a huge quantity of indigestible stones of knowledge."[30] The target of his ire, Thomas Howard points out, was the "*a priori* claims of knowledge among theologians and philosophers alike."[31]

For Nietzsche, the purpose of the historian is not to form self-forgetting laws of history. Countering Plato's "mighty *necessary lie*" of an eternal order of nature with the "necessary truth" of history, he claimed that one is without life or cannot live a full life if one fails to recognize the chaos of existence; "genuine life," he said, is "the basis of culture."[32] The "excess of history," however, prevents that recognition. The remedy for that excess is the interplay between science, on the one hand, and art and religion, on the other hand. Science lauds scientific knowledge and knowledge of "things historical," not art, religion, or "things eternal." Science "hates forgetting, which is the death of knowledge, and seeks to abolish all limitations of horizon and launch mankind upon an infinite and unbounded sea of light whose light is knowledge of all becoming." Nietzsche doubted the efficacy of that scientific aspiration. He insisted that life must rule over science, not science over life; knowledge belongs within the ambit of life, of existence. "Thus science requires superintendence and supervision."[33]

While Strauss regarded Nietzsche as the originary radical historicist, he emphasized the role of Heidegger in determining the shape and substance of radical historicism. In a letter to Karl Löwith dated 15 August 1946 Strauss stated, "With Heidegger, 'historicity' has made nature disappear *completely*, which however has the merit of consistency and compels one to reflect."[34] In a letter to Kojève dated 24 March 1950 Strauss asked, "Have you seen Heidegger's *Holzwege*? Most interesting, much that is outstanding, and on the whole bad: the most extreme historicism." In a letter to Kojève dated 26 June 1950 Strauss remarked, "I have once again been dealing with Historicism, that is to say, with Heidegger, the only *radical* historicist."[35] In these letters Strauss describes Heidegger in a concise but abrupt manner as both original and presenting a radical challenge to Western thought. In chapter 1 of *Natural Right and History* Strauss elaborates this epigrammatic thread of the critique of Heidegger—as radical—he made the epistolary medium. He states, "The most thoroughgoing attempt to establish historicism culminated in the assertion that if and when there are no human beings, there may be *entia*, but there cannot be *esse*, that is, that there can be *entia* while there is no *esse*. There is an obvious connection between this assertion and the rejection of the view that 'to be' in the highest sense means 'to be always.' "[36] Strauss does not name Heidegger as the author of that "attempt," though he likely had Heidegger in mind.[37] In the words of Heidegger, "There is no time when man was not, not because man was from all eternity and will be for all eternity but because time is not eternity and time fashions itself into a time only as a human, historical being-there."[38]

Strauss clearly was preoccupied with the fate of philosophy in modern times. Yet it would be a mistake to argue, as Hwa Yol Jung does, that due to that preoccupation Strauss failed to grasp the import of Heidegger's ontology; namely, its "disclosure of Being."[39] Heidegger's "great achievement," Strauss stated in his lecture "Existentialism," "was the coherent exposition of *Existenz*. . . . Kierkegaard had spoken of existence within the traditional horizon, i.e. within the horizon of the traditional distinction between essence and existence. Heidegger tried to understand existence out of itself."[40]

In his effort to understand the meaning of Being, Heidegger stressed the historicity of man.[41] In his essay "The Anaximander Fragment" he argued, "What can all merely historiological philosophies of history tell us about our history . . . if they explain history without ever thinking out, from the essence of history, the fundamentals of their way of explaining events, and the essence of history, in turn, from Being itself?"[42] In other words, history should be understood in an existential, not historiological, manner; disciplines of history, philosophy, and theology fail to grasp the meaning of Being. *The* question of Being, Heidegger explained in *Existence and Being*, "fixes its attention on the one thing that is the mark of 'truth' of every kind."[43]

Several themes underlie Heidegger's answer or approach to the question of Being. First, he bases truth and the meaning of Being in human temporality, not in general representations of beings.[44] Second, he depicts human temporality as the horizon formed by the putting into time of both past events and futural possibilities upon the flux of the here and now.[45] Third, he sees in finitude the peak and facticity of human existence.[46] And fourth, he replaces philosophy in the classical sense—the quest for knowledge of first principles—with a philosophy of Being—an ontology about the history-bound, worldly character of all thought and all life.[47]

Historicism forgets eternity and claims that the ground of human thought is history, not nature.[48] "Thought," Peter Gordon explains for Heidegger, "is no longer the origin of temporality but is itself awash in the temporality that makes thought possible."[49] The classics did not, Strauss explains, recognize "a 'field,' a 'world' " of existence called "History" that was separate and superior to "that other 'field,' 'Nature'"; nor did the classics recognize "'History' as an object of knowledge."[50] As Heidegger put it, "even Nature is historical. It is *not* historical, to be sure, in so far as we speak of 'natural history'; but Nature is historical as a countryside, as an area that has been colonized or exploited."[51] Strauss took issue with historicism, for he defended the challenge of the philosophic quest for knowledge and truth.[52] Through the act of interpreting past thinkers, he defended philosophy: "We cannot be passionately interested, seriously interested in the past if we know beforehand that the present is in the most important respect superior to the past."[53] Strauss defended the *quest* for *truth*, but he was not an absolutist. He regarded absolutism as foreign to the philosophic quest, and described the attempt to steer a path between absolutism and relativism as "sufficient" for identifying "a universally valid hierarchy of ends" of moral and intellectual perfection. He claimed, however, that such a path "is insufficient for guiding our actions."[54] The philosopher seeks knowledge of the whole, but stops far short of claiming, in a dogmatic manner, *possession* of complete or final knowledge of the whole. One can, then, to echo Strauss's view of what philosophy is, describe the speculative aspect of his idea of history as neither relativistic nor absolutist.[55]

Turning to History

Strauss conveyed his hermeneutic advice, which comes to sight as advice on *how* to study the history of political philosophy, in a pointed manner. In a letter to Voegelin dated 29 April 1953 he wrote, "there is a fundamental distinction between the technique of true philosophy and that of modern philosophy." He then noted that he had "explained" that distinction in his essay, "Persecution and the Art of Writing."[56] The essay was published in the November 1941 issue of *Social Research* and was reprinted in 1952 as chapter 2 in the work of the same name. In the essay Strauss summarized thus the different literary and philosophic techniques of premodern and modern thinkers: "Modern historical research . . . has counteracted or even destroyed an earlier tendency to read between the lines of the great writers."[57]

According to Paul Cantor, "Strauss's theory of interpretation resulted from a great leap of historical imagination." That leap was the thesis that writers and philosophers in past eras who lived under "illiberal and intolerant regimes" concealed the true import of their writings to avoid persecution and punishment.[58] Paul Bagley explains that when the esoteric is different in "form or content" from the exoteric, that is, from the teaching a writer presents in public, the esoteric may be identified by whoever has access to the esoteric text.[59] When the esoteric resides within the form or content of the exoteric, only initiates will be able to identify the teaching, even if access to the exoteric text is available to non-initiates; initiates alone are able to identify the secret teaching of the text.[60] For Brague, though, the "originality" of Strauss's theory of interpretation "does not lie in the claim that there is a difference between (a) levels of readers, more or less gifted and acute, and (b) levels of meaning, more or less superficial. Neither is this originality to be looked for in his asserting that some texts are esoteric."[61] His originality consists in the fact, as Brague sees it, that Islamic and Jewish views of revelation underpin his views on esotericism. Esotericism is not simply a response to "merely exterior causes," such as persecution. "It corresponds to inner features of the Islamic conception of Revelation, that is, to the way it conceives of the basic relationship of man to the Absolute. First, Revelation in Islam is a mere fact, a *factum brutum*. . . . Second, its content is a text, a written text, a book. The phenomenon of the Sacred Book is far more peculiar to Islam than to Christianity." Of that difference between Islam and Christianity Brague notes, "Judaism stands midway: Unlike Christianity and like Islam, it does not admit an incarnation, and what is revealed is a law; unlike Islam, however, its sacred writings are not immediately present but mediated through the very process of their reception, discussion, and interpretation."[62]

The approach to exegesis that esotericism connotes raises certain questions: "Do we need seven seals to keep an uninspired majority in the dark," asks Kenneth Seeskin, "and at what point does esotericism keep even the inspired minority guessing about the real meaning of the text?" To answer his questions, Seeskin offers to define esotericism in two ways: "normal" and "deep." The former "applies to a book that deals with a complex and demanding subject and requires intense concentration to be appreciated. Although the uninspired majority may not be able to follow it, the book contains no booby traps, blind alleys, or concealed doctrines—at least none that the author has put there intentionally." The latter "applies to a book in which the author hides the true meaning behind hints, clues, or cleverly constructed diversions."[63] I would add, then, that numerology, with its religious or Cabalistic stress upon reading between the lines and divining the significance of numeric patterns, would seem to be an important way to uncover the true meaning of a text. Of the numerological aspect of Strauss's "rules for reading," it suffices to say here that numerology was an ancillary way by which he cast light on the esoteric teachings of past thinkers.[64]

James Rhodes, although he does not use the terms "normal" and "deep" esotericism, would say that Strauss combines the two types of esotericism: "At first, his analysis of irony [in *The City and Man*] seems straightforward. As one reads further into his work [see also *Persecution and the Art of Writing*], however, one realizes that *he writes esoterically about esotericism*. Therefore, his account of its purposes is difficult to understand."[65] While it is beyond the scope of this chapter to determine whether Strauss's esotericism is "normal," "deep," or both, I would argue that he aims to understand thinkers as they understood themselves. His esotericism, however understood, is inextricably linked to his close reading of books, of their intentions, surface tensions, and drifts in argument. That he writes at times in an elliptical manner places logographic—as well as philosophic and theological—demands on the reader to understand the texts at hand. In his way, he helps to equip the reader with a sense of cognitive and textual appreciation for the philosopher's unremitting *quest* for knowledge.[66]

Strauss did not claim an *absolute* insight into the meaning of history, as some critics would say; for they insist that his hermeneutic advice is a doctrine, or even an ideology.[67] By his own account, Strauss did not "possess and present a comprehensive doctrine"; he described his "own hermeneutic experience" as "very limited."[68] Although one must, he says, recognize "the transtemporal truth" of the "fundamental problems," he stresses that "history of philosophy is endangered if the historian starts from the acceptance of any solution of the fundamental problems: if he knows in advance that a given philosophic doctrine which he is studying is false, he lacks the incentive for studying that doctrine with sympathy or care."[69]

Notwithstanding its religious import, hermeneutic activity, to Strauss, is a movement toward philosophy or is philosophy itself. In his lecture "Existentialism" he observes, "The scholar faces the fundamental problems through the intermediacy of books. If he is a serious man through the intermediacy of the great books. The great thinker faces the problems directly."[70] Of *how* one faces the problems, Strauss explains elsewhere that one moves from interpretation to explanation—interpretation is the careful, exact commentary of a book; explanation aims to impart critical insight about its intent, teachings, and influence.[71] Strauss clearly is drawing a distinction between literary and philosophic questions, but he does not mean to say that those questions are heterogeneous. Instead, he means that only when one has considered the literary question of the author's presentation of the matter at hand can one properly consider the fundamental problems.[72]

Strauss's call for a return to the classics, to their texts and "signposts," seems diagnostic and palliative. "The signposts which guided the thinkers of the past," he says, "must be *recovered* before they can be used."[73] The study of history has "philosophic significance," for by that study the perplexed of the modern era will find their way to the "fundamental problems," to "the natural horizon of human thought."[74] The return to the classics is not a nostalgic return; it is philosophical.[75] Strauss is explicit in "What Is Liberal Education?": "No deliberation about remedies for our ills can be of any value if it is not preceded by an honest diagnosis—by a diagnosis falsified neither by unfounded hopes nor by fear of the powers that be." Yet in this diagnosis, "we must not mistake palliatives for cures. . . . Liberal education of adults must now also compensate for the defects of an education which is liberal only in name or by courtesy. Last but not least, liberal education is concerned with the souls of men."[76]

The analytical or, as one could thus put it, educative aspect of Strauss's idea of history is inextricably linked with his critique of "the crisis of our time." His 1964 lecture of the same title "tried," he said in the accompanying lecture, "The Crisis of Political Philosophy," "to trace the crisis of our time to the crisis of political philosophy, and I suggested that a way out of the intellectual difficulties with which we are beset is a return to classical political philosophy."[77] (According to John Gunnell, one should not forget that "concrete" problems accompanied those difficulties; perhaps Gunnell means to say that Strauss gave the two "Crisis" lectures at a time of domestic unrest and struggles against Western colonial powers.[78]) Apart from several brief mentions of Oswald Spengler, Strauss in his first lecture did not cite any historian, philosopher, or thinker who was, like Spengler,[79] drawing attention to the "crisis" and "decline" of the West. The decline consists, Strauss says, of the West's doubt in its once strongly avowed purpose of universal society,[80] and of its skepticism about an original purpose of modernity—Hobbes argued that conquering nature relieves the estate of man from the uncertainty of life in the state of nature.[81] Contemporary social science doubts the efficacy of those purposes of modernity; it claims, Strauss explains, "that no distinction between good or bad values is rationally possible."[82]

Strauss, then, declined to examine at length the "fact-value distinction." His concern was "with a somewhat broader issue": how social science today can and must acquire an adequate understanding of "political things."[83] Indeed, as John Hallowell said in 1950, "Western civilization is in its Time of Troubles. It is beset on all sides by challenges which threaten to destroy it. It is the kind of response which we make to those challenges, however, rather than the challenges themselves, which will determine the outcome."[84] Strauss's concern is visible in his earlier examinations of the fact-value distinction. In his essay on Max Weber in chapter 2 of *Natural Right and History* he argued, "value-free social science was neither possible nor desirable."[85] (In an implicit recognition that Weber was no mere positivist, Strauss nowhere in chapter 2 used the word "positivism.") In "What Is Political Philosophy?," Strauss spoke of the necessity to "all political action" of an adequate understanding of "the good life." Having then defined political philosophy as the "quest" for truth about "political things," he described contemporary political thought as diametrically opposed to that goal and its "very possibility."[86]

To cast light on that opposition, Strauss identified in positivistic social science a cluster of problems.[87] First, one cannot "study social phenomena, i.e., all important social phenomena, without making value judgments." Second, an unproven assumption underlies the fact-value distinction. "The rejection of value judgments is based on the assumption that the conflicts between different values or value-systems are essentially insoluble for human reason." Third, due to its assumption "that scientific knowledge" is *the* "peak of human knowledge," positivism blinded itself to "the whole political or politico-social order" in which "political facts" belong. Fourth, "Positivism necessarily transforms itself into historicism." That is, because positivism claims that distinctive social, historical, and political phenomena underpin all eras, it must view itself as a phenomenon; but to take that view "leads to the relativization of social science and ultimately of modern science generally." Indeed, rejecting faith in "the authoritative character of modern science," radical historicism claims that science is but "one form," not the highest form, of human knowledge.[88]

In speaking of the pressing facts of his time, Strauss, like Spengler, raises a *Zeitgeist* of crisis; but unlike Spengler, he deals with and admits the possibility of transcendent, eternal truth; he does not suggest, as Spengler did, that the core of philosophy is the history—and the *history* alone—of philosophy.[89] Contemporary political science cannot, Strauss stated in "The Crisis of Our Time," gain an adequate understanding of "political things" by surveying "the history of political philosophy." An example of the survey-like approach is "that famous work"—*A History of Political Theory*—"by Sabine." According to Strauss, "It is, strictly speaking, absurd to replace political philosophy by the history of political philosophy"; and yet Sabine "replace[s] a doctrine which claims to be true by a survey of errors."[90] The method of "logic" claims that the works of thinkers in the past abound in blunders because they conflated "factual judgments" with "value judgments." In line with "the demands of logical positivism or behavorial science," the "new" way of studying politics "is concerned with discovering laws of political behavior and, ultimately, universal laws of political behavior."[91]

According to Strauss, in its attempt not to confuse the political thought of a past era with another past era or with the present era, "[t]he new political science thus becomes dependent upon a kind of study which belongs to the comprehensive enterprise called universal history."[92] The enterprise, which dates back to ancient Greek, Jewish, and Roman historiography, seeks to describe the history of the world, especially the rise of civilization and of the nation state, from beginning to end.[93] Whereas ancient historiographers sought to elucidate in a teleological fashion the course of history, modern historians replace the metaphysical search for transcendent order in history with an empirical effort to discover laws of, and stages in, history.[94] The scope of universal history, Löwith points out, "is universal in a very limited sense only. ... We do not ask for the meaning of heaven and earth, the stars, the ocean and the mountains ... Our quest seems to be restricted to ourselves and to history as our history."[95]

Strauss goes on to explain that, to differentiate its own era from past eras, and to understand the political teaching of its own era as a transformation of an original teaching, a teaching it deems inferior to its own teaching, the new political science must be able "to grasp the original teaching as such." The new political science must study classical political philosophy, because in reflecting on its own background and premises, it "must at least consider the possibility that the older political science was sounder and truer than what is regarded as political science today."[96] The return to the classics, then, "is both necessary and tentative or experimental."[97]

Not in any sense tentative is the reason for the return. In a letter to Voegelin dated 9 May 1943 Strauss wrote, "An authentic beginning in the social sciences is impossible before the fundamental concepts are clarified, which means an awareness that the fundamental concepts—the very term 'political,' for example— are of Greek, and in particular of Greek philosophic origin."[98] That awareness, Strauss explained elsewhere, will occur only if study of the classics is "accompanied by constant and relentless reflection on the modern principles, and hence by liberation from the naive acceptance of those principles."[99]

Strauss's judgment that the return to the classics is tentative echoes his equivocal affirmation of classical cosmology—as carrying partially "false" or outmoded ideas about nature and the world. In *Philosophy and Law* Strauss stated, "[O]f Aristotle it is the case that everything he says about the world below the lunar sphere is undoubtedly true, while his views about the upper world, especially about the separate intelligences, are in part only probable, and in part actually false."[100] However, in "What Is Political Philosophy?" Strauss refuted the charge that the return to the classics is impossible because of its "antiquated cosmology," explaining, "Whatever the significance of modern natural science may be, it cannot affect our understanding of what is human in man." He went on:

> To understand man in the light of the whole means for modern natural science to understand man in the light of the sub-human. But in that light man as man is wholly unintelligible. Classical political philosophy viewed man in a different light. It was originated by Socrates. And Socrates was so far from being committed to a specific cosmology that his knowledge was knowledge of ignorance. Knowledge of ignorance is not ignorance. It is knowledge of the elusive character of the truth, of the whole. Socrates, then, viewed man in the light of the mysterious character of the whole. . . . This understanding of the situation of man which includes, then, the quest for cosmology rather than a solution to the cosmological problem, was the foundation of classical political philosophy.[101]

Strauss's approach to the problem of cosmology in modern times entails, then, a defense of the possibility of cosmology. He defends Aristotle, Socrates, and Plato in their respective cosmological accounts, though he suggests that the possibility of cosmology, because it is a possibility, "an open question,"[102] does not necessarily conflict with modern, non-teleotheological views of nature, history, and the whole of human things.[103]

Strauss's idea of history is an idea of what history is, how one studies it, and why it is important to do so. The speculative and the analytical aspects of his idea of history correspond to the two levels on which he examined historicism: the ontological and the methodological. For Strauss, history cannot be defined in purely temporal terms; the meaning of history is not revealed by the historicist exploration or ontology of Being. In laying bare the faults of historicism and "the crisis of our time," he raised the hermeneutical issue of how to approach texts written by past thinkers. In raising this issue, he sought to recover knowledge of the good life. He drew attention to transcendent meaning in history, but did not claim an absolute insight into the meaning of history; nor did he analyze the structure of history. Overall, Strauss's idea of history is practical rather than speculative, for in elucidating the meaning of history and directing attention to the fundamental alternatives, he was responding to a particular "historical" problem, namely, "the crisis of our time."

CHAPTER TWO

Revelation and Reason in Leo Strauss

Revelation and reason are pivotal in Strauss's project, yet nearly three decades after his death, questions remain about the essential meaning of this core dimension of his thought. Scholarship of recent years has tended to approach his project by situating its position in relation to revelation and reason—to one or the other or to both.[1] Among those who hold Strauss in high regard and inclusive of his former students, those often called Straussians, the view is far from unanimous.[2] Did Strauss give his allegiance to reason alone, that is, to Athens and classical political philosophy? Did his vocation as a political philosopher and his loyalty to the party of Athens preclude his being open to revelation, that is, open to the possibility that the Bible conveys truths regarding the good life? Or was he beyond a dogmatic attachment whether to reason or to revelation?

Central in Strauss's oeuvre is his delineation of the decisive areas of agreement and disagreement between the Bible and Greek philosophy about what is good, just, virtuous, best, and right. Looking back on his 1936 book on Hobbes, Strauss wrote in 1965 in his "Preface to *Hobbes Politische Wissenschaft*," "My study of Hobbes began in the context of an investigation of the origins of biblical criticism in the seventeenth century, namely, of Spinoza's *Theologico-Political Treatise....* Since then the theological-political problem has remained *the* theme of my investigations."[3] Strauss's thought has been described as "conservative" and he himself as "an atheist," but he did not respond to this "problem" by articulating an atheistic vision of the good life. Instead, he sought to restore both "the authority of the moral order common to philosophy and the Bible" and "the conviction that human life could be well lived only by devotion to the 'high.'"[4] In his own way, Strauss raised "'the all important question' *quid sit deus*."[5] Nor did Strauss respond to the theological-political problem by enunciating a political program. He was not known either to have belonged or given his imprimatur to any political party.[6] His concern about politics "was primarily realized in education: his most passionate polemics were directed against trends or tendencies in the academy."[7]

The elucidation of each fundamental alternative, that they are immiscible, and their mutual opposition to modernity are key themes for Strauss, especially in his works "Jerusalem and Athens," "Progress or Return?" and "The Mutual Influence of Theology and Philosophy." He says in these works that, although the alternatives agree on the importance of morality, revelation proclaims obedience to God as the one thing needful for life, whereas reason proclaims the sufficiency of the autonomous quest for knowledge. Thus, Bloom and Pangle both claim that Strauss's allegiance was with Athens alone; but to Jaffa, Strauss's loyalty to Athens in no way prevented his openness to Jerusalem.[8] Although I agree overall with Jaffa and Orr, this chapter takes its own exegetical and interpretive path to explicating Strauss's openness to revelation. To understand how Strauss remained loyal to Athens while listening with care to the call of Jerusalem, it helps to have an understanding of how he perceived the alternatives—the variety of terms he used and how he employed them. Through the analysis of how Strauss perceived the relation between the alternatives, and focusing on the above works as they eloquently bear witness to his own meditation upon the conflict between revelation and reason, I endeavor in this chapter to explicate his philosophical openness to revelation.[9]

Defining Revelation and Reason

Faith and Belief vs. Biblical Criticism

Knowledge of revelation ("Jerusalem") and reason ("Athens") is crucial if people in the West are to find their way out of the morass of modernity, Strauss emphasizes in the opening paragraph of Part I of his lecture "Jerusalem and Athens: Some Preliminary Reflections."[10] To underscore the contrast, Part I is entitled "The Beginning of the Bible and Its Greek Counterparts." Both the Bible and Greek philosophy claim to represent "true wisdom."[11]

One must be open, then, to Jerusalem and to Athens.[12] Yet, people who pursue knowledge because they "wish to become wise" side with Athens from the very outset of their quest for "wisdom," Strauss states. "By saying that we wish to hear first and then to act to decide, we have already decided in favor of Athens against Jerusalem."[13]

The choice for Athens is made by people who, in seeking wisdom, feel compelled to "accept the principle" of biblical criticism—"all of us who cannot be orthodox," who feel unable to continue as committed believers. Strauss observes that in the orthodox view, the biblical account of the deeds of God and the prophets is "true and authentic"; to biblical criticism the Bible is an unauthentic and "derivative" collection "not of 'histories' but of 'memories of ancient histories,' to borrow a Machiavellian expression."[14] To Strauss, the expression encapsulates the originary spirit of biblical criticism; he referred to *Discourses* I 16, though the expression is from II 5.[15]

Machiavelli speaks in *Discourses* II 5 of the suppression by the "Christian sect" of "that ancient theology" of the "Gentile sect," a theology that maintained "the world is eternal." The "Christian sect"—Christianity in general and the "modes taken by Saint Gregory"—sought by "persecution" to suppress "all the ancient memories." However, because Christianity failed to replace the Latin language "with a new language," it was unable to eradicate completely those "memories" and the Gentile theology. Machiavelli then implies that the Bible is a collection of myths, of fabulous and mendacious memories. "And because these [Gentile and Christian] sects vary two or three times in five or in six thousand years, the memory of the things done prior to that time is lost; and if, however, some sign of them remains, it is considered as something *fabulous* and is not lent faith to—as happened to the history of Diodorus Siculus, which, though it renders an account of forty or fifty thousand years, is nonetheless reputed, as I believe it to be, a *mendacious* thing."[16]

Spinoza carried Machiavelli's critical reflections further. "Biblical criticism reached its first climax in Spinoza's *Theological-Political Treatise*, which is frankly anti-theological," Strauss explains. Spinoza read the Bible as a "poorly" formulated collection "of remnants of ancient prejudices or superstitions."[17] In the words of Spinoza, "Scripture does not explain things by their secondary causes, but only narrates them in the order and the style which has most power to move men, and especially uneducated men, to devotion." Hence, "its object is not to convince the reason, but to attract and lay hold of the imagination."[18]

Strauss goes on to explain that biblical criticism in the nineteenth and twentieth centuries went further than Spinoza's critique of the Bible. "[W]hereas for Spinoza imagination is simply sub-rational, it was assigned a much higher rank in later times; it was understood as the vehicle of religious or spiritual experience, which necessarily expresses itself in symbols and the like." Ascribing the status of myth to the biblical accounts of signs, miracles, and wonders, later biblical criticism insists "that the Bible contains both 'myth and history.'" However, that distinction between myth and history cannot be found in the Bible. Strauss observes, "From the point of view of the Bible the 'myths' are as true as the 'histories': what Israel 'in fact' did or suffered cannot be understood except in the light of the 'facts' of Creation and Election."[19]

Having addressed biblical criticism, which he describes elsewhere as atheistic,[20] Strauss reflects, "It is true that we cannot ascribe to the Bible the theological concept of miracles, for that concept presupposes that of nature and the concept of nature is foreign to the Bible."[21] Strauss's point is that while the Bible does not contain the Greek concept of *nature* as eternal and prior to God, the Prime Mover, it contains a concept of divinely revealed prescriptions for society; and those prescriptions are inextricably linked with an account of beginnings of the heavens, the earth, and the human race.

Theology in the Bible and Greek Philosophy

Strauss continues, however: "We shall not take issue with the findings and even the premises of biblical criticism. Let us grant that the Bible and in particular the Torah consists to a considerable extent of 'memories of ancient histories,' even memories of memories."[22] By so describing the Bible and the Torah, Strauss did not mean to let go unchallenged the trenchant biblical criticism of Machiavelli, Spinoza, and later times. Indeed, toward the end of Part I Strauss replies to biblical criticism by drawing parallels between the notions of the divine enunciated by Aristotle, Plato, and the Bible. He explains, "The Aristotelian god like the biblical God is a thinking being, but in opposition to the biblical god he is only a thinking being." The biblical God is both "a thinking being" and "a creator-god." In contrast, the Aristotelian god does not preside over the world "by giving orders and laws. Hence he is not a creator god: the world is as eternal as god."[23]

Implicit to Aristotle's conception of goodness is an account of the eternal order of nature. God is the first principle upon which the heavens (the sun, the moon, and the planets) and nature (humans, animals, and plants) depend. God presides over nature; he did not create it. God, the Prime Mover, set the heavenly bodies in spatial and circular motion. The good man is good because the object of his thought is not himself; for the good man, unlike the man who is not good, the eternal order of nature is his reference point for his thoughts and thinking about virtue and goodness. The good man is a man whose thinking is at one with the object of his thought; what is good is that which is good by the eternal order of nature, and the proper end of thought is the good. "For both thinking and the act of thought will belong even to one who has the worst of thoughts. Therefore if this ought to be avoided . . . , the act of thinking cannot be the best of things. Therefore it must be itself that thought thinks (since it is the most excellent of things), and its thinking is a thinking on thinking."[24]

Strauss writes in *The City and Man* that Aristotle, like the Bible, "is concerned above all with the truth of religion."[25] In contrast, he says in "Jerusalem and Athens" that Plato's notion about the creation "by an invisible God" of "heaven and earth" is closer to the Bible than is Aristotle's notion of "pure reason." Shortly afterwards Strauss states, "What Plato himself calls *the theology* consists of two teachings: 1) God is good and hence is no way the cause of evil; 2) God is simple and hence unchangeable."[26] Plato aims in his theological teachings to inculcate piety and correct knowledge about God.[27] Socrates opens the first teaching by claiming, "The god must surely always be described such as he is" (*Republic* 379a), namely, as "the cause of a few things for human beings and not responsible for most. For the things that are good for us are far fewer than those that are bad; and of the good things, no one else must be said to be the cause; of the bad things, some other causes must be sought and not the god" (379c). The second teaching opens with Socrates asking, "Now, what about this second one? Do you suppose the god is a wizard, able treacherously to reveal himself at different times in different *ideas* . . . Or is he simple and does he least of all things depart from his own *idea*?" (380d).[28]

Having spoken of Plato's theology, Strauss indicates a preference for Plato's notion of God over Aristotle's notion: "On the divine concern with men's justice and injustice, the Platonic teaching is in fundamental agreement with the biblical teaching; it even culminates in a statement that agrees almost literally with biblical statements."[29] Strauss's observation is compelling. Furthermore, his accompanying footnote is itself illuminating: he instructs the reader to compare Plato's *Laws*, 905a4–b2, with Amos 9:1–3 and Psalm 139:7–10.[30] Plato and the Bible both say that God rewards and supports those who lead just lives, and punishes those who are evil and lead unjust lives; one cannot escape divine justice. The Athenian stranger explains: "This is the justice of heaven, which neither you nor any other unfortunate will ever glory in escaping, and which the ordaining powers have specially ordained; take good heed thereof, for it will be sure to take heed of you. If you say:—I am small and will creep into the depths of the earth, or I am high and will fly up to heaven, you are not so small or so high but that you shall pay the fitting penalty, either here or in the world below or in some still more savage place whither you shall be conveyed. This is also the explanation of the fate of those whom you saw, who had done unholy and evil deeds" (*Laws* 905a–b).[31] Psalm 139:7–10 proclaims,

> Where can I go from your Spirit?
>   Where can I flee from your presence?
> If I go up to the heavens, you are there;
>   if I make my bed in the depths, you are there.
> If I rise on the wings of the dawn,
>   if I settle on the far side of the sea,
> even there your hand will guide me,
>   your right hand will hold me fast.

In Amos 9:1, the shepherd Amos declares,

> I saw the Lord standing by the altar, and he said:
>   "Strike the tops of the pillars
>   so that the thresholds shake.
>   Bring them down on the heads of all the people;
>   those who are left I will kill with the sword.
>   Not one will get away,
>   none will escape."[32]

Strauss's parallel between the Bible and Plato, about divine concern with justice, and his above instruction to the reader, make a crucial point. The point is this: although the Bible does not have a concept of nature, it does have a theology of what is first, sacred, and ultimate, a theology of the true, natural horizon of law, goodness, and moral virtue.[33] By attributing such a theology to the Bible, Strauss, in effect, has modified his earlier statement that the Bible does not have a concept of nature.

Implicit to Strauss's parallel is a twofold pattern. On the one hand, he is acknowledging a Christian view of revelation, insofar as he imputes to the Bible a *theology* of *faith* in divine providence[34] and hence suggests that the core meaning of revelation be defined vis-à-vis revealed theology. On the other hand, underpinning his imputation is a Jewish view of revelation as "the legal interpretation" of sacred doctrines that teach the imperative of obedience to divine law. In the introduction to *Persecution and the Art of Writing* he explained, "Revelation as understood by Jews and Muslims has the character of Law (*torah, shariʿa*) rather than of Faith. . . . For the Christian, the sacred doctrine is revealed theology; for the Jew and the Muslim, the sacred doctrine is, at least primarily, the legal interpretation of the Divine Law (*talmud* or *fiqh*)."[35]

Strauss is making a case for revelation as meaning primarily the interpretation of biblical precepts on goodness and morality. In using such terms to describe his case, one does not speak amiss. In Part III of "Progress or Return?" he uses the terms "miracles," "theology," "revelation," "divine law," "divine code," "divine wisdom," "revealed law," and the "biblical way of life"; and he speaks of "unbelievers" and "believers," of "unbelief" and "faith" in revelation.[36] In addition, he speaks of a "theologians" and a "theological" defense of "revelation" and of "biblical views" about creation, miracles, and prophecies. However, he does not specifically mention revealed theology in the strictly defined sense of a body of systematic principles, built on divinely revealed knowledge, that prove and explain the existence of God.[37]

Strauss defines revelation, then, by identifying what the Bible and Greek philosophy have and do not have in common. In Part II of "Progress or Return?" he explains that "radical disagreement" exists between the Bible and Greek philosophy: whereas the former regards obedience to God as paramount, the latter regards the pursuit of "autonomous" reason as all-important. "Yet this very disagreement presupposes some agreement." Explicating that agreement, Strauss states that the three key traits of modernity "are rejected explicitly or implicitly by both the Bible and Greek philosophy."[38] Earlier in Part II, he had argued that those traits consist of the "anthropocentric" notion that humankind is "the origin of all meaning"; the proclivity to ascribe preeminence to "rights" over "duties"; and the insistence that "freedom" is not "radically limited" by "the whole order of nature or creation," as was claimed in premodern times. Strauss declines, though, to examine further the mutual opposition of the Bible and Greek philosophy to modernity. He observes, "But this agreement is, of course, only an implicit one, and we should rather look at the agreement as it appeared directly in the text."[39]

Biblical and Philosophic Moral Precepts

"[T]he Bible and Greek philosophy agree in regard to what we may call, and we do call in fact, morality," Strauss writes. "They agree" about the "importance of morality," but not about "the basis of morality." Strauss examines their agreement first. He explains that agreement exists between the Bible and

Plato's "specific prescriptions for human society, . . . and what Plato's *Laws* say about this subject agrees fully with what Moses says."[40] That Strauss says "specific prescriptions" indicates he has in mind the detailed discussions in Books VI to XII—especially Book X—rather than the introductory discussions in Books I to V.

Plato sets out laws, rules, and regulations through his specific prescriptions. His characters in the *Laws* discuss the election and appointment of eligible men to public office, promulgation of laws (Book VI),[41] education of children (Book VII), sport and music (Book VIII), criminal offences (Book IX), and divine concern with the actions of unbelievers. In Book X the Athenian stranger identifies three types of unbelievers: those who claim the gods do not exist (888d–899d); those who claim the gods do exist but fail to take heed of man (899d–901c); and those who claim that the gods do exist, with some unbelievers insisting that the gods can be appeased and others insisting that the gods pay no heed to small, everyday matters (901c–903b). The remainder of Book X addresses methods of persuasion, such an imprisonment, designed to turn unbelievers from their impious, evil ways.[42] Books XI and XII discuss regulations about "our business transactions with one another."[43]

Following on from his parallel between Plato and Moses, Strauss draws this further parallel between philosophy and the Bible, about their moral precepts: "Those theologians who identified the second table of the Decalogue as the Christians call it with the natural law of Greek philosophy, were well-advised."[44] By "the second table of the Decalogue" Strauss means both Exodus 20:12–17 and Deuteronomy 5:17–21. That he did not mention the first table—Exodus 20:3–11 and Deuteronomy 5:7–16—is likely because its decisive focus is not morality but God.[45] The Christian theologian Strauss probably has in mind is Thomas Aquinas, who explained in his *Summa Theologiæ* (1a2æ, q. 99, art. 5, reply): "Duty is of two kinds: that which is determined by reason, and that which is determined by a law. Thus Aristotle [*Ethics* 1134b18] distinguishes two ways of being just, one moral, the other legal. Now a moral duty is of two kinds. For reason directs us to do something either because it is essential to virtuous living or because it contributes thereto. Now it is on this basis that certain of the moral precepts of the Law are expressed as absolute commands or prohibitions. Thus, *Thou shalt not kill, thou shalt not steal* [Exodus 20:13, 15; Deuteronomy 5:17, 19]."[46]

Strauss continues, "It is as obvious to Aristotle as it is to Moses that *murder, theft, adultery*, etc., are unqualifiedly bad."[47] Here Strauss clearly is drawing upon the *Nicomachean Ethics*, 1107a9–14 and 1130a17–b5, and the *Eudemian Ethics*, 1220b21–1221b26, though he does not refer to these passages.

The passions, Aristotle says, are excesses or defects of the mean; but some actions, such as adultery, theft, assault, and murder, are themselves unjust.[48] Strauss's very words point to Exodus 20:13–17. Here Moses proclaims to the Israelites that God declared,

> "You shall not *murder.*
> "You shall not commit *adultery.*
> "You shall not *steal.*
> "You shall not give false testimony against your neighbor.
> "You shall not covet your neighbor's house. You shall not covet your neighbor's wife, or his manservant or maidservant, his ox or donkey, or anything that belongs to your neighbor."[49]

The Bible and Greek Philosophy on the Scope of Law and Justice

Though Strauss notes in "Progress or Return?" that the Bible and Greek philosophy both contain a notion of patriarchy,[50] he focuses on their shared notions of law and justice. His thesis is that the "Bible and Greek philosophy agree in assigning the highest place among the virtues, not to courage or manliness, but to justice. And by justice both understand primarily, obedience to the law. The law that requires man's full obedience is in both cases not merely civil, penal, and constitutional law, but moral and religious law as well."[51]

To differentiate between, on the one hand, civil, penal, and constitutional laws, and, on the other hand, moral and religious laws, is to differentiate between *human* law and *divine* law. Divine law aims at the welfare of the soul and to inculcate correct knowledge of God; human law aims at the welfare of the body. As Strauss explained in *Philosophy and Law*, "Divine law differs from human laws in that it serves the highest end, the specific perfection of man; the specific perfection of man is knowledge, the knowledge of God. Thus the end of the law is identical with the end of philosophy."[52]

To support his thesis in "Progress or Return?" that a conception of divine and human law is common to the Bible and Greek philosophy, Strauss draws a series of parallels between the two. He begins by observing, "In the words of the Bible, 'It is your life,' or 'It is the tree of life for those who cling to it'; and in the words of Plato, 'The law effects the blessedness of those who obey it.'" He then explains that Aristotle and the Bible both ascribe "comprehensiveness" to law and justice and speak of the imperative of obedience to the law. Accord exists between Aristotle's view, "'What the law does not command, it forbids,'" and the biblical command, "'Thou shall eat and be full and be fruitful and multiply.' "[53] Although Strauss does not refer to Aquinas, it is worth citing the following passage, which illustrates Strauss's argument that revelation and reason agree about moral direction. According to Aquinas, "Every law aims at this, to be obeyed by its subjects. It is plain, therefore, that leading its subjects into the virtue appropriate to their condition is a proper function of law. Now since virtue is that which makes its possessor good, the consequence is that the proper effect of law on those to whom it is given is to make them good."[54]

Strauss proceeds to explain that the Bible and Greek philosophy "also agree regarding the problem of justice, the difficulty created by the misery of the just and the prospering of the wicked." Indeed, a striking similarity exists between "Plato's description in the second book of the *Republic* of the perfectly just man who suffers what would be the just fate of the most unjust man" and "Isaiah's description of him who has done no violence, neither was any deceit in his mouth, yet who was oppressed and afflicted and brought as a lamb to the slaughter."[55] Isaiah proclaims of the servant of God:

> He was oppressed and afflicted,
>   yet he did not open his mouth;
> he was led like a lamb to the slaughter,
>   and as a sheep before her shearers is silent,
>   so he did not open his mouth. . . .
> He was assigned a grave with the wicked,
>   and with the rich in his death,
> though he had done no violence,
>   nor was any deceit in his mouth.[56]

Strauss's parallel between the *Republic* and the Book of Isaiah serves to show, then, that the Bible and Greek philosophy agree about the paramount character of divine law and justice as well as the existence of providential order in the world.

Either/Or

Revelation and Reason as Mutually Exclusive Opposites

Strauss did not regard, however, the similarity between the Bible and Greek philosophy as extending to agreement about how to realize law and morality.[57]

He notes that in Greek philosophy, magnanimity accompanies justice. "Aristotle's *Ethics* has two foci, not one: one is justice, the other, however, is magnanimity or noble pride." The two foci "comprise all other virtues, as Aristotle says, but in different ways. Justice comprises all other virtues in so far as the actions flowing from them relate to other men; magnanimity, however, comprises all other virtues in so far as they enhance the man himself."[58] There are two possible sources for Strauss's observations about magnanimity: *Nicomachean Ethics* 1123a34–1125a16 and *Eudemian Ethics* 1232a19–1233a30. In both passages Aristotle says that only when one is great in each of the excellences of courage, temperance, liberality, and magnanimity is one's pride justified; excellence in magnanimity is one part of a justified pride.

Aristotle's approval of magnanimity carries with it a criticism of undue or excessive humbleness. "[T]he unduly humble man, being worthy of good things, robs himself of what he deserves, and seems to have something bad about him from the fact that he does not think himself worthy of good things."[59] "Dignity," that is, proper humbleness, "is a mean between self-will and too great obligingness; for the contemptuous man who lives with no consideration for another is self-willed; the man who adapts his whole life to another and is submissive to everybody is too obliging; but he who acts thus in certain cases but in others, and only to those worthy, is dignified."[60]

Like the "magnanimous man" in Greek philosophy, the "perfect gentleman" described in the Bible is worthy of great honor. The latter, though, claims honor not for himself but for his place in a larger whole. Strauss explains that "Biblical humility excludes magnanimity in the Greek sense," but he adds: "There is a close relation between the magnanimous man and the perfect gentleman. There occur a few, very few, gentlemen and ladies in the Bible—I hope that this remark is not understood as a criticism of the Bible."[61] Drawing upon Books 1 and 2 of Samuel,[62] Strauss then gives the examples of Saul, David, Jonathan, and Michal (daughter of Saul, wife of David). That "close relation" concerns pride and impiety. The point Strauss is making with the examples, and by giving them in the context of his discussion of divine law, is that each of the characters, with the exception of Jonathan, display pride and impiety and thus are characteristic of non-gentlemanly elements in the Bible. If the "perfect gentleman" is a "magnanimous man," Jonathan would not seem to qualify; but if the gentlemen is not magnanimous precisely because he displays humility and piety, perhaps Jonathan is the "perfect gentleman" Strauss is citing. Saul disobeyed God's command to destroy the Amalekites, for he spared King Agag and the best of his livestock; when Saul failed to obey God's command, the prophet Samuel elected David king. Jonathan was the son of

Saul but a close friend of David, and thus did not compete with David over the kingship of Israel. Because Michal mocked David when she saw him dancing before the ark of the Lord, God made her barren. Stressing humility and piety, the Bible warns that to claim honor for oneself is a sin of vanity; what is good in man is due not to man but to God. A good man repents his shortcomings and accepts his due punishment. Greek philosophy, though, praises magnanimity. Because man can be virtuous due to his own efforts, a good man does not, and need not, repent his shortcomings, such as his haughtiness towards other people.[63]

For Strauss, then, the Bible and Greek philosophy "agree" about "the importance of justice" and "disagree as to what completes morality."[64] The biblical demand for obedience to God's Law is accompanied by promises of mercy for the repentant and promises of punishment for the unrepentant. In Greek philosophy, though, divine sanction does not reinforce the demand for obedience to law; human reason alone leads to consciousness of morality. In their quest for knowledge of first things, philosophers begin with the traditional notion that divine codes can be traced to God or the gods. Philosophers transcend that notion in their ascent from opinion (belief and illusion) to knowledge; they acquire knowledge from demonstration, sense perception, and reasoning concerning the visible and intelligible natural order. The Bible, however, proclaims that God's Law is the one true divine law; it must be obeyed.[65] Aquinas explains thus the reason for that obedience: "That which is adequate for the completeness of human law, namely the prohibiting of offences and the apportionment of penalties, is not adequate for the completeness of the divine law. This latter is required to make man totally equipped to share in eternal happiness—something which can be achieved only by the grace of the Holy Spirit."[66]

That the Bible and Greek philosophy disagree about how to complete morality follows from their basic disagreement about the place of God in the cosmos. In Part II of "Progress or Return?" Strauss cites Maimonides' observation in his *Guide of the Perplexed* that the Bible teaches that God created the cosmos out of nothing by His very word. Greek philosophy, says Maimonides, did not articulate that notion of "divine omnipotence"; to Aristotle, "the visible universe" is eternal.[67] In Part I of "Jerusalem and Athens" Strauss explains that, although the Bible and Greek philosophy both express theological teachings, the Bible proclaims as true God's creation of the world, whereas "[t]he Platonic teaching on creation does not claim to be more than a likely tale." The "Platonic God" created the world only "after having looked to the eternal ideas which therefore are higher than he. In accordance with this, Plato's explicit theology is presented within the context of the first discussion of education in the *Republic*." Strauss clearly means 376c–412. Indeed, he proceeds to explain: "In the second and final discussion of education—the discussion of the education of the philosophers—theology is replaced by the doctrine of ideas."[68]

In the final paragraph of Part I of "Jerusalem and Athens" Strauss summarizes his discussion of the philosophic and biblical notions of the divine by observing: "The least one would have to say is that according to Plato the cosmic gods are of much higher rank than the traditional gods, the Greek gods."[69] Through Timaeus, Plato explains that only by the generational handing down of customs is the existence and genealogy of the Greek gods known.[70] Aristophanes also speaks of traditions and stories making the gods known; but he has a dim view of the role of the gods in human affairs. In *Peace* he says that "the Moon and that villain the Sun" are capricious and care only for themselves, not for the Greeks.[71] Deuteronomy 4:19, however, reminds the people of Israel that the cosmic bodies are not gods, and must not be revered as such: "And when you look up to the sky and see the sun, the moon and the stars—all the heavenly array—do not be enticed into bowing down to them and worshiping things the Lord your God has apportioned to all the nations under heaven."[72] The Greek gods are known through the natural faculties, whereas the biblical God is known through divine revelation. Strauss observes at the close of Part I of "Jerusalem and Athens" that "according to the Bible the God Who manifests Himself as far as He wills . . . is the only true God. The Platonic statement taken in conjunction with the biblical statement brings out the fundamental opposition of Athens at its peak to Jerusalem: the opposition of the God or gods of the philosophers to the God of Abraham, Isaac and Jacob, the opposition of Reason and Revelation."[73]

By depicting the Bible and Greek philosophy as mutually exclusive opposites, Strauss is saying that one cannot harmonize them in a synthesis. He also gives this impression in his lecture "On the Interpretation of Genesis": "The Bible, therefore, confronts us more clearly than any other book with this fundamental alternative: life in obedience to revelation, life in obedience, or life in human freedom, the latter being represented by the Greek philosophers. This alternative has never been disposed of, although there are many people who believe that there can be a happy synthesis which is superior to the isolated elements: Bible on the one hand, and philosophy on the other. This is impossible. Syntheses always sacrifice the decisive claim of one of the two elements. And I shall be glad if we can take up this point in the discussion."[74] Alluding to this perspective on synthesis in his "Introductory Essay to Hermann Cohen, *Religion of Reason out of the Sources of Judaism*," Strauss explains that Cohen's book "is a philosophic book and at the same time a Jewish book. It is philosophic since it is devoted to the religion of reason, and it is Jewish since it elucidates, nay, articulates that religion out of the sources of Judaism."[75] Perhaps inspired by the "theological orientation"[76] in Franz Rosenzweig, who described Cohen as attempting "a strictly rationalistic reinterpretation of the concept of revelation,"[77] Strauss went on to describe thus the import of Cohen's thought: "For Cohen there are no revealed truths or revealed laws in the precise or traditional sense of the terms."[78] For Cohen, human reason provides the true basis for the experience of God; the grounding of revelation in reason obviates the need to prove God's existence by recourse to traditions, miracles, and prophecies. But to Strauss, Cohen's synthesis of Judaism and philosophy, in emphasizing reason over obedience, undercut the decisive element of Judaism—the laws revealed through the prophets that prescribe a life of obedience to God.[79]

Understanding of goodness, Strauss explains in *Natural Right and History*, is essential to the life of both the individual and community. Yet the Bible and philosophy disagree about how to reach that understanding: whereas the Bible proclaims as indispensable a life of obedience to divine guidance, philosophy proclaims as indispensable "a life of free insight." One acquires knowledge of goodness through philosophy *or* under the direction of the Bible. A synthesis is impossible, because "in every synthesis however impressive, one of the two opposed elements is sacrificed, more or less subtly but in any event surely, to the other: philosophy, which means to be the queen, must be made the handmaid of revelation or vice versa."[80] To the believer, a synthesis is fundamentally unnecessary, for "if man knows by divine revelation what the right path is, he does not have to discover that path by his unassisted efforts."[81]

The Challenge of Openness Between Theology and Philosophy

In Part III of "Progress or Return?" Strauss states his firm position on these questions. Part III has its origin in his lecture, "The Mutual Influence of Theology and Philosophy."[82] Toward the beginning of his lecture, he explains that in their "free quest" for knowledge, "philosophers transcend the dimension of divine codes altogether, the whole dimension of piety and of pious obedience to a pre-given code." The philosopher seeks wisdom but in that search refuses, in this decisive sense, to affirm wisdom that purports to be final and absolute, which is precisely what divinely revealed wisdom claims to be. For "a philosopher, . . . revelation is . . . not more than an unevident, unproven possibility." The philosopher seeks knowledge of the whole, but not through a synthesis of revelation and reason. To the philosopher, a synthesis is impossible; it would require assent to divinely revealed knowledge over knowledge acquired solely through the human faculties. In contrast, "the biblical way of life" is a life of "trust," "faith" and obedience to the revealed word of God.[83]

In claiming to possess *the* truth, believers appeal to what they regard as unimpeachable historical proofs: the biblical accounts of laws, miracles, and prophecies. Yet, to critics of revelation, Strauss notes, the "events" described in the Bible as "miracles," and foretold in "prophecies," "are known only as reported." The critic insists that most of the biblical events "never happened"; those which did "took place in a pre-scientific age" and not "in the presence of first-rate physicists."[84] For the critic, miracles and prophecies are unverifiable phenomena and cannot be experienced in the clear light of day. Revelation, then, claims authority on knowledge of truth on bases the veracity of which philosophy challenges. Philosophy also claims that if "revealed law" is "fully rational," one need not accept it as the word of God alone. If "revealed law," philosophy further claims, "is not fully rational," it is "the product of human unreason."[85] The philosophic campaign against revelation, Strauss admits, "is victorious as long as it limits itself to repelling the attack which theologians make on philosophy with the weapons of philosophy."[86]

Strauss then states, "But philosophy in its turn suffers a defeat as soon as it starts an offensive of its own, as soon as it tries to refute, not the necessarily inadequate proofs of revelation, but revelation itself."[87] "Historical criticism" of revelation is "dogmatic" in its assertion that "an omnipotent God" does not exist. However, to dismiss miracles as "impossible," by arguing that "there is no place for an omnipotent God" in "the whole," "would presuppose that we have perfect knowledge of the whole." Yet to claim to have such knowledge would be tantamount to claiming that one has solved "all riddles," and such a claim is "absurd."[88]

Strauss does not mean that the quest for knowledge of the whole is absurd; he means that the claim by critics of revelation to *possess* that knowledge is absurd. To reject the possibility of miracles is to claim that "miracles are incompatible with the nature of God" and that divine acts of intercession are redundant to both a "perfect" God and to "human perfection." However, those claims require a "natural theology," of the nature of God and His characteristics, which says that God is "comprehensible." Yet, Strauss adds, to say that God is "comprehensible" is to claim complete knowledge of the whole.[89] "Since such a true or adequate, as distinguished from a merely clear and distinct, account of the whole, is certainly not available, philosophy has never refuted revelation. Nor, to come back to what I said before, has revelation, or rather theology, ever refuted philosophy. . . . There seems to be no ground common to both, and therefore superior to both."[90]

Dialogue Between Revelation and Reason

Philosophy vs. Atheism

Though he depicts the revelation-reason question in either/or terms, Strauss did not reject the desirability or the possibility of dialogue between the alternatives. Moreover, he rejects the attempt of atheists to escape the tension between the alternatives. "No one can be both a philosopher and a theologian or, for that matter, a third which is beyond the conflict between philosophy and theology, or a synthesis of both. But every one of us can be and ought to be either the one or the other, the philosopher open to the challenge of theology or the theologian open to the challenge of philosophy."[91] As James Schall forcefully expresses the impetus for that openness, "The biblical scholar who knows no philosophy is a dangerous man. The scientist who is unaware of the higher dimensions of philosophy locks himself into an autonomous ideology."[92]

By his own admission, Strauss was not a theologian.[93] He did not claim to possess the rigor and certitude of a theologian; nor he did claim to operate from within a theological or biblical horizon. That he regarded himself as a scholar not of theology but of the history of political thought suggests his intention to listen more to reason than to revelation. However, by his own reasoning, he could not have been an atheist—a philosopher is open to the possibility of revelation; one cannot seek to be free of the tension between the alternatives, which is precisely what an atheist attempts.

Strauss's manifest interest in matters religious was not a scholarly indulgence or a strategy to conceal an atheistic orientation.[94] Strauss was cognizant of problems in interpreting the extent of his views on religion. Responding to the accusation made by David Spitz in the October 1959 issue of *Commentary* that he was an atheist, that he rejected God, Strauss retorted, "Such accusations at any rate require proof. My accuser has not even tried to prove his accusation. If he should be induced by this remark to try to prove his accusation, I warn him in advance to keep in mind the difference between revealed theology and natural theology or to make himself familiar with it."[95] Strauss, who regarded the accusation as baseless, and not even as specious, gave an approach for interested parties to address the matter. According to Hilail Gildin, "Strauss's point is clear enough: even if one were to show that he rejects revealed theology (something Spitz by no means does) one would still have to show that he rejects natural theology as well (something Spitz may not realize that he must also do) before one could reasonably conclude that he is an atheist." Strauss penned a reply to Spitz, but did not send it to the editor of *Commentary*; instead, it "circulated among his students."[96]

Strauss's injunction to his accuser points to this fundamental difference: whereas revealed theology pertains to faith and the life of obedience to divine revelation, natural theology pertains to the pursuit of unaided human reason in the quest for knowledge of the whole. Given that Strauss saw himself as a Jew, albeit as one who could not believe as his ancestors did, it would be fair to say that he did not regard revealed theology as constituting the principal meaning of revelation. Yet, he did not reject revealed theology, for in the quest for knowledge of the whole, the philosopher must be open to the possibility that revealed theology conveys truth about the whole. Nor did he reject natural theology, for he perceived it to be an integral part of how the philosopher articulates his knowledge, however tentative, of the whole.[97]

Strauss nevertheless maintained that choosing philosophy over religion requires certainty about one's choice that is akin to a leap of faith. Towards the end of his lecture, "The Mutual Influence of Theology and Philosophy," he reflected: "And here when I use the term philosophy, I use it in the common and vague sense of the term where it includes any rational orientation in the world, including science and what have you, common sense. If this is so, philosophy must admit the possibility of revelation. Now that means that philosophy itself is possibly not the right way of life. It is not necessarily the right way of life, not evidently the right way of life, because this possibility of revelation exists. But what then does the choice of philosophy mean under these conditions? In this case, the choice of philosophy is based on faith. In other words, the quest for evident knowledge rests itself on an unevident premise."[98] In response to Strauss Novak asks, "What is the challenge of philosophy to theology? And, what can it mean for theology that philosophy admits the possibility of its prime datum, which is revelation?" Shortly afterwards Novak explains, "The insistence that philosophy must admit the possibility of revelation implies that there are philosophers who would deny any such possibility. Who are they?"[99]

In his epilogue to *Essays on the Scientific Study of Politics*, a 1962 collection of four essays edited by Herbert J. Storing, Strauss, using uncharacteristically polemical rhetoric, states that a "frank" and "dogmatic atheism" typifies the modern intellectual or "scientist." The disciple of the "new science," in the guise of a pose of "intellectual honesty," proclaims the rightness of rejecting both the cogency of belief in God and the very possibility of revelation.[100] In his "Restatement on Xenophon's *Hiero*" Strauss wrote, "For someone who is trying to form his taste or his mind by studying Xenophon, it is almost shocking to be suddenly confronted by the more than Machiavellian bluntness with which Kojève speaks of such terrible things as atheism and tyranny and takes them for granted." Nevertheless, Kojève "does not belong to the many who today are unabashed atheists." A "love" of thinking and of learning animates a philosopher. "Kojève is a philosopher and not an intellectual."[101]

Gildin observes, "According to Strauss, Kojève needs a philosophy of nature in which nature is structured or ordered with a view to history. Strauss claims that nature so understood is incompatible with atheism.... According to Strauss, Kojève was an atheist but had no right to be one."[102] In structuring his philosophy to *the end* of history, Kojève admitted the need for theories of nature and history that affirm that history has *purpose*.[103] Gildin continues, "The presence of a cosmic principle supporting what is highest in man stands in the way of atheism."[104] Gildin's proposition echoes this statement Strauss made in Part II of "Progress or Return?": "One must not forget that even the atheistic, materialistic thinkers of classical antiquity took it for granted that man is subject to something higher than himself, e.g., the whole cosmic order, and that man is not the origin of all meaning." Also in Part II Strauss states, "Even in Aristotle you will find passages where he speaks of certain very crude notions in Greece which pointed fundamentally to what we know in the Bible in a more developed form, e.g., the notion that maybe it is bad to devote oneself to the philosophical rebellion against God."[105] Elsewhere Strauss notes, "Political atheism is a distinctly modern phenomenon. No premodern atheist doubted that social life required belief in, and worship of, God or gods."[106] To the premodern atheist, as Schall observes, "a little religion was useful in controlling the masses. It kept them quiet."[107]

Asking why Werner Dannhauser described Strauss as an undogmatic atheist, and overlooked his reminder about the difference between revealed theology and natural theology, Gildin suggests that Dannhauser's reasoning "may have" been this: "Strauss lived what he taught. He made no secret of the fact that he was not an orthodox Jew. Nor was he a practicing adherent of any other revealed religion. Therefore he rejected all revealed theology."[108] Gildin has in mind here Dannhauser's 1996 essay "Athens and Jerusalem or Jerusalem and Athens?"[109] Yet, as Dannhauser pointed out in an article published in 1990, "any crude description of Leo Strauss as an atheist badly misses the mark." Dannhauser went on to say, "An atheist thinks of religion as an error, an opiate, a delusion. If Leo Strauss was an atheist, one must begin by asking why should he spend so much time and devote so much care to the study of Judaism?"[110] However, Dannhauser later explained, in the essay that Gildin cites: "I have become convinced of what in previous study of Strauss I could not accept, that Leo Strauss was of the party of Athens and not of the party of Jerusalem."[111]

Strauss, Judaism, and Zionism

By his own account, Strauss was receptive to "the party of Jerusalem." Inextricably linked with his reflections on the theological-political problem is a particular concern with what it means to be a Jew in the modern world. As he said towards the beginning of a lecture he gave in 1962, entitled "Why We Remain Jews: Can Jewish Faith and History Still Speak to Us?," "I believe I can say, without any exaggeration, that since a very, very early time the main theme of my reflections has been what is called the 'Jewish Question.'"[112] Strauss's interest in this question arose not simply from a general interest in the theological-political problem, but also from a specifically Jewish standpoint.[113] In 1952, he stated in "Progress or Return?": "It could seem as if progress has led us to the brink of an abyss, and it is therefore necessary to consider alternatives to it. For example, to stop where we are or else, if this should be impossible, to return. Return is the translation for the Hebrew word *t'shuvah*.... Repentance is return; redemption is restoration.... Today, *t'shuvah* sometimes means, not a return which takes place within Judaism, but a return to Judaism on the part of many Jews who, or whose fathers, had broken with Judaism as a whole."[114]

The confluence of return, repentance, redemption, and doubts about progress shaped Strauss's stance on the Jewish Question. As he stated in "Why We Remain Jews," "It is impossible not to remain a Jew. It is impossible to run away from one's origins. It is impossible to get rid of one's past by washing it away." In the same lecture he explained, "I was myself (as you might have guessed) a political Zionist in my youth, and was a member of a Zionist student organization."[115] In his 1965 autobiographical essay, "Preface to *Spinoza's Critique of Religion*," Strauss explained that most Jews in pre-Hitler Germany "assumed that the German state (to say nothing of German society or culture) was or ought to be neutral to the difference between Christians and Jews or between non-Jews and Jews. This assumption was not accepted by the strongest part of Germany and hence by Germany." Shortly afterwards he noted, "At any rate it could seem that in the absence of a superior recognized equally by both parties the natural judge on the Germanness of the German

Jews was the non-Jewish Germans. As a consequence, a small minority of the German Jews, but a considerable minority of German-Jewish youth studying at the universities, had turned to Zionism."[116] In his 1970 exchange with Strauss, entitled "A Giving of Accounts," Jacob Klein noted that Strauss's "primary interests" as a university student "were two questions: one, the question of God; and two, the question of politics."[117] In their exchange Strauss reflected, "When I was seventeen, I was converted to Zionism—to simple, straightforward political Zionism."[118]

I would note here, to return to a recurrent theme in this chapter, that "law," not "revelation," is Strauss's preferred term when he identifies the essential differences as well as the similarities between the Bible and Greek philosophy. In his lecture "How To Study Medieval Philosophy," he perhaps makes his clearest identification of the core sense of what it means to be a Jew. In equally clear terms, he distinguishes that identification from Christianity. "For the Jew and the Muslim, religion is primarily not, as it is for the Christian, a *faith* formulated in dogmas, but a *law*, a *code* of divine origin. Accordingly, *the* religious science, the sacra doctrina is, not dogmatic theology, theologia revelata, but the science of the law, Halachah or Fikh."[119] According to Hillel Fradkin, "The preference for the term 'law' in place of 'revelation' is explained by the fact that revelation is too general a term for a phenomenon that is emphatically particular in its alleged occurrences. It is therefore imprecise. Jewish revelation takes the form of law. Other revelations do not."[120] I would add here, though, that Strauss employs the terms "revelation" and "reason," "Jerusalem" and "Athens" to represent metaphorically the fundamental alternatives represented by the Bible and Greek philosophy.[121]

Like the youthful Strauss, the mature Strauss supported political Zionism, the difference being that the mature Strauss was alert to, but did not despair of solutions for, the problems of a strictly political Zionism.[122] As Strauss said in 1923: "*Zionism retains the separation, effected by assimilation, between Zionism and messianism, between national, worldly ends and spiritual means—but it abandons messianism. In opposition to assimilation's will to perish, it goes back to the galut's* [the Jewish exile's] *will to live.* Nordau rebukes assimilation for its abandonment of Zionism, but he does not acknowledge that, in a deeper sense, this previously mentioned separation prepared the ground for Zionism. . . ." Strauss went on, "Zionism continues and heightens the de-Judaizing tendency of assimilation," but added, "it does so, more precisely, for the sake of its struggle against the illusionism, the lack of grounding in reality [*Entwirklichtheit*] of the *galut*. . . . Assimilation denied the existence of the Jewish Question while Zionism acknowledges it."[123] "Political Zionism is problematic for obvious reasons," Strauss said in a 1957 letter to the editor of the *National Review*. "But I can never forget what it achieved as a moral force in an era of complete dissolution. It helped to stem the tide of 'progressive' leveling of venerable, ancestral differences; it fulfilled a conservative function."[124] Elsewhere Strauss suggested that political Zionism was problematic precisely because it "was strictly limited to political action. The mind was in no way employed, or even the heart was in no way employed, in matters Jewish."[125] Originating with Leon Pinsker's *Autoemancipation* (1882) and Theodor Herzl's *The Jews' State* (1896), the desire of political Zionism to recover Jewish pride culminated in the demand for a Jewish state; but, cultural Zionism claimed, a stress on cultural and historical heritage did not accompany that demand or recovery. Cultural Zionism, which believed that a Jewish state must be based upon Jewish heritage, was itself problematic. "Did one not completely distort the meaning of the heritage to which one claimed to be loyal by interpreting it as a culture like any other high culture?"[126] By situating itself between concerns relating to the State and to religion, between a strictly political position and a strictly religious position, cultural Zionism steered itself away from divine revelation, the ultimate basis of Jewish heritage.[127] "Judaism cannot be understood as a culture. There are folk dances, and pottery, and all that—but you cannot live on that. The substance is not culture, but divine revelation." The shift to religious Zionism involves the recognition that "the only clear solution" to the problem of being a Jew in the modern era is the "return to the Jewish faith, return to the faith of our ancestors."[128]

Nevertheless, Strauss counted himself among those Jews who feel unable fully to return to the faith of their ancestors. He asked in his "Why We Remain Jews" lecture, "What shall those Jews do who cannot believe as our ancestors believed?"[129] Such Jews must, he says, continue to regard themselves as Jews. There are two types of "nonreligious Jews," Strauss explained in "Freud on Moses and Monotheism," a lecture he gave in 1958. "There are those who wish that they had not been born Jews, who regard their Jewish origin as a misfortune; and there are those who do not wish not to be born as Jews or are even perhaps glad to be born as Jews. They feel that the best in them is due to their Jewish origin, or at any rate inextricably linked with that." The second type is better than the first type, Strauss added, for being a good Jew entails regarding oneself as a Jew.[130]

Such good, "passionately committed" Jews, Green explains, are "of two different types": those who follow secular or political Zionism, "and reject divine revelation as defining Judaism"; and "those committed Jews who accept divine revelation but make it theologically conform with modern philosophic or scientific notions and criticisms." The latter "type," says Green, "refers especially to such modern Jewish religious thinkers as the idealist Cohen and the existentialist Rosenzweig."[131] Though drawn to Cohen's attempt to be both a Jew and a philosopher, Strauss, for the reasons mentioned above, could not accept Cohen's synthesis. Strauss, in the preface to his work on Spinoza, a work he had dedicated to the memory of Rosenzweig, spoke of "the return to Judaism" as originating with Rosenzweig. "The new thinking as unqualified empiricism speaks of God, man, and the world as actually experienced, as realities irreducible to one another, whereas all traditional philosophy was reductionist."[132] (Rosenzweig's "new thinking," Strauss went on, was challenged by Heidegger, whose "form of the new thinking...led far away from any charity as well as from any humanity." Heidegger, according to Strauss, sought to separate "biblical morality" from any consideration of "biblical theology," and linked the philosophical understanding of man with a historical sense of being.[133]) Rosenzweig erred, however, Strauss explained, by taking "the Jewish nation" and not "God's Law, the Torah," as his point of departure "when speaking of the Jewish experience."[134]

What of Strauss's own point of departure? What is his understanding of "what is primary or authoritative for the Jewish consciousness"?[135] It is instructive to note here that in his lecture on Freud Strauss proposed, perhaps autobiographically, "another definition of the good Jew, that is, the nonreligious good Jew. He is a man who knows that he is a Jew, that he belongs to the Jewish people, and that the root of his problem is the fact that he cannot believe what his ancestors believed."[136] Elsewhere, Strauss reflected: "I believe—and I say this without any disrespect to any orthodox Jew—that it is hard for people, for most Jews today, to believe in verbal inspiration (I mean, in verbal inspiration of the Torah), and in the miracles—or most of the miracles—and other things.... But a Judaism which is not belief in the 'Creator of the World,' that has problems running through it."[137]

Despite the problem of being unable to "believe what his ancestors believed," Strauss, through reflecting on the difficulties with efforts to solve the Jewish Question, contributed to the continuation of Jewish heritage. Liberal democracy and assimilation failed as solutions in Germany, Strauss argued in the preface to his work on Spinoza, because they both suffer from the presuppositions that every problem has a solution[138] and that German Jews are accepted in non-Jewish German society.[139] Nazi Germany, Strauss said in "Why We Remain Jews," "was based on no principle other than the negation of Jews."[140] Strauss regarded cultural and political Zionism as problematic for the reasons mentioned above. He perceived Rosenzweig's "new thinking" to be problematic, because, as Novak explains, "although certainly religious," its existentialist bent left it "too rooted in subjectivist notions of the primacy of human experience to adequately constitute the objective content of classical Judaism."[141] The above "attempts to solve" the Jewish Question "by purely human means," Strauss argues, have "failed because of the overwhelming power of the past."[142] Hence, Strauss regarded an unqualified return to orthodoxy as the "the only clear solution";[143] but he maintained that the solution "is not feasible, humanly speaking, for all Jews."[144] The reason for that unfeasibility is that "such *teshuvah*, a return . . . to the God of the fathers, is fraught with risk," Michael Morgan explains. "And the core of that risk is what Strauss calls again and again 'intellectual probity,' an honesty of the heart that is at the same time an honesty of the mind."[145]

Strauss, however, was more than a *nonreligious* good Jew. According to David Walsh, "He is not just ethnically or culturally Jewish, but spiritually Jewish as well. I am not referring to his own religious practices, but to his understanding of the nature of Judaism and of the Mosaic revelation." Of that understanding Gregory Smith points out, "Barring such a perfect philosophic system [of the whole], Strauss asserted that it may be true that the world could never be perfectly intelligible without the premise of a mysterious God. Thereby, Strauss publicly defended at least one of the tenets of orthodoxy and by extension, the life of the orthodox believer. He defended that life, . . . but he did not choose [it] . . . for himself as the central venue of his life."[146] Strauss was more than a nonreligious good Jew precisely because he contributed to the continuity of Jewish heritage, to the preservation of the ultimate and specifically Jewish basis of Judaism.

Despite his firm insistence about the necessity of a return to classical political philosophy, that Strauss himself turned to Athens does not mean that he was closed to the call of Jerusalem. Central to both the Bible and Greek philosophy, he argued, is concern with justice, virtue, and the good life. By arguing that revelation and reason agree with each other, he did not overlook their fundamental disagreement about how to complete morality—obedience to God's Law versus a life of free insight. Given that disagreement, he rejected a synthesis of the alternatives; but he maintained that they are compatible as far as moral direction is concerned. He was not open to revelation in spite of his being a political philosopher. He claimed that philosophy must be open to the challenge of revelation, for the philosopher, in the quest for knowledge of the whole, must reflect on the claim to truth made by theologians. His position on the alternatives is open, for it is neither antithetical to revelation nor a defense of revelation before all else. Illustrating his openness to revelation is his argument that atheism is anathema to philosophy and not only to revelation, and by his personal and philosophic-theistic fidelity to Judaism.[147]

PART TWO

Strauss's Machiavelli on Religion
Neither Christian Nor Pagan

In order to judge properly of Machiavelli's doctrine, we must consider that in the crucial respect there is agreement between classical philosophy and the Bible, between Jerusalem and Athens, despite the profound difference and even antagonism between Athens and Jerusalem. According to the Bible man is created in the image of God; . . . righteousness is obedience to the divinely established order, just as in classical thought justice is compliance with the natural order; to the recognition of elusive chance corresponds the recognition of inscrutable providence.

—Leo Strauss, "The Three Waves of Modernity"

CHAPTER THREE

Christianity and the Bible

In a well-known line from the introduction to *Thoughts on Machiavelli* Strauss stated his preference for "the old-fashioned and simple opinion according to which Machiavelli was a teacher of evil." Elsewhere in the introduction he said, "Many of our contemporaries are of the opinion that there are no permanent problems and hence no permanent alternatives. . . . Our critical study of Machiavelli's teaching can ultimately have no other purpose than to contribute towards the recovery of the permanent problems."[1] In chapters 1 to 3 Strauss addressed such themes as Machiavelli's new modes and orders, his anti-Christian and antitheological animus, and his corruption of the minds and morals of the young. Strauss's primary purpose in these chapters was not, however, the critical study of Machiavelli's teaching; Strauss's focus was largely on interpretive, not theological or philosophical, matters. One is justified in saying that by his reflection at the beginning of chapter 4: "It would not be reasonable to claim, or indeed to believe, that the preceding observations suffice to elucidate every obscure passage of the *Discourses*. The utmost we can hope to have achieved is to have pointed to the way which the reader must take in studying Machiavelli's work."[2]

Strauss's critical study of Machiavelli's teaching, though not explicitly divided in a literary manner, is twofold in its scope: in part I of chapter 4 Strauss examines his teaching on religion; in part II Strauss examines his teaching on morality and politics.[3] The thesis in part I is that Machiavelli is neither Christian nor pagan; the thesis in part II is that his moral-political teaching revolts not only against Christianity and all religion, but also against classical political philosophy, that is, against Aristotle, Plato, Socrates, and Xenophon. The structure of part I is also twofold: the first section examines Machiavelli's critique of biblical religion; the second section examines broader aspects of his teaching on religion, about cosmology and the utility of religion.

Considering the issues, themes, and questions singled out in his critical study of Machiavelli's teaching, Strauss clearly felt the intellectual importance and personal challenge of the revelation-reason question. The present chapter, carried further in chapters 4 to 7, shows the arguments and the actions in Strauss's critical study tending to side with "Athens" but listening with care to the dictates of "Jerusalem."

Machiavelli's Judgment on Christianity

Christianity and Matters of the World

Machiavelli set his focus on the here and now, not on venerating God or the gods. Contesting that he was a pagan and a pious one at that, Strauss points out, "He had not reverted from the worship of Christ to the worship of Apollo."[4] Yet, Strauss explains shortly afterwards, "it is not misleading to count Machiavelli among 'the wise of the world.'"[5] In *Discourses* III 30 Machiavelli notes that for Savonarola, the desire of "the wise" to discover, with astrology and divination, the underlying and ultimate causes of the world is impious. In the same chapter Machiavelli explains that Savonarola's failure to act with certainty against those opposed to his reordering of Florence caused his downfall. One cannot rule a state with success if one does not employ cruel and forceful methods. Machiavelli points out, "Moses was forced to kill infinite men who ... were opposed to his plans. Friar Girolamo Savonarola knew this necessity very well ... [but] was not able to conquer it because he did not have the authority to enable him to do it."[6] Strauss continues, "Those 'wise of the world' who transcend the limits of political cleverness reject not only the myths of the pagans but above all revelation and the characteristic teachings of revelation on the ground indicated. They are *falāsifa* or 'Averroists.'"[7] Coby thus notes for Strauss: "Machiavelli is an Averroist, one of the worldly wise who trust in reason and not in revelation."[8] Coby is correct to say that Strauss sees Machiavelli as rejecting trust in revelation; yet, Strauss goes on to show, in trusting reason Machiavelli rejects the existence of an eternal order in the world; and his conception of nature is not a pagan myth of nature.[9] For Strauss Machiavelli is no mere Averroist; he is the harbinger of a "new," temporal conception of reason.

By connecting Machiavelli with the Averroists, the followers of Averroës (1126–1198), the medieval Arabic philosopher and commentator of Aristotle, Strauss casts light on the roots of Machiavelli's "wise" teaching on religion. Strauss does not then discuss Averroës or the Averroists, though he returns to the subject of Averroism when examining Machiavelli's views on Christian theology.

Strauss continues, "The vulgar understanding of Machiavelli is justified to some extent by his reticences. He does not often speak of theological subjects, the Bible, Biblical characters, Biblical events or Christianity." By "vulgar understanding" Strauss means the claim that Machiavelli was a pious pagan. Rather than proving "indifference or ignorance" of theology, the Bible, or Christianity, Machiavelli's reticence shows that he had a political view of the phenomena of the world; his thesis is that Christianity has led the world into weakness.[10]

Explicating that thesis, Strauss turns to *Discourses* I pr., II 2, and III 1, the three instances in the work where Machiavelli specifically mentions Christianity. In countless other passages he deals with core Christian beliefs, but he does so indirectly; in those places, Strauss observes, he compares "the ancients" with "the moderns; for the ancients are primarily the pagan Romans and the moderns are primarily the Christians."[11] In the preface to Book I of the *Discourses* Machiavelli notes, "neither prince nor republic may be found that has recourse to the examples of the ancients." That lack of recourse is due neither to "the weakness into which the present religion has led the world" nor to "the evil that an ambitious idleness has done to many Christian provinces and cities." Here Machiavelli leads his readers to think that, overall, Christianity is not responsible for the contemporary failure to learn from the ancients. Yet he proceeds in the preface to lament that the "infinite number who read" the histories merely dabble. He attributes that dabbling, the failure or incapacity to learn, to the attitude that modern times differ from ancient times, "as if heaven, sun, elements, men had varied in motion, order, and power from what they were in antiquity."[12]

In his second explicit statement on Christianity, in *Discourses* II 2, Machiavelli further discusses the modern failure to learn from the histories; but he addresses not so much Christianity as he does "our religion." "Thinking then whence it can arise that in those ancient times peoples were more lovers of freedom than in these, I believe it arises from the same cause that makes men less strong now, which I believe is the difference between our education and the ancient, founded on the difference between our religion and the ancient. For our religion, having shown the truth and the true way, makes us esteem less the honor of the world, whereas the Gentiles, esteeming it very much and having placed the highest good in it, were more ferocious in their actions."[13] Machiavelli appears to be saying here, Voegelin explains, that "the false interpretation rather than Christianity itself" is responsible for the weakness of the present world, for the "diminished love of freedom."[14] If one interpreted Christianity "according to virtue"—a strong, active, this-worldly virtue—and not to "idleness," one would see "how it permits us the exaltation and defense of the fatherland." The small number of republics in the present world and the corresponding decline in the "love of freedom" is due to "[t]hese educations and false interpretations." Machiavelli then revises his judgment about Christianity. He states, "Still, I believe the cause of this [decline of republics and freedom] to be rather that the Roman Empire, with its arms and its greatness, eliminated all republics and all civil ways of life."[15] He does not revise, however, his claims that greatness is superior to humility and that the modern world is weak and servile.[16]

Machiavelli's "third statement" in the *Discourses* on the core beliefs of Christianity, Strauss points out, "occurs in the first chapter of the Third Book."[17] Here Machiavelli speaks of the need that "sects, republics, and kingdoms" have for "good institutions" that can be renewed. With "the process of time that goodness" once common to all three "is corrupted" by the "ambition" and "tumult" of men who forget their fear and memories of force, violence, punishment, and terror. Such corruption is shown by the tumults in the ancient Roman republic and in "the state of Florence from 1434 to 1494," the period of Medici rule. Machiavelli recommends, then, that executions of those who cause, or could cause, tumults because they "corrupt themselves" be staged every five to ten years.[18] A return to original principles is another way of dealing with tumults. Strauss explains for Machiavelli, "Through poverty and the example of the life of Christ they [both Saint Francis and Saint Dominic] restored Christianity in the minds of men from which it had already vanished. Their new modes and orders prevented the immorality of the prelates and of the heads of religion from ruining the religion."[19] Machiavelli, however, disputes the value of that and of any attempt to restore Christianity. He rejects the Christian teaching, renewed by the two saints, that "it is evil to speak evil of evil" and that one must "let God chastise" evildoers.[20] That nonresistance to evil leaves oneself prey to those who desire to gain dominion over others. "Resistance to evil is natural to men as well as to any other living being.

The counsel against resisting evil can therefore lead only to evasion of that counsel."[21]

One half of Strauss's thesis that Machiavelli is neither Christian nor pagan has become clearer: Machiavelli bases his critique of Christianity on a temporal view of the ends of religion. He targets his ire at the modern, Christian failure to imitate properly the ancient Roman glories. He lauds the merits of modern weapons (for instance, cannons), but regards his contemporaries, be they Italian, German, French, Spanish, or Swiss, as inferior to the ancient Romans in the grasp of politics and the art of war.[22] (Mansfield notes for Machiavelli, "to be *armed* means to have the art of war, a feat of study and intellect rather than of arms."[23]) Generations of incompetent clerics and venal Popes have resulted in the cycle of a politically and militarily irresolute Church hierarchy and an always crisis-riven Italy. Machiavelli's anticlericalism, however, masks this deeper criticism: Christianity itself is responsible for engendering attitudes of neglect and disdain towards matters of the world.[24]

The Tyranny of Religious Authority

For Machiavelli, political authority is superior to religious authority. Good laws depend on good arms; but because priests and prophets do not cultivate the military arts, they cannot defend their peoples.[25] Yet in his argument about "good arms" Machiavelli is in good company.[26] In the *Timaeus* Plato's character Critias recites a story dating from the days of Solon[27] that spoke of the rule of philosophers replacing the rule of the Egyptian priest class (24a–b). The "care of religion," Aristotle says, is essential to the life of a state, but more important is "a power of deciding what is for the public interest"; the priest class should be drawn from members of the warrior and councilor classes "who from age have given up active life."[28] Averroës notes in his *Commentary on Plato's Republic* that the best states come to be that way over "a long [period of] time," under the guidance of "excellent kings," though "their influence is more likely to lead to excellent deeds than good convictions" (II 17.3); states "will not improve by convictions <alone>" (II 17.4); "[s]tates that are excellent in deeds alone are called 'Priestly'" (II 17.5). Indicating that priestly rule is, or can be, tyrannical, Averroës says, "The similarity between the 'priestly' and the tyrannical States often leads the 'priestly' parts that exist in these States to be transformed into tyrannical ones, thus bringing into disrepute him whose aim is 'priestly'" (III 5.6). The "similarity" is this: "The only aim of the homes and the other kinds of men in the Ideal State is a good purpose for one <kind> of the men, namely the rulers. In this respect they resemble the tyrannical State" (III 5.3).[29]

Evidently Strauss has in mind the above passages, particularly from Averroës, when he observes, "The chief reason why Machiavelli opposed the direct or indirect rule of priests was that he regarded it as essentially tyrannical and even, in principle, more tyrannical than any other regime." Citizens in an "ecclesiastical" regime must obey "divine authority" and its orders. Thus, the priestly ruling body, "however excellent," is unaccountable. "On the other hand, if a government is based on arms and if the citizen body is armed and virtuous, misgovernment can easily be prevented."[30]

That Machiavelli opposed *religious* authority gives rise to questions about how he accounted for the spread of Christianity throughout the Roman Empire.[31] He argues, Strauss explains, that the Romans corrupted themselves by allowing their honor, strength, and power to be ceded to, and overcome by, their enchantment with religious cults from abroad. The most threatening of those cults would prove to be Christianity. Stepping into the void created by the Roman Empire's declining political vitality, the strong Christian emphasis on humility and morality attracted the support of the disaffected peoples of the empire.[32]

Machiavelli further argues, contrasting the modern world with ancient Rome, that the moderns, though also adept in not keeping their promises, fail to use cruelty well precisely because their cruelty is pious.[33] To be cruel is to use "fear," "harshness," and "punishment and compliance"; to be kind is to use "humanity and mercy."[34] The ancient Romans, unlike Christians, knew how to be cruel *or* kind and not vacillate between the two. The Bible commands that one love one's neighbor as oneself. Such a command did not restrict the pagan Romans. By the good use of cruel methods to direct the citizenry toward the well-being of "the fatherland," Roman leaders built strong foundations for the republic.[35]

Machiavelli is not simply accusing Christianity of political ineptitude, that its "promulgation of the doctrine of mercy actually produces cruelty."[36] Indeed, he has in mind, Strauss notes, an ancient scriptural command: "According to the Biblical teaching, love of the neighbor is inseparable from love of God whom one is commanded to love with all his heart, with all his soul, and with all his might."[37] The command can be found in Deuteronomy 6:5, though Strauss does not refer to the passage: "Love the Lord your God with all your heart and with all your soul and with all your strength."[38]

Machiavelli is saying, like Averroës, that rulers can compel obedience but not heartfelt conviction. By implying that God is a tyrant, that, as Haig

Patapan explains for Machiavelli, He "imposes impossible demands on His children,"[39] Machiavelli means, I would suggest, that to actualize the teaching to love God and one's neighbors requires the tyrannical use of force.[40] A lasting basis for acceptance of the teaching derives from the capacity of religious authorities to compel obedience among believers. Human nature being rebellious and sinful, the teaching "is very difficult to fulfill." To Machiavelli, Strauss then explains, "it is a most true rule that when difficult things are commanded, harshness, and not sweetness, is needed in order to bring about obedience." Those who disobey God and His commands "deserve infinite pity because they cannot have understood what they did." However, disobedience places oneself against God and the punishment for the unrepentant is eternal damnation. "The God of Love is necessarily an angry God who 'revengeth and is furious' and 'reserveth wrath for his enemies,' a consuming fire," namely, "the fire of hell." Strauss concludes, "Machiavelli tacitly rejects the very notion of divine punishment."[41] In an endnote Strauss indicates that Nahum 1:2 is the biblical passage he is citing when speaking of "fire" and of "hell."[42] The complete passage reads,

> The Lord is a jealous and avenging God;
>   the Lord takes vengeance and is filled with wrath.
> The Lord takes vengeance on his foes
>   and maintains his wrath against his enemies.[43]

Machiavelli holds that not fear of the Lord but fear of human authority best counters the corruption within man. However, he recognizes that Christianity has some merit: he notes, Strauss explains, that the biblical command to love God can produce "good and faithful soldiers." Christian soldiers are loyal to their fatherland and the common good; the soldiers are loyal and fight well, for in fighting for God, they fight for their own good; the good of God is the Good and thus is the basis of their own true good.[44]

Machiavelli clearly is skeptical of religious authority. For him, the good of God is not the true good. He argues that Christianity made "the world weak" by demanding that people not revel "in their virtue and power." Machiavelli, Strauss adds, "means also that Christianity has lowered the stature of man by rejecting the seeking of one's own honor and one's own glory as such." Christianity even taught "the distrust of one's own virtue."[45] In *Discourses* I 11 Machiavelli says that a prince must have recourse to religion when he orders the state. Elsewhere in the *Discourses*, Machiavelli delivers this veiled rebuke to the injunction to trust God: a prince must rely on *himself*, on *his own* judgment and capabilities. Success on a battlefield, Machiavelli explains in III 33, requires that "a good and wise captain" prove to his soldiers by augural means and the like that they have the favor of the gods. "Nevertheless, virtue must accompany these things; otherwise they have no value."[46]

To rely on God or the gods is to invite ruin. Machiavelli reasons, according to Strauss, that "the sins which ruin states are military rather than moral sins." Because the world and human life are always in flux, "states cannot choose the true way or the right mean which consists in keeping what one has and in not taking away from others what belongs to them." Rather than an ever-changing world or man's proclivity for acquisition, it is an external factor that drives nations to war: "Heaven's deficient kindness," namely, "the fulfillment of the divine command to multiply," invariably means that a nation starves to death or engages in a war for its very survival. An "excellent" man may regret, though, allowing "a necessity to sin" to control his actions; he redeems himself by rescuing his "fatherland from foreign or tyrannical domination." Yet, in his public actions and private concerns, an excellent man cannot allow guilt to overcome his desire for excellence; sin is natural and necessary for "everything noble and high."[47]

Machiavelli's Reflections on Biblical/Christian Theology

Theology in Machiavelli

That Machiavelli views biblical religion, religious authority, and matters of the world in a temporal manner suggests that the standpoint from which he censures Christianity itself is temporal.[48] Perhaps, then, what Strauss in *Spinoza's Critique of Religion* said of Hobbes may be said of Machiavelli. "From an agnosticism such as that of Hobbes, it is only a step into atheism, a step which this philosopher himself however never took. Furthermore, his extensive and penetrating preoccupation with theological themes is not to be understood as due to some residue left within him by millennial modes of thought and feeling, but exclusively to the necessity of bringing out the thesis of disbelief in the face of prevailing belief."[49] Elsewhere, however, Strauss suggests that that thesis is, ultimately, atheistic. "The genesis of Hobbes's political philosophy," says Strauss, is marked by "the movement away from the recognition of a superhuman authority—whether of revelation based on Divine will or a natural order based on Divine reason—to a recognition of the exclusively human authority of the State."[50] Hobbes's philosophy, of nature and of politics, combines "political idealism with a materialistic and atheistic view of the whole."[51]

Machiavelli was not, some commentators claim, in any way preoccupied with theology; to some commentators he was, though not so much with theology itself as its basic outcomes. "Machiavelli is concerned not with theological disputation," Sullivan states, "but with the general and practical effect of Christian doctrine."[52] Similarly, Coby explains, "Clearly Machiavelli is displeased with Christianity and from time to time targets its teachings and its practices." Coby adds, "But the *Discourses* presents no sustained assault on Christian principles and is not itself seriously engaged with Christian doctrine; it offers . . . no revisionist retelling of the Sermon on the Mount, where 'Turn the other cheek' is discovered to mean 'Bloody thine enemy's cheek.'"[53] Machiavelli, says Villari, "never concerned himself with religious questions," only with "the formation of the modern State."[54] According to Berlin, "he completely ignores the concepts and categories . . . in terms of which the best known thinkers and scholars of his day were accustomed to express themselves." Berlin later adds, "The absence of Christian psychology and theology— sin, grace, redemption, salvation—need cause less surprise: few contemporary humanists speak in such terms. . . . But, and this is more noteworthy, there is no trace of Platonic or Aristotelian teleology . . . with which the Renaissance thinkers are deeply concerned."[55] In a twist to the above theses, Nederman claims that, although he drew heavily on medieval Christian theology, "[w]here Machiavelli may be said to depart from the medieval framework is in his view that the 'salvation' sought by the ruler is political as well as otherworldly."[56] The above scholars acknowledge, with varying emphases, the extent of Machiavelli's departure from Christianity. The strength of Strauss's analysis is his linkage of that departure with Machiavelli's attack on theology and his linkage of Machiavelli's rejection of Christianity with the rejection of religion in general.

Conscience

Having addressed Machiavelli's this-worldly view of sin and divine punishment, Strauss deems it instructive "to survey" his "teaching regarding the conscience." Of the few instances in which he speaks of conscience, Strauss observes, "In the *Florentine Histories* . . . there occur five mentions of the conscience; four mentions occur in speeches by Machiavelli's characters; the fifth and last mention occurs in Machiavelli's description of Piero de' Medici who was inferior in virtue of the mind and of the body to his father Cosimo and his son Lorenzo."[57] Strauss leaves the survey at that, thus echoing Machiavelli's own rare mentions of "the conscience." Later, when examining Machiavelli's critique of providence, Strauss again refers to the *Florentine Histories*, but he does not cite the five mentions of conscience. Given Strauss's brief reference in this regard, it is fitting to discuss what Machiavelli does say in the passages indicated.

The context of the *Florentine Histories* is manifestly Christian; the work was commissioned in late 1520 by Cardinal Guilio de' Medici as a history of Florence. Machiavelli's own aim in the work was not simply to narrate the history of Florence from the city's origin and up to 1492. His focus, Mansfield explains, is not on history as "history," as " 'our history' or 'my history,' " but as the interplay "between virtue and nature or fortune"; the interplay is "enhanced by a new predictability, even rationality."[58] However, to Fleisher, "Machiavelli is preoccupied not with history, not even with political history, but rather with the history of political greatness—great statesmen and great republics." He focuses on "the political renewal of his own Tuscany and this, he believes, can only come about by the recovery of ancient *modi* and *ordini*, the source of *virtù* and prudence."[59]

When mentioning the conscience while describing pivotal historical events in the *Florentine Histories*, Machiavelli advances against Christianity an anthropocentric view of suprahuman motivational bases to human action.[60] He mentions conscience—one such basis—three times in the *Florentine Histories* III 13. Here Machiavelli conveys his thoughts about conscience through a speech given by a member of a Florentine guild. His plebeian character says: "It pains me much when I hear that out of *conscience* many of you repent the deeds that have been done and that you wish to abstain from new deeds; and certainly, if this is true, you are not the men I believed you to be, for neither *conscience* nor infamy should dismay you, because those who win, in whatever mode they win, never receive shame from it. And we ought not to take *conscience* into account, for where there is, as with us, fear of hunger and prison, there cannot and should not be fear of hell."[61] A ruler or an aspiring ruler, then, must not let his conscience dissuade him from performing whatever actions ensure success. In VI 20, Machiavelli's character, a Milanese ambassador, criticizes a certain count, Francesco Sforza, for reneging on his promise to protect Milan. The ambassador says that the expectations of the Milanese, that the count would protect their city, were too high; on other occasions he had shown he could not be trusted. However, those high expectations do not excuse his faithlessness, the ambassador exclaims. "Nor will it keep the just pricking of your *conscience* from tormenting you when the arms that were prepared by us to injure and frighten others will come to wound and injure us, because you yourself will judge yourself worthy of the punishment parricides have deserved. And even if ambition blinds you, the whole world as witness to your wickedness will open your eyes; God will open them for you, if perjuries, if violated faith and betrayals displease Him, and if He does not always wish to be the friend of wicked men, as up to now He has done for some hidden good. So do not promise yourself sure victory, for that will be kept from you by the just wrath of God."[62] Machiavelli's fifth mention of conscience in the *Florentine Histories* occurs in VII 23. Instead of raising the subject in a speech by a character, he raises it by describing a speech given by Piero de' Medici, who feels guilt for not being able to cure Florence of its recalcitrant citizens. "Nonetheless, to unburden his *conscience* and to see if he could shame them, he called them all to his house and spoke to them." Piero berates the citizens of Florence for putting their own ambitions before the interests of their city; while the rest of Italy is enjoying peace Florence is not. Piero concludes by warning, "I promise you, by the faith that ought to be given and received by good men, that if you continue to carry on in a mode that makes me repent having won, I too shall carry on in a manner that will make you repent having ill used the victory." That Piero listened to his conscience was, Machiavelli suggests, a wasted effort; conscience cannot overcome mortality. "But these very decent thoughts of his were thwarted by death; for, overburdened by the ills of his body and the anxieties of his spirit, he died in his fifty-third year."[63]

When the five usages of conscience in the *Florentine Histories* are regarded collectively, three varied messages emerge. First, it is futile for a ruler to ignore his conscience, for God punishes wrong actions and wicked behavior. Second, fear of a bad conscience cannot, however, stop a ruler from carrying out deeds necessary to achieve greatness. Third, in some circumstances, the protection of the fatherland, for example, God condones wicked deeds, such as murder and deceit. The upshot of Machiavelli's varied messages about conscience in the *Florentine Histories* is that he regards God as a hypocrite and biblical injunctions against evil as inefficacious. As the Apostle Paul stated in Romans 2:12–13, "All who sin apart from the law will also perish apart from the law, and all who sin under the law will be judged by the law. For it is not those who hear the law who are righteous in God's sight, but it is those who obey the law who will be declared righteous."[64]

Machiavelli mentions conscience four times in the *Discourses*. He makes one mention in I 27, another in I 55; and they are both made, Strauss points out, "within a Christian context."[65] Christians perform good actions not only because their neighbors observe them doing so but because God, too, is a witness to their deeds; yet in both I 27 and I 55, Machiavelli is silent about God as a witness.[66] Strauss observes, "The third mention of *coscienza* occurs in a context which is no longer obviously Christian." Machiavelli speaks in *Discourses* II 14–15 about a conspiracy against Rome: the seeming patience of the Romans caused the Latins, that is, gave them the arrogance and the fearlessness, to test the will of, and alienate themselves from, the Romans. Strauss explains on Machiavelli's behalf, "The Latins knew—or, more literally, had awareness (*coscienza*)—of many things which they had done against the will of the Romans." Roman knowledge of the conspiracy did not deter the Latins, because the Latins believed in their own power against Roman capabilities.[67]

Strauss asks, "Could the conscience in Machiavelli's opinion be based on true knowledge of the relation of the power of man to the power of God? In that case, the conscience would be prudence modified by the knowledge of the overwhelming power of God who punishes every action done against his will. Certainly one of Machiavelli's characters identifies the conscience with the fear of hell."[68] To answer his own question, Strauss turns to the fourth mention of conscience in the *Discourses*. In III 6 Machiavelli speaks of the "stained conscience" of those who plotted to kill Caesar.[69] It is not clear whether by "conscience" he means the realization that immoral deeds are abhorrent to God (or the gods).[70] Strauss asks, "Was the bad conscience of these ancient Romans [who conspired against Caesar] caused by the suspicion that they did wrong or by fear of detection by human beings? Machiavelli forces us to raise this question but does not answer it."[71] Nor does Strauss answer the question, though he does examine the meaning of Machiavelli's silence about "bad conscience" when discussing Machiavelli's silence about penitence. In any case, for Strauss the core of his reflections on theology is his rejection of creation *ex nihilo*, not his disavowal of conscience.[72]

Strauss continues, "For the time being we suggest that Machiavelli tried to replace the conscience, or religion, by a kind of prudence which is frequently indistinguishable from mere calculation of worldly gain: 'the true way' consists, not in obeying God's invariable law, but in acting according to the times."[73] Strauss means that Machiavelli takes issue with theological certitude, with precepts based on a final, transcendent end. His criticism is that a virtue informed by conscience should not guide oneself; that is, one cannot transgress a created, providential order that does not exist. In praising the truth of Livy's history, and thereby praising the Romans as superior to the moderns, Machiavelli questions the need for obedience to God's Law. That "praise," Strauss says in chapter 3 of *Thoughts on Machiavelli*, "is an essential element of his wholly new teaching, but it is also, and even chiefly, a mere engine of subversion."[74] The only theology of which he approves, Strauss explains elsewhere, is "civil theology, theology serving the state and to be used or not used by the state as circumstances suggest."[75]

Providence

Moving from the subject of conscience to that of providence, Strauss states, "It is impossible to excuse the inadequacy of Machiavelli's argument by referring to the things he had seen in contemporary Rome and Florence. For he knew that the notorious facts which allowed him to speak of the corruption of Italy proved at the same time the corruption of Christianity in Italy."[76] In short, Machiavelli is correct to say that Italy constantly reels from crisis to crisis, with Florence held captive; but he errs in intimating that Christianity itself is to blame.

Strauss goes on, "It is somewhat worthier but still insufficient to excuse the inadequacy of Machiavelli's argument by the indescribable misuse of the Biblical teaching of which believers in all ages have been guilty." His "argument" and "suggestions" will amaze rather than shock contemporary readers of the Bible. "They have become accustomed, not only to distinguish between the core and the periphery of the Biblical teaching, but to abandon that periphery as unnecessary or mythical. Machiavelli was unaware of the legitimacy of this distinction."[77] Here is a rare instance where Strauss is seeking to understand Machiavelli better than Machiavelli understood himself.[78]

With the above statement about "Biblical teaching," Strauss seems to be imputing a measure of legitimacy to doubts about revelation—about not only the cogency of belief in revelation but also its very possibility. In other words, though Strauss accepts that revelation and reason share a moral horizon, his position on revelation is at times precarious. It is important to remember, then, that the issue of how one should, and must, read the Bible is a leitmotif in Strauss's corpus. It is prominent in his book *Spinoza's Critique of Religion* and in his lectures "Jerusalem and Athens" and "On the Interpretation of Genesis." Strauss's argument, in essence, is that people who read the Bible as a book like any other book, not as the word of God, in effect deny the possibility of revelation, of God revealing Himself to humankind.[79]

One should, Machiavelli insists, read the Bible like any other book. He states in *Discourses* III 30, "And whoever reads the Bible judiciously will see that since he wished his laws and his orders to go forward, Moses was forced to kill infinite men who, moved by nothing other than envy, were opposed to his plans." Machiavelli's reference is to Exodus 32:27–29: "Then he [Moses] said to them, 'This is what the Lord, the God of Israel, says: "Each man strap a sword to his side. Go back and forth through the camp from one end to the other, each killing his brother and friend and neighbor."' The Levites did as Moses commanded, and that day about three thousand of the people died."[80] The point of this passage in Exodus, Fischer notes, is "that those who sin against God shall be justly punished; in truth, [for Machiavelli] it suggests that founders need to murder those who fail to agree with their vision in order to be effective."[81] Similarly, other commentators see Machiavelli as claiming, in *Discourses* III 30 and elsewhere, that the Bible should be read not with reverence but with the desire to discover the "effectual truth" of human action.[82]

Continuing with his analysis of Machiavelli's critique of providence, Strauss turns to the *Florentine Histories*. He explains that "Machiavelli's characters" (in the work), who believe that the success of their cause proves its justice, attribute their success and the misfortune of their enemies to God's favor.[83] "Machiavelli in his own name twice speaks explicitly and without qualifying expressions like 'it seems,' of God's taking care of men insofar as God's providence relates to justice."[84] In VI 32 he notes that Turkish forces took Constantinople in 1453; in VI 33 he notes that Christian forces defeated the Turks at Belgrade in 1455. At the beginning of VI 34, the first of those two examples where he speaks in his own name, he states, "But turning to things in Italy, I say how the year 1456 went . . . ."[85] He explains that the storm that engulfed Tuscany in 1456 was intended by God "to threaten rather than chastise Tuscany." The storm had both political and religious significance, Machiavelli then indicates, when he says that God was reminding people "of his power."[86] In VIII 19–21 Machiavelli likewise speaks of providence and not through a character; he recounts certain events of 1479–80: the forces of Italian dukes and princes, under the papal banner, were confronted with the grave danger of Turkish forces having landed at Otranto and sacked the surrounding areas. At the close of VIII 19 Machiavelli states, "But God, who in such extremities has always had a particular care for it [i.e., Florence], made an unhoped-for accident arise that gave the king, the pope, and the Venetians something greater to think about than Tuscany." Having spoken in VIII 20 of the Turkish attack on Otranto, he explains in VIII 21 that those troubles besetting Florence were an "accident" that presented Florence with the opportunity to atone for its mistakes. Through such atonement, Florence would prove itself, to God, the Pope, and all Christians, worthy of regaining its liberty.[87]

After discussing Machiavelli's mentions of providence in the *Florentine Histories*, Strauss states, "But let us return to the *Prince* and the *Discourses* in which Machiavelli sets forth 'everything he knows.' "[88] Strauss's words, "But let us return," signal that his discussion of the *Florentine Histories* was a digression.[89] It seems fair to say, though, that Strauss had pointed to Machiavelli's depreciation in the *Florentine Histories* of God's intercession in human affairs to reinforce his own proposition that Machiavelli questioned the notion of conscience and the belief in divine providence.

Strauss's précis of Machiavelli's "doctrine regarding providence" is worth quoting in full because it shows that Strauss sees Machiavelli as rejecting outright the belief in divine, particular providence.

> Since man is by natural necessity compelled to be ungrateful to man, he has no reason to be grateful to God. For if there is a natural necessity to sin, one is compelled to ascribe to God the origin of evil; one cannot speak of God as pure goodness or as the highest good which does not contain any evil within itself. Man cannot be expected to be grateful to God for undeserved blessings since he receives with equal abundance sufferings which he does not deserve. Necessity rather than God or necessity governing God or necessity in God, not to say chance, and not human merit or demerit, is the cause of those blessings or sufferings which are not due to man's own prudence or folly. We find just retribution only where just men rule. Every other just government is imaginary. The effective rule of just men depends on good arms, on human prudence and on some measure of good luck. There is no shred of evidence supporting the assertion that chance favors the just more than the unjust. God is not a judge or even an arbiter but a neutral. If it is true that extreme injustice arouses men's hatred, resistance and desire for revenge, it is also true that perfect justice would paralyze the hands of government; states can only be governed by a judicious mixture of justice and injustice. God is with the strongest battalions, which does not mean that he is with the largest number of battalions. Virtue, i.e. man's own virtue, and chance take the place of providence.[90]

The clear implication of the précis is that Machiavelli, according to Strauss, voices an antitheological animus in his doctrine on providence.[91] That he censures Christianity for its theology of a cosmic order created by God implies that he rejects the account of creation in Genesis and its cosmology.[92] Undermining what he sees as the enervating belief in divine providence, and advancing an out-and-out disbelief in biblical religion, he replaces the conscience and belief in divine providence with the imperative of responding to the exigencies of circumstance.[93]

At first glance, Machiavelli's entreaty for a prince to save Italy does not seem amiss. He says in the final chapter of *The Prince* that God has provided Italy with the opportunity for redemption, to save itself from the barbarians. Elsewhere, however, he implies that divine providence is in no way providential, that it does not provide care and protection. Contrasting the moderns, who are Christian, with the ancient pagan Romans, he speaks favorably of cruel deeds whilst saying that unarmed ecclesiastical principalities, as well as imagined principalities and imagined republics, are susceptible to chance.[94]

Machiavelli is expressing a prudence-based view of the means and the ends of human action. The successful ruler acts in line not with justice, nor with eternity, but only with the opportunities presented by circumstances and by the agitations of chance. Ruin occurs when the prince fails to abandon, as the times demand, such qualities as mercy and humanity that are widely regarded as exemplary.[95] Dangers in the here and now, even death, are more dangerous than "the danger of eternal ruin." Underscoring Machiavelli's disregard of the hereafter, Strauss adds: "Or did Machiavelli believe that the danger of damnation can be averted by repentance and perhaps even by repentance on the deathbed? 'Penitence,' he says in his *Exhortation to Penitence*, 'is the sole remedy which can wipe out all evils, all errors of men.' He does not even allude to this possibility in the *Prince* and the *Discourses*."[96] Machiavelli's silence about "the devil," "hell," and "the soul" indicates that he regards such matters as "unimportant simply."[97]

Like Strauss, Dante Germino regards it as significant that Machiavelli mentions penitence and the soul elsewhere than in his two major works. Against Strauss Germino claims, "Surely it is noteworthy that in the 'Exhortation' Machiavelli the alleged blasphemer explicitly condemns blasphemy. He also condemns converting our intellect from an instrument for understanding God's greatness into a means for speculating about the world."[98] Throughout his work, Machiavelli entreats people who are unfriendly to their neighbors, utter impieties, and are ungracious towards God to repent of their wicked ways and let conscience guide them. "Penitence therefore is the only means for annulling all the ills, all the sins of men."[99] At the end of his work, Machiavelli states,

> to repent and to know clearly
> that everything which pleases the world is
> but a brief dream.[100]

According to Andrea Ciliotta-Rubery, the *Exhortation* affirms Strauss's thesis that Machiavelli is a teacher of evil: "[Machiavelli's] reduction of the two great Commandments to '... love the Lord thy God with all thy heart, and with all thy soul ...' and '... love thy neighbor as thyself ....' [Mark 12:29–31] to merely being 'grateful' to God and 'friendly' to neighbors, compromises the original sentiment and intentions of these commandments."[101] Machiavelli's radical alteration of the two commandments indicates that he "cannot be seen as a true believer who respects God's word as the highest Truth," Ciliotta-Rubery stresses. Moreover, that Machiavelli disguises the blasphemous substance of his teaching in the form of a penitential speech given to an audience unaware of its impious, diabolical import shows that he is incorrigibly irreligious. "In its best light," Ciliotta-Rubery states, "Machiavelli's use of a religious forum for the promulgation of his own earthly teaching proves irreverent and at its worst, suggests his own moral indifference to his audience. For this, one may again be brought to the conclusion that Machiavelli is a teacher of evil."[102]

Creation and Miracles

In his views on Creation, Machiavelli amplifies his criticism of conscience and providence as dangerous and untrue doctrines. He holds, Strauss explains: "If all men's being sinners would have to be understood as a consequence of sin, man must have been radically different prior to his original sin from what he is now."[103] Each person is a sinner because Adam and Eve ate the fruit of the forbidden tree in the Garden of Eden. To teach that original sin makes everyone corrupt requires unremitting alertness to the unrest and to the desire for glory caused by sin; but that alertness requires a capacity for cruelty, for meting out punishment, a capacity that Christianity fails to use well.

Without mentioning Adam and Eve, Machiavelli explains in *Discourses* I 2 that people originally lived scattered throughout the earth; gradually they gathered for mutual protection; thus they formed society and civilization. According to Strauss, "Machiavelli's notion of the beginning of the world is not the Biblical but rather the 'Epicurean' notion which presupposes the eternity of 'matter'; by assuming that matter is uncreated, one could admit the necessity of evil or of sin without derogating from God's goodness." In an endnote Strauss instructs, "Consider Averroës' *Commentary on Plato's Republic*, ed. cit., I 11.3–6 and II 7."[104]

Does Strauss mean to draw a parallel between how Averroës and Machiavelli understood the role of God in the world? Averroës says in I 11.3, "Such a statement of the dialectical theologians among the men of our time that Good and Evil cannot be imagined in relation to God, but that all actions in relation to him are good, is indeed a sophistical argument, the fallacy of which is self-evident. For according to this opinion Good and Evil have no definite nature in themselves, but they are good or evil by supposition." At the beginning of II 7.1 Averroës states, "But as regards those of our community known as dialectic theologians, their religious speculation led them to <the opinion> that what God wills has no limited nature." For those theologians, "there is here no <such thing as> beautiful or ugly except by supposition."[105] Elsewhere Averroës says, "it is more appropriate to call someone who makes measured statements about natural phenomena a dialectician than to call him a poet."[106]

Machiavelli elucidates the bases of knowledge of good and evil in a way that seems akin to the "measured statements" of "dialectical theologians." In *Discourses* I 2 he says that from people gathering to form society "arose the knowledge of things honest and good, differing from the pernicious and bad."[107] His statements in *Discourses* I pr., 11, and 39 about man, heaven, and God parallel that discussion in I 2; he makes similar statements in II 5 and III 43. In III 43 he says, "Prudent men are accustomed to say, and not by chance or without merit, that whoever wishes to see what has to be considers what has been."[108] Of II 5 Strauss writes that Machiavelli therein "silently expresses his view on the creation of the world by refuting an argument advanced against the most famous alternative thesis which affirms the eternity of the visible universe."[109] Machiavelli indicated a belief in that thesis in the preface to Book II of the *Discourses*: "I judge that the world has always been in the same manner and there has been (always) as much good as there has been evil."[110]

According to Strauss, "Almost all statements just referred to express mere judgments, i.e., mere conclusions without the reasoning supporting them. The only exception is Machiavelli's summary refutation of an argument in favor of creation."[111] That refutation occurs in *Discourses* II 5. Initially, Machiavelli does not explicitly refute the argument for creation. He opens the chapter thus: "To those philosophers who have meant that the world has been eternal, I believe, one could reply that if so great an antiquity were true, it would be reasonable that there should be memory of more than 5000 years—if it were not visible how those memories of the times are extinguished by various causes."[112] Here Machiavelli is skeptical about arguments for the eternality of the world, though he does not then argue in favor of the account of Creation. Genesis 1:1–2 proclaims that the world came into existence from nothingness by the action of God: "In the beginning God created the heavens and the earth. Now the earth was formless and empty, darkness was over the surface of the deep, and the Spirit of God was hovering over the waters."[113] Machiavelli then explains in *Discourses* II 5 how the ancient memories have been extinguished, and he seems to side with philosophers who say the world is eternal. For instance, he says that "the Christian sect . . . suppressed all . . . [the pagan] orders and all its ceremonies and eliminated every memory of that ancient theology."[114] The thesis Machiavelli affirms teaches that the eternal, inert substance of the world was set into motion by the will and the word of "a First Agent." According to Averroës, "If indeed the world had come into being temporally, it would be more appropriate that it should have come into being, in so far as it was a natural existent, from principles appropriate to natural things, rather than from principles appropriate to artificial things, i.e. the will." Averroës adds this crucial distinction: "Since, however, it is established that the world exists through a First Agent which preferred its existence to its non-existence, it is necessary that this agent should be a willer."[115] For Averroës, then, the disagreement between philosophers and theologians about the cause of the world, of how it came into being, is a disagreement about how God, or divine Creation, proceeded.[116]

Elaborating his earlier observation about the "wise" roots of Machiavelli's teaching on religion, Strauss explains, "Savonarola mentions contemporary 'worldly wise' men who assert that God is not the efficient but the final cause of the world as well as that there is only one soul in all men, i.e., that there is no immortality of individual souls. The men who held these views were the Averroists."[117] Averroës states, "As for the thesis of a numerical plurality of immaterial souls, this is not a theory acknowledged by the philosophers, for they regard matter as the cause of numerical plurality and form as the cause of congruity in numerical plurality. And that there should be a numerical plurality without matter, having one unique form, is impossible."[118] To Plato, "the soul is separated from the body," Averroës explains, "for the soul creates and forms the body, and if the body were the condition for the existence of the soul, the soul would not have created it or formed it."[119] Averroës rejected creation *ex nihilo*, but, Wolfson notes, "[t]he very same persons who damned him for his heresy—Albertus Magnus, Thomas Aquinas, and even Giles of Rome—followed his example and wrote commentaries on Aristotle in his style and manner; and they constantly quoted him."[120] According to Strauss, explicating Averroist views is the key to understanding Machiavelli: "We must turn to the books of the 'Averroists' in order to complete Machiavelli's intimations and to fill the gaps between the seemingly unconnected denials without which his political teaching as a whole would be baseless."[121]

Rather than taking his own advice by turning to those "books," Strauss continues to analyze Machiavelli's views on creation. He observes that Machiavelli "may be said to exclude dogmatically all evidence which is not ultimately derived from phenomena that are at all times open to everyone's inspection in broad daylight." Phenomena such as miracles that support "revealed religion" are "imperfectly known."[122] In the words of Machiavelli, "Men in general judge more by their eyes than by their hands, because seeing is given to everyone, touching to few. Everyone sees how you appear, few touch what you are."[123]

"Whereas Machiavelli does not explicitly discuss the beginnings of Christianity, he explicitly discusses what one may call the beginnings of Judaism," Strauss explains.[124] In Chapter 6 of *The Prince* Machiavelli equates the state founded by Moses to those founded by Cyrus, Romulus, and Theseus, as based "less on fortune" and more on "opportunity" and "their [own] virtue of spirit."[125] Likewise, he says in Chapter 7 that all states, including those founded by the popes, are of human, not heavenly, origin; human virtue rather than divine favor underpins states. Miracles, then, be they biblical—God speaking to Moses—or pagan—Numa claiming a nymph spoke to him—are untrue and impossible but useful for founders, who can use such phenomena to instill in citizens the love or desire to work for the good of their fatherland. Strauss points out for Machiavelli, "one does not hear the words of God but only the words of men."[126] I note, for instance, that Exodus 3:1–22 explains that God called out from within a burning bush and spoke with Moses, instructing him to lead the Israelites out of their slavery in Egypt; and Exodus 4:1–17 explains that God instructed Moses to impart to the Egyptians and Israelites signs to prove that he had spoken with God. In *Discourses* I 11 Machiavelli says, "for Romulus to order the Senate and to make other civil and military orders, the authority of God was not necessary; but it was quite necessary to Numa, who pretended to be intimate with a nymph who counseled him on what he had to counsel the people."[127]

Machiavelli on the Character of Religion

Illustrating the core of Machiavelli's instrumentalist view of the use of religion, Strauss points out that "to Machiavelli, Biblical religion and pagan religion have this in common, that they are both of merely human origin. As for the essential difference between them, he is primarily concerned with its political aspects."[128] The difference pertains to the primacy in pagan Rome of arms—of soldiers, armies, generals, and the pursuit of worldly glory—over the rule of priests. With that primacy of arms, the Romans were not as vulnerable to fickle changes in fortune as are modern, Christian republics. "To repeat Machiavelli's primary contention," says Strauss, "whereas the pagan religion was conducive to the triumph of the world, Christianity has rendered the world weak."[129] Christianity is non-warlike and populist in its origins; in contrast, paganism is warlike and aristocratic in its origins and is preoccupied with political matters. Machiavelli praises the vitality of ancient Roman politics. In particular, defending the plebeian Romans against the charge of fickleness, that they would support a leader only to later plot and rebel against him, he claims that the plebeians always defended with vigor the freedom taken from them by the acquisitive ways of the great.[130]

The tenor of Strauss's analysis of Machiavelli's critique of Christianity is that Machiavelli praises pagan Rome for its pursuit of glory and criticizes Christianity for having made the world weak. Yet Strauss indicated at the beginning of his critical study that his thesis is, and therefore that the tenor of his analysis would be, that Machiavelli is neither Christian nor pagan. Having pointed to Machiavelli's defense of the plebeian Romans, Strauss returns to his original thesis: he suggests that Machiavelli regards paganism as useless, like Christianity. "Paganism is characterized by satisfaction with the present, with the world and its glory, and therefore by despair regarding the future, the ultimate future," Strauss explains for Machiavelli. ". . . Biblical religion is characterized by dissatisfaction with the present, by the conviction that the present, the world, is a valley of misery and sin."[131] This underscoring of the difference between paganism and biblical faith shows a dim view of religion in general. Machiavelli maintains that the most a pagan can hope to achieve is not the succor of eternity, of the afterlife, but merely a brief respite from the anxieties produced by the unceasing flux of the here-and-now present.[132] It is curious, then, that Voegelin claims that Machiavelli reverted to a pagan myth of nature, and that Beiner, Gay, and Parel claim that he sought to paganize Christianity by interpreting it in the light of pagan religiosity.[133]

Strauss goes on to explain, "The peculiar difficulty to which Machiavelli's criticism of the Bible is exposed is concentrated in his attempt to replace humility by humanity. He rejects humility because he believes that it lowers the stature of man. But humanity as he understands it implies the desire to prevent man from transcending humanity or to lower man's goal." Strauss means, in short, that Machiavelli has a political view of the *telos* of humankind. However, Strauss goes on: "As for the other elements of his criticism of the Bible, it would be useless to deny that they were implicit in the teaching of Aristotle and developed by those intransigent Aristotelians [i.e., the Averroists] who knew the Bible."[134] That Strauss acknowledges in a qualified manner—"it is useless to deny"—the link between Machiavelli and Aristotle is because he objects to the unapologetic manner in which Machiavelli takes issue with biblical morality.[135]

Machiavelli issued a comprehensive challenge to the efficacy and truth of Christianity. To revitalize the flagging political virtue of his era, which he attributed to the otherworldly character of Christianity, he articulated a "thesis of disbelief" against prevalent Christian beliefs in divine providence and creation. In his view, not conscience, providence, or even fear of hell but fear of punishment in the here and now makes people good. The closest Strauss came to stating that Machiavelli rejects the existence of God was when he explained, "We would go too far were we to assert that Machiavelli has never heard the Call nor sensed the Presence, for we would contradict his remarks referring to the conscience. But he certainly refuses to heed experiences of this kind."[136] Machiavelli refused to heed those experiences because he regarded them as antithetical to decisive action in political life. In essence, then, an anti-teleotheological animus underpins his critique of Christianity. Whether that animus underpins his view of religion in general remains to be seen.

By explaining that Machiavelli likely affirmed the eternity of the world, Strauss had placed him in the company of Aristotle. Strauss identified, then, a link between Machiavelli and Aristotle, or rather between Machiavelli and the Averroists, regarding the core of religion and its role in the life of founders and princes. However, Strauss did not examine the link in detail; he focused on Machiavelli, not on Averroës or the works of specific Averroists. Strauss's reticence in this regard suggests that he sympathized with a key aspect of Machiavelli's rejection of Christianity, namely, that it denigrates the political aspirations of excellent men.[137] Yet, that Strauss in a theological context examined the theme of providence (before examining doctrines of creation and miracles) is an implicit critique of the *falāsifa* or Averroists, who turned the doctrine of providence into a strictly political theme.[138] At numerous points throughout his critical study of Machiavelli's teaching on religion, Strauss clearly does recognize the possibility of revelation, a possibility that Machiavelli rejected outright. In other words, Strauss was open to the intellectual importance and personal challenge of biblical precepts on the good life. Against Machiavelli, Strauss raises the questions, What is the will of God? What is a person required to do, by God and by others? What is the one thing needful for life? Strauss did not describe himself as a theologian, and thus did not raise those questions from within a theological horizon, but he clearly is, as his analysis of Machiavelli's teaching on religion shows, deeply interested in theological matters.

CHAPTER FOUR

Cosmology and the Utility of Religion

Flatly rejecting Strauss's thesis that Machiavelli is neither Christian nor pagan, Parel states, "Instead of first establishing the ultimate or cosmological basis of his religious thought, critics begin by asking whether he is a Christian or a pagan or an atheist, and so exhaust themselves in the process." Parel adds this caveat: "It is not that these questions are irrelevant. They are indeed relevant; but they become so only when set against the background of his fundamental concept of religion as such. And it is our hypothesis that his concept is derived from his cosmology."[1]

Strauss's critical study of Machiavelli's teaching is exhaustive, but not in Parel's negative sense. By beginning with Machiavelli's critique of Christianity, Strauss did not dissipate the force of his analysis; nor did he ignore Machiavelli's cosmology and fundamental concept of religion. Instead, he elaborated his inclination to the "old-fashioned view" of Machiavelli as "evil," "immoral," and "irreligious." Moreover, he aimed to elucidate the standpoint behind Machiavelli's critiques of Christianity and religion in general. The reason for the elucidation is explained thus by Peterman: "By studying Machiavelli's evil teaching we will appreciate his core, the problem that reveals the unity of his surface and heart, and finally achieve access to the permanent problems."[2]

Chapter 4 of *Thoughts on Machiavelli* continues the thread of analysis that links the preceding chapters. At the close of chapter 1, having examined the basic affinity between *The Prince* and the *Discourses*, Strauss stated that one should understand the perspective of each work by itself, not in the light of the other. In chapter 2 Strauss examined Machiavelli's intention in *The Prince*. He proposed at the end of the chapter that it is necessary to turn to the *Discourses* to understand both how Machiavelli accounted for the ascendancy of Christianity and hoped to achieve the victory of his own enterprise, namely, the challenge to authority. The main theme Strauss raised in chapter 3 is the fundamental challenge in the *Discourses* to *authority*—human and divine.[3]

Machiavelli speaks in the preface to Book I of the *Discourses* of his "desire" to discover "new modes and orders." He hopes that his discoveries, "these labors of mine," will be victorious over the parlous state of knowledge, of things political, military, and governmental, in the present, Christian era.[4] There is no reason to doubt the sincerity of Machiavelli's ambition in this regard or doubt his conviction that his critiques and advice would advance those aims. He bases the hoped-for victory of his discoveries, Strauss argues in chapter 3, on his conviction that the prudence of his teaching will win over parties of Ghibellines, that is, nominal Christians who support secular rule over papal authority. Thus, Strauss concludes the chapter, "We have now answered the question of how Machiavelli can hope for the success of his venture."[5]

Strauss proceeds in chapter 4 to give his promised *critical study* of Machiavelli's *teaching*. In the first section of part I of the chapter Strauss examines Machiavelli's critique of Christianity and biblical religion. In the second section of part I Strauss, as will be seen below, examines his critique of religion in general. The movement between the two sections is in the direction of Machiavelli's standpoint on religion; the movement is a gradual ascent or a careful progression. In part II of chapter 4 Strauss examines his moral-political teaching on virtue, the common good, and good governance; as in part I, Strauss elucidates the anti-teleotheological animus in Machiavelli's "new modes and orders." The movement between the four chapters of *Thoughts on Machiavelli* is, therefore, a movement toward casting light on "the real Machiavelli,"[6] on the standpoint behind both his religious and moral-political teachings; and with each movement in the final chapter Strauss comes closer to his stated goal of achieving access to the fundamental alternatives.

Machiavelli's Cosmological Reflections

Divine Attributes: God, Heaven, and Fortuna

Thus far, Strauss has shown that Machiavelli echoed Aristotelian and Averroist views on the eternality of the world. Now, Strauss proposes: "In order to bring out more clearly the difference between Machiavelli and Aristotle, we must consider Machiavelli's doctrine regarding God and his attributes." Having then summarized the "explicit" mentions of God in *Discourses* I 11–15, Strauss reflects, "On the whole Machiavelli teaches in the section on the Roman religion that fear of God's or the gods' power and wrath can be very useful; he is silent as to whether God and the gods are powerful or exist."[7] Indeed, for Coby, these "five chapters . . . teach us: (1) that religion is the glue of society and is important to national success; (2) that religion is untrue but politically useful to the extent that the rulers feign belief and manipulate the rites; (3) that the control of the plebeian population is the primary use of religion; and (4) that religion used militarily is helpful but of less certain value."[8] Machiavelli's "silence" about God in I 11–15 is not broken by "the only other reference to God which occurs in the First Book," Strauss explains. He then quotes from I 58: "not without cause does one liken the voice of the people to that of God; for a universal opinion visibly produces marvellous effects in its prognostications, so much so that it seems as if the people foresees its evil and its good by an occult virtue."[9] Machiavelli is also somewhat silent about God in *Discourses* II 1, and III 1, 2, 23, 29, and 33: although he speaks of God or the gods watching over and occasionally interceding in human affairs, he is silent about—or, at the very least, is reluctant to discuss—the worth of divine intercessions. Thus, Strauss states, "Whereas the *Discourses* are then in the decisive respect silent about God, they make significant assertions regarding heaven."[10]

By underscoring his silence about God, and by describing the mentions in the *Discourses* about the attributes of God as a "doctrine," Strauss means to show that Machiavelli expresses through his "doctrine" an antitheological animus. Strauss continues, "Following the 'astrologers' or 'scientists' of his age, and perhaps even going beyond them, Machiavelli replaces God by 'heaven.'"[11] Strauss does not identify the people in question; he says (in an endnote) that Savonarola inveighed against philosophers and astrologers, and points out, "According to Savonarola, even the soul has greater power (*virtù*) than heaven."[12] Machiavelli, too, speaks of the influence heaven exerts over human affairs. In *Discourses* I pr., 6, 19, II pr., 2, 5, and III 1 he depicts heaven as a celestial body in the sky above that occasionally deigns to keep an eye on humanity. How Machiavelli goes beyond his contemporaries when he delineates the power of heaven relates to how he expresses the idea that "heaven" is a conscious being. Strauss explains, "There occurs only one passage in the *Discourses* where 'heaven' is described as a thinking and willing being, and in that passage 'heaven' (*il cielo*) is used interchangeably with the Biblical 'the heavens' (*i cieli*)." This passage, which I discuss shortly below, is located near the beginning of II 29. In the passage Machiavelli "tacitly identifies both [*il cielo* and *i cieli*] with Fortuna," Strauss explains. "Fortuna is not the same as heaven or the all-comprising vault. Fortuna can be said to be the goddess which rules the little world of man in regard to extrinsic accidents."[13]

In an endnote Strauss instructs readers to "Cf. *Discourses* III 1 with Dante, *Inferno* 7.67–96."[14] To what end does Strauss place Dante, who writes for a Christian audience and says that God rules over all things, next to Machiavelli, who writes with the desire to teach new modes and orders and says that man should rule over all things? The passage is an exchange between Dante (7.67–69) and Virgil (7.70–96) about Fortune. Dante remarks, " 'My teacher,' I said to him, 'now tell me further: This Fortune you mention to me, what is she, who so has the good things of the world in her clutches?' " Virgil replies: "And he answered me: 'O silly creatures, what great ignorance is this which harms you! Now be sure that you take in my statement about her. He whose wisdom transcends all things, made the heavens and gave them their directors, so that every part shines upon every other part, distributing light uniformly' " (7.70–76). Fortune, Virgil exclaims, " 'is she who so often is crucified even by those who ought to praise her—wrongly blaming and speaking ill of her. But she is blessed and does not hear it. With the other first-created beings, she happily turns her sphere, and rejoices in blessedness' " (7.91–96).[15] In, perhaps, a Dantean-like manner, Machiavelli says in *Discourses* II 29 that Fortuna caused an accident—the French invasion of Roman territory—that led Rome back to its beginnings of strength and discipline; thus, the accident renewed the virtue of the Roman republic. In III 1 he also discusses renewal, that is, within "mixed bodies, such as republics and sects," though the similarity between II 29 and III 1 ends there. In III 1 he speaks of accidents, "extrinsic" and "intrinsic," but he does not attribute, as he did in II 29, accidents to the machinations of Fortuna, as would Dante and Virgil, for both of whom Fortuna is a heavenly agent working for a higher power. In III 1 Machiavelli does not speak of Fortuna as *the* cause of renewal in the Roman republic; instead, he speaks of "the simple virtue of one man" who compels "the wicked" to follow a good "mode of life."[16] When Strauss continues (in his text), "We shall then say that Machiavelli replaces God, not by heaven, but by Fortuna,"[17] he largely has in mind *Discourses* II 29, not III 1; though in III 1 Machiavelli speaks of accidents, he seems to replace Fortuna with a temporal, nonteleological principle of causation.

Prophecy and Heavenly Signs

Strauss follows his survey of Machiavelli's mentions in the *Discourses* about God with a discussion of theological matters. Pointing to *Discourses* I 56 and II 29, Strauss explains, "Machiavelli has explicitly devoted two chapters of the *Discourses* to what one may call theology as distinguished from religion."[18] Strauss's point here is that the cosmology in those chapters is not simply about a general belief in the existence of God; it is about systematic principles on Fortuna, divination, prophecy, and the interpretation of supernatural phenomena.[19]

Machiavelli undercuts the widely held notion that heavenly signs prophesy punishment of humankind for its shortcomings and sins. At first glance, he appears to support that notion. At the beginning of I 56 he writes, "Whence it arises I do not know, but one sees by ancient and by modern examples that no grave accident in a city or in a province ever comes unless it has been foretold either by diviners or by revelations or by prodigies or by other heavenly signs." However, towards the end of I 56 he admits, "Yet it could be, as some philosopher would have it, that since this air is full of intelligences that foresee future things by their natural virtues, and they have compassion for men, they warn them with like signs so that they can prepare themselves for defense." For the philosopher whom Machiavelli does not name, the intelligences are compassionate and all-knowing; their "heavenly signs" enable people to prepare for the travails of life. "Yet however this may be," Machiavelli says, at the end of I 56, "one sees it thus to be the truth, and that always after such accidents extraordinary and new things supervene in provinces."[20]

Machiavelli means to say that, as heavenly signs foresee adverse future events, the absence of the signs is evil, as is heaven itself, for it should cause the signs.[21] Yet, he does not mention God, either as a cause of signs, or at all; he speaks of "knowledge of things natural and supernatural, which we do not have."[22] He suggests, then, that God is irrelevant. For Strauss, Machiavelli's deprecation of "the heavenly signs . . . is in entire agreement with the intention of his whole work." His "silence" in both *The Prince* and the *Discourses* about the "devil and hell" and "divine punishment" reveals that "intention."[23] In an endnote Strauss cross-refers to his own previous discussion. Given that in chapter 3 I examined the pages in question, it suffices to say here that, having spoken of Machiavelli's rejection of biblical injunctions against sin, Strauss cited the warning in Nahum 1:2 that God's vengeance is harsh for those who disobey His commands. Strauss adds in his endnote this parallel between the Bible and Machiavelli: "The intelligences in the air [mentioned in *Discourses*

I 56] may remind us of 'the prince of the power of the air' of *Ephesians* 2.2."[24] Strauss's parallel draws attention to the theo-cosmological import of Machiavelli's notion of effectual truth. Ephesians suggests that the root cause of peoples' rejection of scriptural commands against sin is both this-worldly and supernatural: "As for you, you were dead in your transgressions and sins, in which you used to live when you followed the ways of this world and of the ruler of the kingdom of the air, the spirit who is now at work in those who are disobedient."[25]

Fortuna

Strauss clearly is identifying the main theological strands in Machiavelli's cosmology. "Yet," Strauss points out, "we must not for one moment forget that Machiavelli does not assert the existence of those intelligences in the air; the only superhuman intelligent and willing being whose existence he asserts in the *Discourses* is Fortuna."[26] Nor must one forget that Machiavelli regards the intercessions of the intelligences not as divine (or general) acts of providence but as accidents. Thus, he blurs the distinction between portents and accidents; and by accidents he means calamities that human actions hasten, not the actions of God, the gods, or Fortuna.[27]

Strauss, however, is not ascribing to Machiavelli a *theology* of Fortuna. Strauss notes, "Whereas I 56 leads up to a merely hypothetical suggestion belonging to quasi-theology, II 29 promises by its very heading to contain Machiavelli's assertoric quasi-theology: 'Fortuna blinds the minds of men when she does not wish them to oppose her designs.'"[28] By using the term "quasi-theology" to describe both I 56 and II 29 Strauss means that Machiavelli's views on God and Fortuna resemble, but do not constitute, a theology. His theology is not a theology qua theology, for he replaces God with Fortuna as the Supreme Being and replaces Fortuna with mundane chance. In essence, then, in his quasi-theology Machiavelli advances an anti-teleotheological cosmology.[29]

In *Discourses* II 29 Machiavelli initially speaks of heaven in an abstract sense. Depicting heaven not as a particular being but as a general cosmological body, he opens the chapter thus: "If how human affairs proceed is considered well, it will be seen that often things arise and accidents come about that the heavens have not altogether wished to be provided against." He then explains that "heaven" instigates accidents "for some end," so that people "know its power."[30] Elsewhere he seems to acknowledge God as *the* divine, providential being: he says that these sometimes-unkind actions of the heavens tend to contradict the will of God, the author of specific providential acts.[31] In *Discourses* II 29, however, he goes on to depict heaven as Fortuna, a thinking, active being with her own goals, will, and desires. As Strauss describes this thesis of II 29, ". . . Fortuna takes the place of all gods. Not only is the existence of Fortuna more certain than that of the intelligences in the air; she is also more powerful than they might be . . . ." Fortuna's power over human affairs *is*, her ends unfathomable; but "men ought never to give up, no matter what the condition into which Fortuna may have brought them."[32]

Though all-powerful in her realm, Fortuna bestows her favors in a fickle manner. Machiavelli notes in *Discourses* II 30 that Fortuna is open to persuasion by men of virtue; her variability, he says in Chapter 25 of *The Prince*, governs one half only of human affairs—"she leaves the other half, or close to it, for us to govern."[33] Toward the end of Chapter 25 he describes Fortuna as a woman who likes to be beaten down by audacious young men; toward the end of *Discourses* II 30 he observes, "where men have little virtue, fortune shows its power very much."[34] In II 1 Machiavelli explains that victory in war can be gained by "a very great virtue and prudence mixed with fortune."[35] In II 29 he attributes the periodic renewal of virtue in Rome to Fortuna. In III 1, taking up these discussions in II 1 and II 29, he says that by "either extrinsic accident or intrinsic prudence" can "sects, republics, and kingdoms" be brought "back toward their beginnings," and thereby "regain new life and new virtue." By "extrinsic accident" Machiavelli means both heaven and random accidents; but he suggests, as seen above, that heaven be understood in temporal terms. By "intrinsic prudence" he means the virtue of a single man and the orders that that man enacts through his actions. "[E]xtrinsic force," Machiavelli concludes in III 1, draws a society to "its beginnings," but is too "dangerous" to well-being and security "to be desired."[36]

Fortuna and Nature

When identifying the divine power that governs men and makes them virtuous, Machiavelli at times conflates Fortuna and heaven. That conflation allows him, Strauss observes, "to present Fortuna not merely as the only superhuman being which thinks and wills, or as the only god, but likewise as the all comprehensive order which does not think and will, or as nature." Strauss asks, "What then is the relation between Fortuna and nature?"[37] Strauss means by this question to establish whether Machiavelli believes that Fortuna and her chance accidents, on the one hand, or the qualities within men, on the other hand, decisively determine the path of human action. Fortuna, Strauss explains for Machiavelli, is "a part" of—and her "power . . . based on"—nature; heaven presides over "the whole" of nature. "But if one looks more closely," Strauss states, "one sees that in the most important cases 'the cause of (good) fortune' is not Fortuna but human virtue and good institutions, i.e., the work of prudence and art. Rome owed her greatness decisively to her virtue and not to Fortuna."[38] Machiavelli explains in *Discourses* I 2, 4, 11, and III 9 and 29, as well as in Chapters 6 and 7 of *The Prince*, that accidents and chance events hold some sway over human affairs by providing opportunities for people to prove their mettle. In *Discourses* II 1, though, having said that good fortune combined with virtue makes a republic great, he argues that the greatness of Rome was due more to virtue than to fortune. He means a collective virtue, marked by a measure of competition within the city: the accidents in Rome arose, he claims, not so much from random acts of chance as they did from the tumults between nobles and the people.[39]

Fortuna, then, can be challenged. Striving against her power evinces virtuous action; the outstanding individual is willing, able, and has the qualities (intrinsic, not extrinsic) both to change the times and to adapt as circumstances demand. Such change and adaptation is limited, though. Chance cannot be completely controlled, as Machiavelli shows in the *Florentine Histories* VIII 36 when he links the fall of Italy to the death of Lorenzo de' Medici, who "was loved by fortune and by God in the highest degree."[40] Accidents in a republic that are due to deficient virtues and institutions, Machiavelli says in *Discourses* III 31, can be rectified—if outstanding men of virtue exist in the republic. The foundation of a great republic, he goes on to explain in III 31, is a military composed of the people, that is well-trained, provisioned, armed, and led by capable, spirited commanders who are neither made "insolent" by "good fortune" nor "cowardly" by "defeat."[41] The basis of the Roman "state was the people of Rome," Machiavelli stresses in *Discourses* II 30, "the Latin name, the other partner towns in Italy, and their colonies, from which they drew so many soldiers that with them they were sufficient to combat and hold the world."[42]

Chance, Accidents, and the Natural Order of the World

To Machiavelli, then, *the* underlying principle in human action is not that chance which is due to the agitations of Fortuna. By so replacing Fortuna with accidents, Machiavelli, says Strauss, "deliberately blurs the distinction between nature and chance in order to indicate the common origin of both belief in gods and knowledge of nature." People tend to "arrive at making foreseeable the unforeseeable and at transforming the simply unintended into something intended." Due to "the minds of unwise and undisciplined men," who are "frightened by the extraordinary or new as such," a tendency arises in most men to "identify the extraordinary with the grave." Regardless of whether an accident is grave or accidental, men see in it a sign of the extraordinary. "An event brought about intentionally is an accident for those men who did not intend it or foresee it. Let us now call 'new accidents' such accidents as are not in themselves grave." Grave accidents are signs from heaven; new accidents happen genuinely or through the contrivance of a captain; and an accident through contrivance is a "fabricated" accident. To interpret a genuine or a grave accident to his own benefit, a captain must prevent people "from discovering its true cause."[43] Depending, then, on one's foresight, accidents are anticipated or unanticipated; in addition, they may be rendered consequential or incon-sequential.[44]

Although Machiavelli speaks of the influence that chance and accidents have over human affairs, divine beings, the mighty authors of general and specific providential acts, are largely absent from his cosmology. Strauss states, "In the *Prince*, in which Machiavelli never speaks of 'we Christians,' he never mentions the gods or heaven." His silence about the gods is selective, though. "[W]hile he asserts in the *Prince* the existence both of God and of Fortuna as a willing and thinking being, he never refers there to any demon-stration of the existence or power of Fortuna."[45] Fortuna desires to make new princes great, Machiavelli says in Chapter 20. However, he said in Chapter 8 that Agathocles' greatness and virtue were due to his own capabilities, not to good fortune. In Chapter 6 Machiavelli explained, "the result of becoming prince from private individual presupposes either virtue or fortune, . . . ; nonetheless, he who has relied less on fortune has maintained himself more."[46] Of Chapter 25 Strauss says that Machiavelli "hardly sheds further light on Fortuna, or on chance, by saying at the end of the chapter that For-tuna is like a women who can be vanquished by the right kind of man. For if Fortuna can be vanquished, man would seem to be able to become the mas-ter of the universe."[47]

Having examined Machiavelli's views on Fortuna, Strauss notes, "We have stated the reasons which may induce one to think that Machiavelli's cosmo-logical premises were Aristotelian." Strauss has come full circle to the point at which he began: examining Machiavelli's cosmology to explicate *the* difference between Machiavelli and Aristotle. Upon returning to that originary juncture, Strauss travels forward again, by stating: "Yet there is no place in his [i.e., Machiavelli's] cosmology for a ruling Mind. This by itself does not prove that he consciously broke away from Aristotle's doctrine of God, for that doctrine has been understood in greatly different ways."[48]

Illustrating those "ways," Strauss instructs in an endnote, "Cf. e.g. Cicero, *De natura deorum* I 33–35 and *Acad. Post.* I 29."[49] This brief reference to Cicero serves to remind the reader that the only conscious and willing "force" Machiavelli sees in the world is one that can be ascribed to the action and the thought of the excellent man, a force that, by dint of his virtue, can overcome chance; thus, the force is in no way divine or providential.[50] In *De natura deorum* I 33–35 Cicero speaks of the confusing and confused notions about the corporeality (or otherwise) of God raised by Aristotle, Plato, Xenocrates, Heraclides of Pontus, Theophrastus, and Strato. Of God as a providential, ruling mind, Cicero writes in *Academica* I 29, "this force they say is the soul of the world, and is also perfect intelligence and wisdom, which they entitle God, and is a sort of 'providence.'" But of how one as a result of that "force" conducts oneself in all aspects of life, he says in *Academica* II 92, "No faculty of knowing absolute limits has been bestowed upon us by the nature of things to enable us to fix exactly how far to go in any matter."[51]

For Machiavelli, chance is an underlying force in the world. Though at times he suggests that chance is the ground of all that can be, his basic view of chance is nonteleological. He "indicates" in *Discourses* I 2, Strauss goes on to explain, "his fundamental disagreement with Aristotle's doctrine of the whole by substituting 'chance' (*caso*) for 'nature' in the only context in which he speaks of 'the beginning of the world.'" Whereas Polybius says that regimes change in a cyclical, natural manner, Machiavelli says, in *Discourses* I 2 and 6, and III 1, for example, that regimes change not because of nature but because of chance. Strauss notes, "Among 'the philosophic family' surrounding Aristotle in Dante's Limbo we find 'Democritus who ascribes the world to chance.'"[52] By implying that Machiavelli belongs in Limbo, the first circle of Hell, Strauss places him in esteemed company.[53] But unlike his companions in Limbo, Machiavelli claims that random, chance accidents do not occur under the aegis of a purposeful and divine necessity—God or Fortuna. "We conclude," Strauss explains, "that the movement of fundamental thought which finds expression in both books [*The Prince* and the *Discourses*] consists in a movement from God to Fortuna and then from Fortuna via accidents, and accidents occurring to bodies or accidents of bodies, to chance understood as a non-teleological necessity which leaves room for choice and prudence and therefore for chance understood as the cause of simply unforeseeable accidents."[54]

Of that antiteleological orientation in his cosmology, Strauss explains, "Machiavelli has indicated his fundamental thought also in his *Life of Cas-*

truccio Castracani." Yet shortly afterwards Strauss states, "In considering the *Castruccio*, one must be mindful of the distance between the two books in which Machiavelli expresses 'everything he knows' and all his other utterances."[55] Given the strong emphasis Strauss places on both *The Prince* and the *Discourses* to understand his teaching, it seems odd that Strauss turns, even temporarily, to Machiavelli's other works. However, like his digression into the *Florentine Histories* and the *Exhortation to Penitence*, Strauss's digression into the *Castruccio* casts light on the irreligious and immoral basis to Machiavelli's teaching on religion.

Towards the end of the *Castruccio*, a biography of Castruccio Castracani, a tyrant of Lucca in the thirteenth century, can be found thirty-four sayings that bear "witness" to "his great qualities."[56] Machiavelli adapts thirty-one of his pithy sayings from the *Lives of the Famous Philosophers* by Diogenes Laertius.[57] Diogenes notes that Bion, a self-professed atheist, repented on his deathbed and asked forgiveness for his impious, wicked ways. Machiavelli mentions God three times in his thirty-four sayings,[58] but not once in his description of Castruccio's deathbed speech. Strauss explains, "Castruccio, who speaks in his witty sayings and elsewhere of God, mentions Fortuna in his dying speech five times, but never God. Castruccio, who in his witty sayings speaks of the soul, of hell and of paradise, mentions this world once in his dying speech and the next, never. Similarly, when expressing his own thought, Machiavelli mentions this world once in the *Castruccio* and never the next; and he mentions fortuna eight times and God never."[59]

For Strauss, the significance of the thirty-four sayings consists, I would suggest, in both their form and their content. By "form" I mean that Machiavelli does not state his beliefs; he puts the sayings into the mouth of Castruccio. By "content" I mean the subject matter of the sayings, namely, the need for heartfelt repentance of one's sins. That Machiavelli is silent about God shows that he views morality not from within the traditional horizon of what ought to be, but from within a new horizon—of what is. His horizon is "new" by virtue of its thisworldly view of life; he favors the here and now over the hereafter. Deprecating teleology, eschewing a hierarchy of moral and intellectual ends, he regards autonomy, not divine guidance, as the one thing necessary for life. He favors autonomy, but of a certain kind: autonomy divorced from the autonomous philosophical quest for knowledge of the good life.[60] He regards "philosophy as a useless interference, in the life of a grand, new founder," for like religion, philosophy is concerned with thinking on transcendent norms of human action.[61] In short, the *Castruccio* evinces Machiavelli's antipathy towards not only religion but also philosophy.

The Utility of Religion

Defining Religion

Strauss turns from Machiavelli's cosmological reflections to his claims about the limited usefulness of religion to explicate further his critique of all religion. "Machiavelli uses the term 'religion' in two senses," Strauss observes. "He uses 'religion' synonymously with 'sect' and understands by it a mixed body, or a society of a certain kind. 'Sect' is used also in the sense of 'party,' i.e., an association whose end is not identical with the common good of a particular state."[62] According to Preus, "Machiavelli chose to evaluate religion using norms in no sense intrinsic to religious systems generally, and even antagonistic to the values of Christian believers as he saw them."[63]

In the *Florentine Histories* Machiavelli discusses the disturbances of the Guelfs and Ghibellines. In the Preface and throughout Books I to IV he depicts the fomenting "humors" of, and the internecine conflict between, the Guelfs and Ghibellines as symptomatic of Italy's susceptibility to invasion.[64] For Machiavelli, a "sect" is a "mixed body," for, like any organization or social grouping, it is composed of "simple bodies," that is, of individual human beings.[65] As any given city, state, or country contains "mixed bodies," that is, parties with their own ambitions for power, the common good is difficult to realize in a concrete manner. But to Machiavelli, it was Christianity rather than the bickering of the Ghibellines that posed the greatest danger to the common good of Florence. When speaking of the Guelfs, who supported the papacy, Machiavelli uses interchangeably the expressions, "the sect of the Guelfs" and "the Guelf parties." He uses the term "sect" in reference only to the Guelfs. When speaking of the Ghibellines, who supported the emperor, he uses the expressions, "the Ghibellines," "Ghibelline humors," and "the party of the Ghibellines."[66]

The second sense in which Machiavelli uses "religion," Strauss explains, is of " 'religion' [as] a part of virtue or one of the virtues."[67] Strauss does not refer here to the *Republic*, though his words echo 427e–434d, especially 433b–c. In the latter, Socrates reflects that justice is both a virtue and the whole of virtue: "this—the practice of minding one's own business—when it comes into being in a certain way, is probably justice. . . . [A]fter having considered moderation, courage, and prudence, this is what's left over in the city; it provided the power by which all these others came into being; and, once having come into being, it provides them with preservation as long as it's in the city. And yet we were saying that justice would be what's left over from the three if we found them.”[68] According to Strauss, Machiavelli “may have conceived of the relation between religion as a virtue and religion as a society as parallel to the relation between justice and the other virtues on the one hand and civil society on the other.”[69]

Does Strauss mean that Machiavelli regarded religion both as a part of society and as *the* foundation of society? Machiavelli admits that religion, with its rites and rituals, is a way to order society; religious observances provide a focus for cultural, political, and economic life. Yet, at the basis of those observances he sees artifice, not heartfelt belief. To Machiavelli, Strauss notes, “the belief which is the foundation of religion is not true belief, i.e. not belief based on firm or reliable experience but belief caused by self-deception and to some extent even by deception.”[70] “Indeed,” Fontana explains, “by unveiling the methods used by the founders of pagan religion Machiavelli is simultaneously uncovering the natural and human foundation of revealed religion.”[71]

The Use(s) of Religion

Strauss continues, however: “Machiavelli was not the first man to assert that religion is both untrue and salutary. Religion is a part of virtue or is a virtue.”[72] Rather than explain who that “first man” is—was it Numa Pompilius?— Strauss turns to the section on the Roman religion in Book I of the *Discourses*. Here Machiavelli says that Romulus gave Rome its arms, but that Numa introduced religion into the city, thereby turning its population from their corrupt, ferocious, and uncivilized ways. Yet, having in I 11–15 praised the Roman religion as the cause of the city’s well-being, Machiavelli in I 19 questions that usefulness of religion—he suggests that Numa lacked prudence and arms. “For he who is like Numa will hold it [the state or city] or not hold it as the times or fortune turn under him, but he who is like Romulus, and like him comes armed with prudence and with arms, will hold it in every mode unless it is taken from him by an obstinate and excessive force.”[73]

Religion is useful for ordering a republic, insofar as civic observances of religion inculcate fear of God, a fear that forestalls disquiet amongst nobles and the people. Religion has a similarly pivotal role in kingdoms, though not in the kingdom ruled by a prince who inculcates in his subjects a fear of his rule that replaces fear of God. The prince also enacts modes and orders to counter the problem of hereditary succession. In *Discourses* I 2 Machiavelli warns, “as the prince began to be made by succession, and not by choice, at once the heirs began to degenerate from their ancestors.”[74] By adopting a son of like qualities, the prince ensures the ascension of a capable successor.[75] The qualities relate,

Strauss notes, not to "moral virtue" but to "strong mind and will" and to the judicious use of "moral virtue and vice according to the requirements of the situation." Shortly afterwards Strauss remarks, "Machiavelli does not resist the temptation to say on one occasion that the appearance of religion is more important for the prince than anything else. On the other hand, it seems to be highly desirable that his soldiers should possess fear of God."[76]

Where is that "one occasion"? In his accompanying endnote Strauss refers to Chapters 12, 14, 15, and 18 of *The Prince*.[77] In the preceding note, Strauss (having referred to *Discourses* I 10, 11, 13, and 55) instructed the reader to compare the title of I 12 with the chapter proper.[78] I 12 is entitled "Of How Much Importance It Is to Take Account of Religion, and How Italy, for Lacking It by Means of the Roman Church, Has Been Ruined." Towards the beginning of the chapter Machiavelli emphasizes thus the importance of religion: if rulers of republics or kingdoms keep their states close to their religious foundations, they will easily keep them "religious and, in consequence, good and united. All things that arise in favor of that religion they should favor and magnify, even though they judge them false."[79] Whether religion in general is true or false Machiavelli does not say. What he does say is that the absence of religion is politically problematic in its scope and effects; and in a twist to the chapter title, he hints that it is of little importance to take account of Christian priests.[80] He does not state explicitly in I 12 that Christian *doctrine* has kept Italy divided; but the crux of his critique of Christianity is that its focus on the hereafter has led the world into weakness.

Machiavelli pointedly explains in Chapters 12, 14, 15, and 18 of *The Prince* what a prince must do to rule over his province. These chapters, respectively, advise the prince to cultivate his own arms and not hire mercenaries, who are fickle; to practice assiduously the military arts, for that practice underpins efficacious rule; to forestall ruin by learning about the true ways of the world; and not to worry about breaking his word if it is advantageous or necessary that he not keep to his promises. "A prince should . . . appear all mercy, all faith, all honesty, all humanity, all religion," Machiavelli says in Chapter 18. "And *nothing is more necessary to appear to have than this last quality. . . .* Everyone sees how you appear, few touch what you are; and these few dare not oppose the opinion of many."[81]

Machiavelli is saying that religious faith and conformity are not of essential importance to the virtuous prince. What *is* important is the manifest appearance of religion. Lest his disaffected subjects turn to religion as a counterauthority to his rule and claim that he is acting contrary to the manner in which he should be acting, a prince should cultivate an image of religiosity. If his soldiers fear the gods, he can interpret signs and auguries, arguing that the gods favor his rule, to maintain his hold over his soldiers.[82]

Republics, however, have an additional need for religion that kingdoms do not. As Machiavelli explains in *Discourses* I 12, a republic must possess and keep close to its foundations in religion in order to keep itself free from corruption. In *Discourses* I 13, 33–45, and 46–59 he notes that the prudent use by the Roman nobility of political means protected the well-being of the republic; in I 13 he speaks of the importance of religion to the nobles, but in 33–45 and 46–49 he is silent about religion.[83] Machiavelli suggests, then, that rulers learn to rely not on the favor of the gods but on their own virtue; fear of human, political authority is more useful than religion for shaping soldiers (the people) into dogged fighters. Nevertheless, rulers should use religion to buttress their authority and safeguard social harmony; chaos reigns when people do not feel compelled to obey promises to each other and oaths of allegiance to the republic.[84]

Strauss reflects, "Observations like those just mentioned make one wonder whether Machiavelli was convinced that religion fulfills an important function."[85] What does Strauss mean? He has shown that Machiavelli frequently speaks about the advantages (and disadvantages) of religion for the life and well-being of states, princes, and society. "Even in Machiavelli's system, therefore," says Cassirer, "religion is indispensable. But it is no longer an end itself; it has become a mere tool in the hands of political rulers." However, to view religion as a tool for politicians, states Maritain, "is a perversion of religion which is surely worse and more atheistic than crude atheism."[86] Perhaps, then, Strauss meant that only the temporal usefulness of religion defines the extent of Machiavelli's support of religion.[87] Indeed, Strauss goes on to explain on his behalf, "[s]ociety would be in a state of perpetual unrest" if religion could not make men "incorrupt." Religion is important because it "breeds deference to the ruling class as a group of men especially favored by the gods and reminiscent of the gods. And vice versa, unqualified unbelief will dispose the people not to believe in what they are told by venerable men. The ruling class will not be able in the long run to elicit this kind of deference if it does not contain men, and especially old men, who are venerable by virtue of their piety."[88] In sum, Strauss sees Machiavelli as claiming that religion serves as a tool of social control.

Strauss closes his critical study of Machiavelli's teaching on religion in the next paragraph by anticipating a criticism that he had "devoted" too much "space" to the analysis of Machiavelli's utterances on religion. Strauss argues, "We no longer understand that in spite of great disagreements among those thinkers [in the centuries after Machiavelli], they were united by the fact that they all fought one and the same power—the kingdom of darkness, as Hobbes called it; that fight was more important to them than any merely political issue."[89] In essence, Strauss means that the attack on Christianity and religion in general is a core element of the modern, Machiavellian project—namely, its fight against (what it regards as) ignorance, superstition, otherworldliness, and the claim that morality and religion are inseparable.[90] Underlying the modern insistence that morality and religion are separable is the view that human reason is superior to faith; and because Machiavelli and his successors held reason to be supreme, they regarded not the violation of God's Law but the absence of reason as the true sin. Indeed, in *Natural Right and History* Strauss explained, "When trying to understand the thought of Machiavelli, one does well to remember the saying that Marlowe was inspired to ascribe to him: 'I . . . hold there is no sin but ignorance.'"[91] Given Strauss's inclination to the old-fashioned view of Machiavelli, it is not surprising that in the introduction to *Thoughts on Machiavelli*, Strauss, when citing the same saying, spoke of "the *diabolical* character of Machiavelli's thought."[92] As Marlowe's insinuatingly named character, *Machevill*, exclaimed in the *Jew of Malta*:

> To some perhaps my name is odious,
> But such as love me, gard me from their tongues,
> And let them know that I am *Machevill*,
> And weigh not men, and therefore not mens words.
> Admir'd I am of those that hate me most:
> Though some speake openly against my bookes,
> Yet will they reade me, and thereby attaine
> To *Peters* Chayre: And when they cast me off,
> Are poyson'd by my climing followers.
> I count Religion but a childish Toy,
> And hold there is no sinne but Ignorance.[93]

———

For Strauss, the problem on the surface of things in Machiavelli, regarding his views on religion, is whether he, though critical of the otherworldly Christian religion, is equally critical of pagan Rome for its attempt to combine this-worldly and otherworldly concerns. What is clear, Strauss argues in attempting to resolve that problem, is that Machiavelli articulated a temporal view of religion. Neither Christian nor pagan, condemning both biblical religion and paganism for leading the world into weakness, he favored the pursuit of glory, of action in the here and now. Properly understood, his "theology" about Fortuna, chance, and accidents is antitheological. Counterpoising his theology to the Bible, denying the existence of God or the gods, and eschewing a pagan myth of nature, Machiavelli left no decisive scope for divine influence upon human affairs. As Strauss said toward the beginning of his critical study, "Paganism is a kind of piety and one does not find a trace of pagan piety in Machiavelli's work. He had not reverted from the worship of Christ to the worship of Apollo."[94] When Strauss digressed twice from the strong emphasis he placed on both *The Prince* and the *Discourses* in understanding Machiavelli, he amplified his thesis that Machiavelli is neither Christian nor pagan; the first digression was to the *Florentine Histories* and *Exhortation to Penitence*, the second to the *Castruccio.*

Taken together, the arguments and the actions in his analysis of Machiavelli's teaching of religion show that Strauss was open to the possibility of revelation. In taking seriously—against Machiavelli's rejection of—the claim to truth and authority in biblical religion, Strauss aimed to recover the horizon obscured by Machiavelli and his successors: the biblical horizon of what is good, just, virtuous, best, and right.[95]

PART THREE

Strauss's Machiavelli on Philosophy
Political Virtue

Machiavelli's admiration for the political practice of classical antiquity and especially of republican Rome is only the reverse side of his rejection of classical political philosophy. He rejected classical political philosophy, and therewith the whole tradition of political philosophy in the full sense of the term, as useless: Classical political philosophy had taken its bearings by how man ought to live; the correct way of answering the question of the right order of society consists in taking one's bearings by how men actually do live. Machiavelli's "realistic" revolt against tradition led to the substitution of patriotism or merely political virtue for human excellence or, more particularly, for moral virtue and the contemplative life.

— Leo Strauss, *Natural Right and History*

CHAPTER FIVE

Moral Virtue and Human Action

From arguing that Machiavelli is neither Christian nor pagan, Strauss moves to show that he mounts a radical challenge to classical political philosophy. Machiavelli rejects both Christianity and religion in general on the basis that they are false and antithetical to life; people should order life in line with the here and now, not with ideals of goodness, with ideals that accord with a higher or divine source. He amplifies this view about the right order of life, Strauss argues, in his views on the use and the ends of philosophy. In seeking to discover new modes and orders, Machiavelli rejects the classical ideal that moral norms should underpin human action. Linking virtue not with what *ought* to be but with the "effectual truth" of what *is*, he regards the exigent needs of the state as the root of virtue. He has, then, an atheistic view of what constitutes, and how one gains knowledge of, the good life.[1]

Strauss states, "We are entitled to make a distinction between Machiavelli's teaching regarding religion and his teaching regarding morality since he himself makes a distinction between religion and justice or between religion and goodness."[2] (The distinction made in *Discourses* I 55 is between "goodness" and "religion"; the distinction made in *Discourses* III 1 is between "religion" and "justice."[3]) Machiavelli's deliberations on morality, like those on religion, Strauss explains, consist of "a foreground of 'first statements' which reproduce accepted opinions and a background of 'second statements' which are more or less at variance with accepted opinions." First statements serve to mitigate the

radical qualities of the second statements. "But the explicit discussion of religion occupies much less space than the explicit discussion of morality."
Machiavelli leads the reader to think, then, "that morality appears to be less
comprehensive and hence less fundamental than religion."[4]

The apparent subsuming of morality into religion belies the gravity of
Machiavelli's endeavors. Against that subsuming, Strauss states, "[i]f one desires
not to lose one's way, one must start from Machiavelli's claim, raised at the
beginning of the *Discourses* and in the middle of the *Prince*, that his teaching
which is comprehensive or concerns the foundations is new."[5] As Machiavelli
wrote in the preface to Book I of the *Discourses*, "driven by that natural desire
that has always been in me to work, without any respect, for those things I
believe will bring common benefit to everyone, I have decided to take a path
as yet untrodden by anyone."[6] Machiavelli is a "discoverer," Coby notes, "but
he does not further explain the novelty of his endeavor."[7] His novelty or newness, Strauss suggests, relates more to morality and to politics than to religion.
"In his teaching concerning morality and politics Machiavelli challenges not
only the religious teaching but the whole philosophic tradition as well." He
articulates "his new principle" against the classical principle that "took its
bearings by how one ought to live." Focusing not on "imagined things" but on
what men actually do, he shares the disdain for "book learning" and "the men
of words" that "many practitioners of politics" of all eras have felt.[8]

Machiavelli nevertheless focuses on "reasoning about everything." His
stated enterprise, Strauss adds, is to impart knowledge of new modes and
orders to those people who just study "the things of the world."[9] Of creating
or maintaining "a free state," Machiavelli explains in *Discourses* I 18, "it is very
difficult to do either the one or the other; and although it is almost impossible to give a rule for it, because it would be necessary to proceed according
to the degrees of corruption, nonetheless, since it is good to reason about
everything, I do not wish to omit this."[10] Of the "modes and government"
of princes, he says in Chapter 15 of *The Prince*, "in disputing this matter I depart from the orders of others. But since my intent is to write something useful to whoever understands it, it has appeared to me more fitting to go directly
to the effectual truth of the thing than to the imagination of it."[11]

Machiavelli bases his studies both on his experience in contemporary
affairs and his contemplation of ancient Greek and Roman histories.[12] He
emphasizes, though, the importance of *practice*. In *Discourses* I 47 he remarks,
"one can soon open the eyes of peoples by finding a mode by which they have
to descend to particulars."[13] In III 39 he explains that successful military action
depends on the captain combining general and particular knowledge; the

captain applies to new countries his familiarity with a given site or region, a familiarity gained by hunting and military training. Machiavelli inverts, then, or emulates with a twist, the classical precept that one gains knowledge by moving from general or universal principles to studying particular examples.[14] His twist relates to what he sees as true norms of morality and politics. One ascends to "general knowledge or 'firm science' . . . of the 'nature' of the things of the world . . . by recognizing the universal in the particular." Knowledge thus gained is "at least partly preceptive or normative." But, adds Strauss, "Machiavelli does not oppose to the normative political philosophy of the classics a merely descriptive or analytical political science; he rather opposes to a wrong normative teaching the true normative teaching."[15]

Through examining Machiavelli's "normative teaching," Strauss aims to recover both the biblical and classical moral horizons. His purpose in laying bare the effectual truth of Machiavellian political virtue, I argue, is to recover the agreement between revelation and reason on the nobility and truth of the good life. In showing where Machiavelli stands in relation to the fundamental alternatives, Strauss's own moral stance, his position on morality vis-à-vis the alternatives, is implied in the interstices of his analysis. By studying the arguments and the actions of the analysis, one learns how Strauss himself responds to the personal and intellectual challenge of the revelation-reason question. Retracing the path Strauss takes in tracking Machiavelli's footsteps on his "untrodden" path is germane to explicating Strauss's own position on revelation and reason and how he handles Machiavellian political virtue.

Virtue and Goodness

The Scope of Goodness

Machiavelli engages with classical views on goodness. "He knows that these generally held opinions are not entirely baseless," Strauss explains. "They contain elements which he can preserve. Besides, by reproducing those opinions he furnishes himself with the indispensable 'first statements.'" By way of example of a first statement, Strauss quotes Chapter 15 of *The Prince*: "I know that everyone will confess that it would be most praiseworthy for a prince to possess all the above-mentioned qualities which are held to be good." Those qualities, Strauss goes on, are "liberality, mercy, fidelity, courage, chastity, sincerity, religion, and so on."[16] As a first statement, this passage (from Machiavelli) does not simply reproduce, if at all, traditional moral views. Strauss stated in chapter 1, "No one, I believe, questions the opinion that Machiavelli did doubt the common view regarding the relation between morality and politics, for every one has read chapters 15 ff. of the *Prince*." In the words of Mosca, "In the fifteenth through eighteenth chapters is found the quintessence of Machiavellianism."[17]

There can be no doubt that Machiavelli was aware of traditional morality. Men praise goodness and criticize vice, he notes in those "Machiavellian" chapters. Men praise a prince for his exemplary actions and conduct, for his concern with the good of his subjects; men detest a tyrant, as pursuit of self-advantage, not the good of his subjects or of the public as a whole, motivates him. This common view served as Machiavelli's criterion for preferring republics to princes. For Machiavelli, Strauss points out, "republics are to be preferred to princes because they are morally superior to the latter: they are less given to ingratitude and bad faith than are princes."[18]

At the same time, Machiavelli questions the common view. The essence of his thought is to deny that morality must guide political life. What is "new" in Machiavelli is his temporal or, as Maritain puts it, "merely terrestrial" view of goodness.[19] Machiavelli speaks of "good means" and "good ends," but he sees them in this-worldly terms; for an action is good when it benefits "the common good," or the good of all in "the commonwealth."[20] In *Discourses* I 37, echoing discussions in I 6, 16, and 29, and III 25, he attributes the troubles caused in Rome by the conflict between the plebeians and the nobles— conflict over the sharing out of honors, riches, and land—to the eroded enforcement of the agrarian laws. In I 6, as well as in I 10, he says that to be "honest" is to have the praiseworthy moral virtues, whereas to be "honorable" is to have "extraordinary virtue"; and to be honorable is to be conscious of that latter virtue and to conduct oneself accordingly.[21]

Strauss is arguing that Machiavelli delimits the scope of goodness in an anticlassical manner. It is curious, then, that Strauss goes on to explain that his "implicit distinction between the honest and the honorable reminds us of the distinction between justice and magnanimity, the two peaks of Aristotle's ethics."[22] For Aristotle, justice and magnanimity are the peaks of virtue because they are vital guides to excellence.[23] Aquinas, too, regards them as peaks of virtue, though not as coexistent virtues, as Aristotle seems to.[24] Aquinas explains, "Nothing is adorned save by something worthier than itself. But Aristotle speaks of magnanimity as the adornment of justice and all the virtues." Aquinas replies, "When magnanimity is added to justice the goodness of justice is increased. Yet without justice it would not have the character of virtue."[25]

Machiavelli, however, avoids describing the pursuit of justice and of magnanimity, of a noble and high-minded generosity, as the basis of goodness. Strauss observes, "It is noteworthy that Machiavelli avoids mentioning justice in the most striking passages." For instance, he is silent about justice in Chapter 15 of *The Prince*, in his "most comprehensive enumeration of the praiseworthy qualities."[26]

If Machiavelli does not regard as praiseworthy that justice guides a ruler, that a ruler give each person his or her due, what does he mean by justice? This much is clear: when Machiavelli says that a ruler is praiseworthy when he protects and renews his state, especially if it is a republic, Machiavelli means that goodness and justice share a "factual" basis.[27] "Among all men praised," he says at the beginning of *Discourses* I 10, "the most praised are those who have been heads and orderers of religions. Next, then, are those who have founded either republics or kingdoms." Chief among those who "are infamous and detestable" and not worthy of praise "are destroyers of religions," followed by "squanderers of kingdoms and republics." "And no one will ever be so crazy or so wise, so wicked or so good, who will not praise what is to be praised and blame what is to be blamed." Yet, people do not blame Caesar for turning the Roman republic into a tyranny; "the writers" praise him, for they "are corrupted by his fortune." His "evil" is his destruction of the republic; rather than renewing it, he "spoil[ed] it entirely."[28] Dictatorial authority, Machiavelli says in *Discourses* I 34, can do good to the republic; when a dictator can renew good, but without "undoing the old orders of the city and making new ones," citizens should not be afraid of electing a dictator.[29]

Machiavelli is saying that, although it is fitting that Caesar be praised for building an empire, people err in praising him as the highest among men who are worthy of praise. The reason for this unwarranted praise is that men, in assessing the "particular" reasons behind events, tend to misapprehend "general" causes.[30] In *Discourses* I 47 Machiavelli says, "peoples are deceived generally in judging things and their accidents about which, after they know them particularly, they lack such deception."[31] Deeds belie the praise of goodness. People express themselves not simply through deeds, but through speeches; invariably, at public gatherings speeches are flattering. Though people dwell on the appearance of success, they follow "a middle course" between the outright condemnation and the outright praise of vice; but in especial instances, such as war, men will laud the recourse by their ruler to fraud.[32]

Virtue and the Mean

Strauss goes on, "The common understanding of virtue had found its classic expression in Aristotle's assertion that virtue, being the opposite of vice, is the middle or mean between two faulty extremes (a too little and a too much [*sic*]) which are opposed to each other." Machiavelli "occasionally," Strauss points out, echoes that notion of the virtuous mean.[33] For instance, in *Discourses* III 31 he defines virtue as the ability to adapt to variations in fate; vice consists of becoming insolent and intoxicated by good fortune that one may not have possessed in the first place. In Chapter 17 of *The Prince* he says that a prince "should proceed in a temperate mode with prudence and humanity so that too much confidence does not make him incautious and too much diffidence does not render him intolerable."[34]

Machiavelli also echoes Livy's criticism of the mean. In *Discourses* II 23 and III 40, respectively, Machiavelli describes as "harmful" and "pernicious" the middle way the Samnites followed at the battle of the Caudine Forks.[35] As Livy, speaking through Herennius Pontius, said of the choice the Samnites had to let go unharmed or to kill to the very last man the Roman army they had pinned down at the Caudine Forks, "a middle course . . . 'is in sooth [i.e., in truth] a policy that neither wins men friends nor rids them of their enemies.'"[36] In his own voice Livy says, "Too late and all in vain did they [the Samnites] praise the alternative policies suggested by the aged Pontius, between which they had fallen."[37]

Machiavelli does approve, however, of a certain mean. He says, Strauss notes, that "[t]he Roman people kept its place honorably by neither ruling arrogantly nor serving abjectly. Liberty is the mean between principality or tyranny and license."[38] Citing his criticism of the mean in *Discourses* III 40, Strauss points out for Machiavelli, "On the other hand, however, people condemn 'the middle course' (*la via del mezzo*) as harmful." Strauss then seems to juxtapose Machiavelli with both the Bible and Aristotle: he states, "Mercy and justice despise the undecided, the lukewarm, those who are neither for nor against God. Furthermore, we may add in accordance with what Aristotle has said, justice is not a mean between two vices but is opposed only to one vice."[39] In short, justice is opposed to bad actions. The biblical book of Revelation proclaims, "I know your deeds, that you are neither cold nor hot. I wish you were either one or the other! So, because you are lukewarm—neither hot nor cold—I am about to spit you out of my mouth."[40] According to Aristotle, "Not every action nor every passion admits of a mean; for some have names that already imply badness, e.g. spite, shamelessness, envy, and in the case of actions adultery, theft, murder . . . . It is not possible, then, ever to be right with regard to them; one must always be wrong."[41]

Machiavelli, too, opposes actions that are the antithesis of excellence; but he favors actions that Aristotle would consider the epitome of badness.

Machiavelli rejects *la via del mezzo*, though he had initially adopted it. Strauss observes, "At any rate Machiavelli tacitly rejects the view that virtue is a mean between two vices." He sees "conceit" and "humility" not as "opposite defects" but as similar forms of the same vice that is opposed to virtue; and virtue "is based on 'knowledge of the world.' "[42]

Related to Machiavelli's differentiation (toward the beginning of Chapter 15 of *The Prince*) "between the virtue of liberality and the virtue of giving," Strauss points out, is the differentiation in the Tuscan language "between stinginess and rapacity." For Machiavelli to see "stinginess and rapacity" as "two different vices" implies that he assigns one virtue to stinginess and another virtue to rapacity. "The stingy man abstains 'too much' from using his own; the rapacious man desires to acquire by rapine what belongs to others." The counterpart of the stingy man's "excess" is the "defect" of "prodigality." "Machiavelli tacitly denies this by assigning to liberality only one opposite vice, namely, stinginess. . . . [H]e tacitly substitutes the virtue of giving for justice."[43] I would note here that Machiavelli contrasts the praiseworthy qualities—of being a "giver," "merciful," "faithful," "fierce and spirited," and "humane"—with extreme qualities—of being "rapacious," "cruel," "a breaker of faith," "effeminate and pusillanimous," and "proud." The extreme qualities, which are vices, correspond with defect or excess. Machiavelli identifies in the prince two types of vice: "those vices that would take his state from him," and "vices without which it is difficult to save one's state."[44]

According to Strauss, Machiavelli "alludes to the fact that liberality has two opposite vices and he alludes to justice which is thought to have only one opposite vice. He explains the meaning of these allusions partly in the following chapter."[45] For Strauss to employ the words *alludes* and *tacitly* gives rise to the questions: Does Machiavelli emphatically reject the mean? If so, where? Though shortly after the above statement Strauss examines Machiavelli's emphatic judgments against the mean, he continues in the meanwhile by analyzing Machiavelli's tacit rejections of the mean.

Cultivating a reputation for liberality, Machiavelli warns in Chapter 16 of *The Prince*, leads the prince to impose onerous demands on his subjects. Liberality leads only to poverty and to rapaciousness and hence to the prince being despised by his subjects. If a prince devotes all of his state's resources to lavish displays of his liberality, he will lack the resources to defend his state and subjects. Thus, a reputation for parsimony should not dissuade a prince. Parsimony is "the vice of stinginess," and to Machiavelli, Strauss notes, "this vice is preferable to the virtue of liberality."[46]

By lauding parsimony, Machiavelli not only implies that the mean is difficult to follow and an inefficacious standard of human action; he denies that the mean is possible. To understand that denial, says Strauss, one needs to discuss his ideas about justice.[47] Machiavelli advises republics to maintain what they have and to refrain from acquisition; that refrainment "is the middle course between taking away from others what belongs to them and losing to others what one possesses." The path that "reason" recommends cannot be followed at all times, if ever, for all aspects of human life are perpetually in motion. Necessity compels princes to favor "the vice of rapacity" over "the virtue of giving." By acquiring what belongs to others, the prince gains the resources to indulge "the virtue of liberality." Thus, "Justice as the stable mean between self-denial or giving away what one has on the one hand and injustice on the other is impossible; a bias in favor of the latter is necessary and honorable."[48]

An example of that bias can be found in *Discourses* I 2. Machiavelli observes, "Seeing that if one individual hurt his benefactor, hatred and compassion among men came from it, and as they blamed the ungrateful and honored those who were grateful, and thought too that those same injuries could be done to them, to escape like evil they were reduced to making laws and ordering punishments for whoever acted against them: hence came the knowledge of justice."[49] In other words, the law and its grounding in selfinterest determines what is just; and the processes of creating laws and imposing punishment gives rise to justice. But for Polybius, human action that is mindful of morality and duty establishes a sense of justice. Of a person hurting a benefactor, Polybius says, "those who become aware of it will naturally be displeased and offended by such conduct, sharing the resentment of their injured neighbor and imagining themselves in the same situation. From all this there arises in everyone a notion of the meaning and theory of duty, which is the beginning and end of justice."[50]

Machiavelli's critique of the mean as inefficacious can be seen in *Discourses* I 26 and I 27. At the end of I 26 he states, "they take certain middle courses which are most harmful, for men do not know how to be altogether evil nor how to be altogether good, as will be shown in the following chapter by an example."[51] Machiavelli's contrast here, Strauss explains, is between "honorably evil" and "unqualifiedly evil."[52] Machiavelli underscores the contrast in I 27, that is, by speaking not in his own name but as a narrator, who describes the observations of "the prudent men who were with the pope." Machiavelli explains that "the cowardice of Giovampagolo"—his failure to kill Pope Julius II, who had visited Perugia escorted by only one guard—"arose from men's not knowing how to be honorably wicked or perfectly good; and when malice has greatness in itself or is generous in some part, they do not know how to enter into it."[53]

Machiavelli's argument, Strauss notes, is that the correct mode of princely action "is indeed a mean—yet not the mean between two opposite vices but the mean between virtue and vice."[54] The correct mode is a mean "between humanity and inhumanity" that varies in response to changing times. That mean is the "true," "natural" mean, for it "imitates" the perpetually variable way of nature. "[T]he alternation which Machiavelli calls natural is understood by the tradition which he attacks as the alternation between sin and repentance. The alternation which he praises as agreeing with nature . . . consists in choosing virtue or vice with a view to what is appropriate 'for whom, toward whom, when and where.' "[55] In *Discourses* II 23 and 24, and III 21, Machiavelli advises the prince to base the alternation on what fits the times; that is, when times are dangerous and forceful action will secure his power. The alternation itself, Machiavelli says in Chapters 17 and 18 of *The Prince*, is led by the astute, prudent appraisal of the times and maintained by virtue, by strength of spirit and body.[56] In *Discourses* I 41 and Chapter 8 of *The Prince* Machiavelli speaks of the good and bad use, by tyrants, of both virtue and vice. Religion, too, can be so used; it is both a virtue and a vice.[57] Thus, Strauss notes for Machiavelli, "Whereas the moral virtues and vices (e.g. religion and cruelty) can be well and badly used because their use must be regulated by prudence, prudence cannot be badly or imprudently used."[58] However, in *Discourses* II 26 Machiavelli warns against the failure to be prudent: "I believe that one of the great prudences men use is to abstain from menacing or injuring anyone with words. For neither the one nor the other takes forces away from the enemy, but the one makes him more cautious and the other makes him have greater hatred against you."[59] The implication here is that a prince's failure to be prudent in the manner suggested, and as the times demand, may have dire consequences for his rule.

Machiavelli seeks to do away with the idea of virtue as a mean. Yet, in linking virtue with effectual truth, with knowledge of the true ways of the world, he both inverts and emulates the mean. As Strauss puts it, he upholds "the reality of the generally recognized opposition between (moral) virtue and (moral) vice." Strauss adds, "This fact affords perhaps the strongest proof of both the diabolical character and the sobriety of his thought."[60] Illustrating this "proof" is Chapter 8 of *The Prince*—here he describes Agathocles as a man who "always kept to a life of crime" *and* had great "virtue of spirit and body."[61] This movement between morality and criminality was "guided by prudence and sustained by virtue."[62]

A Prudent Mean

From Machiavelli's tacit rejections of the mean Strauss turns to his "most emphatic references" about the mean's "desirability or possibility." "If one examines his remarks on this subject more carefully, one sees that he favors a 'certain middle course' rather than the extremes in question."[63] Of those "remarks" Strauss notes that *Discourses* II 23 is the only chapter title in the work that speaks of the "middle course."[64] I would add that in II 23 Machiavelli explains that, in taking the Latium towns under its control to increase the size of the Roman republic, Rome "either benefited them or eliminated them. . . ." Rome did not "ever use the neutral way in affairs of moment."[65] Those "affairs" relate to civil, military, and governmental matters. Machiavelli opens the *Florentine Histories* IV 1 thus: "Cities, and especially those not well ordered that are administered under the name of republic, frequently change their governments and their states not between liberty and servitude, as many believe, but between servitude and license." Liberty is a mean between the two humors of "servitude" and "license." If a city sides with one humor or the other, it will be unable to maintain its freedom; "nobles" are "ministers of servitude," and "men of the people" are "ministers of license." Though "it happens rarely," admits Machiavelli, a city is "free" when, due to "good laws and good orders," it "has no necessity, as have others, for the virtue of a single man to maintain it."[66] In *Discourses* III 2 Machiavelli criticizes the man of "quality" who seeks, as would a philosopher, a mean of neutrality between friendship and open conflict with princes. "Such a middle way would be the truest if it could be observed, but because I believe that it is impossible, one must be reduced to the two modes written above—that is, either to distance oneself from or to bind oneself to them. Whoever does otherwise, if he is a man notable for his quality, lives in continual danger." One must *feign* friendship, then. In III 2, shortly after having condemned the mean, he states, "one must play crazy, like Brutus, and make oneself very much mad, praising, speaking, seeing, doing things against your intent so to please the prince."[67]

That Machiavelli condemns the classical mean for its lack of judiciousness and farsightedness implies that he would advocate a mean based on guile, force, and power. Strauss continues, though: "We still have to consider whether the apparently unqualified rejection of the middle course does not convey an important message. Machiavelli is an extremist in the sense that he challenges the whole religious and philosophical tradition."[68] Strauss already has, it would seem, considered what that "message" is. In chapter 3 of *Thoughts on Machiavelli* he said, "Machiavelli censures a half measure once taken by

Florence."[69] In *Discourses* II 23 Machiavelli had praised the Roman senate for not keeping to the mean "in affairs of moment," and stated, "Princes ought to imitate this judgment."[70] The Florentines, he then remarked, failed to imitate fully that judgment. When Arezzo rebelled against Florence in 1502, the Florentines exiled or fined the Arentines and stripped them all of their former honors and offices; rather than destroying Arezzo, Florence was merciful. Strauss went on, "Machiavelli knew that the Bible teaches not only love but fear as well. But from his point of view the Biblical combination of love and fear . . . leads to all extremes of pious cruelty or pitiless persecution."[71]

By explicating Machiavelli's "important message," Strauss indicates his own position on morality vis-à-vis the revelation-reason question. The position is an open one, for Strauss is saying that both revelation and reason convey truth about the good life. Machiavelli's message is not simply that the classical mean, and the biblical equivalent, is a hazardous and impossible standard for human action. He takes issue with classical and biblical views about the proper end of human action; for him, what is highest in humanity has no providential or transcendent basis. He abandons Christian charity, for, rejecting Christian love as false and dangerous, he says that people can be virtuous only through fear, not by dint of the grace of God. His message, his legacy to modernity, is his adamant denial that virtue and civic-mindedness has, or can have, a divine beginning.[72] The upshot of his legacy is that he initiates a new Fall—and the original Fall took place "when men sought to be like gods in a world in which everything was given to them, given to them evidently not in justice but in generosity and kindness."[73]

Virtue vs. Goodness

Machiavelli takes exception to the Good in its traditional meaning of that which is best at all times, in all places, and for all people. He regards the Good as an untruth; good qua good, without evil, is impossible. "Generally stated," Strauss explains, for Machiavelli, "there is no good, simple or combined, without its accompanying evil, so much so that all choice can be said to be a choice among evils. If a certain institution appears to be altogether salutary, one can be certain that it will prove to carry with itself an unsuspected evil so that one will be compelled sooner or later to modify or to abolish that institution: one will always be in need of new modes and orders."[74] That "certain institution" is the republic. In *Discourses* III 17 Machiavelli says, "it is impossible to order a perpetual republic, because its ruin is caused through a thousand unexpected ways." Of that impossibility as it relates to moral conduct, he notes in III 37, "in the actions of men . . . one finds that close to the good there is always some evil that arises with that good so easily that it appears impossible to be able to miss the one if one wishes for the other."[75]

Although arguing that he rejected the Good, Strauss concedes, "Machiavelli seems to admit a *summum bonum;* he praises the pagans for having seen the highest good in worldly honor or, more precisely, in 'greatness of mind, strength of the body and all other things which are apt to make men most strong.' "[76] This passage can be found in *Discourses* II 2, in the midst of Machiavelli's second explicit statement on core Christian beliefs in the work. "To understand this passage," Strauss continues, "we must return to Machiavelli's remarks on Agathocles."[77] Machiavelli explains in Chapter 8 of *The Prince* that for all of his spirit and ability to overcome hardship, Agathocles was far too cruel; he had the strength necessary for exercising political virtue, but he was without moral virtue. An excellent man, Machiavelli explains in *Discourses* III 31, has both the vice and the virtue needful to rise above and prosper in spite— or even because—of unfavorable times. Despite the travails of their times, contemporary princes, Machiavelli says in II 18, have failed to show contrition for deviating from the well-ordered ancient Roman arts of warfare and modes of politics. In III 21, having said that love *or* fear motivates men, he insists that if one lacks the exceptional virtue necessary to correct one's inevitable deviations from the mean, holding to a mean between love and fear is impossible.[78]

Tempering Machiavelli's praise of the excellent man is his realization, Strauss explains, that "no man partakes of all excellences which can ennoble man: no man is complete; a 'universal man' is an imagined being." Even "[t]he most perfect prince or ruler" lacks "the specific excellence of which the people is capable."[79] Indeed, in *Discourses* I 58, II 24, and III 9 and 13, Machiavelli explains that the excellence of the people consists of their love for freedom and their unflagging defense of it by dint of their diverse natures and their obedience to laws. In I 55 he speaks of the *rarity* of the man who is excellent in both "brain and authority."[80]

To elucidate the temporal core of Machiavelli's moral-political teaching, Strauss has thus far drawn attention to his departure from the classical mean. Shifting from that emphasis, Strauss states: "*To sum up*, Machiavelli rejects the mean to the extent to which the notion of the mean is linked up with the notions of a perfect happiness that excludes all evil and of the simply perfect human being or of the 'universal man,' and therefore with the notion of a most perfect being simply which possesses all perfections most eminently and hence cannot be the cause of evil."[81] Strauss's shift is from the mean itself and the relation, or rather the tension, between goodness and virtue to the relation between freedom and virtuous action. Before proceeding, Strauss explains (in an endnote) that Machiavelli's "criticism of neutrality" in Chapter 21 of *The Prince* parallels his "criticism of the middle course in the *Discourses*." Both criticisms recognize "faith in the power of justice. In proportion as the faith in the power of justice or in the imitation of Fortuna is weakened, the case for neutrality (or the middle course) is strengthened."[82]

Free Will, Necessity, and Chance

Virtue and Free Will

Machiavelli defends free will as the domain of the virtuous; but in his argument for human autonomy, he eschews notions of "good" and "bad" that are tied to ideals of the good life. Strauss observes, "The common understanding of goodness had found its classic expression in Aristotle's assertion that virtue is the habit of choosing well and that choosing well or ill as well as the habits of choosing well or ill (the virtues or vices) are voluntary: man is responsible for having become and for becoming virtuous or vicious. Man can choose the good or the bad; he possesses a free will."[83] Strauss's words echo both Aristotle and Aquinas; the reference Strauss gives for the "assertion" is not from Aristotle but from Aquinas, namely, *Summa Theologica*, I, q. 82, a. 1.[84]

By referring to Aquinas, Strauss points to an agreement between the classics and Christianity on the nobility of the good life, and recalls his thesis that Machiavelli revolts against religious and philosophic tradition. However, one commentator goes so far as to say of Strauss: "It seems likely that he quietly agreed with Machiavelli's criticism of Christian scholasticism for having openly promulgated a teaching that denigrated the political nature of man and that led men to aspire to transcend their need for law, their need for closed polities, in the expectation of attaining for themselves a vision of the light beyond the cave."[85] As an analysis of scholasticism is beyond the scope of this chapter, it suffices to say here that even if Strauss took issue with the scholastics' denigration of the political or their attempt to synthesize faith and reason,[86] such disagreements would not diminish his philosophical openness to revelation or vitiate his insight into the fundamental inadequacy of Machiavelli's critique of Christianity.

Machiavelli takes issue with Aristotle and Aquinas, in this sense: one can, he says, choose one's own ends—the ends and how one reaches them—*if* one has the virtue. In Chapter 25 of *The Prince* he says that because Fortuna rules one half of human affairs and leaves free will to rule the other half, men are able to dominate Fortuna; but only if they are young and headstrong. Rationality is as equally important as an impetuous spirit, Machiavelli says in the same chapter, when he uses the metaphor of the prince controlling Fortuna with "dikes and dams." The prince who does not so control or "resist" and "contain" Fortuna "with suitable virtue" leaves himself prey to "the great variability of things."[87] As Strauss summarizes Machiavelli's argument, "Man can be the master of his fate."[88]

Strauss spells out the logical implications: "Yet chance presupposes nature and necessity. Therefore, the question concerns less the relation of freedom and chance than the relation of freedom on the one hand and nature and necessity on the other: can virtue control nature and necessity as it can control chance?"[89] People regard themselves as controlling their lives, not the power of fate and circumstances. Due, though, to that power, it is often impossible for people to act virtuously, in accordance with good laws. When times are in tumult, people tend to forget the power of necessity, for they blame their misfortunes on a prominent individual, not on the preexisting corruption within society. For these reasons, the Romans blamed the fall of the republic on Caesar; they did not realize that their unrest over the agrarian laws and the economic demands of imperial expansion were also to blame.

One cannot wholly change either chance or the times, which arise from chance. Instead, one should adapt as circumstances demand. Yet the capacity to adapt is limited. One's habits or modes of action arise from "natural inclination" and thus are difficult to alter. Only those rare individuals who possess innate virtue and prudence, knowing when not to act morally, can rule over chance and the times. In only these rare individuals do the "Is" and the "Ought" meet. The majority of people lack the capacity to act wisely, that is, to apply moral precepts astutely.[90]

When the prince fails both to exercise his innate virtue and to educate himself and his soldiers in the art of warfare, misfortune prevails. In *Discourses* I 19 Machiavelli says, "He who is like Romulus, and like him comes armed with prudence and with arms, will hold it [his state] in every mode unless it is taken from him by an obstinate and excessive force." In I 21 Machiavelli notes, "It is more true than any other truth that if where there are men there are no soldiers, it arises through a defect of the prince and not through any other defect, either of the site or of nature."[91] In III 8 and 9 he explains that an uncorrupt, well-ordered republic rewards good, wise actions and punishes wicked, unwise actions; "wicked" actions stem from passions that conflict with the times. To reward wicked citizens is to invite ruin; they work for bad ends, and their actions do not bring good fortune to the republic. Only excellent men, due to their virtue and prudence, can change the times, manipulate and dominate chance, and thus not be controlled by chance or the times.

Necessity and Fear

Machiavelli sees a close relation between virtue and the compulsion to act well that arises from the exigencies of the times. In the case of the excellent man, his prudence and free will guides that compulsion. In turn, he compels others to act well, namely, those who lack virtue or instigate tumults in the fatherland. What, then, is necessity? Is it intrinsic to the excellent man or is it extrinsic in origin? Or is it both?

Turning from virtue and free will to necessity, Strauss quotes this passage from *Discourses* III 12: "As has been written by some moral philosophers, men's hands and tongue, two most noble instruments for ennobling him, would not have done their work perfectly nor would they have carried the works of men to the height to which they are seen to have been carried, if they had not been driven on by necessity." Rather than then saying who the "moral philosophers" are, and asking if Machiavelli agrees with them, Strauss indicates that what he means by necessity is unclear: "Yet are not men's failures also due to necessity? Man's nature is such that necessity compels him to be virtuous or good as well as to be vicious or bad. Machiavelli's praise of necessity must then refer to a particular kind of necessity."[92]

It is worth noting here that that praise relates to what Cicero, in his *Academica*, calls the "division" of philosophy that deals "with conduct and morals," viz., "with the right conduct of life." What is good, Cicero claims, "is to be sought in nature and in nature only." The "complete accordance with nature in mind, body and estate is the limit of things desirable and the End of goods." In turn, "some" bodily goods reside "in the whole frame and others in the parts." Cicero goes on, "health, strength and beauty were goods of the whole, goods of the parts were sound senses and the particular excellences of the parts severally, for instance, speed in the feet, power in the hands, clearness in the voice, and also an even and distinct articulation of sounds as a quality of the tongue."[93] The "greatest" of the goods "have their being in the mind itself and in virtue itself." A key "principle of conduct in life and of duty itself" is the protection of "the things that nature prescribed." Happiness, though, requires not "virtue alone" but "the addition of the goods" relating to both "the body" and "the employment of virtue."[94]

Machiavelli agrees with Cicero that "the hands" and "the tongue" ennoble men. However, Machiavelli disagrees that the body, mind, and estate must accord with nature; for him, not nature but glory and survival define "the limits" of what is good, proper, and desirable.[95] The natural end of a soldier, Machiavelli explains in *Discourses* III 12, is to preserve his own life. Depending on the choice his commander or enemies give him to die, fight, flee, surrender, or sue for peace, a soldier chooses the best possible way to achieve the end of survival. In turn, a good, virtuous captain will exhaust every option before committing his soldiers to fight; thus, he maximizes the chance of survival for himself, his soldiers, and his fatherland.[96] In II 27 Machiavelli cited Hannibal as an example of such a captain. When returning to Carthage "to relieve the fatherland" after sixteen years in Italy, Hannibal "was not ashamed to ask for peace since he judged that if his fatherland had any remedy it was in that and not in war. When that was denied him, he did not wish to fail to engage in combat, even if he should lose, since he judged that he was still able to win or, losing, to lose gloriously."[97]

What compels men to be good is not virtue (or the orders of nature) but necessity. Necessity is that "fear of death," ignominious or otherwise, which makes soldiers facing great odds act against the natural desire for survival but act to the utmost of (and beyond) the capacity for combat. "Generalizing from this," Strauss explains, for Machiavelli, "we may say that it is fear, the fundamental fear, which makes men operate well."[98]

Necessity and Virtuous Action

Machiavelli lauds the use of fear, but maintains that war also makes men virtuous. He identifies, Strauss notes, "two kinds of war": "wars caused by necessity and wars caused by choice or ambition." Frequently, "wars of choice" are wars of ambition, because they aim at "acquisition or aggrandizement"; "wars of necessity are waged by whole peoples" when an invading army or overpopulation and hunger force them to flee their homeland for another, conquering and killing, in turn, the population in the new homeland.[99] In *Discourses* I 3 Machiavelli says that men never work for the good of their country (or city) unless forced to do so by necessity; confusion and disorder reign when men are free to indulge their ambitions. "Therefore it is said that hunger and poverty make men industrious, and the laws make them good." In III 12, quoting the speech of a Samnite captain, Machiavelli proclaims, "War is just to whom it is necessary, and arms are pious to those for whom there is no hope save in arms."[100] However, war does not always make men industrious; men, especially "great and rare men," "worthy men," Machiavelli says in III 16, are inherently incapable of forever holding their ambitions in check.[101]

Excellent men operate well because of their expectation of reward. All other men, viz., men who are not excellent, operate well because of their concern for survival. Survival has a close relation to the protection of property. The republic that fails to protect its lands will lack the means to feed and to satisfy its population; thus, the Roman love of property was greater than even their love of glory. "Considering the connection between property and money," Strauss points out, "we are not surprised to learn that while virtue is indeed much more important for winning wars than is money, yet money is necessary in the second place."[102]

Compared to the need for virtue, money would seem, for Machiavelli, to occupy a somewhat distant "second place." Indeed, he entitles *Discourses* II 10 "Money Is Not the Sinew of War, As It Is according to the Common Opinion." Quintus Curtius and other historians, whom Machiavelli does not name, voice the opinion in question.[103] In contrast to the common opinion Machiavelli explains in II 10, "Titus Livy . . . shows that three things are necessary in war: very many and good soldiers, prudent captains, and good fortune. . . . [H]e then comes to his conclusion without ever mentioning money."[104] Nor does Machiavelli always mention money. He opens II 1 by noting, "Many have had the opinion—and among them Plutarch, a very grave writer—that the Roman people in acquiring the empire was favored more by fortune than by virtue." Shortly afterwards, however, he explains, "And Livy seems to come close to this opinion, for it is rare that he makes any Roman speak where he tells of virtue and does not add fortune to it. I do not wish to confess this thing in any mode, nor do I believe even that it can be sustained."[105] Machiavelli goes on to draw this point from Rome's wars for supremacy against the Samnites, Tuscans, and Carthaginians: "Whoever considers well the order of these wars and the mode of their proceeding will see inside them a very great virtue and prudence mixed with fortune." The Romans, though, did not rely upon fortune alone. When they sought to enter "new provinces they always tried to have some friend who should be a step or a gate to ascend there or enter there, or a means to hold it. . . . Those peoples who observe this will see they have less need of fortune than those who are not good observers of it."[106]

Good soldiers, not money, are the sinews of war; good soldiers can find money, whereas money is no substitute for good soldiers.[107] Yet, Machiavelli is not simply saying that possessing money is more important than Fortuna's good graces, or that the need for, and love of, money should supplant reliance upon Fortuna. He says in Chapter 7 of *The Prince* that a talent for acquiring money is less important than an ability to lay firm foundations for one's rule over a state taken with the aid of Fortuna, who may withdraw her favor once one is in power. "Thus," says Mansfield, "when Machiavelli argues that one must not rely on money, he means one must not be dependent on God, or fortune, or faith."[108]

Necessity and Goodness

Love of money notwithstanding, necessity makes men both virtuous and good. In *Discourses* I 3 Machiavelli stresses, "it is necessary to whoever disposes a republic and orders laws in it to presuppose that all men are bad, and that they always have to use the malignity of their spirit whenever they have a free opportunity for it." Badness and malignancy cause disunion when not kept "in check with fear."[109] He states in Chapter 17 of *The Prince*, "one can say this generally of men: that they are ungrateful, fickle, pretenders and dissemblers, evaders of danger, eager for gain." Men, therefore, he says in Chapter 23, "will always turn out bad for you unless they have been made good by a necessity."[110]

Fear, terror, violence, and uncertainty make people good. Seeking "peace and security," people gather in society; laws further make people good, and fear of penalties for disobedience to the laws keeps them good. Though "leaders" instigate the imposed instances of necessity, "virtuous legislators or founders" teach them to "operate well" and to "act freely" as leaders. In turn, "virtuous founders operate well because they are prompted by their natural desire for the common good."[111] A necessity rooted in fear of death and punishment makes most men good; a necessity arising not from that fear but from a drive to acquire property, money, honor, and glory makes leaders and founders good. Choice has a close affinity with ambition and ambition with the desire for honor and glory. Innately prudent men operate well because they can avoid being subject to mere necessity; choice is the preserve of the virtuous. Most men, however, because they are weak and lack prudence, operate well only when subject to that fear of death and hunger which is imposed by the virtuous.[112]

Machiavelli's argument that ambition is a form of necessity compelling man to be *good* is, for Strauss, the one factor alone that justifies his praise of necessity. Here Strauss, his own open position on the revelation-reason question perhaps too open, comes close to imputing a measure of legitimacy to Machiavelli's revolt against religious and philosophic tradition. "Machiavelli's praise of necessity, which surpasses in emphasis everything he says in praise of choice, would be untenable if he had not seen his way toward conceiving of ambition or the desire for honor or glory, and especially of the desire of the founder for supreme glory, as a form of that necessity which makes men operate well." The compulsion to operate well, which arises out of ambition, occurs, Strauss explains for Machiavelli, when one has fulfilled one's "primary wants"; "ambition" is "the desire to acquire, to have more than one needs, not to be inferior to others." However, "ambition does not necessarily make man operate well. Not all men know how to satisfy 'the natural and ordinary desire for acquisition.'"[113] The appetite for acquisition, Machiavelli says in I 37, is greater than the power for achieving it. In I 29 he muses (in the chapter title), "Which Is More Ungrateful, a People or a Prince."[114] Avarice, he says in I 29, moves both princes and people in their relations with captains, whose success in battle is responsible, in the first place, for the prince or the people acquiring glory and empire. In equally pointed terms, Machiavelli states in Chapter 3 of *The Prince*: "And truly *it is a very natural and ordinary thing to desire to acquire*, and always, when men do it who can, they will be praised or not blamed; but when they cannot, and wish to do it anyway, here lie the error and the blame."[115]

Not all men can successfully act upon the natural desire for acquisition. Manlius Capitolinus's unsuccessful pursuit of ambition, Machiavelli explains in *Discourses* III 8, was due both to his impatience and to his failure to adapt to the times; he was a corrupt man in a Rome that did not wish to be corrupted. In virtuous men, the desire for glory has the power of *necessity*, a power that compels them to satisfy that desire. An element of *choice* is also involved, for the compulsion itself to act "arises entirely from within." In weak men, men who lack virtue, the compulsion to act—and to act well—arises not from glory, nor from within, but from the action of an external necessity that plays upon men's fear of death, evil, and misery. Strauss explains for Machiavelli, "The soldiers led by Messius would not have fought well if Messius had not enlightened them as to the necessity to fight well by shouting to them 'Do you believe that some god will protect you and carry you off from here?'"[116]

Rather than being practical and rational but, in the end, "passively obedient" to exterior causes, "[t]he truly virtuous man," Jaffa explains, following Aristotle, "must possess prudence as a conscious and active element within himself."[117] Machiavelli would agree that the virtuous man should possess such an "element," that he be active, not passive; but Machiavelli would stress that men operate well, and can begin to overcome the vicissitudes of chance and of the times, only when they have knowledge of necessity and are mindful of its exigencies. He indicates in *Discourses* III 12 that men, in their efforts, should meet but aim to overpower necessity. In the *Florentine Histories* II 2 he says, "men never maintain themselves in difficulties unless maintained there by some necessity"; in VII 7 he notes, "men always flee more willingly from the evil that is certain."[118] In short, soldiers and the people in general respond to a necessity rooted in fear of death and concern for survival; captains and other virtuous men respond to a necessity rooted in the desire for glory, and they strive to overcome necessity and to subdue Fortuna.

Free Will vs. Necessity and Chance

Machiavelli relates the excellence of an action not to a moral but an expedient basis. The sole or necessary precondition of virtue would seem, then, to be opportunity.[119] Men of supreme virtue who have already acquired or founded kingdoms operate well when they compel the "matter" at hand—namely, the people—to follow new modes and orders. The occasion itself for the virtuous man to operate well arises from events gravely threatening to public safety, such as an invading army. From the threat to public safety arises the opportunity to create a good, obedient populace; a corrupt populace is made obedient by both laws and the force required to impose the laws. In *Discourses* I 17 Machiavelli explains, "where the matter is not corrupt, tumults and other scandals do not hurt; where it is corrupt, well-ordered laws do not help unless indeed they have been put in motion by one individual who with an extreme force ensures their observance so that the matter becomes good." Although questioning "whether this has ever occurred or whether it is possible," he states, "if a city that has fallen into decline through corruption of matter ever happens to rise, it happens through the virtue of one man who is alive then, not through the virtue of the collectivity that sustains good orders."[120]

Does the virtuous man cease to be, or is he less than, a virtuous man if he lacks the opportunity to show that he is virtuous? Such opportunity, Machiavelli says in *Discourses* III 16, is not always readily available: "It has always been, and will always be, that great and rare men are neglected in a republic in peaceful times. For through the envy that the reputation their virtue has given them has brought with it, one finds very many citizens in such times who wish to be not their equals but their superiors."[121] For Machiavelli, Strauss explains, "The highest achievement requires that the necessity to operate well which is effective in the giver of the 'form' and the necessity to operate well which is effective in the 'matter' should meet." The virtuous man is "the giver"; the "form" is laws, modes, and orders; and the "matter" is the people and circumstances. A virtuous man, qua the virtuous man, creates his own opportunities. "[T]here is no necessity that the two supplementary necessities should meet; their meeting is a matter of chance. Still, the man of supreme virtue can create his opportunity to some extent."[122]

Here one can see a critical point of difference between Machiavelli and Aristotle. Aristotle maintains, Strauss notes, that the "multitudes have a natural fitness either for being subject to a despot or for a life of political freedom."[123] I would add that Aristotle seems to say that that "natural fitness" is not for tyranny—which he describes as a "perverted form of government"[124]— but for kingship. "A people who are by nature capable of producing a race superior in the excellence needed for political rule are fitted for kingly government." On the other hand, "the people who are suited for constitutional freedom are those among whom there naturally exists a warlike multitude."[125] Strauss goes on to explain that opposed to Aristotle's view is the view that "fitness for either form of life can be artificially produced if a man of a rare 'brain' applies the required degree of force." Force compels a populace to act against its love for freedom or natural inclination of timidity. "No 'defect of nature' can account for the unwarlike character of a nation; a prince of sufficient ability can transform any nation however pampered by climate into a race of warriors."[126] According to Strauss, "We may express Machiavelli's thought by saying that Aristotle did not see that the relation of the founder to his human matter is not fundamentally different from the relation of a smith to his iron or his inanimate matter: Aristotle did not realize to what extent man is malleable, and in particular malleable by man." Modifying this appreciative statement, Strauss then notes: "Still, that malleability is limited and therefore it remains true that the highest achievement depends on chance."[127]

Strauss seems to be saying that Machiavelli is more insightful than Aristotle is regarding the basis of virtuous action. The Machiavellian virtuous prince imposes his will over exigent circumstances and shapes the people both to the times and to his will as he sees fit. The prince does not act according to transcendent moral norms. On the other hand, Strauss did indicate that Machiavelli errs in claiming that the founder, against chance, can shape his subjects to his will.

Machiavelli clearly does praise the princely ability for decisive action in the face of great odds. But, Strauss emphasizes, he "is far from being a worshipper of success: not the success but the wisdom of an enterprise deserves praise and admiration. The man who has discovered the modes and orders which are in accordance with nature is much less dependent on chance than is any man of action since his discovery need not bear fruit during his lifetime."[128] In an endnote, Strauss refers to his earlier description (in chapter 2) of Machiavelli as a "new Moses" introducing new modes and orders, and to his earlier explanation (in chapter 3) that Machiavelli aims to corrupt and to overturn Christian modes and orders. He also refers to chapter 4, where he explained that Machiavelli's excellent man supplants the power of Fortuna with his own power; he does not seek mere independence alone.[129] Strauss's cross-references recall, then, the newness of Machiavelli's enterprise and that he praised not the virtuous man's mere success or his enduring through travails but his capacity to impose his very will on chance, Fortuna, and necessity. Machiavelli is explicit in Chapter 18 of *The Prince* and in *Florentine Histories* VIII 22. In the former he explains that a prince "needs to have a spirit disposed to change as the winds of fortune and variations of things command him, and . . . [needs to] know how to enter into evil, when forced by necessity."[130] In the latter he notes that Florence "celebrated Lorenzo to the sky, saying that his prudence had known how to gain in peace what bad fortune had taken from it in war and that he had been able to do more with his advice and his judgment than the arms and forces of the enemy."[131]

———————————

Machiavelli grounded the ends of virtue and the possibilities of freedom and human action in a mean between liberty and license, or between liberty and tyranny. That grounding, and its attendant morality, suggests the presence of a principle, of what is highest in man, by which he judged political virtue. Strauss drew attention to the principle and set it against the background of an antiteleological cosmology. While he so identified the ultimate basis of Machiavelli's "new modes and orders," he regarded their author as agreeing with Plato and Aristotle about the human potential, or lack thereof, for good—in deeds, thinking, and thought. The "act of thought" qua "the nature of divine thought," says Aristotle, encompasses contemplation on the character of one's thinking; that is, because not only "thinking" but also "the act of thought" occurs in people with "the worst of thoughts," thinking has "dignity" only when "the faculty of thought" includes "a thinking on thinking."[132] The implication here is that Strauss's own position on morality in the light of the revelation-reason question is open to the point of being precariously so, occasionally verging on openness to the claims of a Machiavellian modernity. But given Machiavelli's seeming agreement with the classics, how was he a teacher of immoral doctrines? Where he departed from, and opened a fundamental rupture with, the classics, as he himself suggested in Chapter 15 of *The Prince*, is in his instrumental views on virtue and good governance. He replaced providence with chance, as the basis of what is good in human action,[133] and replaced chance with a this-worldly virtue. He set virtue against goodness and depicted virtue not as a mean between the extremes of deficiency and excess but as a mean between humanity and inhumanity. The excellent, extraordinary man of virtue, Machiavelli would say, is a man who can rise above and rule over, rather than be subject to, changing times and the vicissitudes of life that Fortuna and mundane chance create.

CHAPTER SIX

Virtue and Governance

Inseparable from Machiavelli's view of political virtue is his firm belief that people are naturally disinclined to moral virtue.[1] He takes issue with the virtuous mean and with the classical grounding of human action in moral norms. The present chapter examines his new approach to principles of human action by examining his political conception of virtue and governance.

Contemporary scholarship influenced by J. G. A. Pocock[2] and by Quentin Skinner[3] tends to situate Machiavelli in a tradition of classical republicanism. Machiavelli, so the argument goes, shares with that tradition the idea that freedom, especially in the well-ordered republic, entails a civil society free from domination and from oligarchic or monarchic tyranny.[4] Skinner notes that Machiavelli espoused civic humanist tenets,[5] but that he emphasized decisive political action in relation to the ceaseless pursuit of power, a pursuit often divorced from moral norms.[6] In fact, says Skinner, his "critique of classical humanism . . . is underpinned by a darkly pessimistic view of human nature."[7] Skinner nonetheless argues that his "allegiance" to "political liberty," not simply to "mere security," shows his commitment to republicanism.[8] John Rawls, discussing "the political good [and the core "ideas"] of a well-ordered society," explains that "civic humanism . . . holds that we are social, even political, beings whose essential nature is most fully achieved in a democratic society in which there is widespread and active participation in political life. . . ." One should not identify civic humanism with "the truism that we must live in society to achieve our good. Rather, civic humanism specifies the chief, if not the sole human good as our engaging in political life."[9] "[C]lassical republicanism," as Rawls, following Skinner, defines the term, ". . . is the view that the safety of democratic liberties . . . requires the active participation of citizens who have the political virtues needed to sustain a constitutional regime." Good citizens are "moved in good part by a concern for political justice and public good."[10] Rawls offers to define "civic republicanism" thus: "The importance of deliberative political discussion is a theme of what is sometimes called 'civic republicanism.'"[11]

Establishing definitively whether Machiavelli was a civic humanist, a classical republican, or a civic republican is beyond the scope of this chapter. Nevertheless, I will argue that his views on virtue and governance are at best ambiguous and at worst antithetical to the democratic participation in political life by the many and the great.[12] He sees not a basic opposition but a causal link between the common good and selfishness. That he questions the worth of the common good, advises both tyrants and republicans about preserving power, and identifies basic, irreducible tensions between human nature, the common good, and the highest good indicates that he links political virtue with "effectual truth." That Strauss responds to Machiavellian political virtue by laying bare (what he sees as) its this-worldly, morally corrosive basis is germane to determining where both Machiavelli and Strauss stand on the revelation-reason question, or more particularly, is germane to explicating the close relation between Strauss's own position on revelation and reason and his handling of Machiavellian political virtue.

The Common Good and Selfishness

Virtue and the Common Good

That Machiavelli rejects Aristotle's normative view of virtue is a recurrent theme in Strauss's critical study of the Florentine's teaching on philosophy. Returning to this theme, Strauss states: "The common understanding of goodness had found its classic expression in Aristotle's assertions that virtuous activity is the core of happiness for both individuals and societies, that virtue or the perfection of human nature preserves society, and that political society exists for the sake of the good life, i.e., of the virtuous activity of its members."[13] Likewise, for Plato, the chief concern of those who rule the city, who judge what is good and noble, is the souls of men.[14] Machiavelli has quite different views about the core of goodness and that with which rulers should be concerned.

The purpose of the "best regime," especially "kingship," is to actualize and to protect virtuous activity. "Its opposite is tyranny," Strauss adds, "the simply worst regime: whereas the king finds his chief support in the gentlemen, the tyrant finds his chief support in the common people."[15] However, because the best regime is defined by virtuous citizens and their concern with the common good, such a regime "exists very rarely, if it has ever existed . . . . From Machiavelli's point of view this means that the best regime, as Aristotle as well as Plato conceived of it, is an imagined republic or an imagined principality." For Machiavelli, these forms of government are "imagined" because they "are based on the premise that rulers can or must exercise the moral virtues and avoid the moral vices even in the acts of ruling." That insistence about "the fact of human badness" shows his departure from the classics, for while both Machiavelli and the classics say that man is predisposed to self-seeking goals and that rulers must know the actual ways of man, and both argue that "most men are bad," they draw different "conclusions" about the nature of virtue and governance and the relation between the two.[16]

Strauss is explicating the difference between Machiavelli and the classics regarding how they assessed the best regime. However, by then expressing the view of Aristotle on the basis and scope of the best regime and restating his view with "the words of Machiavelli," Strauss infers that they agree on the matter. "Yet according to Aristotle, man is the worst of all living beings if he is without law and right, and law and right depend upon political society. In other words, men become virtuous by habituation; such habituation requires laws, customs, examples and exhortations, and is therefore properly possible only within and through political society. In the words of Machiavelli, good examples arise from good education, good education arises from good laws, and good laws arise from most shocking things."[17] Machiavelli echoes both Aristotle and Plato, for he says, in *Discourses* I 2, 4, and 10, for example, that laws, customs, and education make men virtuous. He goes further, though. He claims that it is impossible to create morally the foundation for morality. Belief in the social, political, and teleological imperative of moral virtue does not provide a good basis for society; that belief lacks an experiential core and thus is inefficacious and false. Society should not be founded by "semi-divine or divinely inspired benefactors of the human race," for they lack the ability to respond in a timely fashion to political and military exigencies; they are concerned more with the hereafter than with the here and now. The good, "heroic" founders whom Machiavelli holds to be emulative examples, Strauss then points out, are "men like Cesare Borgia and especially the criminal emperor Severus."[18]

It is worth noting here that Machiavelli, in Chapter 19 of *The Prince*, advises a prince to "avoid those things that make him hateful and contemptible." In particular, he must avoid a reputation for rapacity towards "the property and the women of his subjects." Yet in the same chapter, having said that Severus was "very cruel and very rapacious," "a very fierce lion and a very astute fox," Machiavelli describes him as "feared and revered by everyone, and not hated by the army."[19] In *Discourses* I 10 he describes Severus as a "criminal" with "very great fortune and virtue, two things that accompany few men."[20] In Chapter 7 of *The Prince* Machiavelli says that Cesare Borgia fell from power not because of his moral vice but because of an "extreme malignity of fortune," namely, the death of his patron and father, Pope Alexander VI.[21] The significance of Machiavelli's discussion of Severus, when compared with his point about Cesare Borgia, relates to proper princely conduct: by using "intelligence and excellence" for what Aristotle describes as "the worse ends,"[22] the Machiavellian prince arms himself with injustice, not law and justice, as his chief weapon; his sense of his own good combined with his fortune and virtue decides whether his actions are just. "Machiavelli's prince," according to Maritain, "is a bad political man, he perverts politics, because his chief aim is his own personal power and the satisfaction of his own personal ambition."[23] For Machiavelli, cruelty, rapacity, violence, and murder—conduct that Aristotle says is "most unholy" (*Politics* 1253a36), and that Plato says is "disorderly" (*Laws* 782a), the "most insolent" kind of "desire" arising from "erotic longing" and "the engendering of offspring" (782d–783a)[24]—are not necessarily wrong or unjust.

While Aristotle acknowledged that states eschew noble ends to seek wealth and dominion, often at the expense of other states, he held that the best regime, guided by reason, not by necessity, seeks virtue and justice. Strauss observes, "Classical political philosophy culminates in the description of imagined states and thus is useless because it does not accept as authoritative the end which all or the most respectable states pursue. That end is the common good conceived of as consisting of freedom from foreign domination and from despotic rule, rule of law, security of the lives, the property and the honor of every citizen, ever increasing wealth and power, and last but not least glory or empire." Virtuous citizens sacrifice their private ambitions to keep the republic free from both tyranny and foreign powers. "The common good is the end only of republics," Strauss explains for Machiavelli.[25] "Hence, the virtue which is truly virtue can best be described as republican virtue."

Republics are preferable to principalities not because republics are "morally superior." Republics simply have a closer affinity for the common good than princes, who are interested primarily in their private good. Thus, republics "are to be preferred with a view to the common good in the amoral sense." Governed by a single individual and not, as are republics, by a variety "of men of different natures," monarchies are less able than republics to adapt to "different kinds of times."[26]

Moral Virtue vs. Republican Virtue

Machiavelli differentiates virtue from goodness in order to differentiate republican virtue from moral virtue. In turn, he replaces moral virtue as the focus of governance with the pursuit of republican virtue. "Goodness is not always compatible with the common good, whereas virtue is always required for it." In rare cases, though, humanity is of greater benefit to the giver of the deed—namely, the republic or its leading men—in dealing with the enemies of the republic than is republican virtue, viz., "[a]usterity and severity." "In the chapter which is devoted to proving this proposition," Strauss then explains, "Machiavelli retells the story of how Scipio [the Elder] acquired high reputation in Spain by his chastity: he returned a young and beautiful wife to her husband without having touched her."[27]

In *Discourses* III 20, entitled "One Example of Humanity Was Able to Do More with the Falisci Than Any Roman Force,"[28] Machiavelli conveys the lesson of that story. In III 21, without mentioning Scipio's return of the bride, Machiavelli again speaks of Scipio's humane and merciful conduct; however, qualifying his previous praise of Scipio, he says that fear, not love, humanity, or moral virtue should guide affairs of moment. "For men are so unquiet that however little the door to ambition is opened for them, they at once forget every love that they had placed in the prince because of his humanity." To combat such unquiet, "Scipio was constrained to use part of the cruelty he had fled from."[29] Is that utility of cruelty the rule or the exception in achieving greatness? A "good reputation," Machiavelli says in III 34, based "on fact and on your work, gives you so much name at the beginning that you indeed need to work many things contrary to this later if you wish to annul it."[30] From III 20, and his other accounts of Scipio, Strauss extracts the point that Machiavelli regards Scipio's chastity as "a politically irrelevant virtue," for it was "his generosity," not his chaste conduct, "which redounded to the benefit of Rome."[31]

Implicit in Machiavelli's replacement of moral virtue with republican virtue is a criticism of how Aristotle and Plato see justice as *the* moral virtue.

In the *Republic,* Plato advises that the guardians of a city be savage towards strangers but gentle towards citizens. Against Plato, Aristotle says that guardians should be savage towards whoever acts unjustly. Aristotle, Strauss observes, "refrains from reproving Plato for having purified the luxurious city without having forced it to restore the land which it had taken from its neighbors in order to lead a life of luxury. Cruelty towards strangers cannot be avoided by the best of citizens as citizens."[32] Justice in a ruler, then, for Aristotle and Plato, entails moral rectitude—in his own life and in his conduct as a ruler.[33] Machiavelli, however, in Chapter 17 of *The Prince,* advises the prince to "above all . . . abstain from the property of others, because men forget the death of a father more quickly than the loss of a patrimony. . . . I conclude, then, . . . that since men love at their convenience and fear at the convenience of the prince, a wise prince should found himself on what is his, not on what is someone else's; he should only contrive to avoid hatred."[34] Indeed, having stated that cruelty to strangers is unavoidable, Strauss, evidently on Machiavelli's behalf, stipulates his crucial distinction: "Justice which is the habit of not taking away what belongs to others while defending what belongs to oneself rests on the firm ground of the selfishness of society. 'The factual truth' of moral virtue is republican virtue."[35]

The Factual Truth of Republican Virtue and the Common Good

Machiavelli recasts the basis of the common good: not what is morally best qua the Good, but the protection, survival, and salvation of the fatherland define the common good. In *Discourses* I 16 he says that the disaffected sons of Junius Brutus were killed to prevent their plotting against the newly emerged Roman republic.[36] His point is that a republic must be mindful of both external and internal threats. In the absence of those threats, a republic can hold to laws that allow for individual freedoms. The caveat is this: a virtue that consists of the capacity of rulers for cruel conduct always is required to protect the common good. When faced by enemies, domestic or foreign, or when seeking to revive the lost ancient spirit for freedom, rulers must have recourse to the immoral behavior of criminals and tyrants. Rulers must use all methods to protect the republic; otherwise, the common good, society, and the fatherland cannot exist.

For Machiavelli, not morality but leadership and perspicacity make a ruler a *good* ruler. His claim has a classical antecedent, though. Is it better, Aristotle asks, for a state to have a general who "is a bad man" but a capable general, or is it better to have a man who is "just" and "a friend to the constitution"

(*Politics* 1309b1–3)? He answers, "in the choice of a general, we should regard his experience rather than his excellence; for few have military experience, but many have excellence. In any office of trust or stewardship, on the other hand, the opposite rule should be observed; for more excellence than ordinary is required in the holder of such an office, but the necessary knowledge is of a sort which all men possess" (1309b3–9).[37] For Machiavelli, strong, capable rulers who keep their vices from public view, vices that do not fatally damage the republic, "are infinitely to be preferred to saintly rulers who lack political and military ability." Strauss adds, "To use the words of a historian who is well-known for his strict adherence to moral principle, 'a weak man may be deemed more mischievous to the state over which he presides than a wicked one.'"[38] By using those "words," Strauss seems either to be alluding to the problematic character of modern morality,[39] or recalling Aristotle's preference for office holders who are good men rather than good generals.

Machiavelli's avowal that rulers must be immoral "abolishes" the difference between criminal and noncriminal behavior. Strauss explains, "One may object to Machiavelli's view of the relation between moral virtue and the common good by saying that it abolishes the essential difference between civil societies and bands of robbers, since robbers too use ordinary modes among themselves whenever possible. Machiavelli is not deterred by this consideration."[40] Illustrating that "view," Strauss notes that Machiavelli imputes to a pirate prince the mindset of a good, pious Roman citizen, and that he suggests that Roman rulers, for all of their respectability, sometimes lacked prudence or awareness of imminent dangers.[41] A robber, in this case a pirate prince, knows he is a robber and does not belong to a good community. Although he keeps to his own good, not to virtue and justice, he should be mindful both of the people and of considerations relating to his reputation. Scrupulous adherence to expediency, selfishness, and the exigencies of circumstances, then, forms the basis of the common good.

Strauss, perhaps tacitly acknowledging both Hobbes's *Leviathan* and Meinecke's *Machiavellism*,[42] goes on to explain that closely related to Machiavelli's view of the common good is his view of how the republic distributes power. He reasons, according to Strauss, that "since the common good requires that innocent individuals be sacrificed for its sake, the common good is rather the good of the large majority." Nevertheless, "[t]he majority cannot rule."[43] The majority is easily misled and led to ruin by the general appearance of their times.[44] Only a select minority, consisting mainly of nobles, has the capacity to occupy public offices effectively. Yet, to ensure the republic not be riven by enmity, nobles must share power with the people. Needful for territorial expansion is an armed populace and thus the support of the people.[45] However, when the people have had a taste of power and riches from conquests, they become restless for more than their fair share. Acquisition of wealth results, then, in a populace accustomed to the pursuit of personal wealth and an easy, comfortable life.[46]

An imperial republic, as a republic devoted to expansion, cannot abide by moral virtue; nor can it abide even by the republican virtues of "austerity and severity."[47] To maintain itself, it must satisfy the demands of the common people for wealth; moreover, to increase the size of its military forces, it must increase the size of its population by making citizens out of foreigners.[48] The imperial republic must be willing, then, to open itself to the risk of corruption. That "accompanying evil" of an imperial republic arises from its need to forego (partly) republican virtue and to regard subject and free states as allies.[49] If modern Italian states imitated the Roman imperial republic and united under the aegis of "a single republic or a single prince," further "evil" would arise. For Machiavelli, notes Strauss, pointing to his critique of Christianity, "The successful imitation by modern Italians of the early Roman republic would necessarily be accompanied by a peculiar evil: an Italy unified by a republic or a prince would no longer abound in independent republics and thus would be less likely to abound in excellent men."[50]

Strauss's emphasis in examining Machiavelli's moral-political teaching clearly is on laying bare the anticlassical basis of his teaching. Yet, that when examining his views on the factual truth of republican virtue and the common good Strauss points to Machiavelli's critique of Christianity shows that Strauss himself does not force a decision between revelation and reason. Strauss does not force a decision, for he sees the fundamental alternatives as compatible where moral direction is concerned.

By lauding amoral republican virtue, Machiavelli means to say that what benefits the people and the nobles, not what is *common* and *good* for society *as a whole*, characterizes the common good.[51] He regards "the common good" and thus "republican virtue" as comprised, Strauss explains, of "opposite habits (e.g., severity and gentleness) to the extent to which each is conducive to the common good."[52] The respective virtues of the two groups in society, the nobles and the people, illustrate those "habits." The nobles rule, the people are the ruled, and thus each group possesses its own type of virtue. To the people, virtuous nobles are (or ought to be) venerable, gentle, wise, kind, humane, and liberal. To the nobles, the virtue of the people consists of their regard for religion and their obedience to rulers and to the laws. However, the people are often fickle and faithless; they make unruly and unrealistic demands of their rulers for wealth, glories, and representation. Because those tumults arise from a natural inability to match consistently their actions and expectations with laws, the role of rulers is to lead the people and make them good.[53] To quell tumults, a ruler, Machiavelli says in *Discourses* I 54, "should represent himself before it [the city] with the greatest grace and as honorably as he can."[54]

Rulers, though, need not conform to the praiseworthy qualities. According to Strauss, Machiavelli "is far from denying that there are some men who are genuinely kind and humane, not from fear or calculation but by nature; yet he contends that such men when entrusted with high office can become a public menace."[55] Office holders are virtuous, Machiavelli explains in *Discourses* III 7 and 20–22, when they act to secure the well-being of the republic. The virtuous ruler has an eye for the times. Rather than eliminate their ambitions, rulers need only be prudent when pursuing their ambitions. *Discourses* III 27 bears on this discussion about the effectual truth of maintaining power. Here Machiavelli describes three modes for organizing a divided city. The first, "most secure," is to kill the leaders of the tumults; the second, to expel them from the city; the third, "to make them make peace together under obligations not to offend one another." The third mode poses the most danger—from it further tumults arise. Enemies who see each other daily in close proximity will not be able to restrain themselves forever, especially when the lord who rules the divided city supports one faction, and thus makes an enemy of other factions, or seeks to be a friend to all people. "But all these modes and these opinions diverging from the truth arise from the weakness of whoever is lord."[56]

Forms of Government: Republics, Principalities, and Tyrannies

Republican Rule or Princely Rule?

Machiavelli radically doubts the truth of moral virtue. That doubt issues in a practical view of the means and ends of governance. Of his preferred form of government, Strauss has thus far explained that, overall, he emphasizes the efficacy of republican rule.[57] Now, Strauss proposes that he identifies an inherent problem in republican rule: "If there is no good which is not accompanied by its peculiar evil, we have to keep watch for the peculiar defects of even the best republic." Those "defects" relate to virtue and the common good. "If it is true that the common good is the end only of republics and that the common good is the ground of virtue, the defective character of republics will prove the defective character of the common good and of virtue."[58] In the *Discourses*, an "explicitly republican book," Machiavelli "is indeed slow to introduce the subjects 'kingdoms' or 'principalities,' as a glance at the headings of the first ten chapters will have shown." Drawing upon I 40 and III 6, as well as I 10 and III 28, Strauss then speaks of "the detachment" evidenced by the fact that Machiavelli advises both the leaders of republics and those opposed to republics— potential and actual tyrants.[59]

Machiavelli did not always favor, for all times, people, and places, republics over principalities. The very exigencies of governance justify princely rule. That rule can be more conducive to the security of the state than republican rule.[60] The personal liberties allowed in republics can be inimical to stability— freedoms of speech, opinion, and belief tend to result in individuals placing their own interests above the well-being of the republic.[61] Machiavelli implies, then, that the common good of the best republic is defective. But he is equivocal in his praise of princely rule. In *Discourses* I 12 he writes, "And truly no province has ever been united or happy unless it has all come under obedience to one *republic* or to one *prince*, as happened to France and to Spain. The cause that Italy is not in the same condition and does not also have one *republic* or one *prince* to govern it is solely the church."[62] Pursuit of philosophy is also a cause of disunity. In the *Florentine Histories* V 1 he points out, "virtue gives birth to quiet, quiet to leisure, leisure to disorder, disorder to ruin." Ruin arises from the young of a city imitating a leader who studies philosophy, who leads a life of "leisure," and thus neglects this-worldly matters.[63]

Machiavelli questions not only the scope but also the possibility of republican rule. In *Discourses* I 2, 9, and 11 he suggests that only the very power of a prince to enact new modes and orders can overcome the disorder that predates society. He also identifies a corruption that arises from within society. In *Discourses* I 10, 16, 17, and 55 he warns that private persons agitating for their own benefit and the failure of princes to cultivate an incorrupt multitude causes disquiet and ruin.[64] Men, and not just those of the people, who are incorrigibly corrupt—who lack the will and the knowledge to maintain the freedom of their fatherland—can be made good, and kept that way, only by the extreme actions of one individual.[65] That goodness is possible, Machiavelli explains in I 55, when an individual exists who is "prudent," has "knowledge of ancient civilizations," and "is rare in brain and authority."[66] However, he says in the same chapter that such an individual has never existed in Italy. Summarizing these arguments in the *Discourses* about disorder and corruption, Strauss dryly observes, "It is therefore insufficient to say that republics are not always possible."[67]

One must say instead, Strauss goes on to explain, that Machiavelli regards the poor judgment of rulers as responsible for the absence or failure of republican rule.[68] Machiavelli criticizes princes for failing to use the cruelty that is needful for turning the "corrupt" populace of a principality into an "incorrupt" populace governed by republican rule. To avoid being hated and regarded as inhumane, princes often tolerate the demands of the corrupt masses; those princes neglect the values of severity and austerity that underpin the common good. At the very least, a prince should ensure the security—the basic or mere survival—of his subjects. To do that, a prince needs a special freedom to act. If his concern with his own ambition and glory redounds to the benefit of his subjects, his self-interest is justified. To princes, the people, and nobles, then, what is good, natural, and virtuous is the desire for property, honor, and glory. Thus, a prince should act in accordance not with moral virtue but with intelligence, prudence, and greatness of purpose.

Virtue, Princely Rule, and Tyrants

Machiavelli's advice about virtuous princely rule echoes, Strauss explains, "the kind of virtue praised by Callicles in Plato's *Gorgias* and possessed by the criminals Agathocles and Severus."[69] The parallel between Machiavelli and Callicles is about the right order and the very basis of virtue. Rejecting both the concept of nature and the grounding of virtue in nature (or in the dictates of heavenly entities) as untrue, Machiavelli and Callicles seek to discard the strictures of a mythic, perfect good.[70] For Strauss, Machiavelli's advice about virtuous princely rule "is the most obvious message of the *Prince* as a whole." Closely related to that message is the idea that "men are praised or blamed also with a view to their being good or bad at acquiring."[71]

To illustrate Machiavelli's Calliclean advice to princes, Strauss evaluates (in an endnote) "his utterances and silences regarding chastity."[72] In Chapter 15 of *The Prince* Machiavelli lists chastity as a moral virtue. He is silent, though, in the following chapter, and in *Discourses* I 37 and 40, about chastity when describing what the prince must do to avoid his subjects hating him. In *Discourses* III 5, 6, 19, and 26 Machiavelli says that princes should abstain from hateful acts and from the women of his subjects; but he is silent about the wrongness of the act itself of rape. For instance, in III 26 he draws attention to Aristotle's advice that a tyrant must avoid raping women or otherwise violating their dignity. "Among the first causes Aristotle puts down of the ruin of tyrants is having injured someone on account of women, by raping them or by violating them or by breaking off marriages."[73]

Aristotle's warning against rape is stronger than the above words suggest at first glance.[74] He means to say that the tyrant should respect women to demonstrate rectitude in his rule. That respect is not simply for political expediency or to maintain social harmony; it reflects the right, true order of excellence in a ruler; his moral conduct shows the order of his soul, that is, towards praiseworthy ends. In contrast, Machiavelli is saying that the ruler should avoid not so much the violation of women as the disquiets instigated by offended citizens; to negate threats to his power, the tyrant need only suppress those accidents caused by his immorality.

Tyrants and the Common Good

The Calliclean advice to princes, to replace rectitude with watchfulness for disquiet, applies also to "the ruling class." Strauss points out, "If we look back to Machiavelli's analysis of republics, we see at once that there is no essential difference between the motives of the prince and the motives of the ruling class. The excellent ruling class as exemplified by the Roman senate is not dedicated to the common good as the common good is primarily understood."[75] The senate viewed the common good largely from the point of view of their self-interest. In *Discourses* I 3, 37, 40, and 46, and III 22 Machiavelli says that Roman nobles were preoccupied with their own good; they acknowledged plebeian demands for representation, but only to safeguard stability and the prosperity derived from Roman conquests. The nobles did not easily reach that acknowledgment. Fighting amongst themselves for supremacy in Rome often paralyzed the nobles, Machiavelli says in *Discourses* I 50 and III 11. In the former he explains that the tribunate created a dictatorship to stop the conflict between the consuls and thus redirected the consuls' attention toward the good of the republic. In the latter he notes that the tribunate did not always aim its ambitions at the common good; thus, the renewal of goodness in republics is caused by "the simple virtue of one man" and by "extrinsic force."[76]

Having discussed Machiavelli's analysis of the self-interested Roman nobility, Strauss explains, "What the classics called aristocracy, we may say, is an imagined republic; the factual truth of aristocracies which are known to exist or to have existed is oligarchy." The tendency of nobles to dominate the many manifests in a shift in governance from aristocracy to oligarchy. Excessive oppression, though, being injurious of the women and the property of the many, results in the many rising in revolt against the oligarchy; in turn, the many select a man of ambition to rule over the state. Strauss goes on, "According to Aristotle, the fact that the tyrant is supported by the people as distinguished from the gentlemen is an argument against tyranny; according to Machiavelli, it is the strongest argument in favor of tyranny."[77]

For Aristotle, that moral and practical dangers beset tyranny undercuts the claim that the consent of the people legitimizes tyranny. He warns that demagogues arise in democracies where not the rule of law but the people "is supreme."[78] A tyrant is similar to a king who "rules according to law over willing subjects," but different in that a tyrant rules according to self-interest; his power is "arbitrary," he is "responsible to no one."[79] Aristotle warns, then, against the potential for tyranny in widespread popular support for a ruler. But he seems equally wary of nobles and their ambitions for power. He explains that property ownership standards for assessing eligibility for public office must be "sufficiently comprehensive to secure that the number of those who have the rights of citizens exceeds the number of those excluded."[80] Tyranny arises from the overlong tenure of public office. A tyrant preserves his power by eliminating (actual and potential) rivals and by appearing to the populace as pious, merciful, and generous.[81] Tyranny arises from harming the poor, rather than from their resenting being held back from public office.[82]

For Machiavelli, popular support of a tyrant is "just." As Strauss summarizes his argument, "the end of the people is more just—or, . . . more decent or more respectable—than the end of the great. The common good may well appear to be identical with the good of the many. And just as free states may be established by means of violence, tyranny may be established by consent."[83] The key words here, I note, are "may be." Consent, whether by itself or combined with either fortune or factors intrinsic to the tyrant, is conditional at best. In Chapter 7 of *The Prince* Machiavelli states, "Those who become princes from private individual solely by fortune become so with little trouble, but maintain themselves with much." Troubles happen because fortune is "very inconstant and unstable."[84] A tyrant's power is contingent on a measure of nontyrannical behavior; "his fellow citizens," Machiavelli explains in Chapter 9, "ask of him only that they not be oppressed."[85] The tyrant should not, Machiavelli says in *Discourses* I 41, change abruptly from being "a friend of the plebs" to being their "enemy," for "finding yourself uncovered and without friends, you are ruined."[86]

A tyrant, however reliant upon consent, gains power through less salutary ways than consent. In *Discourses* II 13 Machiavelli says that Philip of Macedon, Agathocles, Cyrus, and the Roman republic established empire and great fortune through "fraud" and not "force alone." The title of the chapter, "That One Comes from Base to Great Fortune More through Fraud Than through Force," indicates that lesson.[87] Fraud and fortune aside, tyranny, Machiavelli explains, is not the unstable form of government critics say it is; no form of government, he reflects in *Discourses* I 2, is immune to the changes in men wrought by chance. Rulers who establish the foundations for centuries of stability, he says in I 1, 10, 29, 37, and 52, and III 6, are praiseworthy. For instance, in I 1 he speaks of "the long peace that was born in the world under Octavian," and explains in I 10, "Let a prince put before himself the times from Nerva to Marcus, and compare them with those that came before and that came later . . . . He will see golden times when each can hold and defend the opinion he wishes."[88] By creating laws and orders to represent the many and the great alike, a tyrant keeps the populace free from corruption, discontent, and suspicion; thus, he negates or holds in check the root causes of changes in government. According to Strauss, "Considerations like these induce Machiavelli frequently to use 'prince' and 'tyrant' as synonyms, regardless of whether he speaks of criminal or non-criminal tyrants."[89]

Strauss emphasizes, "It therefore becomes necessary to reconsider the distinction between criminal and non-criminal tyrants. It is not sufficient to say that the criminal tyrant lacked opportunity, since without opportunity he could never have become a tyrant." To become a tyrant, one needs the opportunity. "The classic example of a potential tyrant who lacked opportunity and *therefore* failed was Manlius Capitolinus."[90] Strauss means that Manlius was waiting for the right moment to turn his potential for tyranny into actuality. However, he failed not simply, if at all, because of lack of opportunity. Manlius, unable to contain his envy over the success of Camillus, "was a calumniator," Machiavelli says in *Discourses* I 8; similarly, he remarks in I 24 that "Manlius was moved . . . by his envy or by his wicked nature to arouse sedition in Rome." Manlius, Machiavelli says in III 8, had "much virtue of spirit and body," but his excessive desire for glory and his excessive envy of Camillus blinded him.[91] Manlius remained a potential tyrant because of factors intrinsic to himself. "[H]e lacked that prudence" to recognize that the Roman republic could not be made corrupt; the Romans did not want to lose their liberty to a tyrant. In short, a love for freedom and a large population help build an empire, but envy and idleness are dangerous to its well-being.[92]

According to Strauss, "It is likewise not sufficient to say that a criminal tyrant, while not lacking opportunity, lacked justification, for where there are opportunities of this magnitude, justification will not fail to be forthcoming." The "potential tyrant of extraordinary gifts" believes he can better protect his city or country than his republican rivals, and uses that belief to justify seizing power. Yet, it is difficult to ascertain after the fact whether his belief was well-founded, for his republican rivals may have been able to achieve the same great deed of acquiring power in the state. Thus for Machiavelli, Strauss concludes, "There is then no essential difference between the public-spirited founder of a republic and the selfish founder of a tyranny: both have to commit crimes and both have to pay due regard to that part of society the cause of which is most just. As for the difference between their intentions, one may say with Aristotle that the intentions are hidden."[93]

What Strauss means by that final observation is not immediately clear. Given that a "public-spirited founder" intends to benefit the public good, it seems strange that he would need to hide his intentions. In contrast, "the selfish founder of a tyranny" believes that the only part of society to whose just cause he is obliged to pay due regard is himself, not the people. He views his own interests as far more important, intrinsically and extrinsically, than the common good. Yet, to gain the support of the people, the tyrant must not make his selfish intentions publicly known; he must appear to serve the people, not himself; the people do not like their office holders to act with self-interest.[94] Indicating why the founder of a republic would need to hide his intentions, Strauss explains for Machiavelli, "farsighted patriotism and farsighted selfishness lead to the same results. . . . [T]o achieve its goal, justice must use injustice and injustice must use justice; for both, a judicious mixture of justice and injustice, a certain middle course between justice and injustice, is required."[95]

Prolonging Tyrannical Rule

Both republics and tyrannies are founded on the use of expedient, unjust methods. "However this may be," Strauss explains, for Machiavelli, "the tyrant as well as any other new prince must arm his subjects. Yet he cannot arm all his subjects."[96] A tyrant need only arm and benefit those whose support he requires. As a new prince, he gains and maintains his power by exploiting the traditional hostility between the "two diverse humors" in society—the people and the great.[97] A tyrant may also need to acquire a new state, to add to his own; he must keep the new populace unarmed, though, lest they revolt against him. If he has the support of soldiers, a tyrant need not worry about harming or depending on the unreliable support of the many, who may desire to regain their ancient freedoms. Nor would he have to depend upon the support of the nobles, who may harbor a great desire to dominate the state and the many. Hence, it is prudent, Machiavelli says in Chapter 19 of *The Prince*, that a prince arms only those who have helped him acquire their state. By "new princes" Machiavelli means any prince of any type of governance; in Chapters 19 and

20 of *The Prince* he speaks of princes, new princes, principalities, and the Roman emperors; in *Discourses* I 40 and 41 he speaks of the Roman republic, tyrants, and the tyranny of Appius Claudius.[98]

Machiavelli dispenses advice about ascension to power with equal fervor to tyrants as he does to the founders of republics. That advice, according to Strauss, "as well as other advice of the same kind, is innocent of any consideration of the common good." If he "can advise" tyrants, Machiavelli is willing likewise to advise "private citizens" and any person who acts "with a view" to self-interest.[99] In *Discourses* III 6 Machiavelli both advises those who covet princely power and warns the prince of the danger to his rule from former ruling families and other dissatisfied people who covet his power. Machiavelli opens the chapter thus: "It did not appear to me that reasoning about conspiracies should be omitted, since it is a thing so dangerous to princes and private individuals; for many more princes are seen to have lost their lives and states through these than by open war."[100] Failure by conspirators to deal properly with dangers that occur before, during, and after the acting out of a conspiracy shows that they lack prudence and spirit. Compromising the secrecy of the enterprise is one danger; another is that the conspirators will not kill the prince when they have the opportunity to do so. Moreover, there is a danger that the prince's relatives or friends may kill the conspirators. One need not regard conspiracy, then, as wrong. What is wrong is not private ambition, conspiracy itself, or such acts as murder and treachery, but the conspirators' lack of foresight to their own survival.[101]

Strauss goes on to explain, "While advice with regard to the private advantage of private men becomes conspicuous only in the Third Book of the *Discourses*, it is not absent from the other parts of Machiavelli's work."[102] In *Discourses* I 29 and 30 Machiavelli advises not only aspiring tyrants but also those hitherto without such aspirations. In I 52 he excuses the failure of Piero Soderini to commit the treachery of turning from being a man of the Florentine people to being an apologist for the Medici. "[I]f he had been exposed as a friend to the Medici, he would have become suspect and hateful to the people. Hence his enemies would have had much more occasion for crushing him than they had at first." What deserves criticism is the lack of forethought given to a hateful or treacherous action, not the action itself. "Therefore, in every policy men should consider its defects and dangers and not adopt it if there is more of the dangerous than the useful in it."[103] In II 28 Machiavelli says that republics and princes must refrain from greatly offending "not only against a collectivity but even against an individual"; regardless of his personal safety or the public good, an offended individual will seek satisfaction if his honor is inadequately avenged.[104]

The thread that runs throughout Machiavelli's advice to private men about their self-advantage is that they develop a presence of mind when manipulating the common good for their own ends. In *Discourses* III 34 Machiavelli elaborates three modes by which a "private" man may acquire a reputation for greatness. The first and least reliable mode is for a man with a well-respected father to gain respect for himself by demonstrating his filial piety in public. He soon loses that respect if the people judge him to be without his own virtue. The second and better mode is to keep the company of wise, cultured, well-regarded men. As opinion underlies respect thus acquired, the respect is susceptible to change. The third, superior mode is for "men who are born in a republic" to strive to gain, maintain, and increase their reputations by contriving to commit great and rare great deeds that benefit the republic. Only by committing "many things" against the public good will a person lose this kind of reputation for greatness. Citizens who give rank to fellow citizens should select men who prove themselves worthy by the fact alone of their great deeds. Yet men who desire fame need only aim few deeds at the public good. "For nothing makes them so much esteemed as to give *rare* examples of themselves with some *rare* act or saying conforming to the common good."[105]

Having discussed Machiavelli's advice about self-advantage, Strauss says, "Let us survey the movement of thought which leads from unselfish patriotism to criminal tyranny."[106] In the *Discourses* Machiavelli initially equates the best or natural function of society with the protection of life: in I 1 and 2 he explains that people formed society to better defend themselves, live longer, and to lead a free, stable, and comfortable life. Yet, to maintain its freedom and to keep its citizens good, a society must return to its beginnings from time to time. In I 6 and 16 Machiavelli observes that protection of mere life is not the sole function of society; if a society wishes not only to maintain itself but also to expand, it must order itself to acquire empire. Patriotism, then, has a close link with selfishness. In I 37 he notes that wars arise from the natural desire of people to possess everything they can. That desire is greater than the actual capacity for acquisition; thus, peoples' dissatisfaction with what they do possess drives them to war against those whom they fear or wish to despoil. In I 46 he warns that lest a republic be discord-riven, laws must control men's ambitions and base tendencies. The threat of a return to the uncertainty of life that predates society does not suffice to keep all men good. In III 16 he suggests that a republic ordered for war will always need worthy men; that need forestalls the agitations of men who do not feel esteemed. Thus to Machiavelli, Strauss explains, the core difference between a republic, principality, and a tyranny pertains to "a difference of degree"—not "a difference of kind"—to which oppression is employed by those in power. "But oppression perhaps exists also where extreme inequality of wealth causes an extreme dependence of the poor on the rich."[107]

Human Nature, the Common Good, and the Highest Good

Goodness and Badness in Human Nature: A Comparison with Hobbes

In describing the factual bases of virtue and governance, Machiavelli delimits the extent of participation in civil society by the many and the great. Underpinning that delimitation is his dim view of human nature. In *Discourses* I 3 he states, "it is necessary to whoever disposes a republic and orders laws in it to presuppose that all men are bad, and that they always have to use the malignity of their spirit whenever they have a free opportunity for it."[108] In Chapter 17 of *The Prince* he writes, "one can say this generally of men: that they are ungrateful, fickle, pretenders and dissemblers, evaders of danger, eager for gain."[109] Men are bad, though not wholly bad, for if they were, necessity and laws could not do them good. "[M]en are more prone to evil than to good," Machiavelli notes in I 9; shortly afterwards he states, "if one individual is capable of ordering, the thing itself is ordered to last long not if it remains on the shoulders of one individual but rather if it remains in the care of many and its maintenance stays with many." However, of such "maintenance" he says in *Discourses* I 29: "men are kept better and less ambitious longer through fear of punishment."[110] Summarizing Machiavelli's blunt analyses, Strauss explains, "One would have to say that man is by nature bad if, to quote Hobbes, this could be said without impiety. At any rate, men do not possess a natural inclination toward the good. They are more inclined toward evil than toward the good."[111]

Does Strauss mean to say that Machiavelli is being impious? Strauss does at least open the door to a less radical judgment of human nature by acknowledging Machiavelli's position in the negative form: that man is not naturally good. But as the Book of Genesis teaches, God made man in His image. Therefore, is it impious and blasphemous for Machiavelli to describe man as he does? Moreover, is Strauss claiming that he rejects both the concept and the existence of the highest good? By raising these questions, Strauss offers an implicit contrast between his position on the fundamental alternatives and Machiavelli's position: whereas Machiavelli seeks to be beyond Jerusalem and Athens, Strauss is open to their respective normative claims.

In his book on Hobbes Strauss asked, "Why could Hobbes not make up his mind to treat the view which is in reality conclusive for him, that man's natural appetite is vanity, unequivocally as the basis of his political philosophy? If this conception of natural appetite is right, if man by nature finds his pleasure in triumphing over all others, then man is by nature evil." Strauss pointed out, though: "But he did not dare to uphold this consequence or assumption of his theory." Instead, Hobbes posited a less critical view: "Because man is by nature animal, therefore he is not by nature evil, therefore he is as innocent as the animals." Appetite for power is characteristic of man as man and as an animal. The appetite is permissible, and is not evil, when it is not contrary to "the preservation of life"—"the *primary* good"—or to "happiness"— "the *greatest* good." Appetite for power helps stave off "death," which "is the *primary* as well as the *greatest* and *supreme* evil."[112]

Hobbes opened the preface of *De Cive* (*On the Citizen*) with an entreaty to "Readers" to read his book "attentive[ly]," for it examines an issue of great consequence: "men's duties, first as men, then as citizens and lastly as Christians. These duties constitute the elements of the law of nature and of nations, the origin and force of justice, and the essence of the Christian Religion."[113] Elsewhere in the preface he held that men are naturally disposed to "fear and distrust of each other." Shortly afterwards, though, he stated, "Some object that if we admit this principle, it follows directly not only that all Men are evil (which perhaps, though harsh, should be conceded, since it is clearly said in holy Scripture), but also (*and this cannot be conceded without impiety*) that they are evil by nature." Denying that "men are evil by nature" or "were made so by nature," Hobbes argued that men's propensity to evil is due both to their failure to exercise reason and to the absence of society. Only when living in "civil society"—to escape the uncertainty of life in "the state of nature," an uncertainty grounded in every man asserting a "right to all things"—do men act in accordance with "natural laws."[114] By those "laws" Hobbes meant "the Dictate of right reason . . . about what should be done or not done for the longest possible preservation of life and limb."[115]

Human Nature and the Common Good

According to Strauss, "Machiavelli takes issue with those who explain the bad conduct of men by their bad nature: men are by nature malleable rather than either bad or good; goodness and badness are not natural qualities but the outcome of habituation."[116] Habituation originated, Machiavelli says in *Discourses* I 2, when people gathered to form society for mutual protection. Over time people stray, he explains in I 3, from the "civil way of life"; hence, they must be rehabituated "by hunger and poverty," or, when "good custom is lacking," by "the laws."[117] In I 26 he explains that "a new prince" who desires to make his power over his state absolute must "make everything in that state anew." The prince should "make the rich poor, the poor rich, as did David when he became king— 'who filled the hungry with good things and sent the rich away empty.' " Such "very cruel" methods are indispensable, though difficult to follow, for men "do not know how to be either altogether wicked or altogether good."[118] The failure of men to commit wicked deeds when necessary or advantageous arises, Machiavelli argues in I 27, "from men's not knowing how to be honorably wicked or perfectly good."[119]

That habituation makes people act for the common good does not eliminate their propensity to act with self-advantage. The root of one's being in society is the selfish perception—of a certain kind—of one's needs and wants. For Machiavelli, Strauss notes, "selfishness is badness as long as it is not molded with a view to the needs of living together; it becomes goodness through such molding; but it always remains selfishness." Machiavelli draws upon the account in Polybius' *Histories* about the beginnings of "sociability" and "political society"; but he "omits even Polybius' extremely brief references to the union of men and women and the generation of children as well as to man's natural rationality, to say nothing of the fact that whereas Polybius speaks in this context of 'nature,' Machiavelli speaks of 'chance.' "[120] By that omission, Machiavelli implies that not reason or rearing children, as important as they are for sociability, but rather chance and the manly ability, free from the strictures of moral reasoning, to overcome chance is the foundation of society. He explains, "variations of governments arise by chance among men. For since the inhabitants were sparse in the beginning of the world, they lived dispersed for a time like beasts."[121] While Polybius also draws attention to the base, selfish tendencies in human nature, he says that reason and rearing children counter such tendencies. In the passage Machiavelli omits, Polybius describes "men [as] being all naturally inclined to sexual intercourse . . . the consequence of this being the birth of children," and remarks that "men are distinguished from the other animals by possessing the faculty of reason."[122]

For Machiavelli, Strauss goes on to explain, though man "is by nature concerned only with his own well-being," he cannot ignore "the well-being of his society on which his own well-being appears to depend."[123] The "good republic" is "good" because it provides the laws and orders that persuade people not to act contrary to the common good. Yet, personal benefit motivates people to work for the common good; people need not abandon self-interest if pursuing it benefits the good of society. The republic, then, need not eliminate selfishness. Ruin to society is caused not by passions, humors, or selfishness—whether selfishness on the part of the individual or of the two groups in society, the many and the great—but by the failure of rulers to vent "the malignant humors." Rulers instill a fear of punishment within the citizenry, and to avoid hatred, temper that fear with acts of liberality and the hope of benefits.[124]

"It is impossible to preserve the perfect combination of being loved and being feared," Strauss notes for Machiavelli, "but deviations from that 'middle course' are unimportant if the governors are men of great virtue."[125] A well-ordered republic allows excellent, not weak or humble, men to rise to high positions of governance; excellent men of action, ferocious in strength of spirit, will, and body, govern more effectively than men of contemplation. While love for personal glory and wealth motivates an excellent man, he gains fame and a reputation for greatness by appearing to the people as working for the common good alone. The well-ordered republic permits the excellent man to acquire public office only by votes, that is, by the authority of the citizenry, and not by deception, violence, or other such means inimical to stability. To ensure that its leaders would not foment discord, out of resentment over not receiving their due rewards, the Roman republic allowed them to acquire glory for themselves from their public actions. The republic hence allowed a commander to decide matters of tactics and to keep the glory gained from his successful conduct of a military campaign.[126]

The Common Good vs. the Highest Good

Believing that people are inclined to evil and that acting in accordance with the highest good cannot make them good or virtuous, Machiavelli favors a temporal conception of governance. The well-ordered republic he praises is a republic that orders the many and the great towards goodness; laws and habituation make and keep people good and virtuous. The expectation of eternal glory, of a glory that will forever remain in the minds of all people, makes rulers good; the many (the ruled) are made good by the inculcation in them by the great of belief in rewards in the hereafter.[127]

Machiavelli clearly does focus on how to order the republic, realize the common good, and counter the propensity of men for evil rather than good.[128] To these ends, he advises men of action; but the men he advises are not only the republicans but also the tyrants. Indeed, Strauss reveals what appears in his view to be a fundamental dilemma, which renders Machiavelli's thought both paradoxical and fraught with danger. Strauss asks, "How can we respect someone who remains undecided between good and evil or who, while benefiting us, benefits at the same time and by the same action our worst enemies?"[129] Strauss's answer may be summarized thus: Machiavelli advises tyrants because he believes that being a teacher of new modes and orders entails defending the truth of political life, regardless of whether tyrants and not just republicans benefit from the teaching of factual truth.

Having explained how Machiavelli can be both a republican and an adviser to tyrants, Strauss states, "This difficulty, however, remains. Machiavelli claims to serve the common benefit of everyone by communicating to all the new modes and orders which he has discovered. Yet, as he points out, the new modes and orders cannot benefit those who benefit from the old modes and orders. There are two ways of solving this difficulty." The first is to understand that Machiavelli directs his advice to the great because it is the many rather than the great who, notwithstanding the role of the great as the "defenders" of the old ways, believe the "untruth" of the old ways, that there exists a highest good, a good superior to the common good. He keeps this advice from the attention of the many because it would be too shocking to their sensibilities. According to Strauss, his advice gives the great "a good conscience in doing what they hitherto did with a more or less uneasy conscience."[130]

Of the second way of solving the difficulty with Machiavelli's claims to be benefiting everyone by his counsel, Strauss points out: "Or else one must say—and this is what Machiavelli in fact says—that there is no good however great which is unqualifiedly good."[131] Here Strauss finally offers his solution to the enigma of Machiavelli's thought and teaching. That Machiavelli eschews the Good, regarding it as an impossible standard for virtuous human action, implies that he has no compunction in advising rulers, even tyrants, to act against religion, morality, and the common good. Strauss explains for Machiavelli, "The common good in the political sense is defective not only because it is inferior *qua* common good to the common good simply, which is the truth." For Machiavelli to say that no good exists that is absolutely good indicates that he means by "the political common good" something other than "the truth." According to Strauss, in *La Mandragola* Machiavelli speaks of a "supplement to the common good which exists on the same level as the common good, i.e., on a level lower than the truth."[132] Machiavelli addresses such themes, for instance, as conspiracy and "the triumph of forbidden love." He conveys, then, the appearance that he is speaking about the difficulties leaders have in following traditional morality whilst defending the fatherland. He conveys this appearance to furnish a publicly defensible basis for questioning morality, for jettisoning the classical precept that the highest good and its attendant moral norms should direct the common good.[133]

Machiavelli aims in *La Mandragola*, as he did in both *The Prince* and the *Discourses*, to uncover truths not only for the good of all but also for his own good; he hopes to gain a measure of personal "benefit" and "reward" for his labors. Strauss adds, "The reward would consist in nothing but praise. The praise for which he could hope is necessarily much smaller than the praise which men bestow on the founders of religions and the founders of kingdoms or republics."[134] In *Discourses* I 10 Machiavelli explains that first among men worthy of praise are "heads and orderers of religions"; second, the founders of states; third, military leaders who have "expanded" the state; and fourth, "literary men . . . and because these are of many types, they are each of them celebrated according to his rank."[135] I would note, though, that Machiavelli indicates in the prologue of *La Mandragola* a doubt that he would earn even praise for his endeavors. He explains that the play's author "is striving with these trifling thoughts to make his wretched life more pleasant," and laments, "[t]he pay he expects is that every man will stand aside and sneer, speaking ill of whatever he sees or hears."[136]

Machiavelli is arguing, here and in the *Discourses*, that supreme glory belongs to the teacher, not to the founder; the teacher alone imparts discovery of the truths of the world to the founder and thereby to future generations. The teacher—"the discoverer"—is not a theoretician, though. The teacher, Strauss explains for Machiavelli, "looks at society not theoretically but, being the teacher of founders, in the perspective of founders. . . . The perspective of the teacher of founders comprises the perspectives of both the tyrant and the republic." The teacher is interested in knowledge about "the most stable, the most happy and the most glorious society." Therefore, the teacher "necessarily has a bias in favor of republics."[137]

In his temporal views on virtue and governance, Machiavelli issued a comprehensive challenge to classical political philosophy. The crux of his notion of civil society is a notion of the common good that, against Aristotle, differentiates moral virtue from republican virtue, settles in favor of the latter, and jettisons the highest good. Virtue as it relates to political and social order may seem to entail love of one's city (or country) and be patriotic in nature.[138] Nevertheless, Machiavelli insisted, free and open civil society is a chimera, for human nature is inclined towards evil, not towards the highest good or even the common good. The ruthless appraisal of exigent circumstances must, he says, guide considerations of virtue; the virtuous ruler possesses all the "habits" necessary to protect himself, his state, and its inhabitants against all enemies, be they from within or without. Machiavelli regarded deliberation as essential to civil society, though not in the sense that the prince entrusts rule over affairs of state to a deliberative assembly of the many and the great. Instead, in the figure of the virtuous prince is combined deliberation and daring, particularly about his own good rather than the good of society as a whole. Although Machiavelli has a bias in favor of republics, his ultimate bias is in favor of (what he sees as) the effectual truth of political action. That ultimate bias connotes an anthropocentric conception of morality and good governance; he regards theo- and cosmocentric conceptions as deficient in their grasp of effectual truth.[139]

In taking issue with these core themes of Machiavellian political virtue, Strauss affirms the philosophical approach to the good life. As a scholar of the history of political philosophy, Strauss focuses on the relation between the philosopher and the city, including why philosophers are unwilling to rule, and sees justice in terms of what is good by nature, not what is good by the might of rulers or the prince.[140] Where, then, does Strauss himself stand regarding biblical truths about morality and the one thing needful for life? That when examining classical views on the good society as seen by Machiavelli Strauss formulated his concept of human nature in religious and theological terms illustrates how Strauss himself perceives the relation between the fundamental alternatives. Although the alternatives differ about what completes morality, they agree on the existence of a highest good and on the paramount character of divine law and justice. But does Strauss see the alternatives as compatible where rule of the city is concerned? This much is clear: To Machiavelli's idea of factual truth Strauss opposes the true factual truth of political virtue: morality has a theoretical, not just a practical, dimension, and practical knowledge realizes its true scope when grounded in the theoretical dimension. For Strauss, the right order between the dimensions has special normative import in the contemporary era when set against the backdrop of contemplation of the fundamental alternatives.

CHAPTER SEVEN

The Legacy of Machiavelli's Moral-Political Teaching

Strauss's oft-mentioned thesis that the origin of modernity can be found in Machiavelli is a clear indication that he held modernity and its core traits to be the legacy of Machiavelli.[1] Modernity is not simply secular, Strauss explained in "The Three Waves of Modernity." Rather than consisting simply of "the loss or atrophy of biblical faith," modernity is characterized precisely by Machiavelli's depiction of "all earlier political philosophy as fundamentally insufficient."[2] His basis for rejecting philosophic tradition is twofold: "The traditional views either lead to the consequence that the political things are not taken seriously (Epicureanism) or else that they are understood in the light of an imaginary perfection—of imagined commonwealths and principalities, the most famous of them being the kingdom of God. One must start from how men do live; one must lower one's sights." Shortly afterwards Strauss noted for Machiavelli, "the establishment of political society and even of the most desirable political society does not depend on chance, for chance can be conquered."[3] Machiavelli's contribution to modernity, then, is his replacement of chance, Nature, and God with history, freedom, necessity, and contingency.[4] In part II of "Progress or Return?" Strauss, but without citing Machiavelli, explained that three traits (may be said to) characterize modernity: anthropocentrism; "a radical change of moral orientation" from an "emphasis on duty" to the emphasis on "rights"; and the linking of "freedom" to the horizon of "history," not to "the whole order of nature or creation."[5]

Strauss identified in the origins of modernity a "methodic" turn to "history." In chapter 6 of *The Political Philosophy of Hobbes* he stated, "This turning is shown by the fact that now for the first time the methodic study of history is demanded." Like philosophy, this "new study" of history seeks "truth." The difference is "that philosophy seeks general precepts, while the study of history seeks the application and realization of precepts."[6] Bacon carried further Hobbes's aim to acquire functional precepts from the study of history. Although Bacon acknowledged "that moral philosophy as the theory of virtue and duty has been perfectly worked out by classical philosophy," he argued, Strauss adds, that "the fundamental shortcoming of ancient philosophy is that it limits itself to a description of 'the nature of good.'"[7] Indeed, "We are much beholden to Machiavel and others, that write what men do, and not what they ought to do." Having quoted Bacon's praise of Machiavelli, Strauss noted, "The reference to Macchiavelli's programme (15th chapter of *Il Principe*) shows the direction and the lines which further investigation of the origins of the modern interest in history should take."[8]

Of Strauss's exploration in his book on Hobbes of the modern turn to history, Kennington observes, "He does not even allude to this earlier turn in *Natural Right and History*, . . . : 'The discovery of history' remained for Strauss an uncompleted inquiry."[9] Even if Kennington is correct, one can still say that in his critical study of Machiavelli's teaching Strauss explicated the founding traits of modernity; and one of those traits is the abandonment of nature for history. In particular, Strauss's closing section of his critical study, Gildin notes, "raise[s] the question of the extent to which *all* modern philosophy or science found a congenial home on the new continent Machiavelli claimed to have discovered."[10]

Strauss's Concluding Thoughts on Machiavelli

Plato and Machiavelli on the Efficacy of the Best Regime

Strauss clearly argues that, in his new modes and orders, tied as they are to a concept of "effectual truth," Machiavelli rejects classical precepts of moral virtue. Strauss shows that he inveighs against Aristotle and Plato for their grounding of the means and ends of politics in moral norms. It is curious, then, that Strauss begins his concluding thoughts on Machiavelli by drawing a parallel between Machiavelli and Plato, on how they assessed the best regime: "The manner in which Machiavelli achieves the transition from neutrality in the conflict between the tyranny and the republic to republicanism, from selfishness to devotion to the common good, or from badness to goodness reminds one of the action of Plato's *Republic*. In the first book of the *Republic* Thrasymachus questions justice, i.e., he raises the question as to whether justice is good."[11] Socrates does not then refute the thesis that the pursuit of self-interest, not of goodness, underpins justice. "Instead he begins to found a city in speech," and in "that speech he takes for granted the goodness of justice which had become thoroughly questionable." To Thrasymachus, the tyrant is the best man; he is the strongest man, for he can achieve great gains in private and public arenas, gains unachievable by others; the highest pleasure is the pleasure he gains from power, not from wisdom, or from education, culture, and knowledge. Socrates, though, says that without a proper and lifelong education, man cannot enjoy the benefits of civilization. A purely literary education will produce a soft man; a purely physical education will produce an ignorant philistine. To protect the city properly, guardians must receive, then, both intellectual and physical training. The "transformation" discussed in the *Republic*, Strauss notes, is about how to convert "the lover of tyranny, to say nothing of the lover of bodily pleasures, into a lover of justice." However, "this transformation proves to be only the preparation for the true conversion from badness to goodness, the true conversion being the transition to philosophy, if not philosophy itself."[12]

When stressing that rulers be educated in the ways of the world, Machiavelli alludes to transforming "man through the desire for glory." Strauss adds, "the second and higher conversion seems to have been forgotten." Here Strauss draws a parallel between Machiavelli and Plato about the best regime; he then retracts it by saying that Machiavelli forgot "the second and higher conversion." Strauss goes on, though, to qualify his retraction or "conclusion." He states, "This conclusion however is not compatible with Machiavelli's clear awareness of the delusions of glory and of the limitations of the political."[13]

What does Machiavelli's excellent man convert to if he does not convert from love of tyranny to love of justice or love of philosophy? This much is clear: the conversion is from ignorance to knowledge. The ignorant lack power against Fortuna, mundane chance, and the perpetual flux in the world. The excellent man subdues those travails; they do not subdue him. With knowledge of the world, he can rise above and rule over chance rather than attempting to conquer it with mere might, as would a tyrant; might alone is not able to conquer chance. The excellent man gains knowledge of the world by intertwining experience and reading histories. However, the soldier, captain, prince, and tyrant do not deserve a reputation for excellence; nor does the founder, who is an excellent man, deserve a reputation for all-comprehensive excellence. The truly excellent man is the teacher who imparts to his students (be they soldiers, captains, princes, tyrants, or founders) the truths of the world.[14]

The Newness of Machiavelli's Moral-Political Teaching and its Opposition to the Classics

The key principle of modernity as it appears in Machiavelli consists of a temporal view of all the things in the world. Strauss states, "Machiavelli claims to have taken a way not yet trodden by anyone and thus to have discovered new modes and orders. His discovery is implied in the principle that one must take one's bearings by how men live as distinguished from how they ought to live." That he voiced such a "principle," and based a "teaching" on it that is opposed to the classics, is shown by his "almost complete silence about Plato, Aristotle, and the political philosopher Cicero, to say nothing of scholasticism." Moreover, in *Discourses* I 2 Machiavelli alters "a philosophic passage" from Polybius's *Histories*, VI 6.2–4. Strauss does not further discuss that alteration, except to underscore its location in the *Discourses*: "he who reserves the full power of his attack rather for the end is not likely to reveal the scope of his deviation from the most revered tradition at the beginning of a book."[15]

If one used the logic in Strauss's point about Polybius in the *Discourses*, one could say that Machiavelli's rejection of the classics is signaled also by his mention of Xenophon's *The Education of Cyrus* near the end of the *Discourses*—in III 39—and near the middle of *The Prince*—in Chapter 14. Indeed, for Strauss, his reading of Xenophon rather than of Polybius shows the full extent of his rejection of the classics. Strauss notes that for Machiavelli, "the representative par excellence of classical political philosophy is Xenophon, whose writings he mentions more frequently than those of Plato, Aristotle, and Cicero taken together or those of any other writer with the exception of Livy." Abandoning the Socratic aspect of Xenophon's works for the tyrannical aspect, "Machiavelli refers only to the *Hiero* and the *Education of Cyrus*," Strauss points out, "not to the *Oeconomicus* or to any other of Xenophon's Socratic writings. Xenophon's thought and work has two foci, Cyrus and Socrates. While Machiavelli is greatly concerned with Cyrus, he forgets Socrates."[16] In outlining these "two foci," Strauss echoes both his earlier work, *On Tyranny: An Interpretation of Xenophon's Hiero* (1948), and foreshadows his later works, *Xenophon's Socratic Discourse: An Interpretation of the "Oeconomicus"* (1970) and *Xenophon's Socrates* (1972).[17]

Machiavelli is not, Strauss goes on to explain, entirely at odds with classical political philosophy.[18] Against the hedonists, Aristippus (founder of the Cyrenaics) and Epicurus (founder of Epicureanism), Machiavelli argues that through the glory and honor derived from political life one gains the highest pleasure. He agrees with the sophists, Gorgias, Hippias, Prodicus, Protagoras, and Thrasymachus, for he stresses that "political science" is "the art of legislation." He disagrees with the sophists, and agrees with Aristotle, for he focuses that "art" not on "collecting renowned laws" but on (the end of) the well-being of the city.[19] Machiavelli's agreement with Aristotle does not extend to the scope of law. For Aristotle, excellence must guide legislators and aspirants to power in a state.[20] For Machiavelli, "the safety of his fatherland" must guide "any citizen who finds himself counseling his fatherland"; and "there ought not to enter any consideration of either just or unjust, merciful or cruel."[21]

It would be a mistake, Strauss observes, to see in Machiavelli Thucydides' "denial of the power of the gods or of justice and the same sensitivity to harsh necessity and elusive chance." Strauss reasons, "Yet Thucydides never calls in question the intrinsic superiority of nobility to baseness."[22] In an endnote Strauss says, "Cf. *Discourses* III 41,"[23] but he does not indicate which passages in Thucydides' *History of the Peloponnesian War* he has in mind. It would be instructive, then, to turn briefly to Strauss's chapter on Thucydides in *The City and Man*. Here Strauss wrote that "Thucydides' horizon is the horizon of the city.... The city, if it is healthy, looks up, not to the laws which it can unmake as it made them, but to the unwritten laws, the divine law, the gods of the city."[24] How far in his horizon Thucydides looked to the gods is open to question, though. "The Funeral speech in which his Pericles sets forth what his Athens stands for is silent about the divine law."[25] In his speech for the Athenian dead, Pericles simply spoke of "Hope, the uncertain goddess."[26] He did not mention in that speech, or in the Melian dialogue, the traditional Greek gods. According to Strauss, "that the gods' existence is not explicitly discussed between the Athenians and the Melians does not prove that it was of no concern to Thucydides."[27] Instead, it proves his piety, "the silent character of the conveyance [of belief in the gods] being required by the chaste character of his piety."[28]

Having spoken of Thucydides in his concluding thoughts on Machiavelli, Strauss, through a criticism of contemporary readers and historical method, takes issue with the historicist view that truth is chimerical and time-bound. "The modern historian disposes of an immense apparatus supplying him with information which can be easily appropriated because it is superficial; he is therefore tempted to try to be wiser than the great men of the past whose work he studies. This is true particularly of his efforts to judge of their positions with respect to their predecessors." Strauss adds, "We repeat therefore that Machiavelli points to Xenophon more strongly than to any other thinker."[29] Anachronism aside,[30] Machiavelli, arguably, is the "modern historian" in question: Strauss has argued throughout his analysis that Machiavelli desired to be wiser than the classics, to find new ways of thinking about politics and the relation between morality and religion, on the one hand, and human action, on the other. Though failing to name names, Strauss does have in mind the scholarship on Machiavelli. As Mansfield notes, "it may well appear that Strauss's only fault in scholarly courtesy was an inability to remember names." According to Jackson, "Since Strauss intended above all to author a critique of Machiavelli, his brief treatment of the secondary literature does not perplex."[31] A further key reason for that "brief treatment" is that Strauss regards the scholarship as founded on (what he sees as) the dubious historicist assertion that the thought of any era is a reflection of its own era.[32]

Strauss continues with this contrast between Machiavelli with his predecessors: "He may be said to start from certain observations or suggestions made by Xenophon and to think them through while abandoning the whole of which they form a part."[33] The contrast here is about virtue and the nature of the state. Machiavelli speaks in a matter-of-fact fashion about relations between states, such as the struggle for supremacy; however, he does not also speak of ideals of what the state itself ought to be. Indeed, says Meinecke, Machiavelli gave the first formulation of the modern doctrine of *raison d'état*.[34] It would be a mistake, Strauss argues, to see in Machiavelli the origin of the theory of "the primacy of foreign policy." He forms a "case for imperialism," but "the principle" that underpins his advice to both princes and the leaders of republics, that they acquire territory, "applies equally to domestic policy; according to him the fundamental human fact is acquisitiveness or competition."[35] As Machiavelli puts the point in Chapter 3 of *The Prince*, "truly it is a very natural and ordinary thing to desire to acquire." In *Discourses* II 2 he says, "the end of the republic is to enervate and to weaken all other bodies so as to increase its own body."[36]

Strauss goes on, "We also cannot accept the assertion that he was the first to realize what some people call the narrowness of the traditional condemnation of tyranny." Aristotle and Machiavelli both wrote about how tyrants preserve their power, but "we see that Aristotle treats tyranny as a monstrosity whereas Machiavelli rather deals with tyranny as essential to the foundation of society itself. In this point, as well as in others of the same character, Machiavelli is closer to Plato than to Aristotle."[37] It is just, Plato explains, that parents rule over their children, the old over the young, masters over their slaves, the strong over the weak, and the wise over the unwise (*Laws* 690a–c). In a like manner, a tyrant rules over his subjects. A tyrant, in a short period, can alter from vice to virtue the habits of the people; within them he instills the practice of moral virtue; overall, then, his role is to help legislators organize the city (*Laws* 709d–710b, 711a, and 735d–e). Tyranny often is, Machiavelli explains in *Discourses* I 18 and 55, and III 26, essential to the founding of republics. In I 55 he equates tyranny with the just scope of kingship: "Where there is so much corrupt matter that the laws are not enough to check it, together with them greater force is needed to give order there—*a kingly hand* that *with absolute and excessive power* puts a check on the excessive ambition and corruption of the powerful."[38] Strauss, qualifying his above parallel between Plato and Machiavelli, notes that Machiavelli abandons the strict limits Plato places on the extent of tyrannical rule. Machiavelli "even argues for tyranny pure and simple. Yet what enables him to do so is not a more thoroughgoing or comprehensive analysis of political phenomena as such than that given by the classics but his destructive analysis of moral virtue."[39]

Strauss's effort here is to underscore what he regards as the innate blindness to morality, to a hierarchy of ends and of excellences, in Machiavelli's "excellent" man. Machiavelli rejects the classical view that tyranny, because it eschews virtue and the good life, is a perverted form of government. However, Strauss states, "Machiavelli's most emphatic attack on 'all writers' is directed, not against the traditional condemnation of tyranny but against the traditional contempt for the multitude."[40] Defending the people, Machiavelli opens *Discourses* I 58 thus: "That nothing is more vain and inconstant than the multitude so our Titus Livy, like all other historians, affirms." Elsewhere in the chapter he explains, against Livy's criticism of the fickle and vainglorious ways of the people, that "a prince unshackled from the laws will be more ungrateful, varying, and imprudent than a people."[41] In III 13 Machiavelli claims that in Rome's battles against the Volsci, "one sees that the virtue of the soldiers"— viz., the virtue of the people—"had given marvelous proofs of itself without a captain."[42] Livy, though, stresses the importance of a capable captain. At the beginning of III 15 Machiavelli notes, "When the Fidenates had rebelled and had killed the colony that the Romans had sent to Fidenae, to remedy this insult the Romans created four tribunes with consular power. They left one of them for the guarding of Rome and sent three against the Fidenates and the Veientes." The Roman forces were unable to respond in a timely fashion to an attack by the Veientes, for the three tribunes "were divided amongst themselves"; they quarreled about who would make the decisions in battle. I would add here that the Livian story (IV 31.3–4) says that the Roman people, their forces defeated due to discord among the tribunes, demanded the election of a dictator to rule Rome. Machiavelli omits the part of the Livian story that says the Roman people feared the tribunate would choose a consul as dictator; but he adds to the story the claim: "the virtue of the soldiers was the cause of [Rome] not receiving harm."[43] Machiavelli agrees, then, with Livy that dictatorial power be used to reorder republics; but, to account for the justness of that power, he explains against Livy that the people and not the nobles are the "repository" of "authority" and "morality."[44]

The Soullessness of Machiavelli's Moral-Political Teaching

One should not interpret Machiavelli's democratic remarks as meaning that he is *the* origin of the "democratic theory" that "Spinoza and Rousseau" passed on to following generations. One must not, Strauss then points out, emphasize his inclination to democracy but fail to consider the nature of that inclination: his support of the multitude, like his support of tyranny, advances "a comprehensive argument" about the proper basis of virtue. "Moral virtue, wished for by society and required by it," Strauss explains for Machiavelli, "is dependent on society and therefore subject to the primary needs of society. It does not consist in the proper order of the soul. It has no other source than the needs of society; it has no second and higher source in the needs of the mind."[45] Thus for Strauss, Machiavelli's notion of virtue is "soulless": "His silence about the soul is a perfect expression of the soulless character of his teaching: he is silent about the soul because he has forgotten about the soul."[46]

For Aristotle, "the soul" consists of "rational" and "irrational" parts. "In the rational part... resides wisdom, readiness of wit, philosophy, aptitude to learn, memory, and so on; but in the irrational those which are called the excellences—temperance, justice, courage, and such other states of character as are held to be praiseworthy." Because of the excellences, "we are called praiseworthy; but no one is praised for the excellences of the rational part. For no one is praised for being philosophical or for being wise, or generally on the ground of anything of that sort. Nor indeed is the irrational part praised, except in so far as it is capable of subserving or actually subserves the rational part."[47] Following Aristotle, McCoy notes that "[h]uman life... is characterized by the activity of a rational element. Man's proper good consists in the activity of his soul according to reason."[48] Aristotle identifies another twofold division in the soul: thought/desire, or thought/appetite—the division relates to both the goal and exercise of reason.[49] Proper movement stems from thoughts and thinking on excellence; in a person whose soul is well-ordered, movement accords with thoughts on excellence,[50] and desire and appetite accord with reason.[51] Machiavelli, though, would say that the excellent man must be moved not by thoughts and thinking on eternity and moral norms but only by a spiritedness in his thinking about the here and now.[52] In sum, by describing Machiavelli and his teaching as "soulless," Strauss is illustrating the scope of the former's rejection of the classics.

Machiavelli is silent about "the soul," but it would be a mistake to claim thus that he completely rejects the philosophic quest for knowledge. To Felix Gilbert, "Machiavelli was not a philosopher" because he declined "to outline a philosophical system."[53] Strauss states, "To avoid the error of denying the presence of philosophy in Machiavelli's thought, it suffices to remember what he indicates regarding the relation between the superiority of 'the most excellent man' to fate and that man's knowledge of 'the world.'"[54] Illustrating that indication, Strauss instructs in an endnote, "Cf. also the strange 'dependence' of the *Castruccio* on Diogenes Laertius (cf. pages 224–225 above)."[55] By these instructions, Strauss reminds the reader that, although in this work Machiavelli speaks of philosophy, he derives its concluding sayings not from Plato and Aristotle (to each of whom he refers once only in both *The Prince* and the *Discourses*) but from Diogenes Laertius. In the sayings, Machiavelli indicates the necessity for founders to value artful conduct over prudence and action over contemplation; the indication follows from the stated aim of the *Castruccio*, namely, that the work will discuss the "very great things" that men of "humble and obscure" birth have undertaken because, and even in spite, of the agitations of Fortuna.[56]

Strauss continues, "One is entitled to say that philosophy and its status is obfuscated not only in Machiavelli's teaching but in his thought as well."[57] The point here is that Machiavelli does not dwell upon the classical precept that moral virtue is needful for excellence and the founding of society. He eschews the precept, though he recognizes it; he emulates but radically changes it in his own conception of the virtuous mean, that is, of liberty as a mean between tyranny and license. The change is radical because Machiavelli, Strauss goes on, "denies that there is an order of the soul, and therefore a hierarchy of ways of life or of goods." He bases his notion of virtue on temporal and not "supra-political" aspects of human existence. His new modes and orders obfuscate the classical meaning of philosophy as quest for knowledge of the good life. He was not voicing, however, any ideas unknown to the classics. Alluding to Heidegger's answer to the question of Being, of his narrowing of the horizon of all thought, from nature to historicity, Strauss states, "A stupendous contraction of the horizon appears to Machiavelli and his successors as a wondrous enlargement of the horizon."[58]

Machiavelli vs. the Classics

Classical political philosophy, however, presents a vision of the city in which the common people contract the horizon of the city, of what is good about political life and the desire to be free, to a core of self-interest. The classics, Strauss continues in his concluding thoughts on Machiavelli's teaching, regarded the city as closed to philosophy, in the sense that the common people—"the *demos*"—is unwilling to act always in line with ideals of what is good, just, and virtuous. To the *demos*, the end of the city is its practical, everyday well-being; but to philosophers, a "good citizen" is always mindful "of man's highest perfection." The "ends," then, of the *demos* and of the philosophers "differ radically." That "gulf" between ends, Strauss adds, "can be bridged only by a noble rhetoric," a rhetoric that philosophers themselves are "incapable of supplying." Philosophers "sketch" the "outlines" of philosophy but leave its implementation "to orators or poets."[59] Strauss then explains in an endnote, and referring to the *Phaedrus* and the *Gorgias*, that Socrates criticizes orators for their being interested not in enlightenment but only in the crafty use of rhetoric.[60] A ruler with a love of learning, the philosopher-king, says Socrates, leads the people into the upper world of enlightenment from the cave of ignorance, wherein the people are trapped by the riddles of poets and their lies that the gods do not care for humankind.[61]

Machiavelli forever changed the meaning of philosophy, precisely because he forever changed the basis and the end of philosophy. He regards the good life as impractical, as an ideal based on how men ought to be, not how they actually are; and thus the good life is impossible. Whereas to the classics the implementation of the best regime depends upon chance, in Machiavelli's "new notion of philosophy," as Strauss puts it, rare men of virtue base society on their conquests of chance and necessity; only the excellent men of virtue can make corrupt men good and keep them that way. To enact his "new philosophy," Machiavelli had to persuade his readers of the truth of his views as compared to the falsity of the classics. "Yet before that grand revolt or emancipation can get under way," Strauss points out, "the hold which the old modes and orders have over the minds of almost all men must be broken." His "new philosophy" is based on "propaganda," which is necessary "to guarantee the coincidence of philosophy and political power. Philosophy is to fulfill the function of both philosophy and religion."[62]

For Strauss, Machiavelli, as the author of new modes and orders, as the originator of modernity, is both a political thinker on the one hand, and akin to a doctrinaire and a propagandist on the other.[63] However, Garrett Mattingly, following Rousseau, who saw *The Prince* as "the book of republicans," argues that satire—not the teaching—of pernicious doctrines is the core of the book.[64] Machiavelli's "real talent," says Lev Kamenev, "is that of the political publicist, writing on urgent contemporary issues, or on past events as recorded by historians of the ancient world."[65] *The Prince*, according to Antonio Gramsci, "is a 'living' book, in which political ideology and political science are fused in the dramatic form of a 'myth.' "[66] The above commentators, those who examine the extent of his concern with religion and theology,[67] and those who situate him in a tradition of civic republicanism[68] recognize his newness, but conceive of it in varying or different ways.[69]

Given Strauss's argument that Machiavelli taught a new political science, it is useful to discuss briefly how political philosophy relates to political science in Strauss's understanding. For the classics, philosophy is the quest for knowledge of the whole and political philosophy is a quest for knowledge of the best regime.[70] With one foot in the ancient, classical world, Machiavelli addressed, even if only to take issue with it, the realm of political philosophy that was situated in the whole and that examined questions of politics and morality in the light of their place in the whole. The subject matter of philosophy is knowledge, or rather the *quest* for knowledge, of the whole—of God and of Nature, of the heavens and the earth, and of plant, animal, and human life. In turn, the political philosopher deals with human life, the best regime, and questions of good and bad.[71] With his other foot planted in the realm of effectual truth, Machiavelli eschewed normative political ideas. His approach to solving problems of moral and intellectual virtue is to relegate traditional reflections on virtue—on the very questions, what is virtue? how should one live?—to the level of ineffectual truth. As a political thinker attached to a specific quest for new modes and orders, as distinct from quest for knowledge of truth qua the Good, he stood in a particular relation to political philosophy: against his classical predecessors he linked the subject matter of the best regime to an inquiry into what people do, what they actually are, rather than what they ought to do. In his way, Machiavelli anticipated modern political science, its empirical spirit, and its eschewal of normative philosophy. Yet, the merit of his thought compared to modern political science, for Strauss, is *reflection* on the regime of the city, on its morality and politics and the totality within which they are grounded and given form and substance.[72] As Strauss said in "An Epilogue": "Only a great fool would call the new political science diabolic: it has no attributes peculiar to fallen angels. It is not even Machiavellian, for Machiavelli's teaching was graceful, subtle, and colorful. Nor is it Neronian. Nevertheless one may say of it that it fiddles while Rome burns. It is excused by two facts: it does not know that it fiddles, and it does not know that Rome burns."[73]

Strauss opens the final paragraph to his critical study of Machiavelli's teaching by observing, "The necessity which spurred on Machiavelli and his great successors spent itself some time ago." That "necessity" was the "effort" to "escape imitating nature." The effort "was meant to be reasonable." Yet the modern project has "become ever more shallow." Unlike "many present day conservatives" (Strauss does not name names), the classics "knew that one cannot be distrustful of political or social change without being distrustful of technological change." Although wary about the usage and development of inventions, the classics, Strauss explains, made two exceptions: to foster complete change in a tyranny (a "manifestly desirable" goal), and to enable the good city to defend itself.[74] "[N]ot only should cities have walls," says Aristotle, "but care should be taken to make them ornamental, as well as useful for warlike purposes, and adapted to resist modern inventions."[75]

The classics, Strauss continues, thus acknowledged that "the good city has to take its bearings by the practice of bad cities or that the bad impose their law on the good. Only in this point does Machiavelli's contention that the good cannot be good because there are so many bad ones prove to possess a foundation."[76] How firm is that "foundation"? Not at all, says McCoy of modern thought in general; it lacks, he says, the "intellectual center" that would make it "capable of knowing the good proper and natural to man."[77] Based on "a soulless psychology and a lifeless biology," modern scientific thought, Maritain points out, rejects "the primary value of transcendental being." According to Maritain, "The grand error of such science has been the desire to protect itself against the intelligence; in the endeavour to keep it out it has risked dying of asphyxia." By "the intelligence," Maritain meant the awareness of intellectual and moral virtues.[78] Strauss also voices concern with the purpose of science, when he qualifies his above "point" about "the good city." He states, "One could say however that it is not inventions as such but the use of science for such inventions which renders impossible the good city in the classical sense. From the point of view of the classics, such use of science is excluded by the nature of science as a theoretical pursuit."[79] In brief, the purpose of science is to gain and to test the veracity of knowledge about the natural processes in the world; the purpose of science is not rampant development of technology.[80] The problem of science, then, necessarily relates to the desire for autonomy.[81] On the one hand, the classics and modern science both see the search for autonomy as preeminent in human life. On the other hand, they disagree about the scope of autonomy—the classics emphasize the whole, transtemporal order of nature, whereas modern science claims the conquest of nature and emphasizes the temporal basis of all knowledge.[82]

"Besides," Strauss goes on, "the opinion that there occur periodic cataclysms in fact took care of any apprehension regarding an excessive development of technology." Natural disasters are acts of "beneficence" that nature intends to redound to the benefit of society. Strauss adds, "Machiavelli himself expresses this opinion of the natural cataclysms."[83] In *Discourses* II 5 he explains that heaven purges "the human race ... either through plague or through famine or through an inundation of waters." That no memory exists of such calamities in an ancient past is "because those who are saved are all mountain men and coarse."[84] In the words of Aristotle, "the primaeval inhabitants, whether they were born of the earth or were the survivors of some destruction, may be supposed to have been no better than ordinary or even foolish people among ourselves."[85]

Of Strauss's discussion about natural disasters, Schall notes that the last endnote in his critical study "cited, among others, St. Thomas, or at least a section of a book attributed to St. Thomas, namely, to Lectio IX of book 7 of the *Commentary on the Politics*.... It is not exactly clear why Strauss referred to this *Commentary* in this context. The text deals with the proper physical location and the proper arrangement, including the defenses, of parts of a city. This may have been the only point."[86] By citing Aquinas Strauss, I would suggest, may also have been recalling his thesis that Machiavelli rejected both Christianity and the classics. The corollary of the thesis is that meditation on the possibility of divine revelation should accompany the return to the classics. The return is indispensable for the quest for knowledge of the good life in the modern era. Yet—and this is the point Strauss may have been making— a return to the classics perhaps by itself does not suffice to, and a *modern philosophy* unmindful of the highest good cannot, ensure rectitude in human action and save civilization from Machiavellianism.[87]

Indeed, Strauss concludes, having cited *Discourses* II 5, "It would seem that the notion of the beneficence of nature or of the primacy of the Good must be restored by being rethought through a return to the fundamental experiences from which it is derived. For while 'philosophy must beware of wishing to be edifying,' it is of necessity edifying."[88] Peterman notes that those sentences change "Hegel's statement on philosophy—'for while "philosophy must beware of wishing to be edifying," it is of necessity edifying'—to the end of supporting the seeming need to 'return to the fundamental experiences' that might restore the notion of the 'primacy of the good.' "[89] In stating thus that the end of philosophy (qua philosophy) is the search for truth—the truth of all things, the ultimate basis of virtue—whereas modern philosophy eschews the theoretical character of philosophy in favor of human, purely practical concerns, Strauss echoed his statement at the end of the introduction, that his critical study would "contribute towards the recovery of the permanent problems."[90]

Strauss achieved his aim by reconnecting knowledge of political things with classical moral virtue. Yet, though he sided with the classics against Machiavelli's amoral republican virtue, he was open to the challenge of revelation. In siding with the classics against Machiavelli's insistence that morality and politics not be directed toward the false and unsalutary quest for knowledge of the good life, Strauss recognized the challenge of the biblical way of life lived in accordance with the highest good.

Conclusion

Through a careful examination of Strauss's idea of history, his conception of the revelation-reason question, and his critical study of Machiavelli's teaching, I have endeavored to explicate Strauss's attentive and wide-ranging engagement with the fundamental alternatives, revelation and reason, with particular emphasis upon the exegetic, narrative, and thematic analysis of Strauss's critical study.

To understand the crux of the matter at hand, one must pay, as Strauss would say, attention to the surface of the matter. The surface of Strauss's idea of history adopts an idea of what history is and how and why one must study it. Against historicism, Strauss upheld the endless challenge of philosophy: "Philosophy in the strict and classical sense is quest for the eternal order or for the eternal cause or causes of all things. It presupposes then that there is an eternal and unchangeable order within which History takes place and which is not in any way affected by History."[1] Not the play of events within the ambit of History but the action of history toward eternity constitutes the meaning of history. Yet, historicism insists that not eternity but History is the horizon of all that is and can be. That historicism so views the sweep of history has, says Strauss, made paramount the return to the classics, to the careful study of Aristotle, Plato, Socrates, Thucydides, and Xenophon; for Strauss, that study counters "the crisis of our time," a crisis of doubt, of atheistic and nihilistic uncertainty about life and whether it has ultimate meaning.

Strauss was himself a political philosopher; but he was open to the challenge that revelation, not philosophy, conveys the right way of life. That openness seems to be a paradox, for he argued that the alternatives are immiscible. Probing his use of such terms as "law," "nature," and "theology" shows that he regards the Bible and Greek philosophy as having a shared understanding of the scope of divine law and justice, but not of the basis of how to realize law and justice. There cannot be, Strauss argued, a synthesis of the life of obedience to God's Law and the life devoted to free philosophic quest for truth. Yet, he also argued, both approaches stress the importance of morality and thereby provide a common front against the morass of modernity. Hence, his interest in matters biblical, religious, and Jewish was an essential part of his being a scholar of the history of political thought; the interest was not a scholarly predilection designed to conceal an atheistic worldview. As Deutsch and Nicgorski explain, "Strauss as a *political* philosopher and a Jew was concerned with both ways of life: that of reason and that of faith."[2]

Concern with both revelation and reason is at the core of Strauss's critical study of Machiavelli's teaching. Strauss perceived in Machiavelli's teaching on religion the thesis that Christianity has made the world weak—on moral, military, and political levels. No mere anticlericalist, Machiavelli rejected the Christian focus on the hereafter; he argued that injunctions against cruel and evil acts prevent priests from timely responses to the exigencies of the here and now. Thus, he regarded political authority (the rule of princes) as superior to religious authority (the rule of priests).

Machiavelli's critique of biblical theology juxtaposed the Bible's proclamation of obedience to God's Law as paramount with Machiavelli's conviction that observance of one's own worldly gain is the one thing needful for life. Reasoning that no act of providence is unaccompanied by extreme hardship, he sought to replace providential order with human modes and orders that can overcome Fortuna and mundane chance. Machiavelli apparently followed the lead of Averroës, who followed Aristotle, in maintaining that the Prime Mover, God, set the eternal matter of the world in motion. Closely related to Machiavelli's rejection of creation *ex nihilo* is his claim that revealed evidential phenomena such as miracles are beyond the bounds of human experience. According to Strauss, "We would go too far were we to assert that Machiavelli has never heard the Call nor sensed the Presence, for we would contradict his remarks referring to the conscience. But he certainly refuses to heed experiences of this kind."[3]

By indicating that Machiavelli likely affirmed the eternality of the world, Strauss had placed him in the company of Aristotle. However, Strauss then surveyed "Machiavelli's doctrine regarding God and his attributes" to identify "more clearly the difference between Machiavelli and Aristotle."[4] In examining that survey, we found that Machiavelli replaced God as the Supreme Being with Fortuna, an always fickle but occasionally malignant entity. In addition, he in turn replaced Fortuna with mundane chance as the governing principle in nature, the world, and human affairs; and by chance he meant truly random accidents. Thus Machiavelli rejected the Aristotelian notion of "a ruling Mind."[5] Machiavelli's blunt view of the importance of religion as a tool of social control underscores his irreligiousness.

That Machiavelli regarded religion as a tool and approached religion, biblical and pagan, from a temporal perspective does not completely account, however, for what Strauss regarded as the problem on the surface of things in Machiavelli. If Strauss's own position on the revelation-reason question is a guide to the matter, it seems that Strauss identified the horizon of that surface as the one thing necessary for life: autonomy versus obedience to God. Indeed, that Machiavelli rejected the otherworldly character of biblical religion suggests that he would support a this-worldly or secularized faith—a faith that emphasizes human autonomy as the path to virtue in the here and now. Yet, the implication of that formulation of his modernity is to place Machiavelli in the company of Plato. Strauss points out in "The Three Waves of Modernity," "This is exactly what Plato claims to do in his *Republic*: to bring about the cessation of all evil on earth by purely human means. And surely Plato cannot be said to have secularized biblical faith."[6] Arguably, then, the problem on the surface of things in Machiavelli is not whether autonomy or obedience to God is necessary for life, but instead concerns the normative underpinnings required for the quest for autonomy. In his effort to seek "new modes and orders," he spoke of taking "a path as yet untrodden by anyone,"[7] and stated, "It has appeared to me more fitting to go directly to the effectual truth of the thing than to the imagination of it."[8]

Illuminating the normative direction of that "path," Strauss perceived an anti-teleotheological orientation in Machiavelli's rejection of both biblical and classical morality.[9] Although Strauss did not explicitly define the orientation as such, he clearly did offer to define what was "new" or distinctive about Machiavelli's new modes and orders. "Machiavelli favored a cosmology which is in accordance with his analysis of morality. His analysis of morality will prove to be incompatible with a teleological cosmology."[10] Elsewhere Strauss employed a range of terms analogous to "teleological cosmology." In chapter 3 of *Thoughts on Machiavelli*, where he examined the Florentine's rejection in the *Discourses* of biblical authority, Strauss spoke of "the comprehensive theo-cosmological scheme implied in the principle of authority."[11] In "What Is Political Philosophy?" Strauss wrote, "The narrowing of the horizon which Machiavelli was the first to effect, was caused, or at least facilitated, by anti-theological ire—a passion which we can understand but of which we cannot approve."[12] The same "passion," Strauss said in his essay on Marsilius of Padua, inspired Machiavelli's revolt against "the classical tradition."[13] Clearly, then, Strauss regarded Machiavelli as neither Christian nor pagan, his cosmology as anti-teleotheological at its very basis, even if, as McAllister claims, he "never labeled Machiavelli's religious beliefs."[14]

Machiavelli amplified his temporal conception of the ends of human action in his moral-political teaching. In that teaching, as Strauss argues, "Machiavelli challenges not only the religious teaching but the whole philosophic tradition as well."[15] Strauss also perceived, according to Green, that "with all his radicalism Machiavelli still wanted to actualize what the classics merely envisaged. He still moved in the sphere of human nature as delineated by the classics, even if he reached different conclusions about what to do with it."[16] Indeed, the classical perception of the base tendency attendant to human nature did not attenuate its emphasis upon the desirability of the good life and the best regime. Machiavelli, however, concluded from his dim view of human nature that good governance, be it in the form of princely rule or republican rule, must seek a singularly practical, temporal goal: controlling the many and the great alike, preventing them from doing harm to the common good.

A dramatic instance of contrast between the classical and Machiavellian themes of human nature and human action is found in Machiavelli's teaching on the moral mean. Aristotle maintained that virtue is the mean between the two extremes of excess and deficiency; some actions, such as murder and theft, do not admit of a mean. Machiavelli spoke of a mean between virtue and vice that varies in accordance with the times; he did not declaim the badness of murder and theft. To Aristotle, the good accords with the eternal order of nature; and man has free will in the sense that he can choose good or bad and choose to act to the highest good, not in the sense that he can choose his own ends. To Machiavelli, freedom to choose one's own ends, irrespective of a highest or a supreme good, is free will. Chance, nature, and necessity limit the range of free will; but the excellent man is capable of freely acting in the face of great odds. The excellent man supplants the necessity that is rooted in fear of death with a necessity that is rooted in his desire for personal benefit and glory; that capacity to overcome, and rule over, chance, nature, and necessity shows his virtue.

We also witnessed Machiavelli's departure from the classical notion of the best regime. Like the classics, he spoke in less than flattering terms about human nature—people are guided by concern for self-interest, not the good of society as a whole; thus, laws and education are needed to make people good. Nevertheless, the classics maintained that the common good and other moral considerations of how one ought to live should guide the individual and society. Machiavelli, though, abandoning classical morality, claimed that the major end of civil society is to ensure that citizens remain free from foreign domination. The protection of the fatherland from external *and* internal threats defines the common good; but for Plato and Aristotle, moral virtue defines the common good.

Machiavelli argued that the common good is the end only of republics, for princes and tyrants are interested primarily in their private good. He attested to the superiority of republican rule compared to the rule of princes and tyrants, for he upheld the constancy of the many against the tendency in the great towards avarice and overweening self-esteem. However, he questioned the efficacy not only of the classical common good but also his own notion of the common good as inspiration for political virtue; moreover, his republican sympathies did not prevent him from advising tyrants about the preservation of their rule. He maintained that the excellent man, who is rare in body and spirit, is essential to the renewal of existing—or to the creation of new— modes and orders. Human nature being what it is, disposed to evil rather than to the Good, rulers must use means of persuasion more cruel than kind to habituate citizens to act in accordance with the good of society as a whole.

Strauss ultimately concluded that Machiavelli's moral-political teaching was not so much new as it was a restriction of the scope of virtue from what ought to be to what is. His legacy to the history of political philosophy is the basic change he initiated in the meaning of philosophy. Whereas Plato spoke of converting the tyrant from a life devoted to power to a life devoted to philosophy or philosophy itself, Machiavelli spoke of converting the tyrant from badness to goodness by appealing to his desire for glory; badness consists not of moral shortcomings but of failing to foresee dangers to the fatherland. However, Machiavelli never considered the ruler who controls chance, rather than being subject to it, as the truly excellent man. Machiavelli, perhaps in an autobiographical reflection, viewed the truly excellent man as the teacher and discoverer of new modes and orders.

Throughout his critical study, then, Strauss elaborated his stated inclination to the "old-fashioned and simple verdict" that Machiavelli was "evil" and his "teaching immoral and irreligious."[17] In grappling with Machiavelli's opposition to biblical religion and to classical political philosophy, Strauss affirmed the validity and authority of both revelation and reason; but he did not aim to give a manifestly practical solution to Machiavelli's abandonment of these alternatives. "The scope and meaning of philosophy are diminished," Gourevitch notes, "its aspirations are lowered, once it confines itself primarily to problems that admit of solutions. By taking its bearings by how men live rather than by how they ought to live, it forfeits every chance of being the city's ruler and becomes, instead, its hostage."[18]

While Strauss listened attentively to the call of Athens, he was open to Jerusalem, for he recognized the acuteness of biblical religion as a way of thinking about moral principles for human action. As Mitchell notes, "Strauss honors Jerusalem but loves Athens."[19] In his own way, Strauss issued a rejoinder to Machiavelli's antipathy to both Athens and Jerusalem. Whereas Machiavelli argued that self-deception underpins belief in God, Strauss recognized the credibility of revelation. Against Machiavelli's replacement of God with Fortuna and of Fortuna with random, nonteleological chance, Strauss upheld the possibility of divine revelation. Strauss's reply, then, to a Machiavellian modernity was to emphasize what classical and biblical thought have in common, as well as how they differ.

Strauss and Machiavelli both aimed to convert the young to philosophy, though they differed fundamentally over what philosophy is. Machiavelli sought to replace classical moral norms with what he saw as true norms; that is, norms based on action in the here and now and on contemplation of "effectual truth." Strauss also emphasized the importance of action, but he sought to re-anchor philosophy in the true, natural horizon of the permanent problems. By so answering Machiavelli, Strauss articulated a theological-political thesis about a return to classical and biblical teachings on the good life and the good society. The paradox of the critical study is that Machiavelli, teacher of "evil," "immoral," and "irreligious" doctrines, aided Strauss in grappling with the revelation-reason question.

Appendix

On the Surface of *Thoughts on Machiavelli,* chapter 4:
An Outline of Strauss's Critical Study of Machiavelli's Teaching

¶¶1–43: Part I: Machiavelli's teaching on religion

  ¶¶1–26: Section One: Machiavelli's critique of Christianity and Biblical religion

    ¶1: Introduction

    ¶2: Strauss states his thesis for part I: Machiavelli is neither Christian nor pagan

    ¶¶3–14: Machiavelli's judgment regarding the weakness(es) of Christianity

      ¶¶4–6 respectively, Strauss examines the three explicit statements in the *Discourses* on the core beliefs of Christianity—I pr., II 2, III 1

    ¶¶15–30: Machiavelli's reflections on biblical/Christian theology

      ¶15: conscience

      ¶¶16–19: divine providence

        ¶¶17, 19: providence as mentioned in the *Florentine Histories* and the *Exhortation to Penitence,* respectively

      ¶¶20–23: creation and miracles

      ¶¶24–26: the weakness of biblical religion and strength of pagan religion

¶¶27–28: divine attributes: God, heaven, and Fortuna

¶¶29–30: prophecy

¶¶27–43: Section Two: Machiavelli's judgments on cosmology and religion in general

¶¶27–37: Machiavelli's cosmological reflections; the theo-cosmological subject matter of both 27–28 and 29–30 bridges sections one and two

¶31: Fortuna

¶¶32–33: the relation between Fortuna and nature

¶34: the power of chance and accidents

¶¶35–37: order in the world: God, Fortuna, or mundane chance?

¶37: order in the world, as mentioned in the *Castruccio*

¶¶38–42: the utility of religion

¶43: Strauss defends the length of his analysis of Machiavelli's teaching on religion

¶44: Bridging paragraph between Parts I and II

¶¶45–87: Part II: Machiavelli's moral-political teaching

¶¶45: Introduction

¶¶46–80: the aspects of Machiavelli's moral-political teaching

¶¶46–51: virtue and goodness

¶¶52–60: free will, necessity, and chance

¶¶61–68: the common good and selfishness

¶¶69–75: forms of government: republics, principalities, and tyrannies

¶¶76–80: human nature, the common good, and the highest good

¶79: human nature, the common good, and the highest good in *La Mandragola*

¶¶81–87: Strauss's concluding thoughts on Machiavelli's moral-political teaching: Machiavelli's legacy to the history of political philosophy

Notes

Introduction

1. David Bolotin, "Leo Strauss and Classical Political Philosophy," *Interpretation* 22, no. 1 (Fall 1994): 130 (original emphasis); Allan Bloom, "Leo Strauss: September 20, 1899–October 18, 1973," *Political Theory* 2, no. 4 (November 1974): 376.

2. WWRJ, 312.

3. OIG, 359. On the above "inkling," see also POR, 265, 289–90; cf. PIH, esp. 246–47, 257. For Strauss's view of himself a scholar, see also FMM, 285, and his semi-autobiographical reflections, GA, P*HPW*, P*SCR*, and UP.

4. JA, 149.

5. Bloom divides Strauss's corpus into three periods: early, middle, and later. The first period is characterized by works on Judaism and Zionism; the second, "by his discovery of esoteric writing"; and the third, "by a complete abandonment of the form as well as the content of modern scholarship." The third period begins with *Thoughts on Machiavelli*. Bloom, "Leo Strauss," 379–87.

6. On this point, see Michael P. Jackson, "Leo Strauss's Teaching: A Study of *Thoughts on Machiavelli*" (Ph.D. diss., Georgetown University, 1985), 245–49. For a guide to the structure of *TM*, ch. 4, see below, appendix. The appendix and the section headings in chs. 3 to 7 draw upon Jackson, "Leo Strauss's Teaching," 204–27, 295.

7. Susan Orr, *Jerusalem and Athens: Reason and Revelation in the Work of Leo Strauss* (Lanham, Md.: Rowman and Littlefield, 1995), 7.

8. See, e.g., Thomas L. Pangle, Editor's introduction to *RCPR*, esp. vii; Gregory Bruce Smith, "Who Was Leo Strauss?" *American Scholar* 66, no. 1 (Winter 1997):

95–104; G. B. Smith, "Leo Strauss and the Straussians: An Anti-democratic Cult?" *PS, Political Science and Politics* 30, no. 2 (June 1997): 180–89. The best or most informative recent accounts about the nature and influence of Strauss's work can be found in Nasser Behnegar, *Leo Strauss, Max Weber, and the Scientific Study of Politics* (Chicago: University of Chicago Press, 2003); Kenneth L. Deutsch and John A. Murley, eds., *Leo Strauss, the Straussians, and the American Regime* (Lanham, Md.: Rowman and Littlefield, 1999); Kenneth L. Deutsch and Walter Nicgorski, eds., *Leo Strauss: Political Philosopher and Jewish Thinker* (Lanham, Md.: Rowman and Littlefield, 1994); Kenneth Hart Green, *Jew and Philosopher: The Return to Maimonides in the Jewish Thought of Leo Strauss* (Albany: State University of New York Press, 1993); K. H. Green, "Editor's Introduction: Leo Strauss as a Modern Jewish Thinker," in *JP*, 1–84; David Novak, ed., *Leo Strauss and Judaism: Jerusalem and Athens Critically Revisited* (Lanham, Md.: Rowman and Littlefield, 1996); Orr, *Jerusalem and Athens*; Michael Zank, "Part I: Introduction," in *LSEW*, 3–49.

9. Shadia B. Drury, "Leo Strauss and the Grand Inquisitor," *Free Inquiry Magazine* 24, no. 4 (June–July 2004), http://www.secularhumanism.org/library/fi/drury_24_4.htm (accessed 18 June 2005). See also, e.g., Seymour M. Hersh, "Selective Intelligence: Donald Rumsfeld Has His Own Special Sources; Are They Reliable?" *New Yorker*, 12 May 2003, 44, 48–49; Laura Rozen, "Con Tract: The Theory Behind Neocon Self-Deception," *Washington Monthly*, October 2003, 11–13; Earl Shorris, "Ignoble Liars: Leo Strauss, George Bush, and the Philosophy of Mass Deception," *Harper's Magazine*, June 2004, 65–71; Mark Lewis Taylor, "Liberation, Neocons, and the Christian Right: Options for Pro-Active Christian Witness in Post-9/11," *Constellation*, Fall 2003, 8–17, http://www.tcpc.org/resources/constellation/fall_03/taylor.pdf (accessed 4 July 2005). Cf. Mark Blitz, "Leo Strauss, the Straussians, and American Foreign Policy," *openDemocracy*, 14 November 2003, 1–4, http://www.opendemocracy.net/content/articles/PDF/1577.pdf (accessed 4 July 2005); Brian Danoff, "Leo Strauss, George W. Bush, and the Problem of Regime Change," *Social Policy* 34, nos. 2–3 (Winter 2003–Spring 2004): 35–40; Joshua Muravchik, "The Neoconservative Cabal," *Commentary* 116, no. 2 (September 2003): 26–33; Peter Singer, *The President of Good and Evil: Taking George W. Bush Seriously* (London: Granta, 2004), 220–24; Thomas G. West, "Leo Strauss and American Foreign Policy: Is There a Neoconservative Connection?" *Claremont Review of Books*, Summer 2004, http://www.claremont.org/writings/crb/summer2004/west. html?FORMAT=print (accessed 4 July 2005).

10. Shadia B. Drury, *Leo Strauss and the American Right* (New York: St. Martin's Press, 1997), xi. Cf. John P. East, "Leo Strauss and American Conservatism," *Modern Age* 21, no. 1 (Winter 1977): 2–3.

11. On that "point," see also Gregory Bruce Smith, "Athens and Washington: Leo Strauss and the American Regime," in Deutsch and Murley, *American Regime*, 105, 124n5.

12. PGS, 434. See also Harvey C. Mansfield, *The Spirit of Liberalism* (Cambridge, Mass.: Harvard University Press, 1978). Mansfield opens his book by stating that it "has been written in defense of liberalism by a friend of liberalism," in response to "the failure of liberals to defend themselves" (vii).

13. *NRH*, 6. For related questions or misgivings about modernity, see, e.g., Harry V. Jaffa, *Thomism and Aristotelianism: A Study of the Commentary by Thomas Aquinas on*

the Nicomachean Ethics (Chicago: University of Chicago Press, 1952; Westport, Conn.: Greenwood Press, 1979), 1–4, 12–13, 18; Jaffa, *Equality and Liberty: Theory and Practice in American Politics* (New York: Oxford University Press, 1965), 13–17, 30, 175–79, 194–96.

14. Peter Emberley and Barry Cooper, introduction to *Faith and Political Philosophy: The Correspondence Between Leo Strauss and Eric Voegelin, 1934–1964*, ed. and trans. Peter Emberley and Barry Cooper (University Park: Pennsylvania State University Press, 1993), xv *n*2. For Peterman, Burnyeat's review essay of Strauss's *Studies in Platonic Political Philosophy* is a "splenetic attack." See M. F. Burnyeat, "Sphinx Without a Secret," *New York Review of Books*, 30 May 1985, 30–36; Larry Peterman, "Approaching Leo Strauss: Some Comments on 'Thoughts on Machiavelli,' " *Political Science Reviewer* 16 (Fall 1986): 318.

15. Shadia B. Drury, *The Political Ideas of Leo Strauss* (New York: St. Martin's Press, 1988). See also Drury, "The Esoteric Philosophy of Leo Strauss," *Political Theory* 13, no. 3 (August 1985): 331–35. Cf. James M. Rhodes, *Eros, Wisdom, and Silence: Plato's Erotic Dialogues* (Columbia: University of Missouri Press, 2003), 85–89.

16. Laurence Lampert, *Leo Strauss and Nietzsche* (Chicago: University of Chicago Press, 1996), 132–33n5.

17. Stephen D. Holmes, *The Anatomy of Antiliberalism* (Cambridge, Mass.: Harvard University Press, 1989), xi, 5. Cf. Ronald J. Terchek, "Locating Leo Strauss in the Liberal-Communitarian Debate," in Deutsch and Murley, *American Regime*, 143–44, 148–50, 152; cf. also Peter Berkowitz, *Virtue and the Making of Modern Liberalism* (Princeton, N.J.: Princeton University Press, 1999), xi–xv, 15–24, 32–34, 170–75; Ronald Lora, *Conservative Minds in America* (Chicago: Rand McNally, 1971; Westport, Conn.: Greenwood Press, 1976), 3–8, 175–78, 191–94.

18. Francis W. Coker, "Some Present-Day Critics of Liberalism," *American Political Science Review* 47, no. 1 (March 1953): 12.

19. Coker, "Critics of Liberalism," 25.

20. Thomas A. Spragens, Jr., review of *The Anatomy of Antiliberalism*, by Stephen Holmes, *Journal of Politics* 57, no. 4 (November 1995): 1200 (I have changed "doesn't" to "does not").

21. Peter Berkowitz, "Liberal Zealotry," review of *The Anatomy of Antiliberalism*, by Stephen Holmes, *Yale Law Journal* 103, no. 5 (March 1994): 1375. I would add that nowhere in that endnote, *Anatomy of Antiliberalism*, 281–84n6, does Holmes refer to any work by Strauss. On the above observations about Strauss on liberalism, see also, e.g., Nasser Behnegar, "The Liberal Politics of Leo Strauss," in *Political Philosophy and the Human Soul: Essays in Memory of Allan Bloom*, ed. Michael Palmer and Thomas L. Pangle (Lanham, Md.: Rowman and Littlefield, 1995), 251–67; Berkowitz, *Modern Liberalism*, 17, 20–22; Wilfred M. McClay, "The Party of Limits," review of *Revolt Against Modernity*, by Ted V. McAllister, *Reviews in American History* 25, no. 1 (March 1997): 97–98; Terchek, "Liberal-Communitarian Debate," 143–56.

22. POR, 257. Here Strauss adds: "No one claims that the faith in America and the hope for America is based on explicit divine premises." Elsewhere, he says that America "was founded in explicit opposition to Machiavellian principles" (*TM*, 13).

23. See also *OT*, 183–85, 191–94. RSW, 155 (col. 1): "Scholarship requires indeed detachment, but detachment is not easily won and easily preserved—scholarship

requires attachment to detachment. Yet the attachment to detachment necessarily leads to attachment to the indispensable conditions of detachment and therewith also to firm rejections."

24. See the works by Drury cited above. See also Fred Dallmayr, "Leo Strauss Peregrinus," *Social Research* 61, no. 4 (Winter 1994): 879, 893–94; George Kateb, "The Questionable Influence of Arendt (and Strauss)," in *Hannah Arendt and Leo Strauss: German Émigrés and American Political Thought After World War II*, ed. Peter Graf Kielmansegg, Horst Mewes, and Elisabeth Glaser-Schmidt (Washington, D.C.: German Historical Institute; Cambridge: Cambridge University Press, 1995), 29, 38–43; Richard Rorty, "Straussianism, Democracy, and Allan Bloom, I: That Old-Time Philosophy," *New Republic*, 4 April 1988, 28–33; Stanley Rothman, "The Revival of Classical Political Philosophy: A Critique," *American Political Science Review* 56, no. 2 (March 1962): 341–52; John H. Schaar and Sheldon S. Wolin, "A Critique," review of *Essays on the Scientific Study of Politics*, ed. Herbert J. Storing, *American Political Science Review* 57, no. 1 (March 1963): 125–50; David Spitz, "Freedom, Virtue, and the New Scholasticism: The Supreme Court as Philosopher-Kings," *Commentary* 28, no. 10 (October 1959): 313–21; Spitz, *The Real World of Liberalism* (Chicago: University of Chicago Press, 1982), ch. 10, esp. 202–3, 210–11.

25. Gary D. Glenn, "Speculations on Strauss' Political Intentions Suggested by *On Tyranny*," *History of European Ideas* 19, nos. 1–3 (1994): 175.

26. Devigne's *Recasting Conservatism* is "neither defensively partisan nor angrily recriminatory," says Steven B. Smith (review of *Recasting Conservatism*, by Robert Devigne, *American Political Science Review* 88, no. 4 [December 1994]: 972). McAllister's *Revolt Against Modernity* "is nonpartisan, fair, and perceptive," says Steven R. McCarl (review of *Revolt Against Modernity*, by Ted V. McAllister, *American Political Science Review* 91, no. 2 [June 1997]: 438 [col. 1]); cf. Scott P. Richert, Review of *Revolt Against Modernity*, by Ted V. McAllister, *Review of Metaphysics* 50, no. 3 (March 1997): 676.

27. Robert Devigne, *Recasting Conservatism: Oakeshott, Strauss, and the Response to Postmodernism* (New Haven: Yale University Press, 1994), xi.

28. *Recasting Conservatism*, 58, 64.

29. André Liebich, "Straussianism and Ideology," in *Ideology, Philosophy, and Politics*, ed. Anthony Parel (Waterloo, Ontario: Wilfrid Laurier University Press for the Calgary Institute for the Humanities, 1983), 226.

30. S. B. Smith, review of *Recasting Conservatism*, 972. Cf. Saul Bellow, *Ravelstein* (London and New York: Viking, 2000), 11–12, 22.

31. Ted V. McAllister, *Revolt Against Modernity: Leo Strauss, Eric Voegelin, and the Search for a Postliberal Order* (Lawrence: University of Kansas Press, 1996), 13.

32. McCarl, review of *Revolt Against Modernity*, 438 (col. 1).

33. James V. Schall, *Christianity and Politics* (Boston: St. Paul Editions, 1981), 254–55. See also Schall, *Another Sort of Learning* (San Francisco: Ignatius Press, 1988), 80, 96ff.

34. Harry V. Jaffa, "Dear Professor Drury," *Political Theory* 15, no. 3 (August 1987): 325. See also Jaffa, *The Conditions of Freedom: Essays in Political Philosophy* (Baltimore: Johns Hopkins University Press, 1975), 4–7.

35. Herbert J. Storing, in Walter Berns et al., "The Achievement of Leo Strauss," *National Review*, 7 December 1973, 1349.

36. Orr, *Jerusalem and Athens*, 4.

37. Cf. Allan Arkush, "Leo Strauss and Jewish Modernity," in Novak, *Leo Strauss and Judaism*, 126–27; Behnegar, *Leo Strauss, Max Weber*, 4; Drury, *Political Ideas of Leo Strauss*, 170–81; Emil L. Fackenheim, "What Is Jewish Philosophy? Reflections on Athens, Jerusalem, and the Western Academy," in *Jewish Philosophers and Jewish Philosophy*, ed. Michael L. Morgan (Bloomington: Indiana University Press, 1996), 165–84, esp. 168, 180–84; Frederick G. Lawrence, "Leo Strauss and the Fourth Wave of Modernity," in Novak, *Leo Strauss and Judaism*, 131–53; Gregory Bruce Smith, "The Post-Modern Leo Strauss?" *History of European Ideas* 19, nos. 1–3 (1994): 191–97; Stanley Rosen, *Hermeneutics as Politics* (New York: Oxford University Press, 1987), 123; Catherine H. Zuckert, *Postmodern Platos: Nietzsche, Heidegger, Gadamer, Strauss, Derrida* (Chicago: University of Chicago Press, 1996), 1–8, 200, 201–3, 261–76.

38. See, e.g., COT, CPP, LHK, *NRH*, POR, and TWM. LHK, 23: "'History' is not in my opinion, as you [Helmut Kuhn] say it is, essentially 'history of decay' but if classical natural right is superior to modern natural right (as you seem to admit), then a decay did take place in fact."

39. Dante Germino, "Blasphemy and Leo Strauss's Machiavelli," in Deutsch and Nicgorski, *Leo Strauss*, 298; but cf. 297: "… I do not agree with Strauss that it is possible to understand a thinker 'as he understood himself,' any more than I agree with Ranke that history can be written *wie sie eigentlich gewesen ist.*"

40. PPH, 66.

41. See, e.g., P*HPW*, 453.

42. Hadley Arkes, "Strauss on Our Minds," in Deutsch and Murley, *American Regime*, 83.

43. See, e.g., *SCR*, 35, 37–39, 40, 52, 100–101, 107–9, 144–46.

44. *PL*, 81–82, 84, 89–90. See also Moses Maimonides, *The Guide of the Perplexed*, trans. Shlomo Pines, intro. Leo Strauss (Chicago: University of Chicago Press, 1963), I 34, III 25–28, 51–52, 54.

45. *PL*, 21. On the themes raised here, see Eve Adler, "Leo Strauss's *Philosophie und Gesetz*," in *Leo Strauss's Thought: Toward a Critical Engagement*, ed. Alan Udoff (Boulder, Colo.: Lynne Rienner Publishers, 1991), 184, 186, 194–95; Adler, "Translator's Introduction: The Argument of *Philosophy and Law*," in *PL*, 1–2. On Strauss's argument in his early works that Cartesian doubt, Spinoza, modern rationalism, and the Enlightenment led to atheism, see David Janssens, "The Problem of the Enlightenment: Strauss, Jacobi, and the Pantheism Controversy," *Review of Metaphysics* 56, no. 3 (March 2003): 605–31; Laurence Lampert, "Nietzsche's Challenge to Philosophy in the Thought of Leo Strauss," *Review of Metaphysics* 58, no. 3 (March 2005): 585–619; Strauss, P*SCR*, 171–73. Concerning the development of modern atheism from Descartes' *cogito* principle, see Cornelio Fabro, *God in Exile: Modern Atheism; A Study of the Internal Dynamic of Modern Atheism, from Its Roots in the Cartesian "Cogito" to the Present Day*, ed. and trans. Arthur Gibson (New York: Newman Press, 1968).

46. See WIPP, 40–55, esp. at 46, where Strauss says of Machiavelli: "He was the first of a long series of modern thinkers who hoped to bring about the establishment of new modes and orders by means of enlightenment. The enlightenment—*lucus a non lucendo*—begins with Machiavelli." See also *NRH*, 61n22.

47. See also *TM*, esp. ch. 4. *TM* is Strauss's major work on Machiavelli; his other writings on Machiavelli are MCL and NM. Discussions of Machiavelli can also be found in *NRH*, *OT*, TWM, and *WIPP*.

48. *PAW*, 142–43.

49. Jackson, "Leo Strauss's Teaching," 250.

50. Harry V. Jaffa, in Berns et al., "Achievement of Leo Strauss," 1353 (col. 1) (emphasis added); Jaffa, *Conditions of Freedom*, 3 (emphasis added): "it was Strauss who, in a long series of works, culminating in *Thoughts on Machiavelli*, laid bare the Machiavellian roots of modernity and of the *specific teachings* of the great moderns."

51. On the modern flight to this-worldly concerns, see G. W. F. Hegel, *Hegel's Philosophy of Right*, trans. T. M. Knox (London: Oxford University Press, 1952), pref., esp. 11, 13; Karl Marx, *Critique of Hegel's "Philosophy of Right,"* trans. Annette Jolin and Joseph O'Malley (London: Cambridge University Press, 1970), 11–20, 76–77, 98, 101–2, 131–32, 138. See also Kojève to Strauss, 2 Nov. 1936, in *OT*, 231–33. Cf. Strauss, *CM*, 2; Exi, 314; GN, 363; OPS, 137–38; *PL*, 37; P*SCR*, 172; cf. also Fabro, *God in Exile*, 155–57, 572–73, 586–92, 636–37, 652–58, 664–71, 697–700, 704–5, 1012.

52. TWM, 88. For the "three wave" thesis, see also WIPP, 40–55; cf. Anthony J. Parel, *The Machiavellian Cosmos* (New Haven: Yale University Press, 1992), 160–61.

53. TWM, 89–91. On Machiavelli and Rousseau, cf. Lionel A. McKenzie, "Rousseau's Debate with Machiavelli in the *Social Contract,*" *Journal of the History of Ideas* 43, no. 2 (April–June 1982): 209–28. On Rousseau's nonteleological view of nature, see Laurence D. Cooper, *Rousseau, Nature, and the Problem of the Good Life* (University Park: Pennsylvania State University Press, 1999).

54. Jean-Jacques Rousseau, *The Social Contract and Other Later Political Writings*, ed. and trans. Victor Gourevitch (Cambridge: Cambridge University Press, 1997), 124. Cf. Rousseau, *A Discourse on Inequality*, trans. Maurice Cranston (London: Penguin Books, 1984), 58.

55. See Frederick Copleston, *Contemporary Philosophy: Studies of Logical Positivism and Existentialism* (London: Burns and Oates, 1956), 175ff., 201–27; Jacques Maritain, "On the Meaning of Contemporary Atheism," *Review of Politics* 11, no. 3 (July 1949): 275–76; Strauss, *OT*, 210–12; PS, 322–27.

56. TWM, 94. On the above "understanding," see also GN, 361–62, 372; OPS, 136–38.

57. *NRH*, 253.

58. TWM, 95–96.

59. *CM*, 1 (emphasis deleted). See also *SA*, 6–8.

60. David Lowenthal, "Leo Strauss's *Studies in Platonic Political Philosophy*," Review of *Studies in Platonic Political Philosophy*, by Leo Strauss, *Interpretation* 13, no. 3 (September 1985): 306. See also Behnegar, *Leo Strauss, Max Weber*, 1–6; East, "Leo Strauss and American Conservatism," 3–6, 17–18; Preston King, introduction to *The History of Ideas: An Introduction to Method*, ed. Preston King (London: Croom Helm; Totowa, N.J.: Barnes and Noble, 1983), 14–16; Zuckert, *Postmodern Platos*, 126–28.

61. G. B. Smith, "Athens and Washington," 107.

62. See, e.g., Bloom, "Leo Strauss," 376–79; Kenneth L. Deutsch, "Leo Strauss, the Straussians, and the American Regime," in Deutsch and Murley, *American Regime*, 56–57; Emberley and Cooper, intro. to *Faith and Political Philosophy*, xxii–xxv; Steven B. Smith, "*Destruktion* or Recovery? Leo Strauss's Critique of Heidegger," *Review of Metaphysics* 51,

no. 2 (December 1997): 357–61; Nathan Tarcov, "On a Certain Critique of 'Straussianism,' " in Deutsch and Nicgorski, *Leo Strauss*, 259–74; Zuckert, *Postmodern Platos*, 116–18, 125, 130. Cf. Raymond Aron, *History, Truth, Liberty: Selected Writings of Raymond Aron*, ed. Franciszek Draus (Chicago: University of Chicago Press, 1985), 354–73; Robert B. Pippin, "Being, Time, and Politics: The Strauss-Kojève Debate," *History and Theory* 32, no. 2 (May 1993): 140, 144–46, 148, 154–55; Dana R. Villa, "The Philosopher versus the Citizen: Arendt, Strauss, and Socrates," *Political Theory* 26, no. 2 (April 1998): 147, 156–57, 162.

63. *NRH*, 304, 314–21; OCPH, 559–86; PPH, 58–60, 69–73; PS, 325–26; R*HH*, 126; TWM, 95–96; WIPP, 53–54.

64. Karl Löwith, *Meaning in History* (Chicago: University of Chicago Press, 1949), 1. See also Friedrich Meinecke, *Historism: The Rise of a New Historical Outlook*, trans. J. E. Anderson (London: Routledge and Kegan Paul, 1972), ch. 2. On philosophy of history and its eschewal of God, theology, and providence for reason and laws of history, see also Jacques Maritain, *On the Philosophy of History*, ed. Joseph W. Evans (London: Geoffrey Bles, 1959); cf. G. W. F. Hegel, *Reason in History: A General Introduction to the Philosophy of History*, trans. Robert S. Hartman (Indianapolis: Bobbs-Merrill, 1953), esp. 13–19, 20–21, 47–48.

65. Harry V. Jaffa, "Leo Strauss's Churchillian Speech and the Question of the Decline of the West," *Teaching Political Science* 12, no. 2 (Winter 1985): 62 (col. 2). See also Milton Himmelfarb, "On Leo Strauss," *Commentary* 58, no. 2 (August 1974): 65–66; Harry V. Jaffa, "The Primacy of the Good: Leo Strauss Remembered," *Modern Age* 26, nos. 3–4 (Summer–Fall 1983): 267–68; on a general level, concerning the above themes, see also James V. Schall, *Reason, Revelation, and the Foundations of Political Philosophy* (Baton Rouge: Louisiana State University Press, 1987), 18, 60, 169–81. Cf. Hwa Yol Jung, "Leo Strauss's Conception of Political Philosophy: A Critique," *Review of Politics* 29, no. 4 (October 1967): 495–96, 510–14; Strauss, COT, 44.

66. OCPH, 575.

67. See, e.g., PPH, 66.

68. Cf. OCPH, 572–73, 585–86; R*HH*, 126. On Strauss's *turn to history*, see James F. Ward, "Political Philosophy and History: The Links Between Strauss and Heidegger," *Polity* 20, no. 2 (Winter 1987): 273–95.

69. *TM*, 13. See also *CM*, 55; OPS, 171, 180.

70. Seth Benardete, *The Argument of the Action: Essays on Greek Poetry and Philosophy*, ed. Ronna Burger and Michael Davis (Chicago: University of Chicago Press, 2000), 408–9; K. H. Green, *Jew and Philosopher*, 7, 145n2; Himmelfarb, "On Leo Strauss," 60, 61; Jackson, "Leo Strauss's Teaching," 40, 140; McAllister, *Revolt Against Modernity*, 90; Robb A. McDaniel, "The Illiberal Leo Strauss," in *Community and Political Thought Today*, ed. Peter Augustine Lawler and Dale McConkey (Westport, Conn.: Praeger, 1998), 195; Susan Orr, review of *Jew and Philosopher*, by Kenneth Hart Green, *Interpretation* 23, no. 2 (Winter 1996): 307–8; Orr, *Jerusalem and Athens*, 24; Peterman, "Approaching Leo Strauss," 332; Stanley Rosen, "Leo Strauss and the Possibility of Philosophy," *Review of Metaphysics* 53, no. 3 (March 2000): 543–44, 552–55; S. B. Smith, "*Destruktion* or Recovery?" 358, 361; Strauss, *CM*, 52–54; OPS, 180–82; Stewart Umphrey, "Natural Right and Philosophy," in Deutsch and Nicgorski, *Leo Strauss*, 275–77, 289, 293–95. Cf. Rhodes, *Eros, Wisdom, and Silence*, 72–73.

71. Orr, *Jerusalem and Athens*, 7–8.

72. Burnyeat, "Sphinx Without a Secret," 30 (col. 1). Cf. Joseph Cropsey et al., "The Studies of Leo Strauss: An Exchange" (responses to Burnyeat, "Sphinx Without a Secret"), *New York Review of Books*, 10 October 1985, 41–44.

73. "Sphinx Without a Secret," 33. Cf. David Lawrence Levine, "Without Malice But With Forethought: A Response to Burnyeat," in Deutsch and Nicgorski, *Leo Strauss*, 353–71, esp. 361–65.

74. Orr, *Jerusalem and Athens*, 8, 9. Orr's quotation is from *TM*, 34. On speaking truth in private and to wise men, see also HBS*GP*, xiv–xv.

75. ET, 55.

76. See below, ch. 1 (section titled, "Turning to History").

77. K. H. Green, *Jew and Philosopher*, 147n4. See also McAllister, *Revolt Against Modernity*, 89.

78. Shadia B. Drury, "The Hidden Meaning of Strauss's *Thoughts on Machiavelli*," *History of Political Thought* 6, no. 3 (Winter 1985): 575–90; "Esoteric Philosophy," 315–37; "Leo Strauss's Classic Natural Right Teaching," *Political Theory* 15, no. 3 (August 1987): 299–315; *Political Ideas of Leo Strauss*, ix–xv, 37–60, 62–71, 114–18.

79. Kateb, "Questionable Influence?" 39.

80. G. B. Smith, "Anti-democratic Cult," 188n4 (col. 2).

81. David Novak, "Philosophy and the Possibility of Revelation: A Theological Response to the Challenge of Leo Strauss," in Novak, *Leo Strauss and Judaism*, 173.

82. Conal Condren, *The Status and Appraisal of Classic Texts: An Essay on Political Theory, Its Inheritance, and the History of Ideas* (Princeton, N.J.: Princeton University Press, 1985), 59; Shadia B. Drury, review of *Carl Schmitt and Leo Strauss*, by Heinrich Meier, *American Political Science Review* 90, no. 2 (June 1996): 411. Cf. Bellow, *Ravelstein*, esp. 15, 47; Rhodes, *Eros, Wisdom, and Silence*, xii.

83. Novak, "Challenge of Leo Strauss," 174.

84. Orr, *Jerusalem and Athens*, 9. Cf. Henry Higuera, "Politics, Poetry, and Prophecy in *Don Quixote*," in Palmer and Pangle, *Political Philosophy*, 176, 178–79, 180, 186; Lampert, "Nietzsche's Challenge to Philosophy," 613–20; Thomas L. Pangle, introduction to *SPPP*, esp. 10–13, 24–25; Plato *Republic* 607a–608b; Strauss, *CM*, 134–37, 142–43; *LAM*, 76–85, 104–5; *LSPS*, 6–11, 169; OPS, 195–205. But compare Pangle's intro. to *SPPP* to his recent works "The Hebrew Bible's Challenge to Political Philosophy: Some Introductory Reflections" (in Palmer and Pangle, *Political Philosophy*, 67–82) and *Political Philosophy and the God of Abraham* (Baltimore: Johns Hopkins University Press, 2003).

85. *Jerusalem and Athens*, 12.

86. *Jerusalem and Athens*, 18.

87. Bloom, "Leo Strauss," 391.

88. My method of analysis in Parts Two and Three is a mean between Orr's close focus and Jackson's broader approach: Jackson examined *Thoughts on Machiavelli* section by section; see his "Leo Strauss's Teaching." Orr examined the forty-one paragraphs of "Jerusalem and Athens" paragraph by paragraph. See Susan Orr, "'Jerusalem and Athens': A Study of Leo Strauss" (Ph.D. diss., Claremont Graduate School, 1992). Orr's dissertation was published in 1995 as *Jerusalem and Athens: Revelation and Reason in the Work of Leo Strauss*. Her book has been described as "a meticulous analysis" (Germaine Paulo Walsh, review of *Jerusalem and Athens*, by Susan Orr, *Journal of Politics* 58, no. 2 [May 1996]: 589), written in "true Straussian fashion" (Douglas Kries,

"Faith, Reason, and Leo Strauss," review of *Jerusalem and Athens*, by Susan Orr, *Review of Politics* 58, no. 2 [Spring 1996]: 354), "a truly Strauss-like reading of Strauss's essay . . . that is, an exceedingly close reading" (Arkes, "Strauss on Our Minds," 78, 79), and "one of a relatively small but rapidly increasing number of attempts to read and understand the writings of Leo Strauss as Strauss read and understood the writings of political philosophers before him" (Michael Palmer, review of *Jerusalem and Athens*, by Susan Orr, *American Political Science Review* 90, no. 2 [June 1996]: 412 [col. 2]).

89. George L. Mosse, review of *Thoughts on Machiavelli*, by Leo Strauss, in *American Historical Review* 64, no. 4 (July 1959): 954. Cf. Drury, "Hidden Meaning," 575–77, 590.

90. Felix Gilbert, "Politics and Morality," review of *Thoughts on Machiavelli*, by Leo Strauss, *Yale Review* 48, no. 3 (March 1959): 468–69.

91. Robert J. McShea, "Leo Strauss on Machiavelli," *Western Political Quarterly* 16, no. 4 (December 1963): 782.

92. Susan Orr, "Strauss, Reason, and Revelation: Unraveling the Essential Question," in Novak, *Leo Strauss and Judaism*, 28. But cf. Lampert, "Nietzsche's Challenge to Philosophy," esp. 589–96, 618–19; Rosen, *Hermeneutics as Politics*, 112; cf. also Drury, "Esoteric Philosophy," 329; "Hidden Meaning," 576–77, 580, 583, 584, 590; "Natural Right," 311.

93. Drury, "Natural Right," 299.

94. Charles Larmore, "The Secrets of Philosophy," review of *The Rebirth of Classical Political Rationalism*, essays and lectures by Leo Strauss, *New Republic*, 3 July 1989, 32 (col. 3).

95. See, e.g., POR, 272–73; *TM*, 14; cf. Drury, "Natural Right," 312.

CHAPTER ONE
Leo Strauss's Idea of History

1. Cf. Deutsch, "Straussians and the American Regime," 51, 52–53; Jürgen Gebhardt, "Leo Strauss: The Quest for Truth in Times of Perplexity," in Kielmansegg, Mewes, and Glaser-Schmidt, *Hannah Arendt and Leo Strauss*, 81–104; K. H. Green, *Jew and Philosopher*, 100, 169n13; Grant Havers, "Between Athens and Jerusalem: Western Otherness in the Thought of Leo Strauss and Hannah Arendt," *European Legacy* 9, no. 1 (February 2004): 19–29; Paul Norton, "Leo Strauss: His Critique of Historicism," *Modern Age* 25, no. 2 (Spring 1981): 143, 149–50; Thomas L. Pangle, intro. to *SPPP*, 1–2; Pangle, "Platonic Political Science in Strauss and Voegelin," in Emberley and Cooper, *Leo Strauss and Eric Voegelin*, 322, 334–35; Strauss, *SPPP*, 175–81; Tarcov, "Straussianism," 269–71.

2. It is useful to consider here McCoy's reminder: "Political science is a practical rather than a speculative science. A speculative science has as its object simply the truth of what is, whereas a practical science, though concerned with the truth of what is, is further ordained to action for the sake of some end." Charles N. R. McCoy, *On the Intelligibility of Political Philosophy: Essays of Charles N. R. McCoy*, ed. James V. Schall and John J. Schrems (Washington, D.C.: Catholic University of America Press, 1989), 276. On the "speculative" and the "practical," see also Aristotle *Nicomachean Ethics* 1103b27–30.

3. Michael Murray, *Modern Philosophy of History: Its Origin and Destination* (The Hague: Martinus Nijhoff, 1970), 13, 24 (original emphasis). On the above themes, cf. Strauss, Exi, 313–14; OCPH, 559; *TPPH*, 84–86; on "History," cf. *OT*, 208–12.

4. Barry Cooper, *The End of History: An Essay on Modern Hegelianism* (Toronto: University of Toronto Press, 1984), 47. Cooper's quotation is from PPH, 57; cf. OCPH, 562–63.

5. See John H. Hallowell, *Main Currents in Modern Political Thought* (New York: Henry Holt and Company, 1950), 258–62, 274–77; Alfred Stern, *Philosophy of History and the Problem of Values* ('S-Gravenhage: Mouton, 1962), 138–39. Cf. Karl R. Popper, *The Poverty of Historicism*, 2nd ed. (London: Routledge and Kegan Paul, 1960), 3. On Popper, who defined historicism by its effort to discover historical laws, cf. Carl Page, *Philosophical Historicism and the Betrayal of First Philosophy* (University Park: Pennsylvania State University Press, 1995), 18–21; here Page explains that Popper's emphasis on methodology obscures the metaphysical aspect of his objection to historicism, namely, to its claim that people cannot resist the laws and movement of history.

6. *NRH*, 12. See also LSPS, 2–3; OPS, 136; PS, 324–25; *WIPP*, 254–56.

7. Letter 23 in SVC, 59. See also PPH, 60.

8. In the preface to *NRH*, Strauss described his book as "an expanded version of six lectures which I delivered at the University of Chicago in October, 1949" (*NRH*, vi). In an undated letter to Helmut Kuhn Strauss wrote, "I myself regard the book as a preparation to an adequate philosophic discussion rather than as a treatise settling the question (cf. the end of the Introduction and of Chapter 1). Such a preparation is necessary because the very notion of natural right has become completely obscured in the course of the last century." While agreeing with Kuhn that this "*précis raisonné* of the history of natural right" evinces a "historical" approach to the issue at stake, Strauss emphasized: "If I understand you correctly, you suspect . . . that in opposing historicism I get entangled in a negative historicism of my own. I do not think that you are right. In regarding Socratics, Plato and Aristotle as the classics of natural right I do not assert, like a historicist, that there is of necessity . . . an absolute moment in history." LHK, 23.

9. *NRH*, 8. On positivism and historicism as the bases of contemporary social science, see also *CM*, 6–11; CPP, 91–92; Exi, 308–11; *LSPS*, 1–3; OPS, 130–38; Rel, 21–25.

10. Strauss to Voegelin, 10 Apr. 1950, Letter 29 in SVC, 66–67: "May I ask you to let me know sometime what you think of Mr. Popper. He gave a lecture here, on the task of social philosophy, that was beneath contempt: it was the most washed-out, lifeless positivism trying to whistle in the dark, linked to a complete inability to think 'rationally,' although it passed itself off as 'rationalism'—it was very bad." Voegelin's reply, dated 18 Apr. 1950, amplified Strauss's astringent condemnation of Popper. Of *The Open Society and Its Enemies* Voegelin wrote: "This book is impudent, dilettantish crap. . . . Briefly and in sum: Popper's book is a scandal without extenuating circumstances; in its intellectual attitude it is the typical product of a failed intellectual; spiritually one would have to use expressions like rascally, impertinent, loutish; in terms of technical competence, as a piece in the history of thought, it is dilettantish, and as a result is worthless." Letter 30 in SVC, 67, 68–69.

11. Thomas J. J. Altizer, "The Theological Conflict Between Strauss and Voegelin," in Emberley and Cooper, *Faith and Political Philosophy*, 268 (emphasis added) (see also Strauss, PPH, 57); I have taken the phrase, "primary opponent," from Eugene F. Miller,

"Leo Strauss: The Recovery of Political Philosophy," in *Contemporary Political Philosophers*, ed. Anthony de Crespigny and Kenneth Minogue (New York: Dodd, Mead, 1975), 94.

12. *NRH*, 13. Cf. Carl Becker, *The Declaration of Independence: A Study in the History of Political Ideas* (New York: Alfred A. Knopf, 1960), 256–73; cf. also Strauss, GN, 372.

13. *NRH*, 13. Cf. GN, 370–71; *NRH*, 295ff., 316.

14. *NRH*, 14.

15. Steven J. Lenzner, "Strauss's Three Burkes: The Problem of Edmund Burke in *Natural Right and History*," *Political Theory* 19, no. 3 (August 1991): 381n5.

16. *NRH*, 14, 15.

17. *NRH*, 16 (interpolation added).

18. WWRJ, 329. Cf. Behnegar, *Leo Strauss, Max Weber*, 183; Eric Hobsbawm, *On History* (London: Weidenfeld and Nicolson, 1997), 144.

19. *NRH*, 16, 17. Cf. Jurgen Herbst, *The German Historical School in American Scholarship: A Study in the Transfer of Power* (Ithaca, N.Y.: Cornell University Press, 1965), 55–57, 101ff.; Maurice Mandelbaum, *The Problem of Historical Knowledge: An Answer to Relativism* (New York: Liveright, 1938), 120ff.

20. *NRH*, 17, 18. Cf. Alan Mittleman, "Leo Strauss and Relativism: The Critique of Max Weber," *Religion* 29, no. 1 (January 1999): 15–19, 21; Norton, "Critique of Historicism," esp. 145–50; and Strauss's discussion of humanism, relativism, and nihilism in SSH, 8–10.

21. *NRH*, 14–16, 18–19, 22–23. Cf. GN, 357–61; *NRH*, 274; POR, 258–67; PPH, 66–67; WIPP, 26.

22. Cf. Meinecke, *Historism*, 58–61, 144–45, 165–71.

23. *NRH*, 37, 39; cf. 41–42, 48–49.

24. RSW, 153 (col. 2).

25. See below and *NRH*, 19–32.

26. *NRH*, 25 (emphasis added).

27. *NRH*, 26 (for the reference to Nietzsche, see 26n9).

28. Friedrich Nietzsche, "On the Uses and Disadvantages of History for Life," in *Untimely Meditations*, trans. R. J. Hollingdale (Cambridge: Cambridge University Press, 1983), 63 (emphasis deleted).

29. Nietzsche, "Uses of History," 66–77. See also Walter Kaufmann, *Nietzsche: Philosopher, Psychologist, Antichrist*, 4th ed. (Princeton, N.J.: Princeton University Press, 1974), 141–45; Catherine Zuckert, "Nature, History and the Self: Friedrich Nietzsche's Untimely Considerations," *Nietzsche-Studien* 5 (1976): 59–64. On the critical use of history, see also Lampert, "Nietzsche's Challenge to Philosophy," 585–88, 598–99.

30. "Uses of History," 78.

31. Thomas Albert Howard, *Religion and the Rise of Historicism: W. M. L. de Wette, Jacob Burckhardt, and the Theological Origins of Nineteenth-Century Historical Consciousness* (Cambridge: Cambridge University Press, 2000), 168.

32. "Uses of History," 118–19 (original emphasis), 119–23. See also Martin Heidegger, *Nietzsche*, vol. 4, *Nihilism*, ed. David Farrell Krell, trans. Frank A. Capuzzi (San Francisco: Harper and Row, 1982), 3–12, 52–57, 246–50. Cf. Strauss, *NRH*, 26–27; Rel, 24–26; SPPP, 176–77.

33. "Uses of History," 120, 121.

34. CCM, 107 (original emphasis). See also PRS, 30.

35. *OT*, 250, 251 (original emphasis; but I have changed the underlining to italics).

36. *NRH*, 32. On Strauss's above depictions of Heidegger, cf. Rémi Brague, "Radical Modernity and the Roots of Ancient Thought," *Independent Journal of Philosophy* 4 (1983): 63ff.; Fabro, *God in Exile*, 624–25, 889–90, 908–38, 939–41, 958–67; Hans Jonas, "Gnosticism and Modern Nihilism," *Social Research* 19, no. 4 (December 1952): 445, 446ff.

37. See Richard H. Kennington, "Strauss's *Natural Right and History*," in Udoff, *Leo Strauss's Thought*, 235–36.

38. Martin Heidegger, *An Introduction to Metaphysics* (New Haven: Yale University Press, 1959), 84, quoted in Kennington, "Strauss's *Natural Right and History*," 252n4.

39. Hwa Yol Jung, "Two Critics of Scientism: Leo Strauss and Edmund Husserl," *Independent Journal of Philosophy* 2 (1978): 86.

40. Exi, 312. For this recognition of the significance of Heidegger's thought, see also Exi, 305, 311, 313; *NRH*, 26–34; PRS, 30–32, 33; P*SCR*, 147–51; Rel, 24–26; Strauss to Voegelin, 17 Dec. 1949, Letter 26 in SVC, 63, and 10 Dec. 1950, Letter 35 in SVC, 75–76; UP, 450; *WIPP*, 55, 246–48, 254.

41. See Brague, "Radical Modernity," 68, 73–74; David Farrell Krell, "Analysis," in Martin Heidegger, *Nietzsche*, vol. 1, *The Will to Power as Art* (New York: Harper and Row, 1979; London: Routledge and Kegan Paul, 1981), 245–57; Herman Philipse, *Heidegger's Philosophy of Being: A Critical Interpretation* (Princeton, N.J.: Princeton University Press, 1998), 151ff., 157–65, 272–76; Ward, "Political Philosophy and History," 282, 287ff.

42. Martin Heidegger, "The Anaximander Fragment," in *Early Greek Thinking*, trans. David Farrell Krell and Frank A. Capuzzi (New York: HarperCollins, 1984), 17. See also Heidegger, *Being and Time*, trans. John Macquarrie and Edward Robinson (Oxford: Basil Blackwell, 1967), 427, 440–41, 449.

43. Martin Heidegger, *Existence and Being* (London: Vision Press, 1949), 319.

44. "Anaximander Fragment," 36ff.; *Being and Time*, 38, 92–95, 126–27, 256–73, 349–52, et passim; *Early Greek Thinking*, 95–98; *Existence and Being*, 319–51; *Nietzsche*, 4:150–66, 207; *Poetry, Language, Thought*, trans. Albert Hofstadter (New York: Harper and Row, 1971; New York: Harper Colophon, 1975), 36–39, 50–56, 60ff., 71–72, 81, 101–2, 123.

45. *Being and Time* II.3–6. On temporality, see also William D. Blattner, *Heidegger's Temporal Idealism* (Cambridge: Cambridge University Press, 1999), esp. 26–28, 89–112, 116–21; Hubert L. Dreyfus, *Being-in-the-World: A Commentary on Heidegger's Being and Time, Division I* (Cambridge, Mass.: MIT Press, 1991), 243–45, 270–71.

46. *Being and Time*, II.1, §§47–53, pp. 281–311, II.5 §§74–75, pp. 434–44; *Early Greek Thinking*, 101; *Poetry, Language, Thought*, 96–97, 124–26.

47. *Being and Time*, Introduction; *Early Greek Thinking*, 79–85; *Existence and Being*, 347–50, 351, 355–92; *Nietzsche*, 4:155–58, 209–13; *Poetry, Language, Thought*, 51, 100ff. See also Blattner, *Heidegger's Temporal Idealism*, 271–76, 277–79, 289–310; Copleston, *Contemporary Philosophy*, 131–35, 176–84; McCoy, *Intelligibility of Political Philosophy*, 86–99; Philipse, *Heidegger's Philosophy of Being*, 77–100, 281–86.

48. See HSMP, 324; PPH, 67ff.; PS, 325, 326–28; SVC, 75.

49. Peter Eli Gordon, *Rosenzweig and Heidegger: Between Judaism and German Philosophy* (Berkeley: University of California Press, 2003), 300–301.

50. PPH, 60.

51. *Being and Time*, 440 (original emphasis). See also *Early Greek Thinking*, 97–98; *Existence and Being*, 334–38; *Nietzsche*, 4:240–42; *Poetry, Language, Thought*, 61–63, 77, 100–103, 106, 109–13, 118–19.

52. See also, e.g., HSS, 191–96; OFKW, 227–29; *PL*, 25–26, 136n2; PRS, 29–34.

53. PPH, 67. See also HSMP, 324–25; OCPH, 586; OFKW, 227–28; *OT*, 25; PPH, 66, 68, 71. On Strauss's defense of philosophy in his "historical studies" (his interpretations of past thinkers), see Victor Gourevitch, "Philosophy and Politics, I," *Review of Metaphysics* 22, no. 1 (September 1968): 60–63; Jackson, "Leo Strauss's Teaching," 2–4; Mittleman, "Strauss and Relativism," 25–26n7; Thomas L. Pangle, "On The Epistolary Dialogue Between Leo Strauss and Eric Voegelin," in Deutsch and Nicgorski, *Leo Strauss*, 250n16; G. B. Smith, "Who Was Leo Strauss?" 98–100.

54. *NRH*, 162–63. See also *LSPS*, 3–5; *NRH*, 5–6; POR, 282–86; Rel, 15–17; SSH, 11–12. Cf. Nasser Behnegar, "Leo Strauss's Confrontation with Max Weber: A Search for a Genuine Social Science," *Review of Politics* 59, no. 1 (Winter 1997): 101–2, 105; Jonas, "Gnosticism and Modern Nihilism," 452; Stern, *Philosophy of History*, 185–86; Stephen P. Turner and Regis A. Factor, *Max Weber and the Dispute Over Reason and Value: A Study in Philosophy, Ethics, and Politics* (London: Routledge and Kegan Paul, 1984), 244n6.

55. On Strauss's view of philosophy what is (i.e., a way of life open to knowledge and to wisdom), cf. Timothy Fuller, "Philosophy, Faith, and the Question of Progress," in Emberley and Cooper, *Leo Strauss and Eric Voegelin*, 286; McShea, "Leo Strauss on Machiavelli," 787–88; James V. Schall, "A Latitude for Statesmanship? Strauss on St. Thomas," in Deutsch and Nicgorski, *Leo Strauss*, 219–20; Strauss, Rel, 17; SCR, 90–91.

56. Letter 43 in SVC, 97–98. For the above distinction, see below and *CM*, 20–21, 141–43; HSS, 187–88, 210–14; OFKW, 221–22, 227.

57. *PAW*, 31, 32. See also OFKW, 224.

58. Paul A. Cantor, "Leo Strauss and Contemporary Hermeneutics," in Udoff, *Leo Strauss's Thought*, 270–71.

59. Paul J. Bagley, "On the Practice of Esotericism," *Journal of the History of Ideas* 53, no. 2 (April–June 1992): 231–35.

60. Bagley, "Practice of Esotericism," 236. See also Rémi Brague, "Athens, Jerusalem, Mecca: Leo Strauss's 'Muslim' Understanding of Greek Philosophy," *Poetics Today* 19, no. 2 (Summer 1998): 249–51.

61. Brague, "Athens, Jerusalem, Mecca," 243. Cf. Cantor, "Leo Strauss and Contemporary Hermeneutics," 271–73; K. H. Green, *Jew and Philosopher*, 113–16, 123–24; Steven B. Smith, "Leo Strauss: Between Athens and Jerusalem," in Deutsch and Nicgorski, *Leo Strauss*, 101–3.

62. Brague, "Athens, Jerusalem, Mecca," 247, 248. On Brague's above points about the "Islamic conception of revelation," cf. K. H. Green, *Jew and Philosopher*, ch. 6.

63. Kenneth Seeskin, "Maimonides' Conception of Philosophy," in Novak, *Leo Strauss and Judaism*, 89 (emphasis deleted). On "deep" esotericism, cf. Strauss, LC*GP*, 56–58, 60, 66, 73–74; LR*K*, 110–11, 111n45.

64. On numerology and numeric patterns, see HBS*GP*, esp. xiii–xiv, xxxiv, xlvii–xlviii; LC*GP*, esp. 51, 63, 87n143; LR*K*, 105n29. For Strauss's "rules for reading," see, e.g., ONI, 351–52; *PAW*, 30. On Strauss, numerology, and his method in general, see Leora Batnitzky and Michael Zank, "Strauss and Textual Reasoning," *Journal of Textual Reasoning* 3, no. 1 (June 2004), http://etext.lib.virginia.edu/journals/tr/volume3/

straussintro.html (accessed 23 July 2005); Bloom, "Leo Strauss," 380–81; Brague, "Athens, Jerusalem, Mecca," 242–45; Jackson, "Leo Strauss's Teaching," 68–71, 73–98; Harvey C. Mansfield, *Machiavelli's Virtue* (Chicago: University of Chicago Press, 1998), 225–29; McAllister, *Revolt Against Modernity*, 93–94; Peterman, "Approaching Leo Strauss," 321–24; Zuckert, *Postmodern Platos*, 121–28.

65. Rhodes, *Eros, Wisdom, and Silence*, 72 (emphasis added). Cf. Alan Verskin, "Reading Strauss on Maimonides: A New Approach," *Journal of Textual Reasoning* 3, no. 1 (June 2004), http://etext.lib.virginia.edu/journals/tr/volume3/verskin.html (accessed 23 July 2005).

66. Cf. Rosen, "Strauss and Philosophy," 543–48, 551–55.

67. Burnyeat, "Sphinx Without a Secret," 30–36; Condren, *Classic Texts*, 160–61, 232–33; Holmes, *Anatomy of Antiliberalism*, 75, 77–78, 85–87; Kateb, "Questionable Influence," 38–42; see also Rhodes, *Eros, Wisdom, and Silence*, 72–103. Cf. McAllister, *Revolt Against Modernity*, 85–94; George H. Sabine, review of *Persecution and the Art of Writing*, by Leo Strauss, *Ethics* 63, no. 1 (October 1952): 220–22; Strauss, OFKW, 231–32.

68. Strauss to Gadamer, 26 Feb. 1961, in *CCWM*, 5. "Strauss's hermeneutic principles," Ward explains, "... are not intended as a formal interpretive methodology." Ward, "Political Philosophy and History," 279. See also Cantor, "Leo Strauss and Contemporary Hermeneutics," 269–70; Nathan Tarcov, "Philosophy and History: Tradition and Interpretation in the Work of Leo Strauss," *Polity* 16, no. 1 (Fall 1983): 5–29. Cf. John G. Gunnell, "The Myth of the Tradition," *American Political Science Review* 72, no. 1 (March 1978): 122–34, esp. 130–31.

69. OFKW, 229.

70. Exi, 306.

71. HSS, 181–82.

72. HSS, 182.

73. HSMP, 325 (original emphasis). See also ONI, 331. Cf. *LSEW*, 215; *SPPP*, 186–90. On this seeming diagnostic and palliative nature of Strauss's call for a return to the classics, see Gunnell, "Myth of the Tradition," esp. 123–25; cf. Ernest L. Fortin and Glenn Hughes, "The Strauss-Voegelin Correspondence: Two Reflections and Two Comments," *Review of Politics* 56, no. 2 (Spring 1994): 337–38, 345–46; K. H. Green, *Jew and Philosopher*, 201n14, 208–9n86; Pangle, "Platonic Political Science," 322, 335, 341, 342n28; Stanley Rosen, "Politics or Transcendence? Responding to Historicism," in Emberley and Cooper, *Leo Strauss and Eric Voegelin*, 261–62; Bernard Susser, "The Restorative Ontology of Leo Strauss," in *The Grammar of Modern Ideology* (London: Routledge, 1988), 137–71; Tarcov, "Philosophy and History," 6–9, 21, 24, 28; Ward, "Political Philosophy and History," 274, 279–80.

74. OCPH, 585, 586. See also Voegelin to Strauss, 12 Mar. 1949, Letter 22 in SVC, 58–59; Strauss to Voegelin, 17 Mar. 1949, Letter 23 in SVC, 59.

75. Lampert, *Leo Strauss and Nietzsche*, 133. See also Kenneth L. Deutsch and Walter Nicgorski, introduction to Deutsch and Nicgorski, *Leo Strauss*, 19–20; King, intro. to *History of Ideas*, 16; Larmore, "Secrets of Philosophy," 32 (cols. 2–3); S. B. Smith, "*Destruktion* or Recovery?" 353, 356–66.

76. WILE, 24, 25. See also Deutsch, "Straussians and the American Regime," 56–57. Cf. John G. Gunnell, "Political Theory and Politics: The Case of Leo Strauss," *Political Theory* 13, no. 3 (August 1985): 341–45, 355–56, 357–59. On the ahistorical orientation in

Strauss's defense of philosophy, see Altizer, "Theological Conflict," 268; Pangle, "Platonic Political Science," 334–37, 341; Umphrey, "Natural Right and Philosophy," 285n21. For an elaboration of Strauss's thesis about importance of liberal education, see Allan Bloom, *The Closing of the American Mind: How Higher Education Has Failed Democracy and Impoverished the Souls of Today's Students* (New York: Simon and Schuster, Touchstone, 1988).

77. CPP, 91. On the above "crisis" and "return," cf. GN, 358–65; *NRH*, 252–53; *OT*, 23–25; *PSCR*, 137–39, 172–73; Rel, 17–18; TWM, 81–98. Bloom, lambasting feminism, political correctness, and "democratic relativism," argues in his *Closing of the American Mind* that the crisis is intellectual and educative.

78. Gunnell, "Political Theory and Politics," 357.

79. Oswald Spengler, *Der Untergang des Abendlandes: Gesalt und Wirklichkeit* and *Der Untergang des Abendlandes: Welthistorische Perspektiven* (Munich: C. H. Beck, 1918, 1922); trans. by Charles Francis Atkinson as *The Decline of the West*, vol. 1, *Form and Actuality* and *The Decline of the West*, vol. 2, *Perspectives of World-History* (New York: Alfred A. Knopf, 1926, 1928).

80. COT, 42, 43.

81. COT, 49. See also *CM*, 3–4; *NRH*, 167–202; *SCR*, 90–92; *TPPH*, 6–29; TWM, 88–89.

82. COT, 50. See also *NRH*, 1–8, 36, 42, 48–50, 52; SSH, 8–11.

83. COT, 50, 51.

84. Hallowell, *Main Currents*, 650.

85. S. J. D. Green, "The Tawney-Strauss Connection: On Historicism and Values in the History of Political Ideas," *Journal of Modern History* 67, no. 2 (June 1995): 268.

86. WIPP, 10–13, 17.

87. "It is not necessary to enter here and now into a discussion of the theoretical weaknesses of social science positivism," Strauss maintains. "It suffices to allude to the considerations which speak decisively against this school." WIPP, 20–21. See also, e.g., *CM*, 9–12; COT, 53–54; OPS, 130–36; Rel, 17–19, 21–26. Regarding Strauss's allusion, cf. Aron, *History, Truth, Liberty*, 354–60; Behnegar, "Strauss's Confrontation with Weber," 97–125; Behnegar, *Leo Strauss, Max Weber*, pt. I; Kennington, "Strauss's *Natural Right and History*," 237–38; Clark A. Merrill, "Spelunking in the Unnatural Cave: Leo Strauss's Ambiguous Tribute to Max Weber," *Interpretation* 27, no. 1 (Fall 1999): 3–26; Eugene F. Miller, "Leo Strauss: Philosophy and American Social Science," in Deutsch and Murley, *American Regime*, 91–100, 102n37; Turner and Factor, *Max Weber*, 208–13, 220–25.

88. WIPP, 21–26.

89. Spengler, *Decline of the West*, vol. 1, intro.

90. COT, 51. See also OPS, 131f.

91. COT, 52.

92. COT, 52.

93. Raymond Aron, *The Dawn of Universal History*, trans. Dorothy Pickles (London: Weidenfeld and Nicolson, 1961), 9–11, 57ff.; Meinecke, *Historism*, 62–65, 322–25; Arnaldo Momigliano, *On Pagans, Jews, and Christians* (Middletown, Conn.: Wesleyan University Press, 1987), 31–52; Leopold von Ranke, *Universal History: The Oldest Historical Group of Nations and the Greeks*, ed. G. W. Prothero, trans. D. C. Tovey and G. W. Prothero, rev. F. W. Cornish (London: Kegan Paul, Trench, 1884), ix–xiv.

94. *NRH*, 13–17; *TPPH*, 79–107; TWM, 90–91, 94–96.

95. Karl Löwith, "Nature, History, and Existentialism," *Social Research* 19, no. 1 (March 1952): 84. Cf. Eric Voegelin, *The Collected Works of Eric Voegelin*, vol. 23, *History of Political Ideas*, bk. 5, *Religion and the Rise of Modernity*, ed. James L. Wiser (Columbia: University of Missouri Press, 1998), 223–26, 232–35; vol. 24, *History of Political Ideas*, bk. 6, *Revolution and the New Science*, ed. Barry Cooper (Columbia: University of Missouri Press, 1998), 31–51.

96. COT, 53, 54. See also *CM*, 10; PPH, 75.

97. COT, 54. See also *CM*, 11; OCPH, 585–86.

98. Letter 9 in SVC, 17.

99. ONI, 328.

100. *PL*, 108. See also *NRH*, 176–77; *PL*, 32–34; P*SCR*, 144–45; WIPP, 36, 38–39. LHK, 24: "I am not an Aristotelian since I am not satisfied that the visible universe is eternal, to say nothing of other perhaps more important reasons. I can only say that what Aristotle and Plato say about man and the affairs of men makes infinitely more sense to me than what the moderns have said or say."

101. WIPP, 38–39. On the above themes of cosmology and science, cf. Larry Arnhart, "Defending Darwinian Natural Right," *Interpretation* 27, no. 3 (Spring 2000): 263–77; David Novak, *Covenantal Rights: A Study in Jewish Political Theory* (Princeton, N.J.: Princeton University Press, 2000), 21–23, 21–22n100, 22n103; Strauss, *CM*, 42–44.

102. *NRH*, 31.

103. See Robert B. Pippin, "The Modern World of Leo Strauss," in Kielmansegg, Mewes, and Glaser-Schmidt, *Hannah Arendt and Leo Strauss*, 151–52.

CHAPTER TWO
Revelation and Reason in Leo Strauss

An earlier version of this chapter was published as "Revelation and Reason in Leo Strauss," *Review of Politics* 65, no. 3 (Summer 2003): 383–408.

1. In this chapter, I focus upon tracking Strauss on revelation and reason, and, to add to this largely interpretive goal, use the work of others who have engaged carefully with this core dimension of his project. For a summary of the revelation-reason gulf and nexus by a former student of Strauss's, see Harry V. Jaffa, "Leo Strauss, the Bible, and Political Philosophy," in Deutsch and Nicgorski, *Leo Strauss*, 195–210. For extended discussions of the matter, see K. H. Green, *Jew and Philosopher*; Orr, *Jerusalem and Athens*. For a variety of essays and perspectives bearing on the revelation-reason question, see Kenneth Hart Green, " 'In the Grip of the Theological-Political Predicament': The Turn to Maimonides in the Jewish Thought of Leo Strauss," in Udoff, *Leo Strauss's Thought*, 41–74; Deutsch and Murley, *American Regime*; Deutsch and Nicgorski, *Leo Strauss*; Emberley and Cooper, *Leo Strauss and Eric Voegelin*, pt. III; Emil L. Fackenheim, "Leo Strauss and Modern Judaism," in *Jewish Philosophers*, 97–105; Jackson, "Leo Strauss's Teaching"; Novak, *Leo Strauss and Judaism*.

2. See, e.g., Harry V. Jaffa, "Crisis of the Strauss Divided: The Legacy Reconsidered," *Social Research* 54, no. 3 (Autumn 1987): 579–603. Himmelfarb, "On Leo Strauss," 64

(col. 1): "There are many excellent teachers. They have students. Strauss had disciples. His disciples are known as Straussians. Straussians of the first generation are those who studied with him, and their students are the second generation. By now there may well be a third generation." Himmelfarb's article was published in 1974; hence, the youngest Straussians may be fifth generation.

3. *PHPW*, 453 (original emphasis). See also *PSCR*, 137.

4. Jaffa, "Leo Strauss, the Bible, and Political Philosophy," in Deutsch and Nicgorski, *Leo Strauss*, 208.

5. S. B. Smith, "*Destruktion* or Recovery?" 369. In response to Strauss's raising of the question, *quid sit Deus*, James Schall points out, "The only question that we can answer, however, as Aquinas maintained, is '*an sit Deus*?' ('whether there is a God?'). It is on the basis of that question, 'whether there is a God?', that the questions about the nature of this God, 'what is God?' can in some sense be answered. . . . [T]he question of Thucydides about what are the gods? About 'what is God?,' is the ultimate question. The question is central if philosophy claims to seek to know the whole." Ken Masugi, "Fr. James V. Schall on Reason and Faith, Part II" (conversation with Fr. Schall, 5 December 2002, Georgetown, Washington, D.C.), http://www.claremont.org/writings/021223masugi_b.html?FORMAT=print (accessed 18 June 2005).

On what Strauss meant by the "theological-political problem," see also K. H. Green, *Jew and Philosopher*, xii–xiv, 111–12; Higuera, "Politics, Poetry, and Prophecy," 178; Michael L. Morgan, "The Curse of Historicity: The Role of History in Leo Strauss's Jewish Thought," *Journal of Religion* 61, no. 4 (October 1981): 348, 356–63; Pangle, intro. to *SPPP*, 18–23; S. B. Smith, "Between Athens and Jerusalem," 78–84; S. B. Smith, "*Destruktion* or Recovery?" 369–74; Walter Soffer, "Modern Rationalism, Miracles, and Revelation: Strauss's Critique of Spinoza," in Deutsch and Nicgorski, *Leo Strauss*, 143, 153–54, 170–73.

6. Arkes, "Strauss on Our Minds," 70.

7. Behnegar, "Liberal Politics of Leo Strauss," 251–52. On the above themes about Strauss on politics, see also Werner J. Dannhauser, "Leo Strauss as Citizen and Jew," *Interpretation* 17, no. 3 (Spring 1990): 433–47; Wilson Carey McWilliams, "Leo Strauss and the Dignity of American Political Thought," *Review of Politics* 60, no. 2 (Spring 1998): 231–32, 244–46; Rosen, *Hermeneutics as Politics*, 16, 118, 120–23, 137; Rosen, "Strauss and Philosophy," 541–42, 549–50; G. B. Smith, "Athens and Washington," 103–4, 120–23; Alfons Söllner, "Leo Strauss: German Origin and American Impact," in Kielmansegg, Mewes, and Glaser-Schmidt, *Hannah Arendt and Leo Strauss*, 123–24.

8. On Jaffa's opposition to Bloom and to Pangle, see Drury, *Political Ideas of Leo Strauss*, 186–90; Lowenthal, "Leo Strauss's *Studies*," 310–11; Orr, *Jerusalem and Athens*, 9–12, 160n24; Peterman, "Approaching Leo Strauss," 319–21; John Ranieri, "Leo Strauss on Jerusalem and Athens: A Girardian Analysis," *Shofar* 22, no. 2 (Winter 2004): 92n28.

9. It is beyond the scope of this chapter, however, to examine the issue of what happens when revelation and reason, despite their agreement on moral direction, part company regarding the righteous religious and reasonable righteous course of action—to kill or not to kill one's implacable enemies.

10. Quoted above, first epigraph to this book.

11. JA, 149.

12. Cf. Fuller, "Philosophy, Faith," 282; Havers, "Between Athens and Jerusalem," 19–24, 28; Lampert, "Nietzsche's Challenge to Philosophy," 589–91; James L. Wiser,

"Reason and Revelation as Search and Response: A Comparison of Eric Voegelin and Leo Strauss," in Emberley and Cooper, *Leo Strauss and Eric Voegelin*, 237–38, 241–42.

13. JA, 150.

14. JA, 150. Cf. Peterman, "Approaching Leo Strauss," 329, 345–47; Strauss, *LSEW*, 133; OIG, 359–61.

15. Cf. Orr, *Jerusalem and Athens*, 50–52, where Orr speaks of *Discourses* III 5, but quotes from II 5 (1970 Pelican edition of Leslie J. Walker's translation of the *Discourses*), for instance, where Machiavelli speaks of "rude mountain dwellers." In a way, then, Orr is echoing Strauss when the latter quoted from II 5 but referred to I 16. For Strauss's reference to *Discourses* I 16, see JA, 150n1.

16. Niccolò Machiavelli, *Discourses on Livy*, trans. Harvey C. Mansfield and Nathan Tarcov (Chicago: University of Chicago Press, 1996), 138–39 (emphasis added). Hereafter cited as *Discourses*, with all quotations from this translation, unless indicated otherwise.

17. JA, 150. Cf. OFKW, 225–27; *SCR*, 226–28; *TM*, 51, 133.

18. *A Theologico-Political Treatise*, in *The Chief Works of Benedict de Spinoza*, vol. 1, *Tractatus Theologico-Politicus, Tractatus Politicus*, trans. R. H. M. Elwes (London: George Bell and Sons, 1883), 91.

19. JA, 150 (I have changed "exept" to "except").

20. *LSEW*, 133. For both Strauss and Rosenzweig, Bible science is atheistic, because its theological views, especially its differentiation of myth from history, teach that "God remains merely an object" (*LSEW*, 133), and that one can know nothing of God as God (creator of the earth, heavens, and human life) or through divine revelation, but can know God only as the human projection of ultimate human desires into the realm of myth and thereafter into the purely this-worldly course of history. See Franz Rosenzweig, "Atheistic Theology" (1914), in *Philosophical and Theological Writings*, ed. and trans. Paul W. Franks and Michael L. Morgan (Indianapolis: Hackett, 2000), esp. 17–19, 21; see also Paul Mendes-Flohr, "Franz Rosenzweig and the Crisis of Historicism," in *The Philosophy of Franz Rosenzweig*, ed. Paul Mendes-Flohr (Hanover, N.H.: University Press of New England, for Brandeis University Press, 1988), 144–45.

21. JA, 151. See also *IPP*, 162; *NRH*, 81–82; *ONL*, 137–38; POR, 282. Cf. Pangle, "Hebrew Bible," 67, 70; Schall, *Reason, Revelation*, 213, 215; Strauss, LRK, 95–96, 96–97n4; *LSEW*, 190, 195. But cf. also 4 Mac. 5:6–9, where Antiochus says to Eleazar (a Hebrew trained in philosophy and law) and others before forcing them to eat the flesh of pigs: " '. . . I respect your age and your grey hairs, although to have worn them so long a time, and still to cling to the Jewish religion, makes me think you no philosopher. For most excellent is the meat of this animal which Nature has graciously bestowed upon us. . . . Truly it is folly not to enjoy innocent pleasures, and it is wrong to reject Nature's favours. . . .' " Eleazar replies: " 'We, O Antiochus, having accepted the Divine Law as the Law of our country, do not believe any stronger necessity is laid upon us than that of our obedience to the Law' " (4 Mac. 5:16). *The Apocrypha and Pseudepigrapha of the Old Testament in English*, vol. 2, *Pseudepigrapha*, ed. R. H. Charles et al. (Oxford: Clarendon Press, 1913), 672.

22. JA, 151. On Strauss's tentativeness in taking issue with biblical criticism, cf. HSS, 184–85.

23. JA, 165. In a footnote, 165n12, Strauss refers to *Metaphysics* 1072b14–30, 1074b15–1075a11; *De Anima* 429a19–20; *Nicomachean Ethics* 1141a33–b2, 1178b1–12; *Eudemian Ethics* 1249a14–15.

24. Aristotle *Metaphysics* 1074b31–34. I have taken all quotations from Aristotle from *The Complete Works of Aristotle: The Revised Oxford Translation*, ed. Jonathan Barnes, 2 vols., Bollingen Series (Princeton, N.J.: Princeton University Press, 1984). On God as the Prime Mover, see *Metaphysics* 1071b3–1075a10, and cf. *Movement of Animals* 699a12–700a25; Maimonides *Guide of the Perplexed* I 69 and II intro.

25. *CM*, 34. Cf. ONI, 338; *WIPP*, 285; cf. also Aristotle *On the Universe* 391a1–b9; *Metaphysics* 1026a6–32.

26. JA, 165–66 (emphasis added). Strauss does not provide citations for those two points, but it would be fair to say that he has in mind Plato *Republic* 379a–380c and 380d–383d. On Plato's "theology," cf. ONI, 363; *XSD*, 148–49, 187–88.

27. Benardete, *Argument of the Action*, 3–4; Strauss, *CM*, 98–99; *LSPS*, 15–16; OPS, 196.

28. *The Republic of Plato*, 2nd ed., trans. Allan Bloom (New York: Basic Books, 1991), 56, 58 (original emphasis). Hereafter cited as *Republic*, with all quotations from Bloom's translation.

29. JA, 166. On Strauss's apparent preference for Plato's notion of God over Aristotle's notion, see K. H. Green, *Jew and Philosopher*, 47–48, 100–102; McCoy, "On the Revival of Classical Political Philosophy," in *Intelligibility of Political Philosophy*, 131–49; Orr, *Jerusalem and Athens*, 112–19; Strauss, LHK, 24; *PL*, 75–79; cf. *NRH*, 144–64; POR, 274–80; *TPPH*, 138–53.

30. JA, 166n13.

31. *The Dialogues of Plato*, rev. 4th ed., trans. B. Jowett (Oxford: Clarendon Press, 1953), 4:476.

32. Ps. 139:7–10, Amos 9:1 (New International Version). All biblical quotations are taken from the NIV.

33. Cf. LR*K*, 133–41; *LSEW*, 78, 130–33, 204–8; Strauss to Voegelin, 25 Feb. 1951, Letter 37 in SVC, 78–79. Cf. also Robert Gordis, *The Root and the Branch: Judaism and the Free Society* (Chicago: University of Chicago Press, 1962), 46–49, 222–25; K. H. Green, *Jew and Philosopher*, 233–36n85; Jacob Klein, "On the Nature of Nature," *Independent Journal of Philosophy* 3 (1979): 101–9; Novak, *Covenantal Rights*, 16–17n67.

34. Consider here Gerald A. McCool, *From Unity to Pluralism: The Internal Evolution of Thomism* (New York: Fordham University Press, 1989), 59–60, 74–80.

35. *PAW*, 9, 19 (original emphasis). See also HSMP, 335. Cf. Gordis, *Root and the Branch*, 28–29; Simon Kaplan, Translator's introduction to *Religion of Reason Out of the Sources of Judaism*, by Hermann Cohen (New York: Frederick Ungar, 1972), xviii; Maimonides *Guide of the Perplexed* epistle dedicatory, pt. I intro.; Orr, *Jerusalem and Athens*, 21, 60–62, 125–33; James V. Schall, "The Right Order of Polity and Economy: Reflections on St. Thomas and the 'Old Law,'" *Cultural Dynamics* 7, no. 3 (November 1995): 427–29; Zuckert, *Postmodern Platos*, 110, 158.

36. On "faith" in revelation, cf. *SCR*, 149, 197, 219–23. Elsewhere, Strauss says that in modern times "biblical morality" has been separated from "biblical theology." See POR, 265; P*SCR*, 151; cf. *LSEW*, 76–78, 87, 130f., 182; *TM*, 141. On "revealed law," cf. LR*K*, 126–29, 131–32.

37. WIPP, 13. On revealed theology, cf. Laurence Berns, "The Relation Between Philosophy and Religion: Reflections on Leo Strauss's Suggestion Concerning the Source and Sources of Modern Philosophy," *Interpretation* 19, no. 1 (Fall 1991): 43.

38. POR, 272–73.

39. POR, 269–72, 273.

40. POR, 274.

41. The second part of Book VI discusses laws with a religious aspect; namely, laws about marriage and procreation. Plato says, "So let these be the things said to encourage marriage, . . . to the effect that one must partake of the eternal coming-into-being of nature by leaving behind children of children, whom one leaves as one's successors in serving the god." *The Laws of Plato*, trans. Thomas L. Pangle (New York: Basic Books, 1980; Chicago: University of Chicago Press, 1988), 773e–774a. Hereafter cited as *Laws* with all quotations from Pangle's translation.

42. Toward the beginning of Book V, Plato says that of all the possessions man has, the soul is the most divine. The role of the legislator is to determine what honors (of the body) are good and noble, as well as what is evil and base; one must act according to standards set by legislators, for evil and base actions do not bring honor to one's soul. Of Book X Strauss explains, "The impiety which is to be condemned is the impiety against the gods of the cosmos, but not the impiety against the gods of the city, which are merely a figment of the imagination. We can say Plato substitutes a natural theology for a civil theology." *LSPS*, 38.

43. *Laws* 913a.

44. POR, 274.

45. On this point, see, e.g., Jaffa, *Conditions of Freedom*, 274–75; Strauss, ONL, 142.

46. St. Thomas Aquinas, *Summa Theologiæ*, vol. 29, *The Old Law*, (1a2æ, qq. 98–105), trans. David Bourke and Arthur Littledale (Blackfriars; London: Eyre and Spottiswoode; New York: McGraw-Hill, 1969). For the above references to Aristotle and the Bible, see 48nn11, 12.

47. POR, 274 (emphasis added).

48. Cf. Aquinas *Summa Theologiæ* vol. 29, 1a2æ, q. 100, art. 5, reply. On adultery, cf. Plato *Republic* 461a–c; *Laws* 841c–e; theft, cf. *Laws* 857a–b, 941b–d; assault, cf. *Laws* 876e–882c; murder, cf. *Laws* 864c–874b.

49. Exod. 20:13–17 (emphasis added).

50. See POR, 274.

51. POR, 275.

52. *PL*, 90. Cf. Aquinas *Summa Theologiæ* vol. 29, 1a2æ, q. 99, arts. 2, 3, replies, and q. 100, arts. 5, 9, replies; Maimonides *Guide of the Perplexed* II 40, III 27; Novak, *Covenantal Rights*, 78–86, 109–16; Plato *Laws* 631b–c; Strauss, OCPP, 91–92; *PL*, 123–24; P*SCR*, 167–68; SR, 4–5, 16–18, 20–22, 27n13.

53. POR, 275. According to Genesis 1:28, "God blessed them [Adam and Eve] and said to them, 'Be fruitful and increase in number; fill the earth and subdue it. Rule over the fish of the sea and the birds of the air and over every living creature that moves on the ground.'" Deuteronomy 32:46–47 instructs parents, "'Command your children to obey carefully all the words of this law. They are not just idle words for you—they are your life.'" Proverbs 3:18 proclaims, "She is a tree of life to those who embrace her; those who lay hold of her will be blessed." By "She" is meant "wisdom" (3:13), the wisdom that arises from keeping from God's "commands" (3:1). Laws, Aristotle explains, command some "acts" and forbid "others"; laws command "excellence" and proscribe "wickedness." *Nicomachean Ethics* 1130a20–25, 1130b22–24. The Athenian stranger says to Kleinias: "It should have been said, 'not in vain are the laws of Crete in especially

high repute among all the Greeks. They are correct laws, laws that make those who use them happy. For they provide all the good things. Now the good things are two fold, some human, some divine. The former depend on the divine goods, and if a city receives the greater it will also acquire the lesser. If not, it will lack both.'" The Stranger goes on, "Where the law is itself ruled over and lacks sovereign authority, I see destruction at hand for such a place. But where it is despot over the rulers and the rulers are the slaves of the law, there I foresee safety and all the good things which the gods have given to cities." Plato *Laws* 631b–c, 715d.

54. St. Thomas Aquinas, *Summa Theologiæ*, vol. 28, *Law and Political Theory* (1a2æ, qq. 90–97), trans. Thomas Gilby (Blackfriars; London: Eyre and Spottiswoode; New York: McGraw-Hill, 1966), 1a2ae, q. 92, art. 1, reply.

55. POR, 275–76.

56. Isa. 53:7, 9.

57. On Either/Or as an encapsulation of Strauss's thought on the relation between revelation and reason, cf. Zachary Braiterman, "Against Leo Strauss," *Journal of Textual Reasoning* 3, no. 1 (June 2004), http://etext.lib.virginia.edu/journals/tr/volume3/braiterman.html (accessed 23 July 2005); Christopher A. Colmo, "Reason and Revelation in the Thought of Leo Strauss," *Interpretation* 18, no. 1 (Fall 1990): 148, 150–51, 154; East, "Leo Strauss and American Conservatism," 9–10; Ranieri, "Leo Strauss on Jerusalem and Athens," 92–94, 97–98, 104; Mari Rethelyi, "Guttmann's Critique of Strauss's Modernist Approach to Medieval Philosophy: Some Arguments Toward a Counter-Critique," *Journal of Textual Reasoning* 3, no. 1 (June 2004), http://etext.lib.virginia.edu/journals/tr/volume3/rethelyi.html (accessed 23 July 2005); Gregory Bruce Smith, "On Cropsey's World: Joseph Cropsey and the Tradition of Political Philosophy," *Review of Politics* 60, no. 2 (Spring 1998): 315n12; S. B. Smith, "*Destruktion* or Recovery?" 359–60; Zank, intro. to *LSEW*, 27, 33–34. Cf. also Lampert, "Nietzsche's Challenge to Philosophy," 605–7; Heinrich Meier, *The Lesson of Carl Schmitt: Four Chapters on the Distinction Between Political Theology and Political Philosophy*, trans. Marcus Brainard (Chicago: University of Chicago Press, 1998), 66, 76–77, 86–88; Strauss, LC*GP*, 42–43; LR*K*, 104–9; RSW, 155 (col. 2).

58. POR, 276. Cf. X*A*, 122, 124, 139–40, and Strauss's description of the "just man" in OPS, 145–46. For an extended analysis of Aristotle on magnanimity, see Jaffa, *Thomism and Aristotelianism*, ch. 6; Mary M. Keys, "Aquinas and the Challenge of Aristotelian Magnanimity," *History of Political Thought* 24, no. 1 (Spring 2003): 37–65.

59. Aristotle *Nicomachean Ethics* 1125a19–22.

60. Aristotle *Eudemian Ethics* 1233b34–38. Cf. Strauss, *SPPP*, 199.

61. POR, 277.

62. See, e.g., 1 Sam. 15:1–11, 16:13, 18:1–4; 2 Sam. 6:14–16, 23.

63. POR, 277–78. Cf. Aristotle *Nicomachean Ethics* 1128a17–35, and Strauss's discussion of Socrates' perfect gentlemen in WILE, 6–7; *XSD*, 128–33, 135, 148–50, 159–70, 175–77, 184–85, 188, 195, 200–205, 209; cf. also Ranieri, "Leo Strauss on Jerusalem and Athens," 102–3; Strauss, *LSPS*, 263–65, 274, 280, 286–88; and Strauss's discussion of magnanimity in *TPPH*, 50–57. On the magnanimous man and his haughtiness, see also Jaffa, *Thomism and Aristotelianism*, 136–38.

64. POR, 279.

65. See *NRH*, 81–92, 163–64; POR, 279–86; Deut. 6:24–25, 12:1–7; Plato *Republic* 531c–534a. Cf. Aristotle *On the Soul* 427a20–428b7; Schall, *Reason, Revelation*, 208–11; Strauss, *LSPS*, 195–97; OPS, 187–90.

66. Aquinas *Summa Theologiæ* vol. 29, 1a2æ, q. 98, art. 1, reply.

67. POR, 281. Cf. HBS*GP*, liv–lvi; ONI, 338.

68. JA, 166. Cf. Plato *Republic* 597a–d. On Plato's "doctrine of the ideas," see also Plato *Timaeus* 28a–29a; Strauss, *CM*, 79, 92–93, 119–21. According to Plato's character Timaeus, "Everyone will see that he must have looked to the eternal; for the world is the fairest of creations and he is the best of causes." By "he" Timaeus means "the creator" (28a), "the father and maker of all this universe" (28c); by "the eternal" Timaeus means "the pattern of the unchangeable" (29a). *The Dialogues of Plato*, rev. 4th ed., trans. B. Jowett (Oxford: Clarendon Press, 1953), 3:714.

69. JA, 166. In a footnote, 166n14, Strauss refers to the *Timaeus* 40d6–41a5; Aristophanes *Peace* 404–13; Deut. 4:19.

70. Plato *Timaeus* 40e–41a: "Oceanus and Tethys were the children of Earth and Heaven, and from these sprang Phorcys and Cronos and Rhea, and all that generation; and from Cronos and Rhea sprang Zeus and Hera, and all those who are said to be their brethren, and others who were the children of these." Timaeus then observes that the creator of the universe proclaims to the pantheon of the visible and retiring gods, ". . . 'Gods, children of gods, who are my works . . . my creations are indissoluble, if I so will' " (41a).

71. Aristophanes, *Peace*, ed. and trans. Alan H. Sommerstein (Warminster, Wiltshire: Aris and Phillips; Chicago: Bolchazy-Carducci, 1985), ll. 404–13.

72. Deut. 4:19. On the above themes and opposition, see also Orr, *Jerusalem and Athens*, 115–18; Strauss, JA, 166. On Aristophanes' condemnation of the gods, see also Strauss, OPS, 147–49, 151; *SA*, 137–59; cf. Rhodes, *Eros, Wisdom, and Silence*, 242–64.

73. JA, 166. See also MITP, 295.

74. OIG, 373.

75. IEHC, 267. On the Jewish-philosophic character of Cohen's book, cf. *SPPP*, 192, 194, 205–7; *WIPP*, 156–59, 161–62.

76. K. H. Green, *Jew and Philosopher*, 16.

77. Rosenzweig, "Atheistic Theology," 15. Cf. Rosenzweig, "It Is Time: Concerning the Study of Judaism," in *On Jewish Learning*, ed. N. N. Glatzer (New York: Schocken Books, 1955; Madison: University of Wisconsin Press, 2002), 27–54, esp. 43–48; Strauss, *PL*, 27; P*SCR*, 163–65.

78. IEHC, 267.

79. IEHC, 271–72. Cf. *LSEW*, 91–95. On the above themes in Strauss's reading of Cohen, cf. also Braiterman, "Against Leo Strauss"; Irene Abigail Piccinini, "Leo Strauss and Hermann Cohen's 'Arch-Enemy': a Quasi-Cohenian Apology of Baruch Spinoza," *Journal of Textual Reasoning* 3, no. 1 (June 2004), http://etext.lib.virginia.edu/journals/tr/volume3/puccinini.html (accessed 23 July 2005).

80. *NRH*, 74–75. "But what is a 'combined' philosopher and theologian?" Jaffa asks. He answers: "Clearly, one who subordinates philosophic to theological principles, and interprets the data of philosophy from the viewpoint of theology. But can the data of philosophy, thus interpreted, be still described as philosophic? . . . [K]nowledge supplied by faith, . . . on Thomas' own principles, is a special gift of God; whereas

philosophic or scientific knowledge is knowledge which is intrinsically capable of communication to all men everywhere, because it is based on evidence which all men everywhere can see with their own eyes, without any special act of Providence." Jaffa, *Thomism and Aristotelianism*, 190, 191.

81. *NRH*, 85. Cf. *NRH*, 7–8, 163–66; Strauss to Voegelin, 25 Feb. 1951, Letter 37 in SVC, 78–79; *WIPP*, 157.

82. Strauss's "mutual influence" lecture (the final of a series of lectures he gave in late 1952 on "progress or return," at the Hillel House at the University of Chicago) was first published in Hebrew, in *Iyyun. Hebrew Philosophical Quarterly* 5, no. 1 (January 1954): 110–26. It was reprinted in an English translation as "The Mutual Influence of Theology and Philosophy" in *The Independent Journal of Philosophy* 3 (1978): 111–18, and as Part III of POR, in *IPP*, 289–310.

83. MITP, 292–98. Cf. *NRH*, 82–94.

84. MITP, 302.

85. MITP, 301–4. On philosophy and its critique of religion as "irrational," cf. Rudolf Otto, *The Idea of the Holy: An Inquiry into the Non-rational Factor in the Idea of the Divine and its Relation to the Irrational*, 2nd ed., trans. John W. Harvey (Oxford: Oxford University Press, 1950), 1–4, 31, 36, 41–42, et passim.

86. MITP, 305.

87. MITP, 305.

88. MITP, 306. Cf. *NRH*, 29–31.

89. MITP, 306–7, 309.

90. MITP, 309. Cf. OIG, 359–61; P*SCR*, 170–71. Given the above discussion, I contend that Sokolowski is correct in saying that Strauss sees a fundamental divide between the life of philosophy and the life of belief and piety, but errs by not acknowledging that Strauss called for dialogue or openness between revelation and reason. See Robert Sokolowski, *The God of Faith and Reason: Foundations of Christian Theology* (Notre Dame, Ind.: University of Notre Dame Press, 1982), 158–63; see also Walter Nicgorski, "Leo Strauss and Christianity: Reason, Politics, and Christian Belief," review of *The God of Faith and Reason*, by Robert Sokolowski, *Claremont Review of Books*, Summer 1985, 20–21. I also contend that Havers, who makes the same points that Sokolowski does, errs by arguing that Strauss "insist[ed] that Jerusalem be subordinated to Athens" in a process that leads to "the elimination of Jerusalem." Havers fails to see that Strauss was both loyal to Athens and acutely aware that Jerusalem requires obedience to God's Law. According to Havers, "The fundamental fact . . . that Strauss evades is that it is the God of Jerusalem, in contrast to the concept of nature found in Greek philosophy and mythology, that requires all human beings . . . to live under one truth, one morality, and one justice." Havers, "Between Athens and Jerusalem," 28.

91. MITP, 290. Cf. *SCR*, 157–60.

92. James V. Schall, "Fides et Ratio: Approaches to a Roman Catholic Political Philosophy," *Review of Politics* 62, no. 1 (Winter 2000): 70–71.

93. See also GN, 362.

94. Cf. Lampert, *Leo Strauss and Nietzsche*, 1–3, et passim; "Nietzsche's Challenge to Philosophy," esp. 589–96, 603–7; Rosen, *Hermeneutics as Politics*, 124–27; cf. also Rhodes, *Eros, Wisdom, and Silence*, 30, 80–86, 96–97.

95. Quoted in Hilail Gildin, "Déjà Jew All Over Again: Dannhauser on Leo Strauss and Atheism," *Interpretation* 25, no. 1 (Fall 1997): 126. In an endnote, 133n2, Gildin refers to David Spitz, "Freedom, Virtue, and the New Scholasticism: The Supreme Court as Philosopher-Kings," *Commentary* 28, no. 10 (October 1959): 315.

96. Gildin, "Déjà Jew," 127. See also K. H. Green, *Jew and Philosopher*, 237–39n1.

97. Schall, "Fides et Ratio," 64; Strauss, WIPP, 9–13. On natural theology, cf. Augustine, *Concerning the City of God Against the Pagans*, trans. Henry Bettinson (Harmondsworth, Middlesex: Penguin, 1972), 6.5–6; cf. also Jaffa, *Equality and Liberty*, 227–29; Strauss, CM, 180; ONI, 334.

98. MITP, 309–10. Cf. Gildin, "Déjà Jew," 130; Himmelfarb, "On Leo Strauss," 64 (col. 1); David Walsh, "The Reason-Revelation Tension in Strauss and Voegelin," in Emberley and Cooper, *Leo Strauss and Eric Voegelin*, 360–61.

99. Novak, "Challenge of Leo Strauss," 175.

100. AE, 322. For the above point about Strauss's rhetoric, see Behnegar, *Leo Strauss, Max Weber*, 142–43. The Storing volume contains essays by Walter Berns, Herbert J. Storing, Leo Weinstein, and Robert Horwitz. Paul F. Kress, "Against Epistemology: Apostate Musings," *Journal of Politics* 41, no. 2 (May 1979): 528–29: "The Storing volume brought the Straussian analysis to bear on the work of the discipline's leading figures of the empirical persuasion in the twentieth century, and could be said to have constituted a manifesto of sorts. Its message is captured in Strauss' epilogue which chides political scientists for a Neronian betrayal of their enterprise, but forgives them on grounds that they know neither that they fiddle nor that Rome burns."

101. OT, 185, 186. On philosophy, thinking, learning, and the intellectual, cf. AE, 322; NRH, 34, 36; OPS, 187, 193–95; PIH, 240, 245, 246–49. Strauss penned his "Restatement" as a reply to the reviews by Voegelin (*Review of Politics* 11 [1949]: 241–44) and by Kojève (*Critique* 6 [1950]: 46–55, 138–55) of the original edition of On Tyranny, published in 1948. Concerning Kojève's statements of atheism, see his "Tyranny and Wisdom," in OT, 152, 161. See also Gildin, "Déjà Jew," 128; Victor Gourevitch, "Philosophy and Politics, II," *Review of Metaphysics* 22, no. 2 (December 1968): 298n128; K. H. Green, *Jew and Philosopher*, 166n119, 237n1; Alexandre Kojève, *Introduction to the Reading of Hegel: Lectures on the "Phenomenology of Spirit,"* assembled by Raymond Queneau, ed. and intro. Allan Bloom, trans. James H. Nichols, Jr. (New York: Basic Books, 1969), 54–57, 89–90, 107–8 (see also Allan Bloom, "Editor's Introduction," viii).

102. Gildin, "Déjà Jew," 128. In an endnote, 133n6, Gildin refers to Kojève's *Introduction à la Lecture de Hegel* (Paris: Gallimard, 1947), 378, and to Strauss's *On Tyranny*, ed. Victor Gourevitch and Michael S. Roth (New York: Free Press, 1991), 237.

103. See OT, 186; cf. 212.

104. Gildin, "Déjà Jew," 128. Cf. Shadia B. Drury, *Alexandre Kojève: The Roots of Postmodern Politics* (New York: St. Martin's Press, 1992), 50, 68; Fabro, *God in Exile*, 41–53, 622–25.

105. POR, 270, 287. Strauss does not give a reference to Aristotle, but, Schall notes, he had in mind *Metaphysics* 982b29. Schall, *Reason, Revelation*, 209–10. Aristotle explains that to pursue and to possess knowledge about life and the world simply for oneself "might be justly regarded as beyond human power; for in many ways human nature is in bondage, so that according to Simonides 'God alone can have this privilege,' and it is unfitting that man should not be content to seek the knowledge that is suited to him." *Metaphysics* 928b29–32.

106. *NRH*, 169. Cf. *LSEW*, 133, 203–8; *SCR*, 209, 299–300n276; *SPPP*, 42–45; *TM*, 51; *TPPH*, 74–75. Cf. also Behnegar, *Leo Strauss, Max Weber*, 197–99; Bolotin, "Strauss and Classical Political Philosophy," 141–42; Gourevitch, "Philosophy and Politics, II," 294–99; Harry Neumann, "Civic Piety and Socratic Atheism: An Interpretation of Strauss' *Socrates and Aristophanes*," *Independent Journal of Philosophy* 2 (1978): 33–37.

107. Schall, *Christianity and Politics*, 101.

108. Gildin, "Déjà Jew," 125, 127.

109. Originally read at a conference about Strauss and Judaism at the University of Virginia, in Charlottesville, 10 and 11 Oct. 1993. Papers from the conference were published in Novak, *Leo Strauss and Judaism*.

110. Dannhauser, "Strauss as Citizen and Jew," 444.

111. Dannhauser, "Athens and Jerusalem or Jerusalem and Athens?" 168. In an endnote, 171n27, Dannhauser refers to his 1990 article.

112. *WWRJ*, 312.

113. On Strauss's Jewishness, see, e.g., Arkush, "Leo Strauss and Jewish Modernity," 111–30; Fackenheim, "Leo Strauss and Modern Judaism," 97–105; K. H. Green, *Jew and Philosopher*; Himmelfarb, "On Leo Strauss," 60–66. But cf. S. B. Smith, "Between Athens and Jerusalem," 82: "It is arguable that Strauss was not interested in Judaism per se but with Judaism insofar as it was an illustration of a more general problem, what he called 'the theological-political' problem. But since this problem, as Strauss himself recognizes, is not peculiar to Judaism but is central to the experiences of the Christian and the Islamic worlds, there is no reason to believe that Strauss's concern was with Judaism as such." Smith is correct that Strauss regards Judaism as illustrating a general, even fundamental, problem; however, it seems equally true that Strauss was concerned with Judaism as such. Consider Exi, 307: "The nobility of Israel is literally beyond praise, the only bright spot for the contemporary Jew who knows where he comes from. And yet Israel does not afford a solution to the Jewish problem. 'The Judaeo-Christian tradition'? This means to blur and to conceal grave differences. Cultural pluralism can only be had it seems at the price of blunting all edges."

114. POR, 249, 250, 251.

115. WWRJ, 317, 319.

116. P*SCR*, 141.

117. GA, 458.

118. GA, 460.

119. HSMP, 333 (original emphasis). Cf. PM, 538–39, 541.

120. Hillel Fradkin, "A Word Fitly Spoken: The Interpretation of Maimonides and the Legacy of Leo Strauss," in Novak, *Leo Strauss and Judaism*, 64.

121. See esp. POR, 272.

122. Cf. *LSEW*, 118–21, 202–4, 208; but see also Zank, "Part I: Introduction," in *LSEW*, 18ff.; Zank, comments in *LSEW*, 63–64.

123. *LSEW*, 86, 87 (original emphasis). The interpolation is Zank's.

124. LE, 414.

125. WWRJ, 319.

126. P*SCR*, 143.

127. P*SCR*, 141–45. See also POR, 251–59; cf. *NRH*, 7–8.

128. WWRJ, 320. On the theological-political core of the dilemma of modern Jews, see also Novak, *Covenantal Rights*, 25–32, 104–5.

129. WWRJ, 320.

130. FMM, 286. Cf. LR*K*, 114–15.

131. K. H. Green, *Jew and Philosopher*, 10.

132. *PSCR*, 146, 147. See also Franz Rosenzweig, "'The New Thinking'" (1925), in *Philosophical and Theological Writings*, 109–39, esp. 115–21.

133. *PSCR*, 147–51. On the relation between the "new thinking" of Rosenzweig and Heidegger, see Gordon, *Rosenzweig and Heidegger*.

134. *PSCR*, 152. Cf. Rosenzweig, *On Jewish Learning*, 59–67, 72–92, 96–102; cf. also Alan Udoff, "Retracing the Steps of Franz Rosenzweig," in *Franz Rosenzweig: "The New Thinking*," ed. and trans. Alan Udoff and Barbara E. Galli (New York: Syracuse University Press, 1999), 153–73, esp. 153–54, 170–73.

135. *PSCR*, 152.

136. FMM, 286, 287–88. Cf. *SCR*, 163–64.

137. WWRJ, 344.

138. *PSCR*, 143–44. On a general level, cf. *OT*, 196.

139. *PSCR*, 137–41. On the failure of liberal democracy and assimilation, see also *LAM*, viii–ix; POR, 254–57.

140. WWRJ, 321.

141. David Novak, introduction to *Leo Strauss and Judaism*, xiii. On Rosenzweig's emphasis on human experience, see his "New Thinking," 138–39. On Strauss's perception of the difficulties with the attempted solutions for the Jewish Question, see Arkush, "Leo Strauss and Jewish Modernity," 111–30; Morgan, "Curse of Historicity," 345–63.

142. POR, 257.

143. WWRJ, 320. Cf. *PSCR*, 170–71.

144. WWRJ, 320. See also *PSCR*, 146–47, 151–54.

145. Morgan, "Curse of Historicity," 351. On "intellectual probity," see, e.g., Strauss; AE, 322; IEHC, 280–81; *PL*, 37–38; *PSCR*, 144, 150–51, 154, 172; Rel, 26, 27; *SPPP*, 177–78; cf. Lampert, "Nietzsche's Challenge to Philosophy," 594–96.

146. D. Walsh, "Reason-Revelation Tension," 351; G. B. Smith, "Athens and Washington," 110. See also Himmelfarb, "On Leo Strauss," 61, 64–65.

147. On the above point about Strauss and theism, see K. H. Green, *Jew and Philosopher*, 26–27, 167n127, 237n1. On fidelity, cf. Strauss, *JP*, 281; POR, 253; *PSCR*, 165, 169; *SCR*, 179–81; WWRJ, 320.

CHAPTER THREE
Christianity and the Bible

1. *TM*, 9, 14. On that "opinion," cf. AE, 327; Strauss to Voegelin, 29 Apr. 1953, Letter 43 in SVC, 97–98.

2. *TM*, 174.

3. Jackson, "Leo Strauss's Teaching," 41, 204, 206; McAllister, *Revolt Against Modernity*, 100; Peterman, "Approaching Leo Strauss," 347–48. Jackson, "Leo Strauss's Teaching," 38: "Strauss did not make the plan of his book obvious; consequently, he does not employ such conventional literary aids and devices as subtitles, numbered sections, or additional spaces between key transition paragraphs."

4. *TM*, 175; see also 109–10, 133, 329n2; cf. 143–44. On piety, cf. K. H. Green, *Jew and Philosopher*, 233n82; Plato *Euthyphro* 5a–6b, 6d–7a, 14b; Strauss, *CM*, 19–20, 65, 67–68; OPS, 167–68, 175; *RCPR*, 187–98, 202–5; *SPPP*, 42–43; *XSD*, 175–76. For a restatement of Strauss's thesis that Machiavelli is neither Christian nor pagan, see Vickie B. Sullivan, "Neither Christian Nor Pagan: Machiavelli's Treatment of Religion in the *Discourses*," *Polity* 26, no. 2 (Winter 1993): 259–80; Sullivan, *Machiavelli's Three Romes: Religion, Liberty, and Politics Reformed* (DeKalb: Northern Illinois University Press, 1996).

For both de Grazia and Ridolfi, Machiavelli is a pious Christian. See Sebastian de Grazia, *Machiavelli in Hell* (London and New York: Harvester Wheatsheaf, 1989); Roberto Ridolfi, *The Life of Niccolò Machiavelli*, trans. Cecil Grayson (London: Routledge and Kegan Paul, 1963). However, for Villari, Machiavelli was, as a Renaissance political thinker, "thoroughly imbued with the Pagan spirit, and merely regarded Christianity as a guide to private morality." Pasquale Villari, *The Life and Times of Niccolò Machiavelli*, popular ed., vol. 2, trans. Linda Villari (London: T. Fisher Unwin, 1898), 92; cf. 2:96–106, 504–6, 509–11. Cf. also Isaiah Berlin, "The Originality of Machiavelli," in *Studies on Machiavelli*, ed. Myron P. Gilmore (Florence: G. C. Sansoni Editore, 1972), 169–75, 177–79, 183–85, 197–98; Joshua Mitchell, *Not by Reason Alone: Religion, History, and Identity in Early Modern Political Thought* (Chicago: University of Chicago Press, 1993), 166n19; Eric Voegelin, *The Collected Works of Eric Voegelin*, vol. 22, *History of Political Ideas*, bk. 4, *Renaissance and Reformation*, ed. David L. Morse and William M. Thompson (Columbia: University of Missouri Press, 1998), 84–86.

5. *TM*, 175. On Machiavelli and "the wise," see also J. Patrick Coby, *Machiavelli's Romans: Liberty and Greatness in the Discourses on Livy* (Lanham, Md.: Lexington Books, 1999), 157, 316–17n20; Strauss, *TM*, 17–19, 28; on a general level, cf. Plato *Apology* 18b–c, 19b, 22e–24c.

6. *Discourses*, 280. Cf. *The Prince*, ch. 6; *Discourses* I 11, 45, 56. Unless otherwise indicated, all quotations I give from *The Prince* are from the translation by Harvey C. Mansfield and Nathan Tarcov, 2nd ed. (Chicago: University of Chicago Press, 1998).

7. *TM*, 175 (original emphasis). See also WIPP, 41. Cf. Clark A. Merrill, "Leo Strauss's Indictment of Christian Philosophy," *Review of Politics* 62, no. 1 (Winter 2000): 96–101; Strauss, LRK, 98–99; *SCR*, 48–49, 96. On Averroism, see also Charles N. R. McCoy, *The Structure of Political Thought: A Study in the History of Political Ideas* (New York: McGraw-Hill, 1963), 127–30.

8. Coby, *Machiavelli's Romans*, 2. See also Zuckert, *Postmodern Platos*, 119–20, 191–92.

9. On Machiavelli's conception of nature, cf. Voegelin, *Collected Works*, vol. 22, bk. 4, 62–64, 83–84; cf. also Ernst Cassirer, *The Individual and the Cosmos in Renaissance Philosophy*, trans. Mario Domandi (Oxford: Basil Blackwell, 1963), 84–87, 99, 101–2, ch. 3 passim; McCoy, *Structure of Political Thought*, 168–70, 179–80.

10. *TM*, 175–76.

11. *TM*, 176.

12. *Discourses*, 6.

13. *Discourses*, 131. See also *TM*, 177–78.

14. Voegelin, *Collected Works*, vol. 22, bk. 4, 69.

15. *Discourses*, 132. For an analysis of Machiavelli's notion of virtue, see Russell Price, "The Senses of *Virtù* in Machiavelli," *European Studies Review* 3, no. 4 (October 1973): 315–45.

16. See *TM*, 179. Cf. Berlin, "Originality of Machiavelli," 170–72.

17. *TM*, 180.

18. *Discourses*, 209–11.

19. *TM*, 180.

20. *Discourses* III 1, quoted in *TM*, 180.

21. *TM*, 180.

22. *Discourses* I 6, 12, II 6, 12, 16–19, 23–24, III 10, 12, 15; *Art of War* II, III, in *Machiavelli: The Chief Works and Others*, vol. 2, trans. Allan Gilbert (Durham, N.C.: Duke University Press, 1965), 595–626, 626–48; *The Prince*, chs. 3, 12–14, 20–21, 26; *TM*, 180–82. Cf. Coby, *Machiavelli's Romans*, 113–36. On Machiavelli's ire over the Christian failure to imitate Roman glories, cf. Coby, *Machiavelli's Romans*, 6–11, 17, 199, 264, 268–75, 341n61; Machiavelli, *Art of War* II, in *Chief Works*, 2:623–24.

23. Mansfield, *Machiavelli's Virtue*, 4 (original emphasis). See also Roger D. Masters, *Machiavelli, Leonardo, and the Science of Power* (Notre Dame, Ind.: University of Notre Dame Press, 1996), 64–65.

24. *TM*, 182–83. See also Coby, *Machiavelli's Romans*, 268, 341n62; Sullivan, *Machiavelli's Three Romes*, 36–38. Cf. Dante Germino, "Second Thoughts On Leo Strauss's Machiavelli," *Journal of Politics* 28, no. 4 (November 1966): 801–3.

25. *The Prince*, chs. 11–12.

26. *TM*, 184–85. In an endnote, 330n24, Strauss refers to Plato *Timaeus* 24a3–b3; Aristotle *Politics* 1328b6–24, 1329a27–34; and instructs the reader to compare those references to Averroës *Commentary on Plato's Republic* II 17.3–5 and III 5.6.

27. ca. 638–559 BC.

28. Aristotle *Politics* 1328b6–24, 1329a27–34. The other essential "things" are "food," "arts," "arms," and "revenue"; *Politics* 1328b6–11.

29. Averroës, *Averroës' Commentary on Plato's Republic*, ed. and trans. E. I. J. Rosenthal (Cambridge: Cambridge University Press, 1956), II 17.3–5, p. 205; III 5.3, p. 216; III 5.6, pp. 216–17.

30. *TM*, 185.

31. *TM*, 185 (cf. 84, 172–73); Sullivan, *Machiavelli's Three Romes*, 141–45, 147–48.

32. *TM*, 185–86.

33. See Coby, *Machiavelli's Romans*, 8–9; Strauss, *TM*, 156–57; Sullivan, *Machiavelli's Three Romes*, 47; see also Miguel E. Vatter, *Between Form and Event: Machiavelli's Theory of Political Freedom* (Dordrecht: Kluwer Academic Publishers, 2000), 297–99.

34. *Discourses* III 19–23; on "punishment and compliance," see III 19; on "humanity and mercy," see III 20–21.

35. *Discourses* III 19–23; *TM*, 185–87. See also Coby, *Machiavelli's Romans*, 179–88, 321n62; Harvey C. Mansfield, *Machiavelli's New Modes and Orders: A Study of the Discourses on Livy* (Ithaca, N.Y.: Cornell University Press, 1979; repr., Chicago: University of Chicago Press, 2001), 372–86; Strauss, *TM*, 160–65; Sullivan, *Machiavelli's Three Romes*, 148–53.

36. Sullivan, *Machiavelli's Three Romes*, 49.

37. *TM*, 187.

38. See also Deut. 11:3; Mark 12:29–31.

39. Haig Patapan, "All's Fair in Love and War: Machiavelli's *Clizia*," *History of Political Thought* 19, no. 4 (Winter 1998): 546. On Machiavelli's above critiques of God and

morality, see also Robert Faulkner, "*Clizia* and the Enlightenment of Private Life," in *The Comedy and Tragedy of Machiavelli: Essays on the Literary Works*, ed. Vickie B. Sullivan (New Haven: Yale University Press, 2000), 30–56, esp. 30–31, 40–47.

40. Tyrannical use of force, however, as Aquinas warns, is antithetical to "the right ordering of rulers in a state." *Summa Theologiæ* vol. 29, 1a2æ, q. 105, art. 1. Here Aquinas examines "the reason for the judicial precepts concerning rulers," and says in obj. 5, "Again, as monarchy is the best form of government, so tyranny is the worst corruption of it. But the Lord, in establishing kingship, set up a tyrannical law; for we read, *This will be the right of the king that shall reign over you: He will take your sons*, etc. Therefore the Law did not make suitable provision for the appointment of rulers." In his reply to obj. 5, Aquinas explains, "This right was not given [to] the king by divine ordinance; here is foretold, rather, how the kings would usurp it and frame unjust laws, degenerate into tyrants and oppress their subjects." While at times "even a good king may, without becoming a tyrant, take away the sons . . . and make many exactions of his subjects," he does so only "in order to promote the common good."

On Machiavelli's suggestion that tyranny underpins biblical teaching, cf. also Strauss, *SCR*, 102.

41. *TM*, 188. Cf. Friedrich Meinecke, "Machiavelli," in *Perspectives on Political Philosophy*, vol. 1, *Thucydides through Machiavelli*, ed. James V. Downton, Jr., and David K. Hart (New York: Holt, Rinehart and Winston, 1971), 405–6. On human nature, see also below, ch. 6.

42. *TM*, 331n35.

43. Nah. 1:2. See also Exod. 20:5; Deut. 32:21–22; Ps. 94:1–3, 97:2–3; Isa. 26:11.

44. *TM*, 189. Strauss takes the phrase, "good and faithful soldiers," from the title of *Discourses* I 43: "Those Who Engage in Combat for Their Own Glory Are Good and Faithful Soldiers."

45. *TM*, 189.

46. See also *Discourses* I 30.

47. *TM*, 191–93, 332n43; on sin and conscience, cf. 148–49.

48. Cf. Coby, *Machiavelli's Romans*, 6–8; Mansfield, *Machiavelli's Virtue*, 48–49, 161; Parel, *Machiavellian Cosmos*, 45–46, 153–58; Haig Patapan, "*I Capitoli*: Machiavelli's New Theogony," *Review of Politics* 65, no. 2 (Spring 2003): 185–207; Sullivan, *Machiavelli's Three Romes*, 38–41.

49. *SCR*, 101. On disbelief, theology, and the critique of religion, cf. *LAM*, 126, 130–31; *LSEW*, 173–96.

50. *TPPH*, 129.

51. *NRH*, 170; cf. 177.

52. Sullivan, *Machiavelli's Three Romes*, 206n37. See also Carnes Lord, "Machiavelli's Realism," in Niccolò Machiavelli, *The Prince*, ed. and trans. Angelo M. Codevilla (New Haven: Yale University Press, 1997), 119, 123n9; J. Samuel Preus, "Machiavelli's Functional Analysis of Religion: Context and Object," *Journal of the History of Ideas* 40, no. 2 (April–June 1979): 171–90, esp. 175–76.

53. Coby, *Machiavelli's Romans*, 274. See also John M. Najemy, "Papirius and the Chickens, or Machiavelli on the Necessity of Interpreting Religion," *Journal of the History of Ideas* 60, no. 4 (October 1999): 663–64.

54. Villari, *Life and Times*, 2:91 (cf. 2:96–97, 116). See also Federico Chabod, *Machiavelli and the Renaissance*, trans. David Moore (London: Bowes and Bowes, 1958), 93–95, 143–48, 187–91, 193–94.

55. Berlin, "Originality of Machiavelli," 160. On Berlin's point about Machiavelli and the Renaissance, cf. Hans Baron, *In Search of Florentine Civic Humanism: Essays on the Transition from Medieval to Modern Thought*, vol. 2 (Princeton, N.J.: Princeton University Press, 1988), esp. 36–39, 101–51; cf. also Peter Gay, *The Enlightenment: An Interpretation*, vol. 1, *The Rise of Modern Paganism* (New York: Alfred A. Knopf, 1966; New York: W. W. Norton, 1977), 256–68, 275–77.

56. Cary J. Nederman, "Amazing Grace: Fortune, God, and Free Will in Machiavelli's Thought," *Journal of the History of Ideas* 60, no. 4 (October 1999): 621. See also Bjørn Qviller, "The Machiavellian Cosmos," *History of Political Thought* 17, no. 3 (Autumn 1996): 326–53, esp. 327, 340ff. Cf. Patapan, "Machiavelli's New Theogony," 186–89, 193, 197–98, 202; Sullivan, "Neither Christian Nor Pagan," 279; Sullivan, *Machiavelli's Three Romes*, 156.

57. *TM*, 193. In 332n44 Strauss refers to *Florentine Histories* III 13, VI 20, and VII 23.

58. Mansfield, *Machiavelli's Virtue*, 127, 136. See also Harvey C. Mansfield, Transalors' introduction to *Florentine Histories*, by Niccolò Machiavelli, trans. Laura F. Banfield and Harvey C. Mansfield, Jr. (Princeton, N.J.: Princeton University Press, 1988), x, xiv–xv. Cf. Markus Fischer, *Well-Ordered License: On the Unity of Machiavelli's Thought* (Lanham, Md.: Lexington Books, 2000), 10–14; Edmund E. Jacobitti, "The Classical Heritage in Machiavelli's Histories: Symbol and Poetry as Historical Literature," in Sullivan, *Comedy and Tragedy of Machiavelli*, 185–92. On Christianity as the context of the *Florentine Histories*, see Mansfield, *Machiavelli's Virtue*, 144–48; cf. Quentin Skinner, *Machiavelli* (New York: Hill and Wang, 1981), 78–86.

59. Martin Fleisher, "The Ways of Machiavelli and the Ways of Politics," *History of Political Thought* 16, no. 3 (Autumn 1995): 338 (original emphasis).

60. On the anthropocentric conception of human action as it relates to modernity in general, see POR, 269–72; see also Jacques Maritain, *True Humanism*, 2nd ed., trans. M. R. Adamson (London: Geoffrey Bles, 1939), esp. 16–26, 27–32, 100.

61. *Florentine Histories*, 123 (emphasis added).

62. *Florentine Histories*, 252 (emphasis added).

63. *Florentine Histories*, 301 (emphasis added), 302.

64. See also, e.g., Ps. 34:12–16; 1 Pet. 3:9–12.

65. *TM*, 193.

66. Ps. 34:15; *TM*, 194; Mansfield, *Machiavelli's New Modes*, 101, 161.

67. *TM*, 194, 195. See also Mansfield, *Machiavelli's New Modes*, 230–32.

68. *TM*, 195.

69. *Discourses*, 230; *TM*, 196. Walker has Machiavelli saying, "bad conscience" (Walker, *Discourses*, 417); Gilbert has him saying, "if your conscience is not clear" (*Machiavelli: The Chief Works and Others*, vol. 1, trans. Allan Gilbert [Durham, N.C.: Duke University Press, 1965], 442).

70. Cf., e.g., Rom. 2:14–15.

71. *TM*, 196.

72. Jackson, "Leo Strauss's Teaching," 211–12.

73. *TM*, 196. See also Jacques Maritain, "The End of Machiavellianism," in *The Social and Political Philosophy of Jacques Maritain: Selected Readings*, ed. Joseph W. Evans and Leo R. Ward (London: Geoffrey Bles, 1956), 320–21, 332–34; Strauss, *NRH*, 161–62.

74. *TM*, 143–44. See also MCL, 16–18, 24; *TM*, 131–32, 148–49. On virtue and of the conscience, see also *NRH*, 163.

75. NM, 314. Cf. *CM*, 22.

76. *TM*, 196.

77. *TM*, 196–97. Cf. HSS, 182–86; JA, 150–52.

78. In an endnote, Strauss continues: "The distinction between core and periphery has taken the place of the distinction between the original teaching and later distortions; in the earlier distinction, the original means either the explicit teaching of the Bible or else that part of the Biblical teaching of which a combination of philology and psychology proves that it is the original." *TM*, 332n52. Cf. *LSEW*, 141–44, 146–47, 153, 154–56, 158; P*SCR*, 150–51, 156–57; *SCR*, 12–13, 17–18, 172, 174f.

79. See, e.g., JA, 150–52; OIG, 359–61; *SCR*, 35, 56, 66–67, 72–73, 75ff., 114–15, 135–36, 140–46, 157–58, 172, 174–76, 258–68. See also *LSEW*, 133; cf. 174, 203–11.

80. *Discourses*, 280.

81. Fischer, *Well-Ordered License*, 183.

82. Angelo Caranfa, *Machiavelli Rethought: A Critique of Strauss' Machiavelli* (Washington, D.C.: University Press of America, 1978), 103–4, 129; Benedetto Fontana, "Love of Country and Love of God: The Political Uses of Religion in Machiavelli," *Journal of the History of Ideas* 60, no. 4 (October 1999): 647n17; John H. Geerken, "Machiavelli's Moses and Renaissance Politics," *Journal of the History of Ideas* 60, no. 4 (October 1999): 579–80, 589–90; Mansfield, *Machiavelli's New Modes*, 398–402; Strauss, *TM*, 51, 114–16, 147–49, 163–68; Vatter, *Between Form and Event*, 280, 289. The phrase, "effectual truth," is from *The Prince*, ch. 15 (cf. *Discourses* I pr., 3, II pr.); on the phrase, see Lord, "Machiavelli's Realism," 116–17; Mansfield, *Machiavelli's Virtue*, 3, 18–19; John M. Najemy, "Language and *The Prince*," in *Niccolò Machiavelli's "The Prince": New Interdisciplinary Essays*, ed. Martin Coyle (Manchester: Manchester University Press, 1995), 96–99, 104; Strauss, MCL, 11–12; *SCR*, 226–27; Vatter, *Between Form and Event*, 31–35.

83. *TM*, 197. Strauss has in mind here (as he indicates in 332n53) *Florentine Histories* IV 7, VI 20–21, VII 4, 17, 28, VIII 10, 11.

84. *TM*, 197–98.

85. *Florentine Histories*, 269.

86. Quoted in *TM*, 198. But of the storm that engulfed Tuscany, de Grazia insists, "the event seems to have no special political or military significance." *Machiavelli in Hell*, 67–68.

87. *Florentine Histories*, 341, 342. On the *Florentine Histories* III 19–21, see also *TM*, 198, 332n54.

88. *TM*, 198.

89. *TM*, 45: "A typical expression indicating a digression is the remark 'But let us return to our subject-matter.'" *TM*, 46: "We do regard as a digression however a passage which is presented as an answer to a possible question or objection of the reader."

Baron speaks of "digressions" but does not see in them the significance that Strauss does. Of Machiavelli's advice in *Discourses* III 6 that princes must act against notions of moral virtue, Baron simply notes, "in the *Discourses* these are digressions, sometimes characterized as such, sometimes splitting up a continuing discussion." Hans Baron, "Machiavelli: The Republican Citizen and the Author of *The Prince*," *English Historical Review* 76, no. 299 (April 1961): 224; Baron, *Florentine Civic Humanism*, 2:111.

90. *TM*, 198–99. Cf. Strauss's discussion of miracles in *PL*, 29–34; *SCR*, 186–92. On the second sentence of Strauss's précis, cf. *CM*, 98–99; JA, 165–66.

91. Cf. *TM*, 73–74, 132–33, 141–49; Sullivan, *Machiavelli's Three Romes*, 50–53.

92. On Genesis and its cosmology, see JA, 151–63, 165–66; OIG, 368–70.

93. Cf. *PL*, 35–38; *SCR*, 37–38, 47–49, 274n2.

94. See, e.g., *The Prince*, chs. 6–7, 11; cf. ch. 13. On *The Prince*, ch. 26, see *TM*, 199 (see also 55, 63, 67–68, 71–75, 79–80).

95. See, e.g., *The Prince*, chs. 15–18.

96. *TM*, 200, 201. The mentions of the *Florentine Histories* and *Exhortation* both occur in the context of Strauss examining Machiavelli's reflections on divine providence and are separated only by a single paragraph, which contains the précis of Machiavelli's doctrine about divine providence. I would suggest, therefore, that the digression to the *Exhortation* adds to the digression to the *Florentine Histories* and that the two digressions form a single, unified digression.

97. *TM*, 31.

98. Germino, "Strauss's Machiavelli," 303. See also Marcia L. Colish, "Republicanism, Religion, and Machiavelli's Savonarolan Moment," *Journal of the History of Ideas* 60, no. 4 (October 1999): 603–6, 616; Germino, "Second Thoughts," 796–803; Parel, *Machiavellian Cosmos*, 54–60, 87; Maurizio Viroli, *Machiavelli* (Oxford: Oxford University Press, 1998), 24–26; Viroli, *Niccolò's Smile: A Biography of Machiavelli*, trans. Antony Shugaar (New York: Farrar, Straus and Giroux, 2000), 257–59. Cf. Patapan, "Machiavelli's *Clizia*," 531ff., 545–47, 547ff.; Viroli, *Niccolò's Smile*, 3–5; Eric Voegelin, "Review of Strauss's *On Tyranny*," in Emberley and Cooper, *Leo Strauss and Eric Voegelin*, 48.

99. Machiavelli, "An Exhortation to Penitence," in *Chief Works*, 1:171.

100. Quoted in Germino, "Strauss's Machiavelli," 303.

101. Andrea Ciliotta-Rubery, "Evil Teachings Without Remorse: An Examination of the Question of Evil Within Machiavelli's 'Exhortation to Penitence' and 'The Life of Castruccio Castracani of Lucca,'" vol. 2 (Ph.D. diss., Georgetown University, 1994), 403 (ellipses are the author's own).

102. "Evil Teachings Without Remorse," 435, 436. See also Strauss, NM, 312; *TM*, 49–52; cf. Sullivan, *Machiavelli's Three Romes*, 218–19n32.

103. *TM*, 201. On Machiavelli's critique of original sin, see also Mansfield, *Machiavelli's Virtue*, 167; Sullivan, *Machiavelli's Three Romes*, 165–67.

104. *TM*, 201, 333n64. On the above comparison between Machiavelli and Epicurean theology, cf. *LAM*, 76–80, 82–83, 86–93; *LSEW*, 186–95; *SCR*, 38–52.

105. Averroës *Commentary on Plato's Republic* I 11.3, II 7.1.

106. Averroës, *Averroës' Middle Commentary on Aristotle's Poetics*, trans. Charles E. Butterworth (Princeton, N.J.: Princeton University Press, 1986), ch. 1, par. 6, p. 65. On dialectics, cf. Aristotle *Prior Analytics* 24a21–b12; *Topics* 101a32–b4; *Sophistical Refutations* 172a12–35; *On the Soul* 403a27–b19; *Metaphysics* 1004b17–26. On poetry, cf. *Poetics* 1448b5–1449a6, 1451a37–b32, 1454b2–14, 1456a4–5, 1458a17–b5, 1459a5–6, 1460b6–15, 1460b34–1461a3.

107. *Discourses*, 11.

108. *Discourses*, 302.

109. *TM*, 202 (for the above references themselves, see 333n65).

110. Quoted in *TM*, 202.

111. *TM*, 202.

112. Quoted in *TM*, 202. Of the identity of the philosophers in question, Mansfield and Tarcov say, "Aristotle, *Physics*, VIII; *Metaphysics*, XII 6–7; *On the Heavens*, I 9 279a12–28. Also Cicero, *Tusculan Disputations*, I 28" (*Discourses*, 138n1).

113. Cf. Strauss, OIG, esp. 361–67.

114. *Discourses*, 139. On Machiavelli and philosophers who say the world is eternal, see Coby, *Machiavelli's Romans*, 340n50; Mansfield, *Machiavelli's New Modes*, 202–3; Strauss, NM, 313–14; cf. de Grazia, *Machiavelli in Hell*, 77f.

115. Averroës, *Averroës' Tahafut Al-Tahafut* (*The Incoherence of the Incoherence*), vol. 1, trans. Simon van den Bergh (London: Luzac and Company, 1969), 12.449, p. 271. Cf. Strauss, OIG, 365–66, 369–70.

116. *Tahafut Al-Tahafut* 12.449–451.

117. *TM*, 202. For Strauss's earlier observation about Machiavelli and Averroism, see *TM*, 175–76. On Machiavelli, Averroism, and the critique of religion, see also K. H. Green, *Jew and Philosopher*, 71–75, 180–82n76.

118. Averroës *Tahafut Al-Tahafut* 1.26–27.

119. *Tahafut Al-Tahafut, About the Natural Sciences* 3.578.

120. Harry Austryn Wolfson, *Studies in the History of Philosophy and Religion*, vol. 1, ed. Isadore Twersky and George H. Williams (Cambridge, Mass.: Harvard University Press, 1973), 383. See also Wolfson, *The Philosophy of the Kalam* (Cambridge, Mass.: Harvard University Press, 1976), 455–65, 589–600. On Averroës and the thesis on eternality, see also Armand A. Maurer, *Medieval Philosophy*, 2nd ed. (Toronto: Pontifical Institute of Mediaeval Studies, 1982), 100–104, 192–207; Strauss, PL, 91–92, 94–98; Wolfson, *Philosophy and Religion*, 1:11–18, 236, 244–45, 374–83, 402–29, 574ff.; Wolfson, *Philosophy of the Kalam*, 358, 373–465, 551–58.

121. *TM*, 203.

122. *TM*, 203; see also 145–46. Cf. *Discourses* I 11–15.

123. *The Prince*, ch. 18, p. 71.

124. *TM*, 204.

125. *The Prince*, 22, 23.

126. *TM*, 205. Cf. *Discourses* II 5, 13, III 22.

127. *Discourses*, 35.

128. *TM*, 205.

129. *TM*, 206. In an endnote, 335n77, Strauss refers to *TM*, 176–77, 184–85; *The Prince*, chs. 10, 13, 19; and *Discourses* II 30.

130. *TM*, 206–7; *Discourses* I 8, 37, 58, II 2.

131. *TM*, 207.

132. *TM*, 207.

133. Voegelin, *Collected Works*, vol. 22, bk. 4, 62–64, 83–84; Ronald Beiner, "Machiavelli, Hobbes, and Rousseau on Civil Religion," *Review of Politics* 55, no. 4 (Fall 1993): 621–24; Gay, *Enlightenment*, 1:55, 195n4, 256–57 (on a general level, see also 1:170–71, 207ff., 216–18); Parel, *Machiavellian Cosmos*, 47–48, 51–59, 61–62.

134. *TM*, 207–8.

135. Jackson, "Leo Strauss's Teaching," 208. Cf. Schall, "Strauss on St. Thomas," 217–19, 221; Strauss, *TM*, 224.

136. *TM*, 203. On experience and the critique of revelation, cf. *SCR*, 126–27; cf. also P*SCR*, 149–50.

137. On the above sympathy, see Merrill, "Christian Philosophy," 98; see also Drury, "Natural Right," 309–11; Drury, "Esoteric Philosophy," 319–20, 329, 331–32; Fuller, "Philosophy, Faith," 279–83; Lampert, *Leo Strauss and Nietzsche*, 139–40; cf. East, "Leo Strauss and American Conservatism," 8–9; Strauss, SR, 4–5.

138. On providence and the Averroists, see Strauss, PM, esp. 542–43.

CHAPTER FOUR
Cosmology and the Utility of Religion

1. Parel, *Machiavellian Cosmos*, 45. See also Parel, "The Question of Machiavelli's Modernity," *Review of Politics* 53, no. 2 (Spring 1991): 320–39.

2. Peterman, "Approaching Leo Strauss," 332. See also Willmoore Kendall, review of *Thoughts on Machiavelli*, by Leo Strauss, *Philosophical Review* 75, no. 2 (April 1966): 252–53.

3. On this point, see Jackson, "Leo Strauss's Teaching," 194–95; cf. Strauss, MCL, 17–19.

4. *Discourses*, 5.

5. *TM*, 172.

6. McAllister, *Revolt Against Modernity*, 95.

7. *TM*, 208.

8. Coby, *Machiavelli's Romans*, 66. See also Najemy, "Papirius and the Chickens," 671–79.

9. *TM*, 208–9.

10. *TM*, 209 (for the references themselves, see 335n81).

11. *TM*, 209.

12. *TM*, 335n82.

13. *TM*, 209 (for the references themselves, see 335n83). Cf. Parel, *Machiavellian Cosmos*, 41–42. On the biblical notion of "the heavens," cf. Robert Sacks, "The Lion and the Ass: A Commentary on the Book of Genesis (Chapters 1–10)," *Interpretation* 8, nos. 2–3 (May 1980): 34, 40–41.

14. *TM*, 335n85.

15. Dante Alighieri, *Inferno*, trans. Allan Gilbert (Durham, N.C.: Duke University Press, 1969), 57.

16. *Discourses*, 209, 210, 211. On Fortuna as seen by Dante (and Virgil), see Ernst Cassirer, *The Myth of the State* (New Haven: Yale University Press, 1946), 160; Cassirer, *Renaissance Philosophy*, 76–77; Parel, *Machiavellian Cosmos*, 65.

17. *TM*, 209.

18. *TM*, 209–10. However, Strauss modifies the above description of *Discourses* I 56 and II 29: see *TM*, 213, 215, where he speaks of Machiavelli's "quasi-theology."

19. On "theology," cf. JA, 150–51, 165–66; *LSEW*, 77–78, 111; MITP, 306–9; NM, 311; *NRH*, 177–80; *TM*, 210–15.

20. *Discourses*, 113, 114. Of the identity of the unnamed philosopher that Machiavelli speaks of, Mansfield and Tarcov, *Discourses*, 114n7, refer to Cicero *De divinatione* I 30.64, and Pietro Pomponazzi, *Tractatus de immortalitate animae* 14. See also *TM*, 335n88.

21. See also *Discourses* I 12, II 5; *TM*, 210.

22. *Discourses*, 114.

23. *TM*, 211.

24. *TM*, 335n90. Strauss's cross-reference instructs, "Cf. pages 188–189 above."

25. Eph. 2:1–2.

26. *TM*, 211.

27. *TM*, 211–13; see also 213–15.

28. *TM*, 213.

29. Cf. *TM*, 165 (line 35). On the above replacement, see also Patapan, "Machiavelli's New Theogony," 185–207.

30. *Discourses*, 197.

31. In a letter to Giovanni Vernacci dated 26 June 1513 Machiavelli wrote, "It is a miracle that I am alive, because my post was taken from me and I was about to lose my life, which God and my innocence have preserved for me. I have had to endure all sorts of other evils, both prison and other kinds. But, by the grace of God, I am well and I manage to live as I can—and so I shall strive to do, until the heavens show themselves to be more kind." Letter 214 in *Machiavelli and His Friends: Their Personal Correspondence*, ed. and trans. James B. Atkinson and David Sices (DeKalb: Northern Illinois University Press, 1996), 239. On the above passage, see *TM*, 336n97.

32. *TM*, 214, 215.

33. *The Prince*, 98.

34. *Discourses*, 202.

35. *Discourses*, 127.

36. *Discourses*, 209, 212.

37. *TM*, 217.

38. *TM*, 217. On the movement or power of Fortuna, and on Fortuna as *a part* of nature, see *Discourses* I 37, II pr., 5; cf. Aristotle *On the Heavens* 286a3–b9, 293a1–10, 300a20–301a19, 308a13–33; *Metaphysics* 1074a15–30; Plato *Timaeus* 39e–40d. On Strauss's above question, cf. *Metaphysics* 1072b1–15, 1073a4–b17.

39. See *TM*, 217, 336n105.

40. *Florentine Histories*, 362. See also *TM*, 218, 336n106.

41. *Discourses*, 281–82. See also *Discourses* III 33.

42. *Discourses*, 201.

43. *TM*, 218–20.

44. *Discourses* III 14, p. 252: "As to seeing new things, every captain ought to contrive to make one of them appear while the armies are hand to hand, which gives spirit to his men and takes it away from the enemy; for among the accidents that give you victory, this is most efficacious."

45. *TM*, 220. In an endnote, 337n112, Strauss instructs the reader to compare chs. 20 and 6 of *The Prince*, and says: "As for the context of both statements, cf. pages 58–60 above. See also pages 74 and 187–188 above." Strauss means that the context consists of Machiavelli's aim "to uproot the Great Tradition" (59).

46. *The Prince*, 22.

47. *TM*, 221.

48. *TM*, 221–22.

49. *TM*, 337n114. The Loeb edition of *Academica* places *Acad. Post.* before *Acad. Priora*. Thus, when Strauss cited *Acad. Post.* I 29, he meant *Posteriora* and *Academica* I 29.

50. Cf. Gay, *Enlightenment*, 1:55, 107–9, 155–56, 259–61.

51. Cicero, *De natura deorum* and *Academica*, trans. H. Rackham, Loeb Classical Library 268 (London: William Heinemann, 1933), 439, 585.

52. *TM*, 222. In an endnote, 337n116, Strauss refers to the *Inferno* 4.136.

53. Dante recounts: "... when I raised my eyes a little more, I saw the teacher of those who understand, sitting amid his philosophic following. All gazed on him [Aristotle]; all did him honor. There I saw Socrates and Plato, who in front of the rest were nearest him; Democritus, who attributed the world to chance, Diogenes, Anaxagoras and Thales, Empedocles, Heraclitus and Zeno." *Inferno* 4.130–138.

54. *TM*, 223. Cf. Parel, *Machiavellian Cosmos*, 45, 65–66, 84–85.

55. *TM*, 223. However, Strauss went on to say of the *Castruccio*, in an article published in 1970: "This graceful little work reveals Machiavelli's moral taste in a more direct or simple and more condensed manner than his great works. At the same time it reveals Machiavelli's relation to the two major trends or schools of classical moral or political thought with unusual explicitness." MCL, 8. The two schools are Socrates and philosophy on the one hand, conventionalism on the other. Strauss declined to examine at length Machiavelli's relation to conventionalism, but explained: "In contradistinction to Aristippus and Diogenes, Machiavelli is a *political* philosopher, a man concerned with the good society; but he understands the good society by starting from the conventionalist assumption, from the premise of extreme individualism: man is not by nature political, man is not by nature directed toward political society. Machiavelli achieves a synthesis of the two classical traditions. He achieves that synthesis by going over to a new plane from the plane on which all classical thought moved. To use what is almost his own expression, he discovered a new continent different from the only continent that was known prior to him." MCL, 10 (original emphasis). The implication here is that, for Strauss, the problem on the surface of things in Machiavelli is that he emulates and subverts but ultimately rejects the classical emphasis on normative thoughts and thinking on excellence.

56. *The Life of Castruccio Castracani of Lucca*, in *The Chief Works*, 2:559.

57. *TM*, 224. See also MCL, 9. Ciliotta-Rubery, "Evil Teachings Without Remorse," 299: "One aphorism dealing with the subject of choosing a wife, comes directly from [Niccolo] Tegrimi's work [*Vita Castrucci Antelminelli Castracani* (1496)]."

58. See *Chief Works*, 2:557 (one mention of God), 558 (two mentions of God).

59. *TM*, 224–25. For Bion's deathbed speech, see Diogenes Laertius, *The Lives and Opinions of Eminent Philosophers*, trans. C. D. Yonge (London: George Bell and Sons, 1895), 175; Machiavelli, *Chief Works*, 2:553–54.

60. On Machiavelli and the good life, see above, present chapter, note 55, where I discuss MCL. Cf. also OIG, 370–71, 373, with *Discourses* I pr., II 2, III 1; *The Prince*, ch. 15.

61. Ciliotta-Rubery, "Evil Teachings Without Remorse," 347. See also James V. Schall, *Jacques Maritain: The Philosopher in Society* (Lanham, Md.: Rowman and Littlefield, 1998), 1–17, 41–42.

62. *TM*, 225. Cf. NM, 314.
63. Preus, "Context and Object," 175.
64. Coby, *Machiavelli's Romans*, 88, 205–6; Sullivan, *Machiavelli's Three Romes*, 28–29.
65. See *Discourses* II 5, III 1; *TM*, 222.
66. *Florentine Histories* pr., I 15, 21–22, 23, 26–28, II 4, 6–12, 17, 30, III 3–5, 18, 20–21, 25, IV 12, 19, 21, 26, 28. On Florence, the Guelfs, and the Ghibellines, see also Hans Baron, *The Crisis of the Early Italian Renaissance: Civic Humanism and Republican Liberty in an Age of Classicism and Tyranny*, rev. ed. (Princeton, N.J.: Princeton University Press, with Newberry Library, 1966), 14–24, 94–98.
67. *TM*, 225.
68. Plato *Republic* 433b–c.
69. *TM*, 225.
70. *TM*, 225–26.
71. Fontana, "Love of Country," 647.
72. *TM*, 226.
73. *Discourses*, 53.
74. *Discourses*, 12.
75. Cf. *Discourses* I 9, 11, 17, 20.
76. *TM*, 227–28.
77. *TM*, 338n124.
78. *TM*, 338n123.
79. *Discourses*, 36, 37.
80. Machiavelli gives two "incontrovertible" explanations to counter "the opinion that the well-being of the cities of Italy arises from the Roman Church." "The first is that because of the wicked examples of that court, this province has lost all devotion and all religion." The "second" reason for the "ruin" of Italy "is that the church has kept and keeps this province divided. And truly no province has ever been united or happy unless it has all come under obedience to one republic or to one prince, as happened to France and to Spain." *Discourses* I 12, p. 38.
81. *The Prince*, 70–71 (emphasis added).
82. *TM*, 227–28.
83. See *TM*, 228–29. See also Mansfield, *Machiavelli's New Modes*, 110–39.
84. See *TM*, 229–30.
85. *TM*, 230. Cf. Preus, "Context and Object," 175–76, 176ff.; Sullivan, *Machiavelli's Three Romes*, 7–8.
86. Cassirer, *Myth of the State*, 138; Maritain, "End of Machiavellianism," 327. Cf. Fabro, *God in Exile*, intro., esp. 9–10, 22–24, 45; cf. also 1144–53.
87. Cassirer says that Machiavelli "was an opponent of the Church but he was no enemy of religion"; Strauss sees Machiavelli as opposed to all religion. Strauss would agree with Cassirer's view that for Machiavelli, "[r]eligion no longer bears any relation to a transcendent order of things and it has lost all its spiritual values," but would—indeed, does—take issue with the claim, which Cassirer makes, that in Machiavelli, "[t]he process of secularization has come to its close." Cassirer, *Myth of the State*, 138, 139. Strauss, TWM, 82: "This is exactly what Plato claims to do in his *Republic* to bring about the cessation of all evil on earth by purely human means. And surely Plato cannot be said to have secularized biblical faith."

88. *TM*, 230–31.

89. *TM*, 231. Cf. Hobbes, *Leviathan*, pt. IV; Spinoza, *Theologico-Political Treatise*, pr., ch. 7.

90. See also *LSEW*, 175, 190–91; *PL*, 35–38; P*SCR*, 171–72; *SCR*, 46–47, 86–87, 111–12, 209–11, 226–29, 245–48; cf. also Lampert, *Leo Strauss and Nietzsche*, 144; Merrill, "Christian Philosophy," 98–102.

91. *NRH*, 177. On the above modern "fight" and its basic claim that reason is supreme, see also Fabro, *God in Exile*, 155–57, 158–69, 226–49, 250–59, 422–25, 430ff.; Lampert, "Nietzsche's Challenge to Philosophy," esp. 607–10, 618–19.

92. *TM*, 13 (emphasis added).

93. Christopher Marlowe, *Jew of Malta*, prologue, lines 5–15, in *The Complete Works of Christopher Marlowe*, vol. 1, ed. Fredson Bowers (Cambridge: Cambridge University Press, 1973), 263 (original emphasis).

94. *TM*, 175. On the above problem on the surface of things, cf. Voegelin, *Collected Works*, vol. 22, bk. 4, 83–84.

95. Cf. Merrill, "Christian Philosophy," 98, 104–5.

CHAPTER FIVE
Moral Virtue and Human Action

1. Cf. Maritain, "End of Machiavellianism," 326–27.

2. *TM*, 231. In an endnote, 338n130, Strauss refers to *Discourses* I 55 and III 1.

3. *Discourses* I 55, pp. 110–11 (emphasis added): "Having first taken an oath to pay the fitting amount [of tax], he throws into a chest so designated what according to his conscience it appears to him he ought to pay. Of this payment there is no witness except him who pays. Hence it can be conjectured how much *goodness* and how much *religion* are yet in those men." III 1, p. 209 (emphasis added): "This return [in republics] toward the beginning is done through either extrinsic accident or intrinsic prudence. As to the first, one sees that it was necessary that Rome be taken by the French, if one wished that it be reborn and, by being reborn, regain new life and new virtue, and regain the observance of *religion* and *justice*, which were beginning to be tainted in it."

4. *TM*, 231–32. On "first" and "second" statements, see also HSS, 212–13; *TM*, 43.

5. *TM*, 232. Cf. Gilbert, "Politics and Morality," 467–68.

6. *Discourses*, 5.

7. Coby, *Machiavelli's Romans*, 21 (see also 207–10, 213, 325–26n35). Cf. Chabod, *Machiavelli and the Renaissance*, 140–42; Condren, *Classic Texts*, 68; Fleisher, "Ways of Machiavelli," 330–38; Mansfield, *Machiavelli's New Modes*, 21–23, 25–28; *Machiavelli's Virtue*, ix–xi, 3, 62, 125–26, 176–80, 235; Masters, *Machiavelli, Leonardo*, 30–32.

8. *TM*, 232–33. Given Strauss's above discussion, I contend that Drury is correct when she states, "Machiavelli's revolt [which takes shape in his new modes and orders] is more a revolt against the pagan tradition of classical philosophy ... than against Christianity." However, Drury errs when she insists, "Strauss does not make this explicit, and his interesting thesis is likely to be missed in the midst of the rhetoric railing against Machiavelli's conscious intention to subvert Christianity." Drury, "Hidden

Meaning," 582; see also Drury, *Political Ideas of Leo Strauss*, 121–32. It suffices to say here that Strauss does make his thesis explicit.

On Machiavelli's "new principle," see also NM, 299–301; *NRH*, 178–79; *OT*, 24–25, 106n5; TWM, 83–88; WIPP, 40–49; cf. MCL, 10, 12; Voegelin, *Collected Works*, vol. 22, bk. 4, 31–34, 42, 60–61, 82–83; cf. also Robert A. Kocis, *Machiavelli Redeemed: Retrieving His Humanist Perspectives on Equality, Power, and Glory* (Bethlehem, Pa.: Lehigh University Press; London: Associated University Press, 1998), 18, 108. On his critique of the contemplative life, cf. also Cassirer, *Myth of the State*, 142–56, 161–62; Patapan, "Machiavelli's New Theogony," 185, 197–98, 203–7; Vatter, *Between Form and Event*, 154–60; Zuckert, *Postmodern Platos*, 118–21, 305n52.

9. Remarks by Machiavelli quoted in *TM*, 233. Strauss has in mind here *The Prince*, ch. 15; *Discourses* I 18, 58; and Machiavelli's letters to Vettori of 9 Apr. and 10 Dec. 1513. For these references, see *TM*, 338n131.

10. *Discourses*, 49.

11. *The Prince*, 61.

12. *TM*, 233; Villari, *Life and Times*, 2:154. In a letter to Francesco Vettori dated 10 Dec. 1513, Machiavelli said of his evening discussions with Dante, Petrarch, and the ancients: "Because Dante says that no one understands anything unless he retains what he has understood, I have jotted down what I have profited from in their conversation and composed a short study, *De principatibus*." Further on in his letter he summarized thus the close relation between his career and his scholarly endeavors: "During the fifteen years I have been studying the art of the state I have neither slept nor fooled around, and anybody ought to be happy to utilize someone who has had so much experience at the expense of others." Letter 224 in *Machiavelli and His Friends*, 264, 265.

13. *Discourses*, 98.

14. Cf. Aristotle *Nicomachean Ethics* 1139b14–1145a11.

15. *TM*, 233 (see also 338n132; cf. 11). Cf. Caranfa, *Machiavelli Rethought*, 37–44, 129, 138, 145; McAllister, *Revolt Against Modernity*, 289n31, 290n54; McCoy, *Structure of Political Thought*, 79, 157–80; Vatter, *Between Form and Event*, 31–35, 100, 307–11; Villari, *Life and Times*, 2:95–98; Viroli, *Machiavelli*, ch. 2. On *Discourses* I 47, see also Mansfield, *Machiavelli's New Modes*, 143–47. On *Discourses* III 39, see also Coby, *Machiavelli's Romans*, 214–15, 319n46; Mansfield, *Machiavelli's New Modes*, 421–23.

16. *TM*, 234.

17. *TM*, 43; Gaetano Mosca, "The Renaissance and Machiavelli," in *A Short History of Political Philosophy*, trans. Sondra Z. Koff (New York: Thomas Y. Crowell, 1972), 83.

18. *TM*, 235.

19. Maritain, "End of Machiavellianism," 322.

20. *TM*, 234–35. Cf. *Discourses* I 9–10, 18, 58; Rousseau, *Social Contract* II 3; Strauss, *SCR*, 226–29.

21. *TM*, 235–36 (for the references themselves, see 338nn137, 138).

22. *TM*, 236.

23. For Aristotle, "Pride, then, seems to be a sort of crown of the excellences; for it makes them greater, and it is not found without them." (*Nicomachean Ethics* 1124a1–3) "[J]ustice is often thought to be the greatest of excellences and 'neither evening nor morning star' is so wonderful ... And it is complete excellence in its fullest sense, because it is the actual exercise of complete excellence." (1129b28–31)

24. See above, ch. 2; see also Keys, "Aristotelian Magnanimity."
25. St. Thomas Aquinas, *Summa Theologiæ*, vol. 37, *Justice* (2a2æ, qq. 57–62), trans. Thomas Gilby (Blackfriars; London: Eyre and Spottiswoode; New York: McGraw-Hill, 1975), q. 58, art. 12, obj. 2 and reply to 2. See also *Summa Theologiæ*, vol. 23, *Virtue* (1a2æ, qq. 55–67), trans. W. D. Hughes (Blackfriars; London: Eyre and Spottiswoode; New York: McGraw-Hill, 1969), q. 60, art. 5, reply.
26. *TM*, 236. In an endnote, 338–39n139, Strauss cites *The Prince*, ch. 15; Aristotle *Nicomachean Ethics* 1106b33–1108b9; and Aquinas *Summa Theologiæ* 1a2æ, q. 60, art. 5, reply.
27. See below and *TM*, 236.
28. *Discourses*, 31–32, 33. Cf. *The Prince*, ch. 16. On praising the praiseworthy and blaming the blameworthy, cf. also Aristotle *Nicomachean Ethics* 1105b29–1106a2.
29. *Discourses*, 74.
30. *TM*, 236. On Machiavelli's criticism of Caesar, see also Coby, *Machiavelli's Romans*, 47–54; cf. Hegel, *Reason in History*, 39–40.
31. *Discourses*, 98. See also *Discourses* I 25, II 22.
32. *TM*, 237. On the mean, see also *TM*, 339n141.
33. *TM*, 237. Strauss does not give references for the above "assertion." I note, then, that in *Nicomachean Ethics* 1108b11–15 Aristotle explains, "There are three kinds of disposition, then, two of them vices, involving excess and deficiency and one an excellence, viz. the mean, and all are in a sense opposed to all; for the extreme states are contrary both to the intermediate state and to each other, and the intermediate to the extremes."
34. *The Prince*, 66.
35. *Discourses*, 184, 300. See also *Discourses* III 41–42.
36. Livy, *History of Rome*, vol. 4, Books VIII–X, trans. B. O. Foster, Loeb Classical Library 191 (London: William Heinemann; New York: G. P. Putnam's Sons, 1926), IX 3.11–12, p. 173.
37. *History of Rome* IX.12.2.
38. *TM*, 238. Strauss is drawing upon *Discourses* I 58 and Chapter 9 of *The Prince*— in that order. In the former Machiavelli states, "The Roman people . . . never served humbly nor dominated proudly while the republic lasted uncorrupt; indeed, with its orders and magistrates, it held its rank honorably" (*Discourses*, 116). In the latter he says, "The people desire neither to be commanded nor oppressed by the great, and the great desire to command and oppress the people. From these two diverse appetites one of three effects occurs in cities: principality or liberty or license" (*The Prince*, 39). On liberty, the people, and the nobles, see also Benedetto Fontana, "Sallust and the Politics of Machiavelli," *History of Political Thought* 24, no. 1 (Spring 2003): 86–108, esp. 89–92.
39. *TM*, 238.
40. Rev. 3:16–17.
41. Aristotle *Nicomachean Ethics* 1107a9–14. On justice and injustice, see also 1129a3–1131a9.
42. *TM*, 238. In an endnote, 339n142, Strauss refers to *The Prince*, chs. 9, 15, 17; *Discourses* I 58, III 31; and instructs, "Cf. Livy IX 3.11 and 12.2."
43. *TM*, 238–39. On Strauss's point about the Tuscan language, cf. Najemy, "Language and *The Prince*," 99–102.
44. *The Prince*, 61–62.

45. *TM*, 239.

46. *TM*, 239. On the above problems Machiavelli sees in liberality, cf. Cicero, *On Duties*, ed. M. T. Griffin and E. M. Atkins, trans. E. M. Atkins (Cambridge: Cambridge University Press, 1991), I 42–59.

47. *TM*, 239.

48. *TM*, 239–40. In 339n145 Strauss cites *Discourses* I 2 and Polybius VI 5.10–6.9.

49. *Discourses*, 11–12.

50. Polybius, *The Histories*, vol. 3, Books V–VIII, trans. W. R. Paton, Loeb Classical Library 138 (London: William Heinemann; New York: G. P. Putnam's Sons, 1923), VI 6.6–8, p. 281. On the contrast between Machiavelli and Polybius, see Qviller, "Machiavellian Cosmos," 229–30.

51. Quoted in *TM*, 240.

52. *TM*, 240.

53. *Discourses*, 62–63.

54. *TM*, 241. Cf. *XS*, 38.

55. *TM*, 241.

56. *TM*, 241–42 (for the references themselves, see 339n149).

57. On the use of religion, see *Discourses* I 11–15.

58. *TM*, 242 (for the references themselves, see 339n150).

59. *Discourses*, 191–92.

60. *TM*, 242.

61. *The Prince*, 34.

62. *TM*, 242. On Agathocles, see also *TM*, 47, 339n151. On virtue, cf. OPS, 189–90.

63. *TM*, 242.

64. *TM*, 339n152.

65. *Discourses*, 181. The title of II 23 is: "How Much the Romans, in Judging Subjects for Some Accidents That Necessitated Such Judgment, Fled from the Middle Way."

66. *Florentine Histories*, 146. See also *Discourses* I 47; *TM*, 339n152.

67. *Discourses*, 213–14. On the man of "quality," see Mansfield, *Machiavelli's New Modes*, 308.

68. *TM*, 242–43.

69. *TM*, 156.

70. *Discourses*, 182.

71. *TM*, 156–57.

72. I thank Fr. James V. Schall for drawing my attention to the significance of the above passage about charity. On Machiavelli's new Fall, cf. Patapan, "Machiavelli's New Theogony," 195–98, 202, 204. On charity, see also, e.g., Aquinas *Summa Theologiæ* vol. 29, 1a2æ, q. 100, art. 10.

73. James V. Schall, "On How Revelation Addresses Itself to Politics," in *Policy Reform and Moral Grounding*, ed. T. William Boxx and Gary M. Quinlivan (Latrobe, Pa.: Saint Vincent College, 1995), 8.

74. *TM*, 243. In an endnote, 340n155, Strauss refers to *The Prince*, ch. 21; *Discourses* I 6, 49, III 11, 17, 37.

75. *Discourses*, 257, 294. On the "actions of men," see also *Discourses* I 6.

76. *TM*, 243. On the phrase *summum bonum*, cf. John Hick, *Faith and Knowledge*, 2nd ed. (Ithaca, N.Y.: Cornell University Press, 1966), 59–61; Thomas Hobbes,

Leviathan, ed. C. B. Macpherson (London: Penguin Books, 1968), ch. 11, at 160; Jaffa, *Thomism and Aristotelianism*, 67–69; Rhodes, *Eros, Wisdom, and Silence*, 92–93; Strauss, *TPPH*, 15–16; Voegelin, *Collected Works*, vol. 22, bk. 4, 70–71.

77. *TM*, 243. In an endnote, 340n157, Strauss refers to *The Prince*, ch. 8, directing the reader to compare it with *Discourses* III 31 and *Discourses* II 18 with *Discourses* III 21.

78. On the contrast between goodness and virtue, cf. OIR, 475–76.

79. *TM*, 244. See also Voegelin, *Collected Works*, vol. 24, bk. 6, 84.

80. *Discourses*, 112.

81. *TM*, 244 (emphasis added).

82. *TM*, 340n159.

83. *TM*, 244. Not until *TM*, 245 (line 14) does Strauss give an accompanying endnote; see 340n160, where he says, "*Prince* ch. 25. Cf. pages 215–221 above.—See Thomas Aquinas, *Summa theologica* I q.82.a.1." On *TM*, 215–21, see above, ch. 4.

84. See *TM*, 340n160. Strauss does not quote the passage, where Aquinas states, "Rational powers embrace opposites, Aristotle says [*Metaphysics* 1046b4]. But will is a rational power, for as the *De Anima* [432b3] says, will is in the reason." Aquinas goes on, "We are masters of our acts in that we can choose this or that. But we choose, not the end, but *things for the sake of the end*, as we read in the *Ethics* [1111b26]. Hence our desire for ultimate fulfilment is not one of the things we are master of." St. Thomas Aquinas, *Summa Theologiæ*, vol. 11, *Man* (1a, qq. 75–83), trans. Timothy Suttor (Blackfriars; London: Eyre and Spottiswoode; New York: McGraw-Hill, 1970), 1a, q. 82, art. 1, obj. 2, and q. 82, art. 1, obj. 3 and reply to 3 (original emphasis). Aristotle argues, "Moral excellence comes about as a result of habit . . . none of the moral excellences arises in us by nature; for nothing that exists by nature can form a habit contrary to its nature." (*Nicomachean Ethics* 1103a16–21) "[W]ish relates rather to the end, choice to what contributes to the end . . . in general, choice seems to relate to things that are in our own power." (1111b26, 30) In fact, "If it is in our power to do noble or base acts, and likewise in our power not to do them, and this was what being good or bad meant, then it is in our power to be virtuous or vicious." (1113b11–14) See also *Nicomachean Ethics* 1103a23–b26, 1109b30–1112a17, 1113b2–1115a6, 1128b16–35; *Eudemian Ethics* 1220a5–1234b13; *Politics* 1337a10-b22; *Rhetoric* 1368b1–1369b29.

85. Merrill, "Christian Philosophy," 98. Cf. Zuckert, *Postmodern Platos*, 120–21.

86. On the latter point, see *NRH*, 7–8, 163–64; cf. Merrill, "Christian Philosophy," 80–88.

87. *The Prince*, 98–99.

88. *TM*, 245. On freedom, rationality, and controlling Fortuna, see also Cassirer, *Myth of the State*, 159; *Individual and the Cosmos*, 73–77.

89. *TM*, 245. The below discussion draws on *TM*, 245–46, 340nn161–63.

90. *TM*, 246–47. On the modern turn from the "Ought" to the "Is," see also Behnegar, *Leo Strauss, Max Weber*, 169–73, 203.

91. *Discourses*, 53, 55.

92. *TM*, 247. See also Rel, 21.

93. Cicero *Academica* I 19. Here Cicero outlines two other divisions in philosophy: "the secrets of nature," and "[the] judgment of truth and falsehood" in rhetoric.

94. *Academica* I 22–23.

95. See Mansfield, *Machiavelli's Virtue*, 31–38.

96. See also *Discourses* I 3, 28, 29, 30, II 12; *The Prince*, chs. 12, 17; *Florentine Histories* IV 14, 18. For these references, see *TM*, 341n165.

97. *Discourses*, 195.

98. *TM*, 248.

99. *TM*, 248. See also *Discourses* I 37, II 6, III 8.

100. *Discourses* I 3, p. 15; III 12, p. 248.

101. *Discourses*, 254, 255. Cf. *Discourses* III 8.

102. *TM*, 249. See also *Discourses* I 1, 2, 7, 32, 36, 37, II 2, 8, III 6, 12, 23; *The Prince*, ch. 17.

103. *Discourses*, 147–48: "But since he [Agis III, King of Sparta] lacked money and feared that for want of it his army would abandon him, he was constrained to try the fortune of battle [against the Macedonians]. So from this cause Quintus Curtius affirms that money is the sinew of war. This sentence is cited every day and is followed by princes who are not prudent enough."

104. *Discourses*, 149. Strauss says of *Discourses* II 10: "As Machiavelli asserts, Livy tacitly contends that money is altogether unimportant for winning wars whereas Livy explicitly contends that chance or good luck is important." *TM*, 341n168.

105. *Discourses*, 125, 126. Plutarch ascribes Rome's greatness to Fortune and Virtue both opposing each other (they "are engaged in a direct and continual strife and discord") and "joining forces" (*Moralia, On the Fortune of the Romans* 316e). "Virtue made Romulus great, but Fortune watched over him until he became great" (321b). *Moralia*, vol. 4, 263d–351b, trans. Frank Cole Babbitt, Loeb Classical Library 305 (London: William Heinemann; Cambridge, Mass.: Harvard University Press, 1936), 325, 349.

106. *Discourses*, 127, 128.

107. See also *Discourses* I 37, 51, II 6, III 10; *TM*, 341n168.

108. Mansfield, *Machiavelli's New Modes*, 218.

109. *Discourses*, 15. On the causes of union and disunion, see also *Discourses* II 25.

110. *The Prince*, 66, 95.

111. *TM*, 249–50.

112. See *TM*, 250–51.

113. *TM*, 251. In an endnote, 342n171, Strauss refers to *Discourses* I 1, 14, 17, 29, 32, 37, III 3, 8, 10, 11, 12, 30; *The Prince*, ch. 3; and directs the reader to compare these references to *Florentine Histories* II 2 and VII 7. He also refers to *TM*, 119–20.

114. *Discourses*, 64. On acquisition, see also *Discourses* III 3, 10.

115. *The Prince*, 14–15 (emphasis added).

116. *TM*, 251, 252. Of the twelve chapters—I 1, 14, 17, 29, 32, 37, III 3, 8, 10, 11, 12, and 30—from the *Discourses* to which Strauss refers in an endnote, *TM*, 342n171, only III 8 speaks of Manlius Capitolinus. As well as directing the reader to compare those references to the *Florentine Histories* II 2 and VII 7, Strauss refers to his previous comments, in ch. 3 (119–20), on *Discourses* III 12. For instance, Strauss said that Machiavelli quoted Livy's speech but left out the part that explains that "some god" would not rescue Messius and his army (*TM*, 120).

117. Jaffa, *Thomism and Aristotelianism*, 89.

118. *Florentine Histories*, 53, 285.

119. See below and *The Prince*, ch. 6; *TM*, 252.

120. *Discourses*, 48.

121. *Discourses*, 254–55.

122. *TM*, 252.

123. *TM*, 253.

124. Aristotle *Politics* 1287b40.

125. *Politics* 1288a8–9, 11–13.

126. *TM*, 252–53. In an endnote, 342n172, Strauss refers to *The Prince*, chs. 6, 26; *Discourses* I 1, 17, 18, 21, 35, 41, 55, III 8, 16; and directs the reader to compare these references to Aristotle *Politics* 1287b37ff. For the phrase, "defect of nature," see *Discourses* I 21; but see also I 41 and III 8. For the phrase, "man of a rare 'brain,'" see *Discourses* I 55.

127. *TM*, 253.

128. *TM*, 253.

129. *TM*, 342n173; Strauss refers to *TM*, 83, 168–72, and 217–18, having referred to *Discourses* III 35, *The Prince*, ch. 18, and *Florentine Histories* VIII 22.

130. *The Prince*, 70.

131. *Florentine Histories*, 344.

132. Aristotle *Metaphysics* 1074b15–34.

133. See above, ch. 3.

CHAPTER SIX
Virtue and Governance

1. Cf. Gen. 8:21.

2. J. G. A. Pocock, *The Machiavellian Moment: Florentine Political Thought and the Atlantic Republican Tradition* (Princeton, N.J.: Princeton University Press, 1975).

3. Quentin Skinner, *The Foundations of Modern Political Thought*, vol. 1, *The Renaissance* (Cambridge: Cambridge University Press, 1978). See also Skinner, introduction to Niccolò Machiavelli, *The Prince*, ed. Quentin Skinner and trans. Russell Price (Cambridge: Cambridge University Press, 1988), ix–xxiv; and Skinner, *Machiavelli*.

4. Gisela Bock, Quentin Skinner, and Maurizio Viroli, eds., *Machiavelli and Republicanism* (Cambridge: Cambridge University Press, 1990); Viroli, *Machiavelli*, esp. chs. 4 and 5. See also Maurizio Viroli, *Jean-Jacques Rousseau and the "Well-Ordered Society,"* trans. Derek Hanson (Cambridge: Cambridge University Press, 1988), 11–12, 120–21, 168–72; Viroli, *From Politics to Reason of State: The Acquisition and Transformation of the Language of Politics 1250–1600* (Cambridge: Cambridge University Press, 1992), 126–77.

5. Skinner, *Foundations*, 1:116–23, 124ff.

6. *Foundations*, 1:128–38. See also Baron, "Machiavelli," 248–51; Gay, *Enlightenment*, 1:258, 261–69, 507–15; Felix Gilbert, *Machiavelli and Guicciardini: Politics and History in Sixteenth-Century Florence* (Princeton, N.J.: Princeton University Press, 1965; repr., 1973), esp. ch. 4. On civic humanism, the spirit of republican freedom, and the Renaissance revival of classical culture and thought, see Baron, *Crisis of Early Italian Renaissance*. For a recent assessment of civic humanism and Machiavelli, see James Hankins, ed., *Renaissance Civic Humanism: Reappraisals and Reflections* (Cambridge: Cambridge University Press, 2000); see also Mark Hulliung, *Citizen Machiavelli* (Princeton, N.J.: Princeton University Press, 1983), esp. 11–30, 189–98, 237–47.

7. Skinner, intro. to *The Prince*, xviii; see also *Foundations*, 1:137. Cf. Kocis, *Machiavelli Redeemed*, 17–19, 68–72.

8. Skinner, *Foundations*, 1:152–58. Cf. Mansfield, *Machiavelli's Virtue*, 233–34; Terchek, "Liberal-Communitarian Debate," 149.

9. John Rawls, *Justice as Fairness: A Restatement*, ed. Erin Kelly (Cambridge, Mass.: Harvard University Press, Belknap Press, 2001), 142, 143. See also Gay, *Enlightenment*; Gilbert, *Machiavelli and Guicciardini*.

10. *Justice as Fairness*, 144; in 144n13 Rawls notes of Skinner's *Machiavelli* that "Machiavelli's *Discourses* is sometimes taken as illustrating classical republicanism as defined in the text."

11. *Justice as Fairness*, 146n16.

12. See, e.g., Fontana, "Politics of Machiavelli," 88ff., 100, 107–8; Mansfield, *Machiavelli's Virtue*, 235–57; Patricia Springborg, "Republicanism, Freedom from Domination, and the Cambridge Contextual Historians," *Political Studies* 49, no. 5 (December 2001): 853–57, 863.

13. *TM*, 253–54. In an endnote, 342n174, Strauss refers to *The Prince*, ch. 15, *Discourses* I 3, and instructs the reader to compare *The Prince*, ch. 25, with Aristotle *Politics* 1311a30–31, *Nicomachean Ethics* 1168b15–28, and Plato *Republic* 408e*ff*.

14. *Republic* 408e–410a.

15. *TM*, 254. See also OPS, 172 (cf. 174–75).

16. *TM*, 254. See also K. H. Green, *Jew and Philosopher*, 159–49; Plato *Republic* 409a–b. Cf. Berkowitz, *Modern Liberalism*, 7–13, 15; Roger D. Masters, "Rousseau and the Rediscovery of Human Nature," in *The Legacy of Rousseau*, ed. Clifford Orwin and Nathan Tarcov (Chicago: University of Chicago Press, 1997), 110. On whether the just city has ever existed, cf. also Strauss, PO, 60–61.

17. *TM*, 254–55. Cf. *Discourses* I 4.

18. *TM*, 255. In an endnote, 342n175, Strauss refers to *Discourses* I 2, 4, 10, 18, 58, II 5, III 36; *The Prince*, ch. 19. He then instructs the reader to compare those references with Aristotle *Politics* 1253a31–37; Plato *Laws* 680d1–5 and 782b–c; and *TM*, 46, 70–71, 133. Concerning Strauss's instruction, see above, present chapter. In *TM*, 46 Strauss mentions Severus and *The Prince*, ch. 19; *TM*, 71 mentions Cesare Borgia and refers to *The Prince*, ch. 7; and *TM*, 133 speaks of the relationship between *The Prince* and the *Discourses*.

In *TM*, 305n62 Strauss explains, "To see the special significance of the discussion of Severus, one should also compare Machiavelli's judgment on his apparent hero Cesare Borgia with his judgment on Severus," and then directs the reader to compare ch. 7 of *The Prince* with ch. 19.

19. *The Prince*, 71–72, 78, 79.

20. *Discourses*, 32.

21. *The Prince*, 27.

22. Aristotle *Politics* 1253a35–36.

23. Maritain, "End of Machiavellianism," 339.

24. Aristotle *Politics* 1253a36; Plato *Laws* 782a, 782e–783a.

25. *TM*, 256. But in an endnote, 342n176, Strauss refers to Aristotle *Nicomachean Ethics* 1102a5–12, 1180a24–28; *Eudemian Ethics* 1248b38*ff*.; *Politics* 1264a1–5, 1293b1–4, 1293b24–26, 1296a32–b2, 1324b1–28, 1333b5–14; Machiavelli, *Discourses* I 9, 10, 16, 29, 34, II 2, 8, III 6, 8.

26. *TM*, 256. On patriotism, cf. *TM*, 11.

27. *TM*, 257. On Machiavelli's point about austerity (keeping the public rich but citizens poor), cf. Coby, *Machiavelli's Romans*, 27–30, 102–4, 107, 151–53.

28. *Discourses*, 261.

29. *Discourses*, 263–64. See also *The Prince*, ch. 17. On affairs of moment, cf. *Discourses* II 23.

30. *Discourses*, 288.

31. *TM*, 257.

32. *TM*, 258.

33. The passage from Aristotle's *Politics*—1327b38–1328a10—to which Strauss refers in an endnote—*TM*, 342n179—does not mention the restoration of confiscated property. Instead, Aristotle says that guardians should be unfriendly to all wrongdoers, be they strangers or not. The passages from Plato's *Republic*—486b10–13, 537a4–7, and 619b7–d1—to which Strauss also refers do not propose that a city confiscate its neighbors' property and territory to live "a life of luxury." In the first passage, Plato says a philosophic person is just and kind; an unphilosophic person is unjust and mean. In the second passage, he speaks of testing children for future roles as guardians. In the third passage, he describes as foolish the choice to lead a life devoid of philosophy and of good, orderly habits. Having in *TM*, 342n179 referred to the *Politics* and then to the *Republic*, Strauss refers to *The Prince*, ch. 17, and adds: "Cf. pages 191–192 and 239–240 above." In those pages, Strauss explained that Machiavelli argues that, given the flux and instability of the world and of human affairs, princes cannot refrain from acquisition.

34. *The Prince*, 67, 68.

35. *TM*, 258.

36. See also *Discourses* III 1. The below discussion draws upon *TM*, 258–59, 342n180; see also Maritain, "End of Machiavellianism," esp. 328–32.

37. Aristotle *Politics* 1309b1–9.

38. *TM*, 259. On Machiavelli's view of a "good" ruler, cf. Cicero *On Duties* I 80–82. The "historian" Strauss has in mind is William H. Prescott, as he indicates in *TM*, 342n180. Here he refers to the *Discourses* I 4, 7, 9, 10, 16, 17, 18, 25, 27, 34, 40, 55, III 3, 7, 11, 21, 29, 40, 41 (cf. *Florentine Histories* II 5), 44; *The Prince*, ch. 18; and instructs the reader to compare these references with both William H. Prescott, *History of the Reign of Ferdinand and Isabella*, ed. J. F. Kirk (Philadelphia, 1872), I, 233, and Aristotle *Politics* 1309a39–b6.

39. Mansfield, *Machiavelli's Virtue*, 224.

40. *TM*, 259. See also Schall, *Jacques Maritain*, 30–31. Cf. McShea, "Leo Strauss on Machiavelli," 785–86.

41. *TM*, 259. *Discourses* I 40: "Men often act like certain lesser birds of prey, in whom there is such desire to catch their prey, to which nature urges them, that they do not sense another larger bird that is above them so as to kill them." III 29: "Titus Livy . . . narrates that as the Roman legates were carrying the booty of the Veientes to Apollo, they were taken by pirates of Lipari in Sicily and led to that town. When Timasitheus, their prince, learned what gift this was, where it was going, and who was sending it, though born at Lipari, he bore himself as a Roman man and showed the people how impious it was to seize a gift such as this. So with the consent of the collectivity,

he let the legates go with all their things. The words of the historian are these: 'Timasitheus filled the multitude, which is always like the ruler, with religion.'" *Discourses*, 89, 278.

42. See Hobbes, *Leviathan*, chs. 10, 21; Friedrich Meinecke, *Machiavellism: The Doctrine of Raison d'État and Its Place in Modern History*, trans. Douglas Scott (London: Routledge and Kegan Paul, 1957), ch. 1, esp. 29–31, 38–40; ch. 2, 54ff.; ch. 6, 150–51. Strauss, however, censures the Meineckian argument that the doctrine of *raison d'état* has its origin in Machiavelli; see below, ch. 7.

43. *TM*, 260.

44. *Discourses* I 25, 47–48, 53.

45. *Discourses* I 5, 6, 40, 44, 49, 50, 60, II 2; *The Prince*, ch. 9; *Florentine Histories* III 1; *TM*, 260. Cf. *Discourses* I 37; *The Prince*, ch. 3; Coby, *Machiavelli's Romans*, 38–39, 64–66, 114ff., 254–58.

46. *Discourses* II 19; *TM*, 261–62.

47. *TM*, 261.

48. *Discourses* I 5, 6, II 2, 3, 4, 19, III 49.

49. *TM*, 261–62. Cf. Coby, *Machiavelli's Romans*, 127–30, 308nn16–18, 309–10n32.

50. *TM*, 262. Cf. *TM*, 307–8n29; Coby, *Machiavelli's Romans*, 270–74.

51. Cf. Cassirer, *Myth of the State*, 145–49; Maritain, "End of Machiavellianism," 328–29.

52. *TM*, 262.

53. *TM*, 262–63, 343n185; *Discourses* I 32, 34, 37, 54, 55. For Machiavelli's dim view of the people, see *Discourses* I 53; *Florentine Histories* II 34, 41, III 17, 18, 20, VI 24; cf. *Discourses* I 44, 58.

54. *Discourses*, 109.

55. *TM*, 265. In an endnote, 343n187, Strauss says, "*Discourses* III 20–22 and 7 end."

56. *Discourses*, 274, 276.

57. See also NM, 314–15; *TM*, 20–21, 25; cf. *TM*, 111, 127. Cf. also Baron, "Machiavelli," 220–21; Cassirer, *Myth of the State*, 155–56.

58. *TM*, 265.

59. *TM*, 266 (for the references themselves, see 343n188).

60. *Discourses* I 10, 11, 12, 43, II 2; *Florentine Histories* V 1.

61. See *TM*, 266 (for the references themselves, see 343n189).

62. *Discourses*, 38 (emphasis added).

63. *Florentine Histories*, 185. Cf. *Discourses* I 10.

64. See also *Discourses* I 33–35, II 19, III 1; *TM*, 266–67.

65. *Discourses* I 17, 18, 55, III 4–6, 8, 30.

66. *Discourses*, 112.

67. *TM*, 268; cf. 266 (lines 37–39).

68. The discussion below draws on *TM*, 268–69.

69. *TM*, 269.

70. Callicles asks, "On what principle of justice did Xerxes invade Hellas, or his father the Scythians?" Callicles answers: "Nay, but these men, I suggest, act in this way according to the nature of justice; yes, by Heaven, and according to the law of nature, though not, perhaps, according to that law which we enact; we take the best and strongest of our fellows from their youth upwards, and tame them like young

lions,—enslaving them with spells and incantations, and saying to them that with equality they must be content, and that the equal is the honourable and the just. But if there were a man born with enough ability, he would shake off and break through, and escape from all this; he would trample under foot all our formulas and spells and charms, and all our laws which are against nature: the slave would rise in rebellion and be lord over us, and the light of natural justice would shine forth." Plato *Gorgias* 483d–484b, in *The Dialogues of Plato*, rev. 4th ed., trans. B. Jowett (Oxford: Clarendon Press, 1953), 2:577. Is Callicles the cynical villain that the above passage, at first glance, and Strauss's parallel suggest? Callicles voices notions of justice, virtue, nobility, and civic mindedness, but seems unable or unwilling to face the moral consequences of the philosophic life and of attachment to virtue; love of the good is not, says Socrates, identical with love of glory, honor, or pleasure. See Devin Stauffer, "Socrates and Callicles: A Reading of Plato's *Gorgias*," *Review of Politics* 64, no. 4 (Fall 2002): 627–57.

71. *TM*, 269.

72. *TM*, 343n192.

73. *Discourses*, 273. Mansfield and Tarcov, *Discourses*, 273n4, refers to *Discourses* III 6, and to Aristotle *Politics* 1314b27 and 1303b17–1304a18.

74. *Politics* 1303b17–28: "In revolutions the occasions may be trifling, but great interests are at stake. Even trifles are most important when they concern the rulers, as was the case of old at Syracuse; for the Syracusan constitution was once changed by a love-quarrel of two young men, who were in the government. The story is that while one of them was away from home his beloved was gained over by his companion, and he to revenge himself seduced the other's wife. They then drew the members of the ruling class into their quarrel and so split all the people into portions. We learn from this story that we should be on our guard against the beginnings of such evils, and should put an end to the quarrels of chiefs and mighty men." *Politics* 1314b21–25: "It is hard for him [a tyrant] to be respected if he inspires no respect, and therefore whatever virtues he may neglect, at least he should maintain the character of a great soldier, and produce the impression that he is one. Neither he nor any of his associates should ever assault the young of either sex who are his subjects."

75. *TM*, 269–70.

76. *Discourses*, 211, 212. On the Roman senate and the common good, see also *TM*, 270, 344n193.

77. *TM*, 270–71. Of Aristotle, Strauss, in an endnote, 344n194, refers to the *Politics* 1297b1–10 and 1308b33–1309a9. On Strauss's observation about tyranny, cf. Roger Boesche, *Theories of Tyranny, From Plato to Arendt* (University Park: Pennsylvania State University Press, 1996), 116–17, 127–28, 161–65; Mansfield, *Machiavelli's New Modes*, 171; Sullivan, *Machiavelli's Three Romes*, 61ff., 72–75.

78. Aristotle *Politics* 1292a4–37.

79. *Politics* 1295a8–23. See also *Nicomachean Ethics* 1160a31–b12.

80. *Politics* 1297b1–5.

81. *Politics* 1308a13–24, 1313a34–1315b10.

82. *Politics* 1297b1–10: "Even if they have no share in office, the poor, provided only that they are not outraged or deprived of their property, will be quiet enough. But to secure gentle treatment for the poor is not an easy thing, since a ruling class is not always humane." On the dissolution of democracy into tyranny, cf. Rousseau, *Social*

Contract III 10–11. On Aristotle's account of how tyrants preserve their power, cf. Boesche, *Theories of Tyranny*, 76–84.

83. *TM*, 271. See also Mansfield, *Machiavelli's New Modes*, 115–18.

84. *The Prince*, 25, 26. Ch. 8 says that a man who "becomes prince from private individual" neither by "fortune" nor by "virtue" becomes prince "by some criminal and nefarious path or … by the support of his fellow citizens." To become prince by criminal means, and to maintain such power that one gains, is to use fraud, violence, and "cruelties … well used." *The Prince*, 34, 37.

85. *The Prince*, 39, 40.

86. *Discourses*, 90.

87. *Discourses*, 155.

88. *Discourses* I 1, p. 8; I 10, pp. 32, 33. See also *TM*, 272. For the criticism that tyranny is an unstable form of government, see, e.g., Aristotle *Politics* 1315a11–39.

89. *TM*, 272.

90. *TM*, 272 (emphasis added).

91. *Discourses* I 8, p. 28; I 24, p. 60; III 8, p. 237.

92. See *TM*, 272–73, 344n195. On Manlius Capitolinus and the Romans' desire to keep their liberty, see also Coby, *Machiavelli's Romans*, 93–95, 243ff.; Mary Jaeger, *Livy's Written Rome* (Ann Arbor: University of Michigan Press, 1997), ch. 3, esp. 84–85, 88; Mansfield, *Machiavelli's New Modes*, 345–47.

93. *TM*, 273.

94. Cf. Aristotle *Politics* 1308b32–37.

95. *TM*, 273.

96. *TM*, 273.

97. I have taken the phrase, "two diverse humors," from *The Prince*, ch. 19, p. 76.

98. On Machiavelli's above views of the principles of princely, republican, and tyrannical rule, see *TM*, 274.

99. *TM*, 274. Strauss then discusses, in approximately this sequence, *Discourses* III 1, 2, 3, 4–5, 6, 8, 9, 11, 22, 23, 30, 34, 35, and 42. See *TM*, 274–76; for most of the references themselves, see 344n197.

100. *Discourses*, 218.

101. See also *TM*, 275–76; Mansfield, *Machiavelli's New Modes*, 339–41. Cf. Coby, *Machiavelli's Romans*, 165–69.

102. *TM*, 276. In an endnote, 344n198, Strauss refers to *Discourses* I 9, 18, 29, 30, 52, II 26, 28; *The Prince*, chs. 22, 23.

103. *Discourses*, 104. See also *TM*, 277.

104. *Discourses*, 196.

105. *Discourses*, 288, 289 (emphasis added). See also *TM*, 276.

106. *TM*, 278. In an endnote, 344n199, Strauss refers to *Discourses* I 1, 2, 6, 16, 37, 46, III 16.

107. *TM*, 278, 279.

108. *Discourses*, 15. On the above themes of virtue, human nature, and governance, see Maritain, "End of Machiavellianism," 321–22; Strauss, *TM*, 279.

109. *The Prince*, 66.

110. *Discourses* I 9, p. 29; I 29, p. 66.

111. *TM*, 279. Cf. Kocis, *Machiavelli Redeemed*, 29, 62–63, 66, 98, 197–98.

112. *TPPH*, 13–16 (original emphasis).

113. Thomas Hobbes, *On the Citizen*, ed. and trans. Richard Tuck and Michael Silverthorne (Cambridge: Cambridge University Press, 1998), 7.

114. *On the Citizen*, 11–12 (emphasis added).

115. *On the Citizen*, 33. Cf. *TPPH*, 17–21.

116. *TM*, 279. In an endnote, 344n200, Strauss refers to *The Prince*, chs. 15, 17, 18; *Discourses* I pr., 3, 9, 26–27, 29, 35, 37, 40, 42, 47–48, 57, 58, II pr., III 12, 29. Strauss then instructs, "Cf. Hobbes, *De Cive*, praef. See page 249 above."

117. *Discourses*, 15.

118. *Discourses*, 61, 62. Mansfield and Tarcov, *Discourses*, 61n1, refers to Luke 1:53, and points out, "Said of God, not of David."

119. *Discourses*, 62–63.

120. *TM*, 280. See also *TM*, 344n201; but cf. *MCL*, 18–19. I have taken the term "sociability" from Polybius *Histories* VI 5.10. On Machiavelli's reading of Polybius, see also Coby, *Machiavelli's Romans*, 23; Fischer, *Well-Ordered License*, 111–12; Mansfield, *Machiavelli's New Modes*, 36–41, 79–80n2, 206–7; *Machiavelli's Virtue*, 82–83, 116–17, 274; Sullivan, *Machiavelli's Three Romes*, 90–95, 210n18; Vatter, *Between Form and Event*, 47–59, 202; Voegelin, *Collected Works*, vol. 22, bk. 4, 62–64.

121. *Discourses* I 2, p. 11.

122. Polybius *Histories* VI. 6.2, 6.4. See also VI 5.1, 5.8.

123. *TM*, 280–81. In an endnote, 344n202, Strauss refers to *The Prince*, ch. 17; *Discourses* I 7, 9, 20, 29, 30, 35–36, 40, 43, 45, 48, 60, II 2, 24, 33, III 10, 15, 21, 28.

124. *TM*, 281; on the humors within the republic, see also *Discourses* I 7, 45.

125. *TM*, 281. Cf. *Discourses* I 7, II 2; *The Prince*, ch. 17.

126. See *TM*, 281–82. Cf. *Discourses* I 20, 29, 34–36, 43, II 33.

127. See *TM*, 282. Cf. *Discourses* I 20, II 2, 24, III 28.

128. Cf. *Discourses* I 40, 41, III 28; *The Prince*, ch. 17.

129. *TM*, 282; for Strauss's answer to the above question, see 282–83.

130. *TM*, 283 (cf. 28).

131. *TM*, 283, 284. In an endnote, 344n203, Strauss refers to his previous observations on Machiavelli's "emphatic references" to the classical mean—having referred to *The Prince*, chs. 6, 7, 15; *Discourses* I pr., 58, III 2, 27, Strauss instructs, "Cf. pages 242–244 as well as notes 152 and 159 above." See my discussion in ch. 5 of those pages and notes.

132. *TM*, 284.

133. *TM*, 284–85. Cf. Faulkner, "*Clizia* and Private Life," 33, 35–37, 40, 49–53; Carnes Lord, "Allegory in Machiavelli's *Mandragola*," in Palmer and Pangle, *Political Philosophy*, 149–73, esp. 152–54, 165–67; Harvey C. Mansfield, "The Cuckold in Machiavelli's *Mandragola*," in Sullivan, *Comedy and Tragedy of Machiavelli*, 1–29, esp. 1, 5, 8, 28–29; Masters, *Machiavelli, Leonardo*, 82–84, 290n4; Vickie B. Sullivan, introduction to *Comedy and Tragedy of Machiavelli*, xi–xiii. Cf. also de Grazia, *Machiavelli in Hell*, 27, 61f., 140–42; Wayne A. Rebhorn, *Foxes and Lions: Machiavelli's Confidence Men* (Ithaca, N.Y.: Cornell University Press, 1988), esp. ch. 2.

134. *TM*, 286. Cf. Lord, "Allegory in Machiavelli's *Mandragola*," 153–54.

135. *Discourses*, 31.

136. *Chief Works*, 2:778.

137. *TM*, 288.

138. Cf. *CM*, 27, 30–32, 239–40; OPS, 184, 187–89; cf. also *TM*, 10–11.

139. See POR, 269–70.

140. LR*K*, 95–96. On the philosophers' reluctance to rule the city, see, e.g., PO, 57–59; Strauss explains here that because philosophers are concerned solely with the quest for knowledge, for truth, they have no time to devote either to mundane, every day matters or to the rule of the city.

CHAPTER SEVEN
The Legacy of Machiavelli's Moral-Political Teaching

1. For Strauss's thesis, see NM, 297ff.; *NRH*, 61n22, 177–80; *OT*, 23–25, 192; *TPPH*, xv–xvi; TWM, 83–89; WIPP, 40–49.

2. TWM, 83–84.

3. TWM, 86, 87. See also *OT*, 106n5, 183–85; *SPPP*, 144.

4. See also Mansfield, *Machiavelli's Virtue*, 37–38, 109, 127–30, 258–63; Vatter, *Between Form and Event*, 133, 193, 307–38. Cf. Jacobitti, "Classical Heritage in Machiavelli's Histories," 176–92; Parel, *Machiavellian Cosmos*, 5–10, 59–61, 153–61.

5. POR, 269–72. On the first point, see also *SCR*, 94–95; on the second point, see also *CM*, 44–45; CPP, 97–98; *SPPP*, 144; on the third point, cf. Hegel, *Reason in History*, 9–10, 11–13, 22–27, 44–46, 54; John Paul II, *Veritatis Splendor: Regarding Certain Fundamental Questions of the Church's Moral Teaching*, Encyclical Letter, 6 August 1993, nos. 31–34, 35, 40–45, 53, 66–67, 70, 72, 75, 84–89, 96–99, 103, 111–12, http://www.vatican.va/holy_father/john_paul_ii/encyclicals/documents/hf_jp-ii_enc_06081993_veritatis-splendor_en.html (accessed 23 July 2005).

6. *TPPH*, 83, 85. On the above difference between philosophy and the study of history, see also *CM*, 141–45.

7. *TPPH*, 86–87.

8. *TPPH*, 88n5.

9. Kennington, "Strauss's *Natural Right and History*," 228.

10. Hilail Gildin, introduction to *IPP*, ix (original emphasis). On that new "continent," see also Strauss, MCL, 10–13; *OT*, 24; WIPP, 40.

11. *TM*, 288. Cf. William B. Allen, "Machiavelli and Modernity," *The Prince* (Codevilla ed.), 105–9; Strauss, *CM*, 121–24; OPS, 157–58, 183–87.

12. *TM*, 289. On politics, philosophy, and the just life, see also OPS, 187–89.

13. *TM*, 289.

14. See *TM*, 289–90, 345n208.

15. *TM*, 290–91; cf. 134. On the extent to which a single characteristic may be identified in modernity, see TWM, 82–84; WIPP, 40.

16. *TM*, 291. See also MCL, 12–13; OPS, 161–63, 165, 175–76; *OT*, 56.

17. On Strauss's foci in *On Tyranny*, see Gourevitch, "Philosophy and Politics," I and II.

18. *TM*, 291.

19. *TM*, 292. In an endnote, 345n212, Strauss refers to Aristotle *Nicomachean Ethics* 1181a12–17. On hedonism, see *TM*, 291–92; on Machiavelli and the sophists, see also MCL, 13; on hedonism and Epicureanism, see also *NRH*, 109–11. *Nicomachean Ethics* 1181a12–17: "Those of the sophists who profess the art [of legislation] seem to be very

far from teaching it. For, to put the matter generally, they do not even know what kind of thing it is nor what kinds of things it is about; otherwise they would not have classed it as identical with rhetoric or even inferior to it, nor have thought it easy to legislate by collecting the laws that are well thought of."

20. See, e.g., *Nicomachean Ethics* 1102a5–25, 1160a9–17; *Politics* 1273a32–b24, 1283a22–b42, 1331b24–1332b11, 1337a10–21; cf. *Politics* 1265a19–24, 1267a18–24.

21. *Discourses* III 31, p. 301.

22. *TM*, 292.

23. *TM*, 345n213.

24. *CM*, 153.

25. *CM*, 161. See also POG, 2.

26. Thucydides, *The History of the Peloponnesian War*, ed. R. W. Livingstone, trans. Richard Crawley, rev. Richard Feetham (London: Oxford University Press, 1943), II 42.

27. *CM*, 190. See also POG, 7–8 (cf. 10, 11, 12).

28. *CM*, 153. Cf. *TPPH*, 74–75. On Thucydides' emphasis on "nobility" over "baseness," see *CM*, 210–19; cf. 186–87, 192ff.

29. *TM*, 292–93. Cf. *CM*, 141–45; GH, 657, 662–64; OCPH, 559–64, 566ff.; ONI, 326–32; *OT*, 22–28; *XSD*, 83–84. On Machiavelli's "historical" method, see *TM*, 145–55.

30. Perhaps foreshadowing Strauss's censure of the "modern historian," James Shotwell wrote in 1922: "To see in the author of the *Peloponnesian War* a 'modern of moderns,' facing history as we do, equipped with the understanding of the forces of history such as the historian of today possesses, is to indulge in an anachronism almost as naïve as the failure to appreciate Thucydides because he lacks it!" James T. Shotwell, *An Introduction to the History of History* (New York: Columbia University Press, 1922), 166–67. In his review of the revised 1939 edition of Shotwell's book (retitled *The History of History*, vol. 1) Strauss stated: "Only one question must be raised. He judges the classical historians with reference to the demand of the modern scientific spirit 'to find the truth and set it forth.' There can be no doubt that the writers concerned [e.g., Herodotus and Thucydides] were interested in finding the truth. But to what extent were they interested in telling it, or able to tell it, without reserve?" *RHH*, 126–27.

31. Mansfield, *Machiavelli's Virtue*, 225; Jackson, "Leo Strauss's Teaching," 54. On Strauss's brief treatment of Machiavelli scholarship, see also the reviews of *TM* by Felix Gilbert, John Hallowell, Willmoore Kendall, and George Mosse.

32. *OT*, 25. See also, e.g., PPH, 57ff.

33. *TM*, 293.

34. Meinecke, *Machiavellism*, esp. intro., chs. 1, 17.

35. *TM*, 293. In an endnote, 345n214, Strauss refers to *The Prince*, ch. 3; *Discourses* II 2, III 11, 30. Machiavelli "managed to articulate the most pressing problems of international relations theory in a forceful and provocative manner," Walker observes. "After all, whatever else he may have written, he did write specifically about the prince (read statesman) in a situation of extreme danger (read international relations)." R. B. J. Walker, *Inside/Outside: International Relations as Political Theory* (Cambridge: Cambridge University Press, 1993), 36. Yet Walker admits that Machiavelli's "primary concern was not international relations at all." Rather, his concern was to formulate a theory of virtue that would enable the prince to respond in a timely manner to the perpetual flux of the world. Walker, *Inside/Outside*, 36, 37–48, 62, 108–9. Cf. Michael W.

Doyle, "Fundamentalism: Machiavelli," in *Ways of War and Peace: Realism, Liberalism, and Socialism* (New York: W. W. Norton, 1997), 93–110.

36. *The Prince*, 14; *Discourses*, 133.

37. *TM*, 293. What references Strauss gives are to Plato and to Machiavelli; for the above references themselves to the *Laws* and the *Discourses*, see *TM*, 345n215. Strauss does not refer to the passages where Aristotle condemns tyranny, probably because he had discussed the matter previously; see *TM*, 270–71.

38. *Discourses*, 111–12 (emphasis added). Cf. *OT*, 68f.

39. *TM*, 293. Cf. Boesche, *Theories of Tyranny*, 25–48, 115–19, 129–33, 161–65; Viroli, *Machiavelli*, 33–38.

40. *TM*, 293–94. In an endnote, 345n216, Strauss refers to *Discourses* I 58 and then instructs, "Cf. also the defense of the people against Livy in *Discourses* III 13 and the corresponding change of a Livian story (IV 31.3–4) in III 15 beginning." Concerning that instruction, see above. Strauss goes on, "Cf. I 49 beginning and end with the plebeian speeches in Livy IV 4.1–4 and 35.5–9. Cf. pages 127–132 above." In those pages Strauss spoke of Machiavelli's censure of the widely held "prejudice" against "the multitude."

41. *Discourses*, 115, 117.

42. *Discourses*, 249. See also Mansfield, *Machiavelli's New Modes*, 358–59.

43. *Discourses*, 253; Livy, *History of Rome*, vol. 2, Books III and IV, rev. ed., trans. B. O. Foster, Loeb Classical Library 133 (London: William Heinemann; Cambridge, Mass.: Harvard University Press, 1939), IV 31.3–4, p. 359.

44. *TM*, 130. Cf. Aristotle *Politics* 1281a11–39.

45. *TM*, 294. Cf. *CM*, 133–34; *LSPS*, 7–8, 57, 241–43. On Strauss's comment about Machiavelli, democracy, and Rousseau, cf. Rousseau, *Social Contract* III 6; Strauss, *NRH*, 274, 278–79; *OIR*, 455, 456–59, 485–87; *ONI*, 357–58, 360; *TPPH*, 155–56. On Machiavelli and Spinoza, cf. *SCR*, 223–29.

46. *TM*, 294. Cf. Caranfa, *Machiavelli Rethought*, 129f., 145–47.

47. Aristotle *Magna Moralia* 1185b4–13. While the authenticity of *Magna Moralia* as Aristotle's own work is disputed, the division of the soul into rational and irrational parts is representative of Greek thought of the time. See Aristotle *Nicomachean Ethics* 1102a27–1103a10; *Eudemian Ethics* 1219b26–1220a11; Plato *Republic* 435b–441b. Here Plato both speaks of that twofold division and proposes a tripartite division of the soul, into rational, spirited, and appetitive parts; on the latter division, see also Aristotle *Nicomachean Ethics* 1105b19–1106a12, 1139a17–18; *On Virtues and Vices* 1249a25–1250a3; *On the Soul* 405b10–30, 432a15–b7 (cf. 407b27–408a18).

48. McCoy, *Intelligibility of Political Philosophy*, 277.

49. Aristotle *Nicomachean Ethics* 1139a3–16; McCoy, *Intelligibility of Political Philosophy*, 277–78; Strauss, OPS, 190.

50. Aristotle *On the Soul* 403b24–26: "Two characteristic marks have above all others been recognized as distinguishing that which has soul in it from that which has not—movement and sensation." 433b13: "All movement involves three factors, (1) that which originates the movement, (2) that by means of which it originates it, and (3) that which is moved."

51. *On the Soul* 433a23–27 (original emphasis): "Thought is never found producing movement without appetite (for wish is a form of appetite . . .), but appetite can originate

movement *contrary* to calculation, for desire is a form of appetite. Now thought is always right, but appetite and imagination may be either right or wrong." 433b5–6: "Appetites run counter to one another, which happens when a principle of reason and a desire are contrary."

52. Cf. *On the Soul* 433b7–10; *Nicomachean Ethics* 1139a17–b35. Cf. also Markus Fischer, "Machiavelli's Political Psychology," *Review of Politics* 59, no. 4 (Fall 1997): 789–829; Mansfield, *Machiavelli's Virtue*, 52, 273–80; Strauss, *LAM*, 105–13; *LSPS*, 57–58; OPS, 190–93.

53. Gilbert, *Machiavelli and Guicciardini*, 193.

54. *TM*, 294.

55. *TM*, 345n217.

56. *Chief Works*, 2:533. On Machiavelli's sayings, see also above, ch. 4; Ciliotta-Rubery, "Evil Teachings Without Remorse," 343–48; Strauss, MCL, 9–10.

57. *TM*, 294.

58. *TM*, 295. On Heidegger, see also above, ch. 1.

59. *TM*, 296. See also OPS, 158, 168–69, 185, 195–96, 200–205; cf. *SPPP*, 77, 83, 87.

60. *TM*, 345n219.

61. Plato *Republic* 484a–541b. See also *TM*, 296; cf. *LSPS*, 171–72, 229; OPS, 196–205.

62. *TM*, 296–97. Cf. McAllister, *Revolt Against Modernity*, 103–5.

63. See also Voegelin, *Collected Works*, vol. 22, bk. 4, 33–34, 34n3. Cf. de Grazia, *Machiavelli in Hell*, 142.

64. Garrett Mattingly, "Machiavelli's *Prince*: Political Science or Political Satire?" *American Scholar* 27, no. 4 (Autumn 1958): 482–91, esp. 489–90. Rousseau, *Social Contract* III 6, p. 95 (emphasis added): "A political sermonizer may well tell them [i.e., kings] that since the people's force is their force, their greatest interest is to have the people flourishing, numerous, formidable; they know perfectly well that this is not true. Their personal interest is first of all that the People be weak, wretched, and never able to resist them. I admit that, assuming always perfectly submissive subjects, it would be in the Prince's interest that the people be powerful, so that this power, being his, might render him formidable to his neighbours; but since this is only a secondary and subordinate interest, and the two assumptions are incompatible, it is natural that Princes always prefer the maxim that is most immediately useful to them. This is what Samuel forcefully represented to the Hebrews; it is what Machiavelli has conclusively shown. *While pretending to teach lessons to Kings, he taught great lessons to peoples*. Machiavelli's *Prince* is the book of republicans." On Machiavelli as a satirist, see also Gay, *Enlightenment*, 1:285–87; Rousseau, *Discourses on Political Economy*, in *Later Political Writings*, 9.

65. Lev Kamenev, "Preface to Machiavelli," *New Left Review*, no. 15 (May–June 1962): 40.

66. Antonio Gramsci, "The Modern Prince: Essays on the Science of Politics in the Modern Age," in *The Modern Prince and Other Writings*, trans. Louis Marks (New York: International Publishers, 1957), 135. On myth, ideology, and Gramsci's interpretation of Machiavelli, see also Louis Althusser, *Machiavelli and Us*, ed. François Matheron, trans. Gregory Elliot (London: Verso, 1999), esp. 89–92, 97–103, and appendix, "Machiavelli's Solitude" (trans. Ben Brewster), 127–30.

67. See above, ch. 3 (sub-section entitled "Theology in Machiavelli").

68. See above, ch. 6 (intro.).

69. On the variance of views about Machiavelli's newness, see Berlin, "Originality of Machiavelli," 149–63.

70. *TM*, 295. See also WIPP, esp. 9–17.

71. See also Cicero, *Tusculan Disputations*, trans. J. E. King, Loeb Classical Library 141 (London: William Heinemann; New York: G. P. Putnam's Sons, 1927), V 1.1–2, 4.10–11.

72. See also *OT*, 183–86.

73. AE, 327. On how philosophy and political philosophy relate to political science in Strauss's view, see also, e.g., AE, OCPP, WIPP. For an account of Strauss's critique of the new political science, see Behnegar, *Leo Strauss, Max Weber*, pt. III.

74. *TM*, 298. On technology, see also WIPP, 37.

75. Aristotle *Politics* 1331a11–15.

76. *TM*, 298–99. Cf. Fischer, *Well-Ordered License*, 169–71; Schall, "Strauss on St. Thomas," 217.

77. McCoy, *Structure of Political Thought*, 312.

78. Jacques Maritain, *The Degrees of Knowledge* (London: Geoffrey Bles, 1937), 241.

79. *TM*, 299.

80. AE, 312–15; Exi, 316–17; NCS, 114; *NRH*, 259–63; OPS, 134–38; *OT*, 23, 208; POR, 266–67; Rel, 22–23; SSH, 8–9. See also Aristotle *Metaphysics* 981a25–982a2; *Nicomachean Ethics* 1094a1–b7; *Politics* 1268b22–36. Cf. Martin Heidegger, *The Question Concerning Technology and Other Essays*, trans. William Lovitt (New York: Harper and Row, 1977), esp. 3–35 ("The Question Concerning Technology").

81. Exi, 308–9 (original emphasis): "While science has increased man's power in ways that former men never dreamt of, it is absolutely incapable to tell men how to *use* that power. Science cannot tell him whether it is wiser to use that power wisely and beneficently or foolishly and devilishly. From this it follows that science is unable to establish its own meaningfulness or to answer the question whether and in what sense science is good. . . . Someone has spoken of a flight from scientific reason. This flight is not due to any perversity but to science itself. . . . The flight from scientific reason is the consequence of the flight *of* science *from* reason—from the notion that man is a rational being who perverts his being if he does not act rationally." Cf. OIR, 460–61, 462, 464–68, 471–75, 484–85.

82. See Michael Davis, *Ancient Tragedy and the Origins of Modern Science* (Carbondale: Southern Illinois University Press, 1988); see also Fabro, *God in Exile*, 61–63, 988, 1025–28, 1122–43.

83. *TM*, 299.

84. *Discourses*, 139, 140. Mansfield and Tarcov, *Discourses*, 139n6, refer to Plato *Timaeus* 22a–23c, *Laws* 676b–678a; Aristotle *Politics* 1269a4–8, *Metaphysics* 1074b1–14; Polybius *Histories* VI 5.

85. *Politics* 1269a4–6.

86. Schall, "Strauss on St. Thomas," 228. In *TM*, 345n222, Strauss refers to *Discourses* II 5 and instructs the reader to compare it with Aristotle *Nicomachean Ethics* 1094a26–b7, *Politics* 1268b22ff., 1331a1–18; and Xenophon *Hiero* 9.9–10. Strauss also instructs the reader to compare the passages from Aristotle with Aquinas *Commentary on the Politics* VII, lectio 9; and directs the reader's attention to *TM*, 309–10n53, where Strauss said that Machiavelli equated criminal rule with non-criminal rule. Machiavelli described Cesare Borgia, Agathocles, Nabis, Cyrus, Hannibal, Severus, and Giovampagolo Baglioni as impious and cruel, but he also described them as excellent men.

87. Cf. John Paul II, *Fides et Ratio: On the Relationship Between Faith and Reason*, Encyclical Letter, 14 September 1998, nos. 3–6, 14–15, 18–23, 33, 41, 45–56, 62–63, 75–79, 81–91, 100–108, http://www.vatican.va/holy_father/john_paul_ii/encyclicals/documents/hf_jp-ii_enc_15101998_fides-et-ratio_en.html (accessed 23 July 2005); Maritain, "End of Machiavellianism," 339–40, 346–47, 352–53; Strauss, *NRH*, 36. Cf. also Havers, "Between Athens and Jerusalem," 19–21, 23–24; McCool, *From Unity to Pluralism*, 7–10, 87–88, 89, 100–102, 136–46, 151–53; McCoy, *Intelligibility of Political Philosophy*, 122–30, 131, 143–49.

88. *TM*, 299.

89. Peterman, "Approaching Leo Strauss," 324–25. See also Jaffa, "Leo Strauss Remembered," 268–69; Lampert, *Leo Strauss and Nietzsche*, 143–45; McAllister, *Revolt Against Modernity*, 107–9. On Hegel's statement, cf. Strauss, OCPP, 88–89; *RCPR*, 57–58.

90. *TM*, 14.

Conclusion

1. *OT*, 212.

2. Deutsch and Nicgorski, intro. to *Leo Strauss*, 11 (original emphasis).

3. *TM*, 203.

4. *TM*, 208.

5. *TM*, 221.

6. TWM, 82.

7. *Discourses* I pr., p. 5.

8. *The Prince*, ch. 15, p. 61. On the modern horizon of autonomy and truth, cf. Fabro, *God in Exile*, 3–5, 91–92, 168, 1144–53.

9. On the term teleotheological, cf. *XSD*, 148–49; cf. also *LAM*, 100; *NRH*, 154.

10. *TM*, 222.

11. *TM*, 165.

12. WIPP, 44.

13. MP, 294.

14. McAllister, *Revolt Against Modernity*, 289n34.

15. *TM*, 232.

16. K. H. Green, *Jew and Philosopher*, 159n49. Cf. Berlin, "Originality of Machiavelli," 193–96.

17. *TM*, 10, 12.

18. Gourevitch, "Philosophy and Politics, II," 317. See also Strauss, *OT*, 196–207; Tarcov, "Straussianism," 266. Cf. John G. Gunnell, "Strauss Before Straussianism: Reason, Revelation, and Nature," in Deutsch and Nicgorski, *Leo Strauss*, 124–25.

19. Mitchell, *Not by Reason Alone*, 210n111.

Bibliography

Primary Sources

Works by Leo Strauss

The Political Philosophy of Hobbes: Its Basis and Its Genesis. Translated by Elsa M. Sinclair. Oxford: Clarendon Press, 1936; repr., Chicago: University of Chicago Press, 1963.

Review of *The History of History*, vol. 1 (rev. and retitled ed. of the 1922 work, *Introduction to the History of History*, vol. 1), by James T. Shotwell. *Social Research* 8, no. 1 (February 1941): 126–27.

"On a New Interpretation Of Plato's Political Philosophy." Review article of *Plato's Theory of Man: An Introduction to the Realistic Philosophy of Culture*, by John Wild. *Social Research* 13, no. 3 (September 1946): 326–67.

"On the Intention of Rousseau." Review article of Jean-Jacques Rousseau, *Discours sur les sciences et les arts*, edited by George R. Havens. *Social Research* 14, no. 4 (December 1947): 455–87.

"On Collingwood's Philosophy of History." Review article of *The Idea of History*, by R. G. Collingwood. *Review of Metaphysics* 5, no. 4 (June 1952): 559–86.

Persecution and the Art of Writing. Glencoe, Ill.: Free Press, 1952.

Natural Right and History. Chicago: University of Chicago Press, 1953; repr., 1965.

Thoughts on Machiavelli. Chicago: University of Chicago Press, 1958; repr., 1978.

What Is Political Philosophy? And Other Studies. Glencoe, Ill.: Free Press, 1959.

"An Epilogue." In *Essays on the Scientific Study of Politics*, edited by Herbert J. Storing, 307–27. New York: Holt, Rinehart and Winston, 1962.

"Replies to Schaar and Wolin" (no. 2). *American Political Science Review* 57, no. 1 (March 1963): 152–55.

"How To Begin To Study *The Guide of the Perplexed*." Introductory essay to Moses Maimonides, *The Guide of the Perplexed*, translated by Shlomo Pines, xi–lvi. Chicago: University of Chicago Press, 1963.

The City and Man. Chicago: University of Chicago Press, 1964.

"The Crisis of Our Time" and "The Crisis of Political Philosophy." In *The Predicament of Modern Politics*, edited by Harold J. Spaeth, 41–54, 91–103. Detroit: University of Detroit Press, 1964.

Spinoza's Critique of Religion. Translated by E. M. Sinclair. New York: Schocken Books; Chicago: University of Chicago Press, 1965. Originally published as *Die Religionskritik Spinozas als Grundlage seiner Bibelwissenschaft Untersuchungen zu Spinozas Theologisch-Politischem Traktat*. Berlin: Academie-Verlag, 1930.

Socrates and Aristophanes. Chicago: University of Chicago Press, 1966.

"Greek Historians." Critical study of *Greek Historical Writing: A Historiographical Essay Based on Xenophon's "Hellenica,"* by W. P. Henry. *Review of Metaphysics* 21, no. 4 (June 1968): 656–66.

Liberalism Ancient and Modern. New York: Basic Books, 1968.

Xenophon's Socratic Discourse: An Interpretation of the "Oeconomicus." Ithaca, N.Y.: Cornell University Press, 1970.

"Machiavelli and Classical Literature." *Review of National Literatures* 1, no. 1 (Spring 1970): 7–25.

Xenophon's Socrates. Ithaca, N.Y.: Cornell University Press, 1972.

"Preliminary Observations on the Gods in Thucydides' Work." *Interpretation* 4, no. 1 (Winter 1974): 1–16.

The Argument and the Action of Plato's Laws. Chicago: University of Chicago Press, 1975; paperback ed., 1978.

"Xenophon's *Anabasis*." *Interpretation* 4, no. 3 (Spring 1975): 117–47.

"Correspondence Concerning *Wahrheit und Methode*." Exchange of letters with Hans-Georg Gadamer, beginning 26 February 1961 and ending 14 May 1961. *Independent Journal of Philosophy* 2 (1978): 5–12.

"Letter to Helmut Kuhn." *Independent Journal of Philosophy* 2 (1978): 23–26.

"Correspondence Concerning Modernity." Exchange of letters with Karl Löwith, beginning 10 January 1946 and ending 26 November 1946. *Independent Journal of Philosophy* 4 (1983): 105–19.

Studies in Platonic Political Philosophy. Chicago: University of Chicago Press, 1983.

"Exoteric Teaching." Edited by Kenneth Hart Green. *Interpretation* 14, no. 1 (January 1986): 51–59.

"Plato," "Marsilius of Padua," and "Niccolò Machiavelli." In *History of Political Philosophy*, 3rd ed., edited by Leo Strauss and Joseph Cropsey, 33–89, 276–95, 296–317. Chicago: University of Chicago Press, 1987.

"The Three Waves of Modernity" and "Progress or Return? The Contemporary Crisis in Western Civilization." In *An Introduction to Political Philosophy: Ten Essays by Leo Strauss*, edited with an introduction by Hilail Gildin, 81–98, 249–310. Detroit: Wayne State University Press, 1989.

"Social Science and Humanism" and "Relativism." In *The Rebirth of Classical Political Rationalism: An Introduction to the Thought of Leo Strauss*. Essays and lectures by Leo Strauss, selected and introduced by Thomas L. Pangle, 3–12, 13–26. Chicago: University of Chicago Press, 1989.

"Some Remarks on the Political Science of Maimonides and Farabi." Translated by Robert Bartlett. *Interpretation* 18, no. 1 (Fall 1990): 3–30.

"The Strauss-Voegelin Correspondence, 1934–1964." Part I in *Faith and Political Philosophy: The Correspondence Between Leo Strauss and Eric Voegelin, 1934–1964*, edited and translated by Peter Emberley and Barry Cooper, 4–106. University Park: Pennsylvania State University Press, 1993.

"Existentialism" and "The Problem of Socrates." Edited by David Bolotin, Christopher Bruell, and Thomas L. Pangle. *Interpretation* 22, no. 3 (Spring 1995): 303–20, 322–38.

Notes on Carl Schmitt, *The Concept of the Political*. In Heinrich Meier, *Carl Schmitt and Leo Strauss: The Hidden Dialogue*, including Strauss's notes on Schmitt's *Concept of the Political* and three letters from Strauss to Schmitt, translated by J. Harvey Lomax, 88–119. Chicago: University of Chicago Press, 1995.

Philosophy and Law: Contributions to the Understanding of Maimonides and His Predecessors. Translated by Eve Adler. Albany: State University of New York Press, 1995. Originally published as *Philosophie und Gesetz: Beiträge zum Verständnis Maimunis und Seiner Vorlaüfer*. Berlin: Schocken Verlag, 1935.

"The Origins of Political Science and the Problem of Socrates: Six Public Lectures by Leo Strauss." Edited by David Bolotin, Christopher Bruell, and Thomas L. Pangle. *Interpretation* 23, no. 2 (Winter 1996): 129–207.

"How To Study Medieval Philosophy." Edited by David Bolotin, Christopher Bruell, and Thomas L. Pangle. *Interpretation* 23, no. 3 (Spring 1996): 319–38.

Jewish Philosophy and the Crisis of Modernity: Essays and Lectures in Modern Jewish Thought. Edited by Kenneth Hart Green. Albany: State University of New York Press, 1997.

"German Nihilism." Edited by David Janssens and Daniel Tanguay. *Interpretation* 26, no. 3 (Spring 1999): 353–78.

On Tyranny. Revised and expanded edition, including the Strauss-Kojève correspondence. Edited by Victor Gourevitch and Michael S. Roth. Chicago: University of Chicago Press, 2000.

Leo Strauss on Plato's Symposium. Edited by Seth Benardete. Chicago: University of Chicago Press, 2001.

Leo Strauss: The Early Writings (1921–1932). Edited and translated by Michael Zank. Albany: State University of New York Press, 2002.

"The Place of the Doctrine of Providence According to Maimonides." Translated by Gabriel Bartlett and Svetozar Minkov. *Review of Metaphysics* 57, no. 3 (March 2004): 537–49.

Works by Niccolò Machiavelli

Machiavelli: The Chief Works and Others. 3 vols. Translated by Allan Gilbert. Durham, N.C.: Duke University Press, 1965.

The Discourses. Edited by Bernard Crick. Translated by Leslie J. Walker. Revised by Brian Richardson. London: Penguin, 1983.

Florentine Histories. Translated by Laura F. Banfield and Harvey C. Mansfield, Jr. Princeton, N.J.: Princeton University Press, 1988.
Discourses on Livy. Translated by Harvey C. Mansfield and Nathan Tarcov. Chicago: University of Chicago Press, 1996.
Machiavelli and His Friends: Their Personal Correspondence. Edited and translated by James B. Atkinson and David Sices. DeKalb: Northern Illinois University Press, 1996.
The Prince. Edited and translated by Angelo M. Codevilla. New Haven: Yale University Press, 1997.
The Prince. 2nd ed. Translated by Harvey C. Mansfield. Chicago: University of Chicago Press, 1998.

Secondary Sources

On Strauss

Adler, Eve. "Leo Strauss's *Philosophie und Gesetz.*" In *Leo Strauss's Thought: Toward a Critical Engagement,* edited by Alan Udoff, 183–226. Boulder, Colo.: Lynne Rienner Publishers, 1991.
———. "Translator's Introduction: The Argument of *Philosophy and Law.*" In Leo Strauss, *Philosophy and Law: Contributions to the Understanding of Maimonides and His Predecessors,* translated by Eve Adler, 1–19. Albany: State University of New York Press, 1995.
Altizer, Thomas J. J. "The Theological Conflict Between Strauss and Voegelin." In *Faith and Political Philosophy: The Correspondence Between Leo Strauss and Eric Voegelin, 1934–1964,* edited and translated by Peter Emberley and Barry Cooper, 267–77. University Park: Pennsylvania State University Press, 1993.
Arkes, Hadley. "Strauss on Our Minds." In *Leo Strauss, the Straussians, and the American Regime,* edited by Kenneth L. Deutsch and John A. Murley, 69–89. Lanham, Md.: Rowman and Littlefield, 1999.
Arkush, Allan. "Leo Strauss and Jewish Modernity." In *Leo Strauss and Judaism: Jerusalem and Athens Critically Revisited,* edited by David Novak, 111–30. Lanham, Md.: Rowman and Littlefield, 1996.
Arnhart, Larry. "Defending Darwinian Natural Right." *Interpretation* 27, no. 3 (Spring 2000): 263–77.
Bagley, Paul J. "On the Practice of Esotericism." *Journal of the History of Ideas* 53, no. 2 (April–June 1992): 231–47.
Batnitzky, Leora, and Michael Zank. "Strauss and Textual Reasoning." *Journal of Textual Reasoning* 3, no. 1 (June 2004). http://etext.lib.virginia.edu/journals/tr/volume3/straussintro.html (accessed 23 July 2005).
Behnegar, Nasser. "The Liberal Politics of Leo Strauss." In *Political Philosophy and the Human Soul: Essays in Memory of Allan Bloom,* edited by Michael Palmer and Thomas L. Pangle, 251–67. Lanham, Md.: Rowman and Littlefield, 1995.
———. "Leo Strauss's Confrontation with Max Weber: A Search for a Genuine Social Science." *Review of Politics* 59, no. 1 (Winter 1997): 97–125.
———. *Leo Strauss, Max Weber, and the Scientific Study of Politics.* Chicago: University of Chicago Press, 2003.

Berkowitz, Peter. "Liberal Zealotry." Review of *The Anatomy of Antiliberalism*, by Stephen Holmes. *Yale Law Review* 103, no. 5 (March 1994): 1363–82.

Berns, Laurence. "The Relation Between Philosophy and Religion: Reflections on Leo Strauss's Suggestion Concerning the Source and Sources of Modern Philosophy." *Interpretation* 19, no. 1 (Fall 1991): 43–60.

Berns, Walter, Herbert J. Storing, Harry V. Jaffa, and Werner J. Dannhauser. "The Achievement of Leo Strauss." *National Review*, 7 December 1973, 1347–57.

Blitz, Mark. "Leo Strauss, the Straussians, and American Foreign Policy." *OpenDemocracy*, 14 November 2003, 1–4. http://www.opendemocracy.net/content/articles/PDF/1577.pdf (accessed 4 July 2005).

Bloom, Allan. "Leo Strauss: September 20, 1899–October 18, 1973." *Political Theory* 2, no. 4 (November 1974): 372–92.

Bolotin, David. "Leo Strauss and Classical Political Philosophy." *Interpretation* 22, no. 1 (Fall 1994): 129–42.

Brague, Rémi. "Athens, Jerusalem, Mecca: Leo Strauss's 'Muslim' Understanding of Greek Philosophy." *Poetics Today* 19, no. 2 (Summer 1998): 235–59.

Braiterman, Zachary. "Against Leo Strauss." *Journal of Textual Reasoning* 3, no. 1 (June 2004). http://etext.lib.virginia.edu/journals/tr/volume3/braiterman.html (accessed 23 July 2005).

Burnyeat, M. F. "Sphinx Without a Secret." Review of *Studies in Platonic Political Philosophy*, by Leo Strauss. *New York Review of Books*, 30 May 1985, 30–36.

Cantor, Paul A. "Leo Strauss and Contemporary Hermeneutics." In *Leo Strauss's Thought: Toward a Critical Engagement*, edited by Alan Udoff, 267–314. Boulder, Colo.: Lynne Rienner Publishers, 1991.

Colmo, Christopher A. "Reason and Revelation in the Thought of Leo Strauss." *Interpretation* 18, no. 1 (Fall 1990): 145–60.

Cropsey, Joseph, et al. "The Studies of Leo Strauss: An Exchange." Responses to M. F. Burnyeat, "Sphinx Without a Secret." *New York Review of Books*, 10 October 1985, 41–44.

Dallmayr, Fred. "Leo Strauss Peregrinus." *Social Research* 61, no. 4 (Winter 1994): 877–904.

Dannhauser, Werner J. "Leo Strauss as Citizen and Jew." *Interpretation* 17, no. 3 (Spring 1990): 433–47.

———. "Athens and Jerusalem or Jerusalem and Athens?" In *Leo Strauss and Judaism: Jerusalem and Athens Critically Revisited*, edited by David Novak, 155–71. Lanham, Md.: Rowman and Littlefield, 1996.

Danoff, Brian. "Leo Strauss, George W. Bush, and the Problem of Regime Change." *Social Policy* 34, nos. 2–3 (Winter 2003–Spring 2004): 35–40.

Deutsch, Kenneth L. "Leo Strauss, the Straussians, and the American Regime." In *Leo Strauss, the Straussians, and the American Regime*, edited by Kenneth L. Deutsch and John A. Murley, 51–67. Lanham, Md.: Rowman and Littlefield, 1999.

Deutsch, Kenneth L., and John A. Murley, eds. *Leo Strauss, the Straussians, and the American Regime*. Lanham, Md.: Rowman and Littlefield, 1999.

Deutsch, Kenneth L., and Walter Nicgorski. Introduction to *Leo Strauss: Political Philosopher and Jewish Thinker*, edited by Kenneth L. Deutsch and Walter Nicgorski, 1–40. Lanham, Md.: Rowman and Littlefield, 1994.

Devigne, Robert. *Recasting Conservatism: Oakeshott, Strauss, and the Response to Post-modernism.* New Haven: Yale University Press, 1994.

Drury, Shadia B. "The Esoteric Philosophy of Leo Strauss." *Political Theory* 13, no. 3 (August 1985): 315–37.

———. "The Hidden Meaning of Strauss's *Thoughts on Machiavelli.*" *History of Political Thought* 6, no. 3 (Winter 1985): 575–90.

———. "Leo Strauss's Classic Natural Right Teaching." *Political Theory* 15, no. 3 (August 1987): 299–315.

———. *The Political Ideas of Leo Strauss.* New York: St. Martin's Press, 1988.

———. Review of *Carl Schmitt and Leo Strauss: The Hidden Dialogue*, by Heinrich Meier. *American Political Science Review* 90, no. 2 (June 1996): 410–11.

———. *Leo Strauss and the American Right.* New York: St. Martin's Press, 1997.

———. "Leo Strauss and the Grand Inquisitor." *Free Inquiry Magazine* 24, no. 4 (June–July 2004). http://www.secularhumanism.org/library/fi/drury_24_4.htm (accessed 18 June 2005).

East, John P. "Leo Strauss and American Conservatism." *Modern Age* 21, no. 1 (Winter 1977): 2–19.

Emberley, Peter, and Barry Cooper. Introduction to *Faith and Political Philosophy: The Correspondence Between Leo Strauss and Eric Voegelin, 1934–1964*, edited and translated by Peter Emberley and Barry Cooper, ix–xxvi. University Park: Pennsylvania State University Press, 1993.

Fackenheim, Emil L. "Leo Strauss and Modern Judaism" and "What Is Jewish Philosophy? Reflections on Athens, Jerusalem, and the Western Academy." In Emil L. Fackenheim, *Jewish Philosophers and Jewish Philosophy*, edited by Michael L. Morgan, 97–105, 165–84 (endnotes, 256, 261–62). Bloomington: Indiana University Press, 1996.

Fortin, Ernest L., and Glenn Hughes. "The Strauss-Voegelin Correspondence: Two Reflections and Two Comments." *Review of Politics* 56, no. 2 (Spring 1994): 337–57.

Fradkin, Hillel. "A Word Fitly Spoken: The Interpretation of Maimonides and the Legacy of Leo Strauss." In *Leo Strauss and Judaism: Jerusalem and Athens Critically Revisited*, edited by David Novak, 55–85. Lanham, Md.: Rowman and Littlefield, 1996.

Fuller, Timothy. "Philosophy, Faith, and the Question of Progress." In *Faith and Political Philosophy: The Correspondence Between Leo Strauss and Eric Voegelin, 1934–1964*, edited and translated by Peter Emberley and Barry Cooper, 279–95. University Park: Pennsylvania State University Press, 1993.

Gebhardt, Jürgen. "Leo Strauss: The Quest for Truth in Times of Perplexity." In *Hannah Arendt and Leo Strauss: German Émigrés and American Political Thought After World War II*, edited by Peter Graf Kielmansegg, Horst Mewes, and Elisabeth Glaser-Schmidt, 81–104. Washington, D.C.: German Historical Institute; Cambridge: Cambridge University Press, 1995.

Germino, Dante. "Second Thoughts on Leo Strauss's Machiavelli." *Journal of Politics* 28, no. 4 (November 1966): 794–817.

———. "Blasphemy and Leo Strauss's Machiavelli." In *Leo Strauss: Political Philosopher and Jewish Thinker*, edited by Kenneth L. Deutsch and Walter Nicgorski, 297–307. Lanham, Md.: Rowman and Littlefield, 1994.

Gilbert, Felix. "Politics and Morality." Review of *Ethics in a World of Power: The Political Ideas of Friedrich Meinecke*, by Richard W. Sterling. Review of *Thoughts on Machiavelli*, by Leo Strauss. *Yale Review* 48, no. 3 (March 1959): 465–69.

Gildin, Hilail. Introduction to *An Introduction to Political Philosophy: Ten Essays by Leo Strauss*, edited by Hilail Gildin, vii–xxiv. Detroit: Wayne State University Press, 1989.

———. "Déjà Jew All Over Again: Dannhauser on Leo Strauss and Atheism." *Interpretation* 25, no. 1 (Fall 1997): 125–33.

Glenn, Gary D. "Speculations on Strauss' Political Intentions Suggested by *On Tyranny*." *History of European Ideas* 19, nos. 1–3 (1994): 171–77.

Gourevitch, Victor. "Philosophy and Politics," I and II. *Review of Metaphysics* 22, no. 1 (September 1968): 58–84; no. 2 (December 1968): 281–328.

Green, Kenneth Hart. "'In the Grip of the Theological-Political Predicament': The Turn to Maimonides in the Jewish Thought of Leo Strauss." In *Leo Strauss's Thought: Toward a Critical Engagement*, edited by Alan Udoff, 41–74. Boulder, Colo.: Lynne Rienner Publishers, 1991.

———. *Jew and Philosopher: The Return to Maimonides in the Jewish Thought of Leo Strauss*. Albany: State University of New York Press, 1993.

———. "Editor's Introduction: Leo Strauss as a Modern Jewish Thinker." In Leo Strauss, *Jewish Philosophy and the Crisis of Modernity: Essays and Lectures in Modern Jewish Thought*, 1–84. Albany: State University of New York Press, 1997.

Green, S. J. D. "The Tawney-Strauss Connection: On Historicism and Values in the History of Political Ideas." *Journal of Modern History* 67, no. 2 (June 1995): 255–77.

Gunnell, John G. "The Myth of the Tradition." *American Political Science Review* 72, no. 1 (March 1978): 122–34.

———. "Political Theory and Politics: The Case of Leo Strauss." *Political Theory* 13, no. 3 (August 1985): 339–61.

———. "Strauss Before Straussianism: Reason, Revelation, and Nature." In *Leo Strauss: Political Philosopher and Jewish Thinker*, edited by Kenneth L. Deutsch and Walter Nicgorski, 107–28. Lanham, Md.: Rowman and Littlefield, 1994.

Hallowell, John H. Review of *Thoughts on Machiavelli*, by Leo Strauss. *Midwest Journal of Political Science* 3, no. 3 (August 1959): 300–303.

Havers, Grant. "Between Athens and Jerusalem: Western Otherness in the Thought of Leo Strauss and Hannah Arendt." *European Legacy* 9, no. 1 (February 2004): 19–29.

Himmelfarb, Milton. "On Leo Strauss." *Commentary* 58, no. 2 (August 1974): 60–66.

Holmes, Stephen D. *The Anatomy of Antiliberalism*. Cambridge, Mass.: Harvard University Press, 1989.

Jackson, Michael P. "Leo Strauss's Teaching: A Study of *Thoughts on Machiavelli*." Ph.D. diss., Georgetown University, 1985.

Jaffa, Harry V. "The Primacy of the Good: Leo Strauss Remembered." *Modern Age* 26, nos. 3–4 (Summer–Fall 1983): 266–69.

———. "Leo Strauss's Churchillian Speech and the Question of the Decline of the West." *Teaching Political Science* 12, no. 2 (Winter 1985): 61–67.

———. "Dear Professor Drury." *Political Theory* 15, no. 3 (August 1987): 316–25.

———. "Crisis of the Strauss Divided: The Legacy Reconsidered." *Social Research* 54, no. 3 (Autumn 1987): 579–603.

————. "Leo Strauss, the Bible, and Political Philosophy." In *Leo Strauss: Political Philosopher and Jewish Thinker*, edited by Kenneth L. Deutsch and Walter Nicgorski, 195–210. Lanham, Md.: Rowman and Littlefield, 1994.

Janssens, David. "The Problem of the Enlightenment: Strauss, Jacobi, and the Pantheism Controversy." *Review of Metaphysics* 56, no. 3 (March 2003): 605–31.

Jung, Hwa Yol. "Leo Strauss's Conception of Political Philosophy: A Critique." *Review of Politics* 29, no. 4 (October 1967): 492–517.

————. "Two Critics of Scientism: Leo Strauss and Edmund Husserl." *Independent Journal of Philosophy* 2 (1978): 81–88.

Kateb, George. "The Questionable Influence of Arendt (and Strauss)." In *Hannah Arendt and Leo Strauss: German Émigrés and American Political Thought After World War II*, edited by Peter Graf Kielmansegg, Horst Mewes, and Elisabeth Glaser-Schmidt, 29–43. Washington, D.C.: German Historical Institute; Cambridge: Cambridge University Press, 1995.

Kendall, Willmoore. Review of *Thoughts on Machiavelli*, by Leo Strauss. *Philosophical Review* 75, no. 2 (April 1966): 247–54.

Kennington, Richard H. "Strauss's *Natural Right and History*." In *Leo Strauss's Thought: Toward a Critical Engagement*, edited by Alan Udoff, 227–52. Boulder, Colo.: Lynne Rienner Publishers, 1991.

Kojève, Alexandre. Review of *On Tyranny*, by Leo Strauss. *Critique* 6 (1950): 46–55, 138–55.

Kress, Paul F. "Against Epistemology: Apostate Musings." *Journal of Politics* 41, no. 2 (May 1979): 526–42.

Kries, Douglas. "Faith, Reason, and Leo Strauss." Review of *Jerusalem and Athens: Reason and Revelation in the Work of Leo Strauss*, by Susan Orr. *Review of Politics* 58, no. 2 (Spring 1996): 354–56.

Lampert, Laurence. *Leo Strauss and Nietzsche*. Chicago: University of Chicago Press, 1996.

————. "Nietzsche's Challenge to Philosophy in the Thought of Leo Strauss." *Review of Metaphysics* 58, no. 3 (March 2005): 585–613.

Larmore, Charles. "The Secrets of Philosophy." Review of *The Rebirth of Classical Political Rationalism*, essays and lectures by Leo Strauss. *New Republic*, 3 July 1989, 30–35.

Lawrence, Frederick G. "Leo Strauss and the Fourth Wave of Modernity." In *Leo Strauss and Judaism: Jerusalem and Athens Critically Revisited*, edited by David Novak, 131–53. Lanham, Md.: Rowman and Littlefield, 1996.

Lenzner, Steven J. "Strauss's Three Burkes: The Problem of Edmund Burke in *Natural Right and History*." *Political Theory* 19, no. 3 (August 1991): 364–90.

Levine, David Lawrence. "Without Malice But With Forethought: A Response to Burnyeat." In *Leo Strauss: Political Philosopher and Jewish Thinker*, edited by Kenneth L. Deutsch and Walter Nicgorski, 353–71. Lanham, Md.: Rowman and Littlefield, 1994.

Liebich, André. "Straussianism and Ideology." In *Ideology, Philosophy, and Politics*, edited by Anthony Parel, 225–45. Waterloo, Ontario: Wilfred Laurier University Press for the Calgary Institute for the Humanities, 1983.

Lowenthal, David. "Leo Strauss's *Studies in Platonic Political Philosophy*." Review of *Studies in Platonic Political Philosophy*, by Leo Strauss. *Interpretation* 13, no. 3 (September 1985): 297–320.

McAllister, Ted V. *Revolt Against Modernity: Leo Strauss, Eric Voegelin, and the Search for a Postliberal Order.* Lawrence: University of Kansas Press, 1996.

McCarl, Steven R. Review of *Revolt Against Modernity: Leo Strauss, Eric Voegelin, and the Search for a Postliberal Order,* by Ted V. McAllister. *American Political Science Review* 91, no. 2 (June 1997): 437–38.

McClay, Wilfred M. "The Party of Limits." Review of *Revolt Against Modernity: Leo Strauss, Eric Voegelin, and the Search for a Postliberal Order,* by Ted V. McAllister. *Reviews in American History* 25, no. 1 (March 1997): 95–100.

McDaniel, Robb A. "The Illiberal Leo Strauss." In *Community and Political Thought Today,* edited by Peter Augustine Lawler and Dale McConkey, 191–208. Westport, Conn.: Praeger, 1998.

McShea, Robert J. "Leo Strauss on Machiavelli." *Western Political Quarterly* 16, no. 4 (December 1963): 782–97.

McWilliams, Wilson Carey. "Leo Strauss and the Dignity of American Political Thought." *Review of Politics* 60, no. 2 (Spring 1998): 231–46.

Merrill, Clark A. "Spelunking in the Unnatural Cave: Leo Strauss's Ambiguous Tribute to Max Weber." *Interpretation* 27, no. 1 (Fall 1999): 3–26.

———. "Leo Strauss's Indictment of Christian Philosophy." *Review of Politics* 62, no. 1 (Winter 2000): 77–105.

Miller, Eugene F. "Leo Strauss: The Recovery of Political Philosophy." In *Contemporary Political Philosophers,* edited by Anthony de Crespigny and Kenneth Minogue, 67–99. New York: Dodd, Mead, 1975.

———. "Leo Strauss: Philosophy and American Social Science." In *Leo Strauss, the Straussians, and the American Regime,* edited by Kenneth L. Deutsch and John A. Murley, 91–102. Lanham, Md.: Rowman and Littlefield, 1999.

Mittleman, Alan. "Leo Strauss and Relativism: The Critique of Max Weber." *Religion* 29, no. 1 (January 1999): 15–27.

Morgan, Michael L. "The Curse of Historicity: The Role of History in Leo Strauss's Jewish Thought." *Journal of Religion* 61, no. 4 (October 1981): 345–63.

Mosse, George L. Review of *Thoughts on Machiavelli,* by Leo Strauss. *American Historical Review* 64, no. 4 (July 1959): 954–55.

Muravchik, Joshua. "The Neoconservative Cabal." *Commentary* 116, no. 2 (September 2003): 26–33.

Neumann, Harry. "Civic Piety and Socratic Atheism: An Interpretation of Strauss' *Socrates and Aristophanes.*" *Independent Journal of Philosophy* 2 (1978): 33–37.

Nicgorski, Walter. "Leo Strauss and Christianity: Reason, Politics, and Christian Belief." Review of *The God of Faith and Reason: Foundations of Christian Theology,* by Robert Sokolowski. *Claremont Review of Books,* Summer 1985, 18–21.

Norton, Paul. "Leo Strauss: His Critique of Historicism." *Modern Age* 25, no. 2 (Spring 1981): 143–54.

Novak, David. Introduction and "Philosophy and the Possibility of Revelation: A Theological Response to the Challenge of Leo Strauss." In *Leo Strauss and Judaism: Jerusalem and Athens Critically Revisited,* edited by David Novak, vii–xvi, 173–92. Lanham, Md.: Rowman and Littlefield, 1996.

Orr, Susan. "'Jerusalem and Athens': A Study of Leo Strauss." Ph.D. diss., Claremont Graduate School, 1992.

————. *Jerusalem and Athens: Reason and Revelation in the Work of Leo Strauss.* Lanham, Md.: Rowman and Littlefield, 1995.

————. "Strauss, Reason, and Revelation: Unraveling the Essential Question." In *Leo Strauss and Judaism: Jerusalem and Athens Critically Revisited*, edited by David Novak, 25–53. Lanham, Md.: Rowman and Littlefield, 1996.

————. Review of *Jew and Philosopher: The Return to Maimonides in the Jewish Thought of Leo Strauss*, by Kenneth Hart Green. *Interpretation* 23, no. 2 (Winter 1996): 307–16.

Palmer, Michael. Review of *Jerusalem and Athens: Reason and Revelation in the Work of Leo Strauss*, by Susan Orr. *American Political Science Review* 90, no. 2 (June 1996): 412–13.

Pangle, Thomas L. Introduction to *Studies in Platonic Political Philosophy*, by Leo Strauss, 1–26. Chicago: University of Chicago Press, 1983.

————. Editor's introduction to *The Rebirth of Classical Political Rationalism: An Introduction to the Thought of Leo Strauss*, essays and lectures by Leo Strauss, selected and introduced by Thomas L. Pangle, vii–xxxviii. Chicago: University of Chicago Press, 1989.

————. "Platonic Political Science in Strauss and Voegelin." In *Faith and Political Philosophy: The Correspondence Between Leo Strauss and Eric Voegelin, 1934–1964*, edited and translated by Peter Emberley and Barry Cooper, 321–47. University Park: Pennsylvania State University Press, 1993.

————. "On The Epistolary Dialogue Between Leo Strauss and Eric Voegelin." In *Leo Strauss: Political Philosopher and Jewish Thinker*, edited by Kenneth L. Deutsch and Walter Nicgorski, 231–56. Lanham, Md.: Rowman and Littlefield, 1994.

Peterman, Larry. "Approaching Leo Strauss: Some Comments on 'Thoughts on Machiavelli.'" *Political Science Reviewer* 16 (Fall 1986): 317–51.

Piccinini, Irene Abigail. "Leo Strauss and Hermann Cohen's 'Arch-Enemy': A Quasi-Cohenian Apology of Baruch Spinozi." *Journal of Textual Reasoning* 3, no. 1 (June 2004). http://etext.lib.virginia.edu/journals/tr/volume3/piccinini.html (accessed 23 July 2005).

Pippin, Robert B. "Being, Time, and Politics: The Strauss-Kojève Debate." *History and Theory* 32, no. 2 (May 1993): 138–61.

————. "The Modern World of Leo Strauss." In *Hannah Arendt and Leo Strauss: German Émigrés and American Political Thought After World War II*, edited by Peter Graf Kielmansegg, Horst Mewes, and Elisabeth Glaser-Schmidt, 139–60. Washington, D.C.: German Historical Institute; Cambridge: Cambridge University Press, 1994.

Ranieri, John. "Leo Strauss on Jerusalem and Athens: A Girardian Analysis." *Shofar* 22, no. 2 (Winter 2004): 85–104.

Rethelyi, Mari. "Guttmann's Critique of Strauss's Modernist Approach to Medieval Philosophy: Some Arguments Toward a Counter-Critique." *Journal of Textual Reasoning* 3, no. 1 (June 2004). http://etext.lib.virginia.edu/journals/tr/volume3/rethelyi.html (accessed 23 July 2005).

Rhodes, James M. *Eros, Wisdom, and Silence: Plato's Erotic Dialogues.* Columbia: University of Missouri Press, 2003.

Richert, Scott P. Review of *Revolt Against Modernity: Leo Strauss, Eric Voegelin, and the Search for a Postliberal Order*, by Ted V. McAllister. *Review of Metaphysics* 50, no. 3 (March 1997): 675–76.

Rorty, Richard. "Straussianism, Democracy, and Allan Bloom, I: That Old-Time Philosophy." *New Republic*, 4 April 1988, 28–33.

Rosen, Stanley. "Politics or Transcendence? Responding to Historicism." In *Faith and Political Philosophy: The Correspondence Between Leo Strauss and Eric Voegelin, 1934–1964*, edited and translated by Peter Emberley and Barry Cooper, 261–66. University Park: Pennsylvania State University Press, 1993.

———. "Leo Strauss and the Possibility of Philosophy." *Review of Metaphysics* 53, no. 3 (March 2000): 541–64.

Rothman, Stanley. "The Revival of Classical Political Philosophy: A Critique." *American Political Science Review* 56, no. 2 (March 1962): 341–52.

Rozen, Laura. "Con Tract: The Theory Behind Neocon Self-Deception." *Washington Monthly*, October 2003, 11–13.

Sabine, George H. Review of *Persecution and the Art of Writing*, by Leo Strauss. *Ethics* 63, no. 1 (October 1952): 220–22.

Schaar, John H., and Sheldon S. Wolin. "A Critique." Review of *Essays on the Scientific Study of Politics*, edited by Herbert J. Storing. *American Political Science Review* 57, no. 1 (March 1963): 125–50.

Schall, James V. "A Latitude for Statesmanship? Strauss on St. Thomas." In *Leo Strauss: Political Philosopher and Jewish Thinker*, edited by Kenneth L. Deutsch and Walter Nicgorski, 211–30. Lanham, Md.: Rowman and Littlefield, 1994.

Seeskin, Kenneth. "Maimonides' Conception of Philosophy." In *Leo Strauss and Judaism: Jerusalem and Athens Critically Revisited*, edited by David Novak, 87–110. Lanham, Md.: Rowman and Littlefield, 1996.

Shorris, Earl. "Ignoble Liars: Leo Strauss, George Bush, and the Philosophy of Mass Deception." *Harper's Magazine*, June 2004, 65–71.

Smith, Gregory Bruce. "The Post-Modern Leo Strauss?" *History of European Ideas* 19, nos. 1–3 (1994): 191–97.

———. "Who Was Leo Strauss?" *American Scholar* 66, no. 1 (Winter 1997): 95–104.

———. "Leo Strauss and the Straussians: An Anti-democratic Cult?" *PS, Political Science and Politics* 30, no. 2 (June 1997): 180–89.

———. "Athens and Washington: Leo Strauss and the American Regime." In *Leo Strauss, the Straussians, and the American Regime*, edited by Kenneth L. Deutsch and John A. Murley, 103–27. Lanham, Md.: Rowman and Littlefield, 1999.

Smith, Steven B. "Leo Strauss: Between Athens and Jerusalem." In *Leo Strauss: Political Philosopher and Jewish Thinker*, edited by Kenneth L. Deutsch and Walter Nicgorski, 81–105. Lanham, Md.: Rowman and Littlefield, 1994.

———. Review of *Recasting Conservatism: Oakeshott, Strauss, and the Response to Postmodernism*, by Robert Devigne. *American Political Science Review* 88, no. 4 (December 1994): 971–72.

———. "*Destruktion* or Recovery? Leo Strauss's Critique of Heidegger." *Review of Metaphysics* 51, no. 2 (December 1997): 345–77.

Soffer, Walter. "Modern Rationalism, Miracles, and Revelation: Strauss's Critique of Spinoza." In *Leo Strauss: Political Philosopher and Jewish Thinker*, edited by Kenneth L. Deutsch and Walter Nicgorski, 143–73. Lanham, Md.: Rowman and Littlefield, 1994.

Söllner, Alfons. "Leo Strauss: German Origin and American Impact." In *Hannah Arendt and Leo Strauss: German Émigrés and American Political Thought After World War II*, edited by Peter Graf Kielmansegg, Horst Mewes, and Elisabeth Glaser-Schmidt, 121–37. Washington, D.C.: German Historical Institute; Cambridge: Cambridge University Press, 1994.

Spitz, David. "Freedom, Virtue, and the New Scholasticism: The Supreme Court as Philosopher-Kings." *Commentary* 28, no. 10 (October 1959): 313–21.

Spragens, Thomas A., Jr. Review of *The Anatomy of Antiliberalism*, by Stephen Holmes. *Journal of Politics* 57, no. 4 (November 1995): 1198–1201.

Susser, Bernard. "The Restorative Ontology of Leo Strauss." In *The Grammar of Modern Ideology*, 137–71. London: Routledge, 1988.

Tarcov, Nathan. "Philosophy and History: Tradition and Interpretation in the Work of Leo Strauss." *Polity* 16, no. 1 (Fall 1983): 5–29.

———. "On a Certain Critique of 'Straussianism.'" In *Leo Strauss: Political Philosopher and Jewish Thinker*, edited by Kenneth L. Deutsch and Walter Nicgorski, 259–74. Lanham, Md.: Rowman and Littlefield, 1994.

Taylor, Mark Lewis. "Liberation, Neocons, and the Christian Right: Options for Pro-Active Christian Witness in Post-9/11." *Constellation*, Fall 2003, 1–21. http://www.tcpc.org/resources/constellation/fall_03/taylor.pdf (accessed 4 July 2005).

Terchek, Ronald J. "Locating Leo Strauss in the Liberal-Communitarian Debate." In *Leo Strauss, the Straussians, and the American Regime*, edited by Kenneth L. Deutsch and John A. Murley, 143–56. Lanham, Md.: Rowman and Littlefield, 1999.

Udoff, Alan, ed. *Leo Strauss's Thought: Toward a Critical Engagement*. Boulder, Colo.: Lynne Rienner Publishers, 1991.

Umphrey, Stewart. "Natural Right and Philosophy." In *Leo Strauss: Political Philosopher and Jewish Thinker*, edited by Kenneth L. Deutsch and Walter Nicgorski, 275–95. Lanham, Md.: Rowman and Littlefield, 1994.

Verskin, Alan. "Reading Strauss on Maimonides: A New Approach." *Journal of Textual Reasoning* 3, no. 1 (June 2004). http://etext.lib.virginia.edu/journals/tr/volume3/verskin.html (accessed 23 July 2005).

Villa, Dana R. "The Philosopher versus the Citizen: Arendt, Strauss, and Socrates." *Political Theory* 26, no. 2 (April 1998): 147–72.

Voegelin, Eric. "Review of Strauss's *On Tyranny*." In *Faith and Political Philosophy: The Correspondence Between Leo Strauss and Eric Voegelin, 1934–1964*, edited and translated by Peter Emberley and Barry Cooper, 44–49. University Park: Pennsylvania State University Press, 1993.

Walsh, David. "The Reason-Revelation Tension in Strauss and Voegelin." In *Faith and Political Philosophy: The Correspondence Between Leo Strauss and Eric Voegelin, 1934–1964*, edited and translated by Peter Emberley and Barry Cooper, 349–68. University Park: Pennsylvania State University Press, 1993.

Walsh, Germaine Paulo. Review of *Jerusalem and Athens: Reason and Revelation in the Work of Leo Strauss*, by Susan Orr. *Journal of Politics* 58, no. 2 (May 1996): 589–91.

Ward, James F. "Political Philosophy and History: The Links Between Strauss and Heidegger." *Polity* 20, no. 2 (Winter 1987): 273–95.

———. Review of *Leo Strauss and the American Right*, by Shadia B. Drury. *American Political Science Review* 92, no. 3 (September 1998): 679–80.

West, Thomas G. "Leo Strauss and American Foreign Policy: Is There a Neoconservative Connection?" *Claremont Review of Books*, Summer 2004, http://claremont.org/writings/crb/summer2004/west.html?FORMAT=print (accessed 4 July 2005).

Wiser, James L. "Reason and Revelation as Search and Response: A Comparison of Eric Voegelin and Leo Strauss." In *Faith and Political Philosophy: The Correspondence Between Leo Strauss and Eric Voegelin, 1934–1964*, edited and translated by Peter Emberley and Barry Cooper, 237–48. University Park: Pennsylvania State University Press, 1993.

Zank, Michael. "Part I: Introduction." In Leo Strauss, *Leo Strauss: The Early Writings (1921–1932)*, edited and translated by Michael Zank, 3–49. Albany: State University of New York Press, 2002.

Zuckert, Catherine H. *Postmodern Platos: Nietzsche, Heidegger, Gadamer, Strauss, Derrida.* Chicago: University of Chicago Press, 1996.

On Machiavelli

Allen, William B. "Machiavelli and Modernity." In Niccolò Machiavelli, *The Prince*, edited and translated by Angelo M. Codevilla, 101–13. New Haven: Yale University Press, 1997.

Althusser, Louis. *Machiavelli and Us.* Edited by François Matheron. Translated by Gregory Elliot. Appendix, "Machiavelli's Solitude," translated by Ben Brewster. London: Verso, 1999.

Baron, Hans. "Machiavelli: The Republican Citizen and the Author of *The Prince*." *English Historical Review* 76, no. 299 (April 1961): 217–53.

———. *In Search of Florentine Civic Humanism: Essays on the Transition from Medieval to Modern Thought.* Vol. 2. Princeton, N.J.: Princeton University Press, 1988.

Beiner, Ronald. "Machiavelli, Hobbes, and Rousseau on Civil Religion." *Review of Politics* 55, no. 4 (Fall 1993): 617–38.

Berlin, Isaiah. "The Originality of Machiavelli." In *Studies On Machiavelli*, edited by Myron P. Gilmore, 149–206. Florence: G. C. Sansoni Editore, 1972.

Bock, Gisela, Quentin Skinner, and Maurizio Viroli, eds. *Machiavelli and Republicanism.* Cambridge: Cambridge University Press, 1990.

Caranfa, Angelo. *Machiavelli Rethought: A Critique of Strauss' Machiavelli.* Washington, D.C.: University Press of America, 1978.

Chabod, Federico. *Machiavelli and the Renaissance.* Translated by David Moore. London: Bowes and Bowes, 1958.

Ciliotta-Rubery, Andrea. "Evil Teachings Without Remorse: An Examination of the Question of Evil Within Machiavelli's 'Exhortation to Penitence' and 'The Life of Castruccio Castracani of Lucca.'" 2 vols. Ph.D. diss., Georgetown University, 1994.

Coby, J. Patrick. *Machiavelli's Romans: Liberty and Greatness in the Discourses on Livy.* Lanham, Md.: Lexington Books, 1999.

Colish, Marcia L. "Republicanism, Religion, and Machiavelli's Savonarolan Moment." *Journal of the History of Ideas* 60, no. 4 (October 1999): 597–616.

Doyle, Michael W. "Fundamentalism: Machiavelli." In *Ways of War and Peace: Realism, Liberalism, and Socialism*, 93–110. New York: W. W. Norton, 1997.

Faulkner, Robert. "*Clizia* and the Enlightenment of Private Life." In *The Comedy and Tragedy of Machiavelli: Essays on the Literary Works*, edited by Vickie B. Sullivan, 30–56 (endnotes, 200–203). New Haven: Yale University Press, 2000.

Fischer, Markus. "Machiavelli's Political Psychology." *Review of Politics* 59, no. 4 (Fall 1997): 789–829.

———. *Well-Ordered License: On the Unity of Machiavelli's Thought.* Lanham, Md.: Lexington Books, 2000.

Fleisher, Martin. "The Ways of Machiavelli and the Ways of Politics." *History of Political Thought* 16, no. 3 (Autumn 1995): 330–55.

Fontana, Benedetto. "Love of Country and Love of God: The Political Uses of Religion in Machiavelli." *Journal of the History of Ideas* 60, no. 4 (October 1999): 639–56.

———. "Sallust and the Politics of Machiavelli." *History of Political Thought* 24, no. 1 (Spring 2003): 86–108.

Gay, Peter. *The Enlightenment: An Interpretation.* Vol. 1, *The Rise of Modern Paganism.* New York: Alfred A. Knopf, 1966; New York: W. W. Norton, 1977.

Geerken, John H. "Machiavelli's Moses and Renaissance Politics." *Journal of the History of Ideas* 60, no. 4 (October 1999): 579–95.

Gilbert, Felix. *Machiavelli and Guicciardini: Politics and History in Sixteenth-Century Florence.* Princeton, N.J.: Princeton University Press, 1965; repr., 1973.

Gramsci, Antonio. "The Modern Prince: Essays on the Science of Politics in the Modern Age." In *The Modern Prince and Other Writings,* translated by Louis Marks, 135–88. New York: International Publishers, 1957.

de Grazia, Sebastian. *Machiavelli in Hell.* London and New York: Harvester Wheatsheaf, 1989.

Hankins, James, ed. *Renaissance Civic Humanism: Reappraisals and Reflections.* Cambridge: Cambridge University Press, 2000.

Hulliung, Mark. *Citizen Machiavelli.* Princeton, N.J.: Princeton University Press, 1983.

Jacobitti, Edmund E. "The Classical Heritage in Machiavelli's Histories: Symbol and Poetry as Historical Literature." In *The Comedy and Tragedy of Machiavelli: Essays on the Literary Works,* edited by Vickie B. Sullivan, 176–92 (endnotes, 230–38). New Haven: Yale University Press, 2000.

Kamenev, Lev. "Preface to Machiavelli." *New Left Review,* no. 15 (May–June 1962): 39–42.

Kocis, Robert A. *Machiavelli Redeemed: Retrieving His Humanist Perspectives on Equality, Power, and Glory.* Bethlehem, Pa.: Lehigh University Press; London: Associated University Press, 1998.

Lord, Carnes. "Machiavelli's Realism." In Niccolò Machiavelli, *The Prince,* edited and translated by Angelo M. Codevilla, 114–23. New Haven: Yale University Press, 1997.

———. "Allegory in Machiavelli's *Mandragola.*" In *Political Philosophy and the Human Soul: Essays in Memory of Allan Bloom,* edited by Michael Palmer and Thomas L. Pangle, 149–73. Lanham, Md.: Rowman and Littlefield, 1995.

Mansfield, Harvey C. *Machiavelli's New Modes and Orders: A Study of the Discourses on Livy.* Ithaca, N.Y.: Cornell University Press, 1979; repr., Chicago: University of Chicago Press, 2001.

———. Translators' introduction to *Florentine Histories,* by Niccolò Machiavelli, translated by Laura F. Banfield and Harvey C. Mansfield, vii–xv. Princeton, N.J.: Princeton University Press, 1988.

———. *Machiavelli's Virtue.* Chicago: University of Chicago Press, 1998.

———. "The Cuckold in Machiavelli's *Mandragola.*" In *The Comedy and Tragedy of Machiavelli: Essays on the Literary Works*, edited by Vickie B. Sullivan, 1–29 (endnotes, 197–200). New Haven: Yale University Press, 2000.

Maritain, Jacques. "The End of Machiavellianism." In *The Social and Political Philosophy of Jacques Maritain: Selected Readings*, edited by Joseph W. Evans and Leo R. Ward, 319–53. London: Geoffrey Bles, 1956.

Masters, Roger D. *Machiavelli, Leonardo, and the Science of Power.* Notre Dame, Ind.: University of Notre Dame Press, 1996.

Mattingly, Garrett. "Machiavelli's *Prince:* Political Science or Political Satire?" *American Scholar* 27, no. 4 (Autumn 1958): 482–91.

McKenzie, Lionel A. "Rousseau's Debate with Machiavelli in the *Social Contract.*" *Journal of the History of Ideas* 43, no. 2 (April–June 1982): 209–28.

Meinecke, Friedrich. *Machiavellism: The Doctrine of Raison d'État and Its Place in Modern History.* Translated by Douglas Scott. London: Routledge and Kegan Paul, 1957.

———. "Machiavelli." In *Perspectives on Political Philosophy.* Vol. 1, *Thucydides through Machiavelli*, edited by James V. Downton, Jr., and David K. Hart, 401–24. New York: Holt, Rinehart and Winston, 1971.

Mosca, Gaetano. "The Renaissance and Machiavelli." In *A Short History of Political Philosophy*, translated by Sondra Z. Koff, 70–98. New York: Thomas Y. Crowell, 1972.

Najemy, John M. "Language and *The Prince.*" In *Niccolò Machiavelli's "The Prince": New Interdisciplinary Essays*, edited by Martin Coyle, 89–114. Manchester: Manchester University Press, 1995.

———. "Papirius and the Chickens, or Machiavelli on the Necessity of Interpreting Religion." *Journal of the History of Ideas* 60, no. 4 (October 1999): 659–81.

Nederman, Cary J. "Amazing Grace: Fortune, God, and Free Will in Machiavelli's Thought." *Journal of the History of Ideas* 60, no. 4 (October 1999): 617–38.

Parel, Anthony J. "The Question of Machiavelli's Modernity." *Review of Politics* 53, no. 2 (Spring 1991): 320–39.

———. *The Machiavellian Cosmos.* New Haven: Yale University Press, 1992.

Patapan, Haig. "All's Fair in Love and War: Machiavelli's *Clizia.*" *History of Political Thought* 19, no. 4 (Winter 1998): 531–51.

———. "*I Capitoli:* Machiavelli's New Theogony." *Review of Politics* 65, no. 2 (Spring 2003): 185–207.

Pocock, J. G. A. *The Machiavellian Moment: Florentine Political Thought and the Atlantic Republican Tradition.* Princeton, N.J.: Princeton University Press, 1975.

Preus, J. Samuel. "Machiavelli's Functional Analysis of Religion: Context and Object." *Journal of the History of Ideas* 40, no. 2 (April–June 1979): 171–90.

Price, Russell. "The Senses of *Virtù* in Machiavelli." *European Studies Review* 3, no. 4 (October 1973): 315–45.

Qviller, Bjørn. "The Machiavellian Cosmos." *History of Political Thought* 17, no. 3 (Autumn 1996): 326–53.

Rebhorn, Wayne A. *Foxes and Lions: Machiavelli's Confidence Men.* Ithaca, N.Y.: Cornell University Press, 1988.

Ridolfi, Roberto. *The Life of Niccolò Machiavelli.* Translated by Cecil Grayson. London: Routledge and Kegan Paul, 1963.

Skinner, Quentin. *Machiavelli*. New York: Hill and Wang, 1981.

—————. Introduction to *The Prince*, by Niccolò Machiavelli, edited by Quentin Skinner and Russell Price, translated by Russell Price, ix–xxiv. Cambridge: Cambridge University Press, 1988.

Sullivan, Vickie B. "Neither Christian Nor Pagan: Machiavelli's Treatment of Religion in the *Discourses.*" *Polity* 26, no. 2 (Winter 1993): 259–80.

—————. *Machiavelli's Three Romes: Religion, Liberty, and Politics Reformed.* DeKalb: Northern Illinois University Press, 1996.

—————, ed. with introduction. *The Comedy and Tragedy of Machiavelli: Essays on the Literary Works.* New Haven: Yale University Press, 2000.

Vatter, Miguel E. *Between Form and Event: Machiavelli's Theory of Political Freedom.* Dordrecht: Kluwer Academic Publishers, 2000.

Villari, Pasquale. *The Life and Times of Niccolò Machiavelli.* Popular ed. 2 vols. Translated by Linda Villari. London: T. Fisher Unwin, 1898.

Viroli, Maurizio. *Machiavelli.* Oxford: Oxford University Press, 1998.

—————. *Niccolò's Smile: A Biography of Machiavelli.* Translated by Antony Shugaar. New York: Farrar, Straus and Giroux, 2000.

Other References

Aquinas, Thomas, St. *Summa Theologiæ.* Vol. 11, *Man* (1a, qq. 75–83). Translated by Timothy Suttor. Blackfriars; London: Eyre and Spottiswoode; New York: McGraw-Hill, 1970.

—————. *Summa Theologiæ.* Vol. 23, *Virtue* (1a2æ, qq. 55–67). Translated by W. D. Hughes. Blackfriars; London: Eyre and Spottiswoode; New York: McGraw-Hill, 1969.

—————. *Summa Theologiæ.* Vol. 28, *Law and Political Theory* (1a2æ, qq. 90–97). Translated by Thomas Gilby. Blackfriars; London: Eyre and Spottiswoode; New York: McGraw-Hill, 1966.

—————. *Summa Theologiæ.* Vol. 29, *The Old Law* (1a2æ, qq. 98–105). Translated by David Bourke and Arthur Littledale. Blackfriars; London: Eyre and Spottiswoode; New York: McGraw-Hill, 1969.

—————. *Summa Theologiæ.* Vol. 37, *Justice* (2a2æ, qq. 57–62). Translated by Thomas Gilby. Blackfriars; London: Eyre and Spottiswoode; New York: McGraw-Hill, 1975.

Aristophanes. *Peace.* Edited and translated by Alan H. Sommerstein. Warminster, Wiltshire: Aris and Phillips; Chicago: Bolchazy-Carducci, 1985.

Aristotle. *The Complete Works of Aristotle: The Revised Oxford Translation.* Edited by Jonathan Barnes. 2 vols. Bollingen Series. Princeton, N.J.: Princeton University Press, 1984.

Aron, Raymond. *The Dawn of Universal History.* Translated by Dorothy Pickles. London: Weidenfeld and Nicolson, 1961.

—————. *History, Truth, Liberty: Selected Writings of Raymond Aron.* Edited by Franciszek Draus. Chicago: University of Chicago Press, 1985.

Augustine. *Concerning the City of God Against the Pagans.* Translated by Henry Bettinson. Harmondsworth, Middlesex: Penguin, 1972.

Averroës. *Averroës' Commentary on Plato's Republic.* Edited and translated by E. I. J. Rosenthal. Cambridge: Cambridge University Press, 1956.

———. *Averroës' Tahafut Al-Tahafut* (*The Incoherence of the Incoherence*). Vol. 1. Translated by Simon van den Bergh. London: Luzac and Company, 1969.

———. *Averroës' Middle Commentary on Aristotle's Poetics*. Translated by Charles E. Butterworth. Princeton, N.J.: Princeton University Press, 1986.

Baron, Hans. *The Crisis of the Early Italian Renaissance: Civic Humanism and Republican Liberty in an Age of Classicism and Tyranny*. Rev. ed. Princeton, N.J.: Princeton University Press, with Newberry Library, 1966.

Becker, Carl. *The Declaration of Independence: A Study in the History of Political Ideas*. 1922. New York: Alfred A. Knopf, 1960.

Bellow, Saul. *Ravelstein*. London and New York: Viking, 2000.

Benardete, Seth. *The Argument of the Action: Essays on Greek Poetry and Philosophy*. Edited by Ronna Burger and Michael Davis. Chicago: University of Chicago Press, 2000.

Berkowitz, Peter. *Virtue and the Making of Modern Liberalism*. Princeton, N.J.: Princeton University Press, 1999.

Blattner, William D. *Heidegger's Temporal Idealism*. Cambridge: Cambridge University Press, 1999.

Bloom, Allan. *The Closing of the American Mind: How Higher Education Has Failed Democracy and Impoverished the Souls of Today's Students*. New York: Simon and Schuster, Touchstone, 1988.

Boesche, Roger. *Theories of Tyranny, From Plato to Arendt*. University Park: Pennsylvania State University Press, 1996.

Brague, Rémi. "Radical Modernity and the Roots of Ancient Thought." *Independent Journal of Philosophy* 4 (1983): 63–74.

Cassirer, Ernst. *The Myth of the State*. New Haven: Yale University Press, 1946.

———. *The Individual and the Cosmos in Renaissance Philosophy*. Translated by Mario Domandi. Oxford: Basil Blackwell, 1963.

Charles, R. H., et al., eds. *The Apocrypha and Pseudepigrapha of the Old Testament in English*. Vol. 2, *Pseudepigrapha*. Oxford: Clarendon Press, 1913.

Cicero. *Tusculan Disputations*. Translated by J. E. King. Loeb Classical Library 141. London: William Heinemann; New York: G. P. Putnam's Sons, 1927.

———. *De natura deorum* and *Academica*. Translated by H. Rackham. Loeb Classical Library 268. London: William Heinemann, 1933.

———. *On Duties*. Edited by M. T. Griffin and E. M. Atkins. Translated by E. M. Atkins. Cambridge: Cambridge University Press, 1991.

Cohen, Hermann. *Religion of Reason Out of the Sources of Judaism*. New York: Frederick Ungar, 1972.

Coker, Francis W. "Some Present-Day Critics of Liberalism." *American Political Science Review* 47, no. 1 (March 1953): 1–27.

Condren, Conal. *The Status and Appraisal of Classic Texts: An Essay on Political Theory, Its Inheritance, and the History of Ideas*. Princeton, N.J.: Princeton University Press, 1985.

Cooper, Barry. *The End of History: An Essay on Modern Hegelianism*. Toronto: University of Toronto Press, 1984.

Cooper, Laurence D. *Rousseau, Nature, and the Problem of the Good Life*. University Park: Pennsylvania State University Press, 1999.

Copleston, Frederick. *Contemporary Philosophy: Studies of Logical Positivism and Existentialism.* London: Burns and Oates, 1956.

Dante Alighieri. *Inferno.* Translated by Allan Gilbert. Durham, N.C.: Duke University Press, 1969.

Davis, Michael. *Ancient Tragedy and the Origins of Modern Science.* Carbondale: Southern Illinois University Press, 1988.

Diogenes Laertius. *The Lives and Opinions of Eminent Philosophers.* Translated by C. D. Yonge. London: George Bell and Sons, 1895.

Dreyfus, Hubert L. *Being-in-the-World: A Commentary on Heidegger's Being and Time, Division I.* Cambridge, Mass.: MIT Press, 1991.

Drury, Shadia B. *Alexandre Kojève: The Roots of Postmodern Politics.* New York: St. Martin's Press, 1992.

Fabro, Cornelio. *God in Exile: Modern Atheism; A Study of the Internal Dynamic of Modern Atheism, from Its Roots in the Cartesian "Cogito" to the Present Day.* Edited and translated by Arthur Gibson. New York: Newman Press, 1968.

Gordis, Robert. *The Root and the Branch: Judaism and the Free Society.* Chicago: University of Chicago Press, 1962.

Gordon, Peter Eli. *Rosenzweig and Heidegger: Between Judaism and German Philosophy.* Berkeley: University of California Press, 2003.

Hallowell, John H. *Main Currents in Modern Political Thought.* New York: Henry Holt and Company, 1950.

Hegel, G. W. F. *Hegel's Philosophy of Right.* Translated by T. M. Knox. London: Oxford University Press, 1952.

―――. *Reason in History: A General Introduction to the Philosophy of History.* Translated by Robert S. Hartman. Indianapolis: Bobbs-Merrill, 1953.

Heidegger, Martin. *Existence and Being.* London: Vision Press, 1949.

―――. *An Introduction to Metaphysics.* New Haven: Yale University Press, 1959.

―――. *Being and Time.* Translated by John Macquarrie and Edward Robinson. Oxford: Basil Blackwell, 1967.

―――. *Poetry, Language, Thought.* Translated by Albert Hofstadter. New York: Harper and Row, 1971; New York: Harper Colophon, 1975.

―――. *The Question Concerning Technology and Other Essays.* Translated by William Lovitt. New York: Harper and Row, 1977.

―――. *Nietzsche.* Vol. 4, *Nihilism.* Edited by David Farrell Krell. Translated by Frank A. Capuzzi. San Francisco: Harper and Row, 1982.

―――. *Early Greek Thinking.* Translated by David Farrell Krell and Frank A. Capuzzi. New York: HarperCollins, 1984.

Herbst, Jurgen. *The German Historical School in American Scholarship: A Study in the Transfer of Power.* Ithaca, N.Y.: Cornell University Press, 1965.

Hersh, Seymour M. "Selective Intelligence: Donald Rumsfeld Has His Own Special Sources; Are They Reliable?" *New Yorker,* 12 May 2003, 44–51.

Hick, John. *Faith and Knowledge.* 2nd ed. Ithaca, N.Y.: Cornell University Press, 1966.

Higuera, Henry. "Politics, Poetry, and Prophecy in *Don Quixote.*" In *Political Philosophy and the Human Soul: Essays in Memory of Allan Bloom,* edited by Michael Palmer and Thomas L. Pangle, 175–87. Lanham, Md.: Rowman and Littlefield, 1995.

Hobbes, Thomas. *Leviathan.* Edited by C. B. Macpherson. London: Penguin Books, 1968.

———. *On the Citizen.* Edited and translated by Richard Tuck and Michael Silver-thorne. Cambridge: Cambridge University Press, 1998.

Hobsbawm, Eric. *On History.* London: Weidenfeld and Nicolson, 1997.

Howard, Thomas Albert. *Religion and the Rise of Historicism: W. M. L. de Wette, Jacob Burckhardt, and the Theological Origins of Nineteenth-Century Historical Consciousness.* Cambridge: Cambridge University Press, 2000.

Jaeger, Mary. *Livy's Written Rome.* Ann Arbor: University of Michigan Press, 1997.

Jaffa, Harry V. *Thomism and Aristotelianism: A Study of the Commentary by Thomas Aquinas on the Nicomachean Ethics.* Chicago: University of Chicago Press, 1952; Westport, Conn.: Greenwood Press, 1979.

———. *Equality and Liberty: Theory and Practice in American Politics.* New York: Oxford University Press, 1965.

———. *The Conditions of Freedom: Essays in Political Philosophy.* Baltimore: Johns Hopkins University Press, 1975.

John Paul II. *Veritatis Splendor: Regarding Certain Fundamental Questions of the Church's Moral Teaching.* Encyclical Letter, 6 August 1993. http://www.vatican.va/holy_father/john_paul_ii/encyclicals/documents/hf_jp-ii_enc_06081993_veritatis-splendor_en.html (accessed 23 July 2005).

———. *Fides et Ratio: On the Relationship Between Faith and Reason.* Encyclical Letter, 14 September 1998. http://www.vatican.va/holy_father/john_paul_ii/encyclicals/documents/hf_jp-ii_enc_15101998_fides-et-ratio_en.html (accessed 23 July 2005).

Jonas, Hans. "Gnosticism and Modern Nihilism." *Social Research* 19, no. 4 (December 1952): 430–52.

Kaplan, Simon. Translator's introduction to *Religion of Reason Out of the Sources of Judaism,* by Hermann Cohen, xi–xxii. New York: Frederick Ungar, 1972.

Kaufmann, Walter. *Nietzsche: Philosopher, Psychologist, Antichrist.* 4th ed. Princeton, N.J.: Princeton University Press, 1974.

Keys, Mary M. "Aquinas and the Challenge of Aristotelian Magnanimity." *History of Political Thought* 24, no. 1 (Spring 2003): 37–65.

King, Preston. Introduction to *The History of Ideas: An Introduction to Method,* edited by Preston King, 3–20. London: Croom Helm; Totowa, N.J.: Barnes and Noble, 1983.

Klein, Jacob. "On the Nature of Nature." *Independent Journal of Philosophy* 3 (1979): 101–9.

Kojève, Alexandre. *Introduction to the Reading of Hegel: Lectures on the "Phenomenology of the Spirit."* Assembled by Raymond Queneau. Edited with an introduction by Allan Bloom. Translated by James H. Nichols, Jr. New York: Basic Books, 1969.

Krell, David Farrell. "Analysis." In Martin Heidegger, *Nietzsche.* Vol. 1, *The Will to Power as Art,* 230–57. New York: Harper and Row, 1979; London: Routledge and Kegan Paul, 1981.

Livy. *History of Rome.* Vol. 4, Books VIII–X. Translated by B. O. Foster. Loeb Classical Library 191. London: William Heinemann; New York: G. P. Putnam's Sons, 1926.

———. *History of Rome.* Vol. 2, Books III and IV. Rev. ed. Translated by B. O. Foster. Loeb Classical Library 133. London: William Heinemann; Cambridge, Mass.: Harvard University Press, 1939.

Lora, Ronald. *Conservative Minds in America.* Chicago: Rand McNally, 1971; Westport, Conn.: Greenwood Press, 1976.

Löwith, Karl. *Meaning in History*. Chicago: University of Chicago Press, 1949.

———. "Nature, History, and Existentialism." *Social Research* 19, no. 1 (March 1952): 79–94.

Maimonides, Moses. *The Guide of the Perplexed*. Translated by Shlomo Pines. Introductory essay by Leo Strauss. Chicago: University of Chicago Press, 1963.

Mandelbaum, Maurice. *The Problem of Historical Knowledge: An Answer to Relativism*. New York: Liveright Publishing Corporation, 1938.

Mansfield, Harvey C. *The Spirit of Liberalism*. Cambridge, Mass.: Harvard University Press, 1978.

Maritain, Jacques. *The Degrees of Knowledge*. London: Geoffrey Bles, 1937.

———. *True Humanism*. 2nd ed. Translated by M. R. Adamson. London: Geoffrey Bles, 1939.

———. "On the Meaning of Contemporary Atheism." *Review of Politics* 11, no. 3 (July 1949): 267–80.

———. *On the Philosophy of History*. Edited by Joseph W. Evans. London: Geoffrey Bles, 1959.

Marlowe, Christopher. *The Jew of Malta*. In *The Complete Works of Christopher Marlowe*. Vol. 1. Edited by Fredson Bowers. Cambridge: Cambridge University Press, 1973.

Marx, Karl. *Critique of Hegel's "Philosophy of Right."* Translated by Annette Jolin and Joseph O'Malley. London: Cambridge University Press, 1970.

Masters, Roger D. "Rousseau and the Rediscovery of Nature." In *The Legacy of Rousseau*, edited by Clifford Orwin and Nathan Tarcov, 110–40. Chicago: University of Chicago Press, 1997.

Masugi, Ken. "Fr. James V. Schall on Reason and Faith, Part II." Conversation with Fr. Schall, 5 Dec. 2002 (Georgetown, Washington, D.C.). http://www.claremont.org/writings/021223masugi_b.html?FORMAT=print (accessed 18 June 2005).

Maurer, Armand A. *Medieval Philosophy*. 2nd ed. Toronto: Pontifical Institute of Mediaeval Studies, 1982.

McCool, Gerald A. *From Unity to Pluralism: The Internal Evolution of Thomism*. New York: Fordham University Press, 1989.

McCoy, Charles N. R. *The Structure of Political Thought: A Study in the History of Political Ideas*. New York: McGraw-Hill, 1963.

———. *On the Intelligibility of Political Philosophy: Essays of Charles N. R. McCoy*. Edited by James V. Schall and John J. Schrems. Washington, D.C.: Catholic University of America Press, 1989.

Meier, Heinrich. *The Lesson of Carl Schmitt: Four Chapters on the Distinction Between Political Theology and Political Philosophy*. Translated by Marcus Brainard. Chicago: University of Chicago Press, 1998.

Meinecke, Friedrich. *Historism: The Rise of a New Historical Outlook*. Translated by J. E. Anderson. London: Routledge and Kegan Paul, 1972.

Mendes-Flohr, Paul. "Franz Rosenzweig and the Crisis of Historicism." In *The Philosophy of Franz Rosenzweig*, edited by Paul Mendes-Flohr, 138–61. Hanover, N.H.: University Press of New England, for Brandeis University Press, 1988.

Mitchell, Joshua. *Not by Reason Alone: Religion, History, and Identity in Early Modern Political Thought*. Chicago: University of Chicago Press, 1993.

Momigliano, Arnaldo. *On Pagans, Jews, and Christians.* Middletown, Conn.: Wesleyan University Press, 1987.

Murray, Michael. *Modern Philosophy of History: Its Origin and Destination.* The Hague: Martinus Nijhoff, 1970.

Nietzsche, Friedrich. "On the Uses and Disadvantages of History for Life." In *Untimely Meditations,* translated by R. J. Hollingdale, 59–123. Cambridge: Cambridge University Press, 1983.

Novak, David. *Covenantal Rights: A Study in Jewish Political Theory.* Princeton, N.J.: Princeton University Press, 2000.

Otto, Rudolf. *The Idea of the Holy: An Inquiry into the Non-rational Factor in the Idea of the Divine and its Relation to the Irrational.* 2nd ed. Translated by John W. Harvey. Oxford: Oxford University Press, 1950.

Page, Carl. *Philosophical Historicism and the Betrayal of First Philosophy.* University Park: Pennsylvania State University Press, 1995.

Pangle, Thomas L. "The Hebrew Bible's Challenge to Political Philosophy: Some Introductory Reflections." In *Political Philosophy and the Human Soul: Essays in Memory of Allan Bloom,* edited by Michael Palmer and Thomas L. Pangle, 67–82. Lanham, Md.: Rowman and Littlefield, 1995.

———. *Political Philosophy and the God of Abraham.* Baltimore: Johns Hopkins University Press, 2003.

Philipse, Herman. *Heidegger's Philosophy of Being: A Critical Interpretation.* Princeton, N.J.: Princeton University Press, 1998.

Plato. *The Dialogues of Plato.* Rev. 4th ed. 4 vols. Translated by B. Jowett. Oxford: Clarendon Press, 1953.

———. *The Laws of Plato.* Translated with notes and an interpretative essay by Thomas L. Pangle. New York: Basic Books, 1980; Chicago: University of Chicago Press, 1988.

———. *The Republic of Plato.* 2nd ed. Translated with notes and an interpretive essay by Allan Bloom. New York: Basic Books, 1991.

Plutarch. *Moralia.* Vol. 4, 263d–351b. Translated by Frank Cole Babbitt. Loeb Classical Library 305. London: William Heinemann; Cambridge, Mass.: Harvard University Press, 1936.

Polybius. *The Histories.* Vol. 3, Books V–VIII. Translated by W. R. Paton. Loeb Classical Library 138. London: William Heinemann; New York: G. P. Putnam's Sons, 1923.

Popper, Karl R. *The Poverty of Historicism.* 2nd ed. London: Routledge and Kegan Paul, 1960.

von Ranke, Leopold. *Universal History: The Oldest Historical Group of Nations and the Greeks.* Edited by G. W. Prothero. Translated by D. C. Tovey and G. W. Prothero. Revised by F. W. Cornish. London: Kegan Paul, Trench, 1884.

Rawls, John. *Justice as Fairness: A Restatement.* Edited by Erin Kelly. Cambridge, Mass.: Harvard University Press, Belknap Press, 2001.

Rosen, Stanley. *Hermeneutics as Politics.* New York: Oxford University Press, 1987.

Rosenzweig, Franz. "It Is Time: Concerning the Study of Judaism." In *On Jewish Learning,* edited by N. N. Glatzer, 27–54. New York: Schocken Books, 1955; Madison: University of Wisconsin Press, 2002.

————. "Atheistic Theology" (1914) and " 'The New Thinking' " (1925). In *Philosophical and Theological Writings*, edited and translated by Paul W. Franks and Michael L. Morgan, 10–24, 109–39. Indianapolis: Hackett, 2000.

Rousseau, Jean-Jacques. *A Discourse on Inequality.* Translated by Maurice Cranston. London: Penguin Books, 1984.

————. *The Social Contract and Other Later Political Writings.* Edited and translated by Victor Gourevitch. Cambridge: Cambridge University Press, 1997.

Sacks, Robert. "The Lion and the Ass: A Commentary on the Book of Genesis (Chapters 1–10)." *Interpretation* 8, nos. 2–3 (May 1980): 29–101.

Schall, James V. *Christianity and Politics.* Boston: St. Paul Editions, 1981.

————. *Reason, Revelation, and the Foundations of Political Philosophy.* Baton Rouge: Louisiana State University Press, 1987.

————. *Another Sort of Learning.* San Francisco: Ignatius Press, 1988.

————. "On How Revelation Addresses Itself to Politics." In *Policy Reform and Moral Grounding*, edited by T. William Boxx and Gary M. Quinlivan, 1–20. Latrobe, Pa.: Saint Vincent College, 1995.

————. "The Right Order of Polity and Economy: Reflections on St. Thomas and the 'Old Law.' " *Cultural Dynamics* 7, no. 3 (November 1995): 427–40.

————. *Jacques Maritain: The Philosopher in Society.* Lanham, Md.: Rowman and Littlefield, 1998.

————. "Fides et Ratio: Approaches to a Roman Catholic Political Philosophy." *Review of Politics* 62, no. 1 (Winter 2000): 49–75.

Shotwell, James T. *An Introduction to the History of History.* New York: Columbia University Press, 1922.

Singer, Peter. *The President of Good and Evil: Taking George W. Bush Seriously.* London: Granta, 2004.

Skinner, Quentin. *The Foundations of Modern Political Thought.* Vol. 1, *The Renaissance.* Cambridge: Cambridge University Press, 1978.

Smith, Gregory Bruce. "On Cropsey's World: Joseph Cropsey and the Tradition of Political Philosophy." *Review of Politics* 60, no. 2 (Spring 1998): 307–41.

Sokolowski, Robert. *The God of Faith and Reason: Foundations of Christian Theology.* Notre Dame, Ind.: University of Notre Dame Press, 1982.

Spengler, Oswald. Introduction to *The Decline of the West.* Vol. 1, *Form and Actuality*, translated by Charles Francis Atkinson, 3–50. New York: Alfred A Knopf, 1926.

de Spinoza, Benedict. *A Theologico-Political Treatise.* In *The Chief Works of Benedict de Spinoza.* Vol. 1, *Tractatus Theologico-Politicus, Tractatus Politicus.* Translated by R. H. M. Elwes. London: George Bell and Sons, 1883.

Spitz, David. *The Real World of Liberalism.* Chicago: University of Chicago Press, 1982.

Springborg, Patricia. "Republicanism, Freedom from Domination, and the Cambridge Contextual Historians." *Political Studies* 49, no. 5 (December 2001): 851–76.

Stauffer, Devin. "Socrates and Callicles: A Reading of Plato's *Gorgias.*" *Review of Politics* 64, no. 4 (Fall 2002): 627–57.

Stern, Alfred. *Philosophy of History and the Problem of Values.* 'S-Gravenhage: Mouton, 1962.

Thucydides. *The History of the Peloponnesian War*. Edited by R. W. Livingstone. Translated by Richard Crawley. Revised by Richard Feetham. London: Oxford University Press, 1943.

Turner, Stephen P., and Regis A. Factor. *Max Weber and the Dispute Over Reason and Value: A Study in Philosophy, Ethics, and Politics*. London: Routledge and Kegan Paul, 1984.

Udoff, Alan. "Retracing the Steps of Franz Rosenzweig." In *Franz Rosenzweig: "The New Thinking*," edited and translated by Alan Udoff and Barbara E. Galli, 153–73. New York: Syracuse University Press, 1999.

Viroli, Maurizio. *Jean-Jacques Rousseau and the "Well-Ordered Society."* Translated by Derek Hanson. Cambridge: Cambridge University Press, 1988.

———. *From Politics to Reason of State: The Acquisition and Transformation of the Language of Politics 1250–1600*. Cambridge: Cambridge University Press, 1992.

Voegelin, Eric. *The Collected Works of Eric Voegelin*. Vol. 22, *History of Political Ideas*, bk. 4, *Renaissance and Reformation*, edited by David L. Morse and William M. Thompson. Vol. 23, *History of Political Ideas*, bk. 5, *Religion and the Rise of Modernity*, edited by James L. Wiser. Vol. 24, *History of Political Ideas*, bk. 6, *Revolution and the New Science*, edited by Barry Cooper. Columbia: University of Missouri Press, 1998.

Walker, R. B. J. *Inside/Outside: International Relations as Political Theory*. Cambridge: Cambridge University Press, 1993.

Wolfson, Harry Austryn. *Studies in the History of Philosophy and Religion*. Vol. 1. Edited by Isadore Twersky and George H. Williams. Cambridge, Mass.: Harvard University Press, 1973.

———. *The Philosophy of the Kalam*. Cambridge, Mass.: Harvard University Press, 1976.

Zuckert, Catherine. "Nature, History and the Self: Friedrich Nietzsche's Untimely Considerations." *Nietzsche-Studien* 5 (1976): 55–82.

Index

absolutism: and relativism, 23

accidents, 70, 86, 95, 103, 133, 203n44, 209n65; caused by Fortuna, 82, 85; caused by heaven, 14; extrinsic, 82, 85, 206n3; grave, new, and fabricated, 87; intrinsic, 82; and natural disasters, 158; and portents, 84; and providence, 84; random, 85, 163; unforeseeable, caused by nonteleological chance, 88

acquisition, 64, 106, 118, 126, 129, 132, 135–36, 138, 142, 214n33; acquisitive ways of the great, 77; in domestic and foreign policy, 114, 151; and Fortuna, 115–16; of good things, 188n53; of knowledge, by philosophers, 41, 43, 44; as natural and ordinary desire, 117, 151; necessity of, 116; by rapine, 105

Agag, King, 40

Agathocles, 87, 107, 110, 134, 223n86

Agis III, King, 211n103

Alexander VI, Pope, 125

Amalekites, 40

ambition, 59, 60, 114–15, 133; affinity with choice, honor, and glory, 116; and base tendencies, 138; blinds people, 67; as cause of tumults, 60; as cause of war, 114; common good and, 133; as desire for acquisition, 117; and discord in republics, 138; door to, opening, 126; excessive, 152; as form of necessity, 116–17; and human nature, 139; makes men operate well, 117; of nobles, for power, 134; private, 125, 137; prudent pursuit of, 130; satisfaction of, by princes, 125, 132; and the times, 117

Amos, 35

Anaxagoras, 204n53

Antiochus, 186n21

Apollo, 58

Aquinas, Thomas, 75, 158, 185n5, 190n80, 223n86; on free will, 111, 210n84; on justice and magnanimity, 102; on law, 37, 39, 41; on tyranny, 197n40

Arezzo, 109

Aristippus, 150, 204n55

248

philosophy/thought, 1, 6, 45, 145, 162.
    See also Strauss, Leo, idea of history
Hobbes, Thomas, 6, 7, 26, 30, 64–65, 94,
    128, 147; on human nature, 139–40
Holmes, Stephen J., 3–4, 171n21
honor, 62, 63, 102, 104, 109, 125, 130, 132,
    137, 204n53, 208n38, 215n70; of body,
    188n42; derived from political life,
    150; esteemed by Gentiles, 60; "hon-
    orably evil" and "unqualifiedly evil,"
    106; "honorably wicked," 106, 141; and
    magnanimity, 40–41; as necessity,
    116–17; and *summum bonum,* 110
horizon: of all thought, 154; biblical, 35,
    45, 95, 101; of city, 150, 155; classical,
    101; of history, 147, 161; limits of, 21;
    modern, 21, 22, 155, 164; moral, shared
    by revelation and reason, 69; natural,
    26, 35, 166; of one thing necessary for
    life, 163; theological, 78; traditional vs.
    new, 22, 89
Horwitz, Robert, 192n100
Howard, Thomas Albert, 21
human action, 84, 85, 86, 106, 151, 166;
    and conscience, 66–69; effectual truth
    of, 70; free will and, 164; the mean
    and, 105–6, 109, 120; means and ends
    of, 72; norms of, 89, 99, 122; rectitude
    in, 158; and virtue, 12, 143
human law, 38–39, 41
human nature, 7, 63, 113, 116, 122, 123, 124,
    144, 164–65; "in bondage," 192n105;
    and common good, 140–42; and
    highest good, 139, 143; Machiavelli on,
    compared with Hobbes, 139–40
humility: biblical, excludes magnanimity,
    40–41; Christian emphasis on, 62;
    inferior to greatness, 60; replaced by
    humanity, 77
humors, 90, 136, 142; diverse, 136; "diverse
    appetites," 208n38; of servitude and
    license, 108

imperialism, 151. *See also* republics, impe-
    rial; Rome, imperial expansion of

intelligence(s): of air, 83–84; as awareness
    of moral and intellectual virtues, 157;
    biblical, 84; and Fortuna, 84–85; and
    heavenly signs, 83; intercessions of, 84;
    perfect, God as, 88; separate, 28–29; use
    of, by princes, 125, 132; and virtue, 157
Isaiah, 39
"Is" and "Ought," 112
Italy, 67, 70, 86, 114; and Christianity, 61, 69,
    72, 90, 92, 205n80, 131; unified, 129, 131

Jackson, Michael P., xii, 151, 169n6,
    176n88, 194n3
Jaffa, Harry V., 5, 8, 11, 13, 31, 117, 174n50,
    190n80
Jerusalem, v, 2, 30, 31–32, 42, 48, 49, 52,
    55, 58, 139, 166, 191n90
Jew(s)/Jewish, 4, 36, 48–52, 186n21; and
    assimilation, 49; nonreligious, 50;
    orthodox, 32, 47, 51, 52; question, 48,
    52. *See also* Judaism
Jonathan, 40–41
Judaism, 4, 6, 47–52, 53, 76. *See also*
    Strauss, Leo, Judaism of; revelation,
    Jewish
Julius II, Pope, 106
Jung, Hwa Yol, 22
justice, 40, 55, 70, 72, 104, 109, 123, 140,
    145; Calliclean, 215n70; divine, 34–35,
    145, 162; factual basis of, 103, 127, 128;
    and injustice, 34, 71, 106, 125, 136; and
    law, scope of, 38–39, 106; and magna-
    nimity, 40–41, 102–3; and the mean,
    103, 106, 111; perfect, 71; praiseworthy
    qualities, 103, 105; problem of, 39; as
    rectitude, 127; religion and, distinc-
    tion between, 99, 206n3; and virtue,
    90–91. *See also* Aquinas, Thomas, on
    justice and magnanimity; Aristotle,
    on justice; Plato, on justice

Kamenev, Lev, 156
Kant, Immanuel, 10
Kennington, Richard H., 147

Kierkegaard, Søren, 22
kingdoms, 60, 85, 103, 118, 131; founders
   of, as praiseworthy, 144; need for religion in, 91, 92–93
Klein, Jacob, 49
Kleinias, 188n53
knowledge, 68, 80, 83, 86, 99, 117–18, 128,
   131, 144; atheistic pursuit of, 192n105;
   conversion to, from ignorance, 148;
   empirical/scientific, 19, 21, 27, 157–58;
   evident, quest for, 46; faith in, 19; of a
   fundamental question, v; general and
   particular, 100–101; of God, 34, 36, 38;
   of good and evil, 74; of good life, 17;
   of ignorance, 29; "indigestible stones
   of," 21; of justice, 106; of new modes
   and orders, 100; philosophic quest
   for, 22, 23, 27, 30, 31, 41, 43, 89, 154,
   156, 158, 159, 219n140; of revelation
   and reason, 31–32; supplied by faith,
   as a gift of God, 190n80; time-bound,
   18; of universal principles, 18–19; of
   whole, 23, 43–44, 46, 53; of world, 105,
   107, 148–49, 154
Kojève, Alexandre, 47
Kress, Paul, 192n100
Kries, Douglas, 176n88
Kuhn, Helmut, 173n38, 178n8
Kulturkritik, 3

Larmore, Charles, 13
Lasch, Christopher, 3
Latins, 68, 108
Laurence, Lampert, 3
law, 19, 20, 28, 33, 102, 110, 111, 112, 125, 135,
   152, 157; and art of legislation, 150,
   219n19; biblical accounts of, 44, 67,
   69–70; and common good, 127,
   129–30, 141; depend on good arms,
   61, 71; divine (*see* divine law); and
   education, 124; and general will, 7;
   grounded in self-interest, 106; of history, 8, 21, 28, 178n5; human (*see*
   human law); and human reason, 41;
   and justice, scope of, 38–39, 106,

215n70; make people good, 114, 116,
   118, 142, 165; natural, 7, 37, 140; natural
   horizon of, 35; ordered, in republics,
   108, 116, 138, 139; revealed, 36, 43, 44;
   rule of, 125. *See also* Aquinas, Thomas,
   on law; Aristotle, on law; God, law(s)
   of; Plato, on law; Plato, on marriage
   and procreation; Plato, specific
   prescriptions of; revelation, Jewish
Lessing, Gotthold Ephraim, 10
liberal democracy, 4, 51; and conditions
   for scholarship, 171n23
liberal education, 26
liberalism, 2–4; ills of, 4, 170n12
liberal relativism, 2–3
liberty, 122, 135; and principality and
   license, 208n38
Liebich, André, 4
Livy, Titus, 68, 104, 115, 149, 152–53,
   211n104, 211n116, 214n41, 221n40
love, 126, 127, 143, 144, 216n74; of fatherland, 76; and fear, combination of,
   109, 110, 142; of freedom, 59–60, 135;
   of good, vs. of glory, honor, and
   pleasure; of money, 115, 116; of thinking and learning, 47, 155; of tyranny,
   vs. of justice and philosophy, 148. *See
   also* God, command to love
Lowenthal, David, 8
Löwith, Karl, 8, 21, 28

Machiavelli, Niccolò: admires classical
   antiquity, 97; admits a *summum
   bonum*, 110; anti-teleotheological
   cosmology of, 84–85, 163–64; anti-
   theological animus/ire in, 57, 71, 81,
   164; Aristotelian and Averroist cosmological premises of, 80–81, 87–88;
   "assertoric quasi-theology" of, 84;
   and atheism, 78, 79, 93, 99; author/
   discoverer/teacher of new modes and
   orders, 57, 80, 82, 99, 100, 120, 143, 144,
   147, 149, 154, 156, 162, 163, 165, 173n46,
   206n8; blasphemer, 72–73; Calliclean
   advice to princes, 132–33; challenge to

modernity (*cont.*)
and specific features of, 6–7, 174n50;
and historicism, 17–23; key principle
of, 149; Machiavellian, 166; morass
of, 1, 31, 162; as new continent, 147,
204n55; original purpose of, 26; and
political philosophy, 156–57; predicament inherent in, 5; and science,
157–58; three waves of, 7; traits of, 36,
146–47
modes and orders: Christian, 60, 120; of
Machiavelli (*see* Machiavelli, Niccolò,
author/discoverer/teacher of new
modes and orders); and nature, 119;
new, in republics, 109–10; new, of
virtuous men, 118; new vs. old, 143,
155; of princes, 91–92, 131
morality, 7, 10, 12, 15, 17, 23, 31, 57, 62, 92,
97, 99–101, 112, 119, 129, 151, 185n9; biblical, 51, 77, 187n36; biblical and philosophic, 36–38, 39, 41, 52, 69, 109, 145,
162, 163, 191n90; and criminality, 107;
of excellent man, 152, 154; and expediency, 118; first and second statements
on, 99–100; immoral foundation for,
124–25; immorality, 60, 68, 89, 120,
127, 128; and the mean, 106, 107, 109;
modern, 128, 147–48; and praiseworthy qualities, 101–3, 130; private,
195n4; and religion, as separable, 94;
in rulers, 127–28, 133; traditional vs.
Machiavellian, 89, 101–2, 143–44, 163,
164–66, 204n55. *See also* goodness, vs.
virtue; moral virtue; philosophy,
moral; sin, moral vs. military
moral virtue, 12, 35, 102, 107, 110, 124, 130,
132, 147, 199n89; and common good,
128, 165; destructive analysis of, 152;
ignorance of, in modern science, 157;
ineffectual truth of, 156; judicious use
of, 92, 133; vs. political virtue, 97,
122–23, 145; practice of, instilled by
tyrants, 152; vs. republican virtue,
126–27, 144, 159; vs. "soulless" virtue,
153–54
Morgan, Michael L., 52

Moses, 37, 38, 58, 69–70, 76; "new Moses,"
Machiavelli as, 12, 120
Mosse, George L., 12
Murray, Michael, 17

Nabis, 223n86
Nahum, 63, 83
natural theology, 44, 188n42; and
revealed theology, difference between,
45–46, 47
nature, 19, 20, 28–29, 101, 119, 156, 157, 162,
163, 164, 204n55, 210n93, 214n41; and
Bible, 33–35, 186n21, 191n90; and
chance, 141; chance, accidents, and
natural order of world, 86–89; of
divine thought, 120; eternal order of,
21, 33–34, 164, 188n41; and Fortuna,
85–86; of God, 44, 185n5; and good,
113–14, 145, 147; of good and evil, 74;
and heavenly signs, 83, 84; and history, 18–23, 47, 66, 146, 147; human
(*see* human nature); law of, 215n70;
natural disasters, 158; natural function of society, 138; natural law, 7, 37,
140; natural right, 7, 18, 173n38, 178n8;
natural science, 19, 29; natural theology (*see* theology, natural); and
necessity, controlled by chance, 112;
pagan myth of, 59, 77, 95; state of, 7,
26, 140; of state, 151; variable ways of,
107; virtue grounded in, 132. *See also*
horizon, natural; order, eternal
necessity, 58, 106, 108, 139, 146, 150, 155,
157, 186n21; ambition as, 116; and
chance, vs. free will, 118–20, 164;
divine, 88; and divine providence, 71;
and fear, 113–14, 116, 164; and freedom, 112; and goodness, 116–18; and
nature, controlled by chance, 112;
nonteleological, 88; to sin, 64, 71, 73;
and virtuous action, 114–16, 125
Nederman, Cary J., 65
Nerva, Nervus, 135
Nicgorski, Walter, 162
Nietzsche, Friedrich, 3, 7, 8, 20–21

Sabine, George H., 27

salvation: by arms, 114; of fatherland, 127; of Italy, 72; necessity of vice for, 105; political and otherworldly, 65

Samnites, 104, 114, 115

Samuel, 40

Samuel, prophet, 40, 222n64

Saul, King, 40, 41

Savonarola, Girolamo, 58, 75, 81

Schall, James V., 5, 45, 47, 158, 185n5, 192n105, 209n72

Schmitt, Carl, 3

scholasticism, 111, 149

science: behavioral, 27–28; "firm," 101; modern, flight from reason, 223n81; modern, problem of, 21, 45, 157–58; natural, 19, 29; object of, 19; and positivism, 19, 27; religious, 49; social, 1, 18, 26–27, 28; on revelation, 46–47, 51. *See also* modernity, as new continent; political science

Scipio Africanus Major, Publius Cornelius (Elder), 126

Seeskin, Kenneth, 24

Severus, 125, 132, 213n18, 223n86

Sforza, Francesco, 66

Shotwell, James T., 220n30

sin, 65, 67, 70, 72, 77, 83, 84, 89; moral vs. military, 64; as natural and necessary, 64, 71, 73; original, 73; and repentance, alternation between, 107; true, ignorance as, 94; of vanity, 41

Skinner, Quentin, 122, 123, 213n10

Smith, Gregory Bruce, 8, 52

Smith, Steven B., 4–5, 172n26, 193n113

Socrates, 29, 34, 58, 90, 148, 149, 155, 161, 178n8, 204n53, 215n70

Soderini, Piero, 137

Sokolowski, Robert, 191n90

Solon, 61

sophists, 150, 219n19

soul, 5, 62, 72, 73, 75, 81, 88, 89; and liberal education, 26. *See also* Aristotle, on soul; Plato, on soul

Spengler, Oswald, 26, 27

Spinoza, Benedict de, 6, 30, 32, 33, 153

Spitz, David, 45–46

Spragens, Thomas A., Jr., 3

Storing, Herbert J., 5, 46, 192n100

Strato, 88

Strauss, Leo: on America, 2–3, 4; as atheist, ix, 13, 30–31, 45–46, 47–48, 53, 162; as "authoritarian antidemocratic," 10; as closet Machiavellian, 10; as conservative, 2–5, 10, 30; defense of philosophy by, 23, 25–26, 27, 29; on God, 38, 44, 45, 49, 78; idea of history in, 9–10, 17, 161; illiberalism of, 4; inclination to "old-fashioned view" of Machiavelli, 12, 57, 79, 94, 166; Judaism of, 47–52, 53, 162, 193n113; as "latter day Cato," 11; as nihilist, 3; "obvious perplexities" in, 10, 11; Orthodoxy of, 32, 47, 51, 52; as philosopher, 1, 13, 162; as political philosopher, 1, 162; project of, 5, 10, 30–31; self-understanding of, 1–2, 5, 6, 9; and Zionism, 48–52

Straussian, 9, 192n100; and conservatives, 4; defined, 30, 184n2; East and West Coast, 11

Sullivan, Vickie B., 65

summum bonum, 110

"surface of things," 9, 163, 204n55

Tarcov, Nathan, 201n112, 203n20, 216n73, 218n118, 223n84

teleology, 7, 28, 65; antiteleological cosmology, 88, 120, 163; nonteleological chance, 88, 166; teleological imperative of moral virtue, 124; temporal, nonteleological principle of causation, 82

teleotheological: modern, nonteleotheological views, 29; antiteleotheological animus, 78, 80; anti-teleotheological cosmology, 84, 164

telos, 77

temporality, 17, 19, 22, 29, 75; temporal conception of virtue and governance, 142, 144–45, 154–55; temporal conception of reason, 59; temporal view of

KIM A. SORENSEN

is a Visiting Research Fellow at the University of Adelaide.